Middle-class Blacks in a White Society

Middle-class Blacks in a White Society

Prince Hall Freemasonry in America

by

WILLIAM A. MURASKIN

UNIVERSITY OF CALIFORNIA PRESS
BERKELEY   LOS ANGELES   LONDON

University of California Press
Berkeley and Los Angeles, California

University of California Press, Ltd.
London, England

Copyright © 1975, by
The Regents of the University of California

ISBN 0-520-02705-1
Library of Congress Catalog Card Number: 73-94435
Printed in the United States of America

Contents

Preface

"So? Why should a nice Jewish boy like you worry about Negroes? You don't have enough problems already?" How often I heard that complaint in the early 1960s! Invariably I answered that if you are Jewish you have to be interested in the most oppressed of American ethnic groups. By the time I was job hunting in the early 1970s the question had become academic—with a vengeance.

This time it wasn't my relatives who looked at me with disbelief; it was the faculty committees at the universities where I was a job candidate. By 1971 the races had become so polarized that in one instance I was flown to New York for a job interview because they assumed I had to be black (despite my name) since I had written a number of journal articles, a master's thesis, and a Ph.D. dissertation on black topics. Who but a black would waste his time doing research like that? Another university department (within a branch of the most prestigious state university on the West Coast) went so far as to call me at home, tell me that I was the greatest historian since Gibbon, and beg me to reject all other offers and fly there immediately. They did, however, wish to confirm that I was black. When I said I was not, they politely terminated the conversation.

With minor variations this theme was repeated again and again, and I began to ask myself what a nice Jewish boy was getting himself into? After a year of looking for a position I finally understood how bad the situation really was. It was bad enough that I turned down, with regret, a post-doctoral fellowship awarded by the National Endowment for the Humanities, a grant which would have allowed me to work under St. Clair Drake at Stanford and to finish this book earlier. But I had no choice. I was already too closely identified with a field in which I was unemployable. So I got out.

When the department of urban studies at Queens College flew me to New York, only then discovering I was not black, they were willing to forgive me and hire me as a hybrid urban historian and sociologist. I grabbed the job. I have been working ever since to dissociate myself from the past and carve a niche where color doesn't matter.

As a result, this book is both my overture and finale in Afro-American studies. But that may not be so unfortunate for me as it seems. Having left the field to avoid repeated humiliations at the hands of white universities, I found changes occurring within Afro-American studies which should have made me think twice about staying in it regardless of job opportunities. Beginning in the late 1960s the study of black history and culture became politically charged. Whether you are a white or black scholar, it is increasingly necessary to look over your shoulder to see what is politically fashionable and what is taboo (i.e., "racist"). Should African roots be emphasized or played down? Should one dwell on the injuries of slavery or the fortitude of the slave? Is it reasonable to see the black experience as similar to that of other ethnic groups or not? Fall behind the times and one is stupid; get ahead and one is charged with malevolence. Some may thrive in such a charged climate. But if someone calls me a racist, I am hurt; as a good liberal, I even feel guilty about such matters—maybe they know something about me I don't know.

This book is about the black middle class, a group I claim to understand better than most people, in part because I am Jewish. Like the blacks who are studied here, in my youth I experienced some confusion over my identity. As an "assimilated," upper-middle-class Jew, I was drawn, on one level, to the values and attitudes (and even the physical apearance) of the WASP upper-middle class. I wanted to be blond-haired, blue-eyed, pugged-nosed, and athletic looking. I fantasized the football helmet in one hand and the hunting rifle in the other. I did not want to be associated with the stereotype of the small, hunched, frail, intellectual-looking—and thereby unattractive—Jew. On another level I was repulsed by the image of the Anglo-American. (I use the word "image" because I do not think I met more than a dozen WASPS in the flesh until I went to college. My familiarity with lower-middle-class religious Jews was equally limited. In the isolation of the gilded ghetto, stereotypes flourish.) I thought of Anglo-Americans as anti-intellectual Babbits, whose games and sports and physical prowess served only to mask their basic inferiority; pretty but dumb—and potentially vicious as well. I was drawn to Jews, especially those who excelled in intellectual pursuits, those who looked down upon gentile "low-browness" with the contempt it deserved. As an adolescent I couldn't make up my mind where to place my loyalities—neither group seemed wholly attractive. The problem was compounded by my perception of recent European Jewish history. When I was very young a major preoccupation of mine was to find hiding places in my house where I could go when the Nazis returned, which of course they would do. Hitler was a major topic of conversation at home for years. It was important to be a part of the people they tried and failed to destroy, to be identified with the people who had all the virtues the Nazis lacked—intellect, compassion, and charitableness.

There was, however, another side of the coin. The Nazis were strong and the Jews weak, the Nazis were (in my mind's eye) tall, blond, and powerful. The Jews were defenseless, pitiful, and thereby contemptible—the perennial victim. Who wants to be a victim? There is a joke that says the Israelis fight the Arabs every day and win, and the Nazis every night and lose. There are many "assimilated" American Jews who fight the same nighttime enemy, with similar results. While I "knew" I would rather be the slave than the enslaver, the concentration camp inmate than the S.S. guard, beneath that knowledge were less noble and edifying emotions. I secretly would have preferred being the victimizer, not the victim.

On an emotional level, the German and the WASP merged into each other, as did the American and European Jews. (Power, strength, violence, and earthy passions were opposed to powerlessness, weakness, intellectuality, and compassion.) Both groups attracted and repelled me. There was no peace between them. As I have grown older I have chosen, rather strongly, not to be a pseudo-WASP (or German) and to positively affirm my Jewishness. But I don't claim to have exorcized the image of the other group, only to have understood and controlled its attractiveness.

I believe my own marginality allows me to understand a key facet of black experience: the black middle class is simultaneously attracted to and repelled by *both* the white middle class and the black lower class. Middle-class blacks share many of the values, aspirations, biases, and prejudices of the dominant white group, which draw them away from the black masses. At the same time, they are repelled by the white group and are sensitive to feelings of loyalty, affection, and sympathy toward their own racial brethren. The black bourgeoisie is suspended between those above and below them and in American society it has not been able to resolve the problem by embracing one and disowning the other. This situation and its effect is the major dilemma of the black middle class.

This work attempts to comprehend the black bourgeois experience by looking at one of its major institutions, Prince Hall Freemasonry. It discusses the ways in which the Order works to teach (and reinforce) a black commitment to the bourgeois life style, and to help its adherents live with dignity, self-respect, and pride as defined by the larger American society. Masonry is examined in both rural and urban locations and in a variety of social settings. Its accomplishments and failures in areas such as civil rights, charity, and business are presented at length. The entire discussion is placed within the context of the black bourgeoisie's ambivalent relations with other social groups and helps illuminate the black middle class's basic tragedy as a group uncomfortably located—one may even say trapped—between the white bourgeoisie and the black lower class.

An introductory word should be said concerning the research technique employed in this work. The method I have used to study the Masons involved the selection of six "representative" states: New York ("The East"), Georgia and Alabama ("The Deep South"), Illinois ("The Middle West"), California ("The West"), Texas (A Rural and Urban, Southern and Western Mixture). These were subjected to in-depth analysis. To make sure the generalizations they produced were reliable for the Masonic Order as a whole, the records of other areas were later perused—especially Ohio, Indiana, Virginia, Mississippi, North Carolina, South Carolina, and Washington, D.C. For all states the key records available were the yearly Proceedings of the Grand Lodge. These were supplemented by Masonic newspapers and magazines, constitutions, rule books, etc. The Grand Lodge proceedings include (in toto or summary) the reports of the major Grand Lodge officials and the membership lists of the Masonic jurisdiction by lodge. Because all information is presented in the form of reports or speeches by easily identified officials (e.g., Grand Master, Grand Secretary, Chairman of the Committee on Foreign Correspondence—usually referred to as C.C.F.C.) and they are relatively short and divided by topics. I will identify my sources in the following chapters by speaker rather than by page number within each proceeding.

No work of scholarship is ever the product of one mind working in a vacuum, and my debts are many. Professors Lawrence Levine, Walton Bean, and Robert Blauner, at the University of California, Berkeley, taught me most of what I know about history, sociology, and research. Even more than in most cases, however, it is necessary that I should absolve them from errors of fact or conception; in particular, I should mention at the outset that Professor Levine and I disagree on the existence of something I call "white middle-class values," discussed in Chapter II.

I should also like to thank the following persons, for their varied contributions: Lieutenant Royal E. Towns, the former editor of *Prince Hall Masonic Digest* (California), who aided me greatly in understanding both the social and philosophical dimensions of the Prince Hall Fraternity; the librarians at the Schomburg Library (New York) and Bancroft Library (Berkeley); my dedicated and conscientious research assistant, Robert Spiegel; Rita Klemczak, my typist; and University of California Press editors Grant Barnes and Russell Schoch. Finally, I wish to thank Lana Brown Muraskin of Rutgers University, without whose creative and critical and loving assistance this book could not have existed.

Chapter I

Introduction

Part 1. The Concept of the Black Middle Class

This is a study of the black middle class, analyzed through one of its oldest social institutions—Prince Hall Freemasonry. The black Masonic Order, through its chapters and affiliates, comprises a significant segment of the Afro-American middle class. By highlighting its salient characteristics and examining its development, I am attempting to view the black bourgeoisie in greater detail and with more clarity than has been done before.

While there is a small literature on the black middle class, on the whole that group has been slighted by researchers. The black lower class is generally a more attractive subject because of its social-problem status, its exotic nature, and its alleged potential as a revolutionary force. Usually, the middle class is discussed only for purposes of contrast, to better illuminate lower-class traits. The comparative neglect from which the black bourgeoisie suffers is also caused by the disdain in which it is held by many scholars. The liberal academic community is contemptuous of the American middle class—whether white or black—and radical academics are even more hostile, for obvious ideological reasons.

One of the few scholars to attempt a full-scale treatment of the black middle class was E. Franklin Frazier in his famous book *Black Bourgeoisie*.[1] That work attempted in a short but powerful presentation to capture the essence of the middle and upper strata of black society. Unfortunately, Frazier's seminal work had a side effect shared by many pioneering studies. Rather than helping to open new areas for study, it appeared to answer all the questions, making further investigation un-

[1] New York, 1957.

1

necessary. It is especially lamentable that Frazier's work should have had this effect because, despite its perceptiveness, it created a basically distorted vision of its subject.

Frazier studied the black middle class, not as a neutral observer (even granting the normal limits of objectivity), but as a participant. While much can be learned from an insider's view, especially an alienated and brilliant insider, a great deal is lost. Frazier's hostility to the group he set out to describe often overflowed into moralistic polemic, which lost sight of reality.

The most obvious flaw in Frazier's study is his attempt to delimit the boundaries of the black bourgeoisie. Frazier's black middle class is primarily a white-collar group with most of its recent growth in the clerical and kindred occupations, though it also includes professional and technical workers, managers and proprietors, craftsmen and foremen.[2] This group is estimated at 16 percent of the male black work force nationally and 20 percent in the north and west—in other words, the class is a significant minority of the black population.[3] The book itself, however, is not about this group, most of which is ignored in the text. Rather, the study focuses on the small elite at the top of the black bourgeoisie—the professionals, businessmen, and to a lesser extent college graduates generally. Most of the important examples he provides of the new middle class's ethics, or lack of them, involve doctors, college professors, or other successful professionals. This is true throughout the work, but is most obvious in his very influential chapter "Society: Status without Substance" where he explicitly says "Negro 'society' is constituted largely of [sic] *professional* and *businessmen* and women with large incomes that enable them to engage in conspicuous consumption."[4] Frazier's formal definition and his actual discussion do not cover the same people.

This distorted emphasis comes directly out of Frazier's emotional involvement with the black elite, a group whose behavior he finds personally threatening, as witnessed by his comment that:

[2] Frazier, pp. 45, 47.
[3] Ibid., p. 46.
[4] Ibid., p. 166. Italics added.

Educated Negroes have been constantly subjected to the pressures of the black bourgeoisie to conform to its values [especially
the struggle for status]. Because of this pressure some gifted
Negroes have abandoned altogether their artistic and scientific
aspirations, while others have chosen to play the role of phoney
intellectual. ... Middle Class Negroes who have made real
contributions in science and art have had to escape from the
influence of the 'social' life of the black bourgeoisie.[5]

In his preoccupation with this elite,[6] Frazier ignores the
vast majority of the black bourgeoisie, especially the white-
collar clerical and kindred workers whom he claims are so
fundamental to its existence. Frazier does draw a fascinating
picture of a vital part of the middle class. He convincingly
argues that, by their example, this group influences the behavior
of the entire black group, the lower class as well as the greater
middle class. In this respect the study has much value.[6] There
is a great difference, however, between the majority of the
middle class being influenced by Frazier's group, and identifying that small, influential minority as *the* middle class.

My study examines a much larger and more representative

---

[5] Ibid., pp. 194-195.

[6] But this is not to say his analysis is not deeply flawed even for this elite group.
Oliver C. Cox in an introduction to Nathan Hare's *Black Anglo-Saxon* (New York,
1970), makes a sweeping critique of Frazier's position. He says of *Black Bourgeoisie*:
"There is hardly a consequential assertion regarding traits of the Negro middle class
that does not prove to be unreliable or egregiously misleading. Its critical evidence
is a composite of personal anecdotes, hearsay, erratic news items, and distorted social
science information" (Hare, p. 20). Cox also emphasizes Frazier's personal and emotional
bias—a bias that develops over time. For example, in 1925 Frazier was very laudatory
of the black middle class and said: " 'These younger men are truly modern business
men [sic].... They work hard .... They have the same outlook on life as the middle
class everywhere .... They have little sympathy with waste of time .... Middle-class
respectability is their ideal' " (quoted by Cox on pp. 29-30 from Frazier's "Durham:
Capital of the Black Middle Class" in *The New Negro*, edited by Alain Locke, [New
York, 1925], pp. 338-339). Yet, Cox says, "Five years later, according to the chronology
of *Black Bourgeoisie*, the middle class had vanished" and was replaced by a "pathological" new bourgeoisie (Hare, pp. 18, 30). Cox is also critical of Frazier's "loose definition
of the Negro middle class." He contends that Frazier has two definitions: one for
occupation and one for income. The size of the group varies greatly under the two
definitions. (Using the income definition of $2,000 or more per year, 40 percent of the
northern blacks are middle class.) Cox feels that this approach creates a picture of
a "black bourgeoisie [which] does not constitute a sociological group but rather
statistical categories of unstable dimensions"—a poor basis for studying the social
characteristics of a class (Hare, p. 17).

segment of the black middle class.[7] Characteristics, values, and behavior that are missing from Frazier's elite are discussed here. However, it is not necessary to dispute his characterization of the black upper-middle class so much as to limit its applicability. By focusing on the majority of the black bourgeoisie, we will see that there is far more continuity in lifestyle between what Frazier called the "Old" and "New" middle classes than he hypothesized; that traditional petty-bourgeois values and behavior did not disappear among middle-class blacks after 1930 or 1940 as Frazier believed. If, for Frazier's elite, divorce and sex scandals "do not affect one's social status . . . rather the notoriety which one acquires in such cases adds to one's prestige," this is not true for the bulk of the middle class.[8] It is also questionable that the one overriding value accepted by the middle class is really the obsession with conspicuous consumption that Frazier's elite possesses. And there is little support for the contention that the majority of the black bourgeoisie has "not taken over the patterns of behavior of the white-collar and professional white workers, but [rather] the values and as far as possible the patterns of behavior of wealthy whites."[9]

I am not directly confronting Frazier's view here, not only because he deals mainly with only the "top" of the middle class, but because most of my material covers the years before the rise of Frazier's "New" middle class. There is less disagreement between us for the decades preceding World War II because Frazier does not claim that the black elite lacked traditional bourgeois morality or behavior before that time. I part company with him only after the war, and even here our differences are muted. Prince Hall Freemasonry has always attracted a significant portion of the black elite. Indeed, until the Depression it attracted the majority of that group. After World War II it continued to attract a disproportionately high percentage of such people, though its relative attractiveness and its social importance for elite status declined. Thus a growing part of the elite is outside my area of study after 1945.

[7] See the end of this chapter for my definition of the term "black middle class."

[8] Frazier, p. 109.

[9] Ibid., p. 141. Interestingly enough, a similar view has been quite popular with "sympathetic" whites. They believe that lower-class blacks, rather than middle-class ones, lack a "work ethic" because they accepted the white plantation-owning class, with its aristocratic disdain of work, as their model.

To this extent, conflict between my view and Frazier's is minimized, since we may not be talking about the same people—even though we both call them the "black bourgeoisie."

One of the real differences between my study and Frazier's concerns the effectiveness of the black middle class as leaders of the race. While we both view the bourgeoisie's effectiveness as severely compromised, Frazier emphasizes the alienation of the middle class (i.e., the elite) from the masses, their identification with the white upper-middle and upper classes, and their withdrawal into a land of make-believe—a land where they lead the style of life of wealthy whites and dissipate their energies.[10] I maintain that acceptance by the black bourgeoisie of white lower-middle-class morality and behavior had the effect of alienating them from the black masses, tying them to the white middle class, and interfering with their ability to lead their race.[11] This is as true for 1850 as for 1950. The result, compromised leadership, is the same but the reasons for it are different.

My view, unlike Frazier's, is that the middle class is a tragic group more deserving of respect and empathy than condemnation. It is a class that is marginal to both the black and white racial communities. Divided in its allegiances, forced to turn in two directions at once, wracked by its own ambivalence, it has been unable even to develop the economic base to be securely worthy of the name "bourgeoisie." The black middle class is not a willing betrayer of itself or its race but is the victim of its own precarious economic and social position. American society's racial and socioeconomic structure conspires against it, cruelly entangling it in an impossible series of contradictions. Frazier is well aware of the economic, social, and cultural restraints on the black middle class, but he ignores the logic of his evidence. Out of hostility he adopts a moralistic stance that assumes the middle class is responsible for its actions even though such moral culpability requires a freedom of choice that he knows it lacks.

Another important and more recent work on the black middle class, quite different from Frazier's and illuminating very different aspects of black society, is Ivan Light's perceptive *Ethnic Business in America*, a study of Japanese, Chinese, West

---

[10] Ibid., pp. 140-141.
[11] See Chapter II for discussion.

Indian, and black American business.[12] Intended not as a general overview of the middle class, it instead highlights some key characteristics of that group. Light attempts to give substance to the contention of Frazier and others that the central value and obsession of the black middle class, "Race Progress" through "black business," is a myth. He does this by describing in detail the failure of the black middle class to develop the economic base necessary for the creation of a true bourgeoisie.

Light's major hypothesis is that American blacks lack a key socioeconomic institution, the Rotating Credit Association, which other groups (the Chinese, Japanese and West Indians) have utilized effectively to generate the funds needed to capitalize a business community. Without this "folk" institution black would-be businessmen have been forced to rely upon formal lending institutions such as banks—which have been notoriously uncooperative with small, fledgling businesses, and equally notorious in their hostility to nonwhite people.[13]

As useful and enlightening as Light's work is in clarifying aspects of the black business tradition, his discussion shares Frazier's weakness. Light's description of the black community includes only two groups, a small "rich" elite and the poverty-stricken mass. Once again, the black middle class below elite status does not exist; Light doesn't even allow for it in theory as Frazier does. Though Light does not explicitly develop his vision of the black class structure, his view becomes clear in his discussion of the need for black businessmen, as represented in the National Negro Business League, to train lower-class blacks to succeed them:

> The growth of Negro-owned business clearly required a continuous expansion of its base of recruitment. . . . Hence, the success of the Business League's attempt to expand Negro business depended crucially on its ability to recruit and train lower-class blacks.
>
> This sine qua non of business development, the Business League was chronically unable to attain. Since the league chapters were structurally isolated voluntary associations of the *wealthy*, they were unable to reach lower-class black youth. The

[12] Ivan Light, *Ethnic Business in America* (Berkeley, 1972).

[13] Abram Harris in *The Negro as Capitalist* (Gloucester, Mass., 1968), p. 57, contends that "When all of the facts are considered, it appears to us that economic rather than racial causes are the primary determinants of the credit policy of white banks to Negro business."

social worlds of the young *slum-dwelling* black and the *prosperous* businessmen could not interpenetrate.[14]

The entire strata of blacks found in Freemasonry—which is representative of the greater black middle class—is ignored. This is the group that would naturally supply Light's "rich" businessmen with recruits, which an undifferentiated black lower class could not do. The details of elite interaction with the larger black bourgeoisie are not given by Light since he takes no note of the existence of that strata. In saying this I am ignoring the question of whether the National Negro Business League really was composed of "wealthy" and "prosperous" black entrepreneurs at all. I am merely saying that a discussion of black business and its failures must include the aspirations, attitudes, and skills of a much larger portion of the black middle class than the practicing (and successful) businessmen.

It is my belief that the best way to see the black bourgeoisie is not to concentrate on the small elite at the top (doctors, lawyers, professors, rich businessmen); nor to focus on outstanding or gifted individual leaders (such as DuBois, Washington, or Wilkins); but rather to study in depth an institution such as Prince Hall Freemasonry, an institution with a large membership and its own spokesmen, men who are more in touch with the average black middle class man than are more prominent black leaders.

Before attempting to understand the black middle class, one must first define it, a task immediately complicated by the fact that the scholarly literature in this field reflects little agreement on the question of who constitutes the black bourgeoisie. The problem exists in the study of white as well as black society because different researchers use differing concepts to define class structure. Sometimes "objective" criteria—income, occupation, education—are used (and there is no agreement as to which ones are paramount); other times reputation within the community or ease of social interaction in informal groups is emphasized. Even when the same criteria are used, the specific subdivisions within the classes are often not directly comparable across several studies.[15] For the investigation of

---

[14] Light, pp. 116-117. Italics added.
[15] The problem is ubiquitous. For example, W. E. B. Du Bois in *The Philadelphia*

blacks the standard problems have been magnified by a retarded development of the "objective" criteria of class. Discrimination during most of our history artificially limited the development of a complete black occupational, income, and educational continuum. Scholars have been explicit about this problem, and the difficulties it has created have not been restricted to studies of small-town southern black communities, or late nineteenth-century urban centers.[16] St. Clair Drake and Horace Cayton, for example, recognized the problem as important in their work on Chicago in the 1930s. They noted that "neither occupation nor income is, in the final analysis, the decisive measuring rod [of middle-class status]. Rather, the middle class is marked off from the lower class by a pattern of behavior expressed in stable family and associational relationships, in great concern with 'front' and 'respectability,' and in a drive for 'getting ahead.' "[17] Drake and Cayton point out that Frazier in his *Negro Family in the United States*[18] attempted to use objective criteria for a definition of middle class but his efforts were not successful.[19] Frazier himself in a later work, while emphasizing the increasing significance of objective criteria of class among blacks, allows that the slow pace with which socioeconomic class criteria has emerged even in large southern cities has meant that "social as opposed to occupational or economic bases of social stratification have continued" to be important.[20] Indeed, even for northern urban centers, Frazier states that " 'middle class' . . . is essentially a social class though

---

Negro (New York, 1899), attempts both a socio-moral definition and a definition based on income and occupation. The number of gradations in the two definitions differ, three in the former and four in the latter. (See Du Bois, p. 311, n.14.) In his study Du Bois hypothesizes a black upper class. E. Franklin Frazier, on the other hand, in *Black Bourgeoisie* postulates only a middle class. G. Franklin Edwards in *The Negro Professional Class* (New York, 1959), limits his discussion of the middle class to professionals alone (and not all professionals at that). Exactly what he feels are the boundaries of the class is obscure. (See Edwards, pp. 17, 20, 161.) Charles Johnson in *Growing Up in the Black Belt* (Washington, D.C., 1941), sees an upper class and middle class with many of his upper-class blacks identical with Edwards' middle class.

[16] Hylan Lewis, *Blackways of Kent* (Chapel Hill, N.C., 1955); Allison Davis, Burleigh and Mary Gardner, *Deep South* (Chicago, 1941); or W. E. B. Du Bois, *The Philadelphia Negro*.

[17] St. Clair Drake and Horace Cayton, *Black Metropolis* (New York, 1962), pp. 661-662.

[18] E. Franklin Frazier (Chicago, 1966).

[19] Drake and Cayton, p. 662.

[20] E. Franklin Frazier, *The Negro in the United States* (New York, 1957), p. 286.

occupation and income play some part in determining its place in the class structure of the Negro community."[21]

Observers of the black, as opposed to the white, class structure, then, have been forced to rely more heavily on behavioral, moral, and value differences to mark class divisions. Unfortunately, it is hard to obtain information on classes built on nonobjective characteristics; for example, a janitor can be termed lower class, stable working class, middle class, or upper class depending upon his behavior, reputation, or associations. The problem is magnified when it is realized that the reputational and perceived value and behavioral differences upon which black classes are supposed to be based may be distorted. The black "middle class" and scholarly observers may agree that the lower class has its own value system; but that perception may be incorrect.

The problem of defining the black middle class is even more acute because the class definitions currently available in the literature on black society are deficient. Most researchers have taken note of the scarcity of objective criteria for class status and have made use of moral, value, or behavioral definitions. They have maintained that blacks can be divided into those who accept standard American petty-bourgeois values and act accordingly, and those who do not.[22] However, the attempt to utilize value and behavioral attributes to distinguish the black middle class from the lower class has raised major problems. First, the assumption that the difference between lower-class and middle-class blacks rests on moral and value differences is highly problematic. This assumption, which has enabled scholars to talk about a black bourgeoisie in the absence of more standard characteristics, has been persuasively challenged by the anti-culture-of-poverty theorists—especially Elliott Liebow, Charles Valentine, and Ulf Hannerz.[23] In their attempt

[21] Frazier, *Negro in U.S.*, p. 301.

[22] Herbert Gans, "Culture and Class in the Study of Poverty: An Approach to Anti-Poverty Research" in *On Understanding Poverty*, edited by D. Moynihan (New York, 1969), and Charles Valentine in *Culture and Poverty* (Chicago, 1968), review from a critical perspective the extensive literature based on this division. Jesse Bernard in *Marriage and Family Among Negroes* (Englewood Cliffs, 1965), ch. 2, gives one of the most ambitious formulations of the concept from a proponent's perspective.

[23] For example, Charles Valentine's *Culture and Poverty* mentioned above, Elliott Liebow's *Talley's Corner* (Boston, 1967), Ulf Hannerz' *Soulside* (New York, 1969), among others. The anti-culture-of-poverty writers are to some extent reviving the ideas of the Chicago School of Sociology. Drake and Cayton in *Black Metropolis*, Davis

to discredit Oscar Lewis' "culture of poverty" concept, they have raised significant doubts about the viability of the concept of "class culture."

In the wake of these criticisms, Herbert Gans, whose brilliant and influential *Urban Villagers*[24] is built on the view that different classes have different values and cultures, has reexamined and repudiated his earlier position. Gans now maintains that "descriptions of class culture pay little attention to the distinction between behavioral and aspirational culture on the one hand and situational responses on the other hand. . . . Dichotomies such as working class and lower class . . . can be used to describe the existential condition . . . and the situational responses which they make . . . but they cannot be used as *cultural* [i.e., value and aspirational] typologies, for people [in the same situation] . . . may respond with different behavioral norms and aspirations."[25] Gans, along with other anti-culture-of-poverty theorists like Valentine and Liebow, contends that all blacks, lower-class and middle-class, have the same values (i.e., standard American middle-class), but that the lower class is forced to adapt its life style in ways that violate those values. Their thesis is that if you change the macrostructural restraints that control the lower class's behavior the black poor will be able and willing to act out "mainstream" bourgeois values without the need for cultural or value "resocialization." The anti-culture-of-poverty scholars may disagree among themselves on whether to call the lower-class

---

and Gardner in *Deep South* and John Dollard in *Caste and Class in a Southern Town*, (New Haven, 1937) paint a picture in which racism and economic and social restraints are basic to black lower-class characteristics—from knivings to weak egos. The Chicago School made it quite clear that the cause of black problems was external to the group (e.g., the racial job ceiling, discrimination). The interpretation emphasizing deeply ingrained "pathology" came later. The new revisionists do not acknowledge their predecessors because they see one of the Chicago School, E. Franklin Frazier, as the "father" of the culture-of-poverty idea. This identification has been unfortunate. It is true that the Chicago School emphasized lower-class disorganization and pathology rather than "healthy adaptation," and that their studies imply that the middle-class life style is superior to the lower-class one, but their stress on socioeconomic structure as the cause of lower-class problems places them clearly against those who "blame the victim" or hypothesize great psychological obstacles to change. The Chicago sociologists (including Frazier) assume no deeply held lower-class value system. In this respect Frazier is paradoxically as much, if not more, the "father" of the anti-culture-of-poverty writers as he is of their opponents.

[24] Herbert Gans, *Urban Villagers* (New York, 1962).
[25] Moynihan, *Understanding Poverty*, pp. 217-218.

life style a "behavioral culture" or simply a noncultural, temporary adaptation, but they all agree that behavior is a doubtful indicator of what men desire and of what they would choose voluntarily if they were free to make a choice.[26] Their arguments against the "orthodox" position are very persuasive.[27]

If this situation was not damaging enough to the standard analyses of black society, the idea that one can tell class by general behavior (rather than value) differences has also been challenged—though, thus far, less thoroughly.[28]

The challenge to the "behavior differentiates class" argument stems from the weakness of our knowledge of how different social strata actually behave. Does the lower class really commit more crime than the middle class? Is the broken matriarchal family really characteristic of black lower-class life? The answers to these questions are not known, though scholars act as if they were. Recently a large literature has developed that contends that crime, juvenile delinquency, and other deviancy statistics broken down by class are worthless since the laws are enforced unequally, with arrests reflecting selective enforcement rather than actual behavior. James Q. Wilson, a fairly conservative scholar, confesses in *Varieties of Police Behavior* that "One might suppose that criminologists would long since have satisfied themselves that lower-income people commit more common crimes . . . than middle- or upper-income groups. I find to my surprise (and irritation) that this is not the case."[29] Wilson strongly "believes" that behavioral differences between classes exist but he admits that "my opinion [is] . . . based, I confess, as much on the experience of living in lower-class as well as rich areas as on the fragmentary . . . studies" available.[30] At the same time the historian Herbert

---

[26] See Hannerz, pp. 177-200, for an explicit discussion of differences and agreements within the anti-culture-of-poverty camp. Hannerz himself attempts to synthesize the strengths of Oscar Lewis and those of his opponents. (While I place him firmly in the anti-culture-of-poverty camp, others might disagree.)

[27] See William Muraskin, "The Moral Basis of a Backward Sociologist: Edward Banfield, the Italians and the Italian-Americans," *American Journal of Sociology* (May 1974), for a detailed critique of a cultural explanation of poverty in southern Italy.

[28] Interestingly, most of the anti-culture-of-poverty writers, while questioning the existence of value differences between classes, do not dispute behavioral ones. Indeed, their theories are based on an acknowledgement of behavioral differences and on an explanation of their cause and meaning.

[29] James Q. Wilson, *Varieties of Police Behavior* (Cambridge, Mass., 1968), p. 40.

[30] Ibid., p. 41.

Gutman has tried to prove that for many decades the average black family has been a standard one of husband, wife, and their own children.[31] Among part of the educated public generally there is a growing suspicion that behavioral differences between middle- and lower-class people have been severely exaggerated by middle-class ethnocentrism, and that observers theorize about the causes of lower-class problems (e.g., alcoholism) while ignoring their high frequency among middle- and upper-class people. I do not claim that anyone has conclusively proved that lower- and middle-class people do not hold different values or manifest differences in behavior. The new scholarship does, however, make a comfortable assertion of the orthodox theory impossible.[32]

Given the difficulties in using income and occupational characteristics or value and behavior differences as the basis for a definition of the black middle class, what criteria can be used to characterize the black bourgeoisie? There are two possible ways out of this predicament. The first involves emphasizing social perception, not "objective reality." Since one cannot define the black lower class, and since too little is known about the actual characteristics, motivation, and practice of that group, one can stress the class-defining differences that black people believe exist. If those blacks who think of themselves as middle class believe their value system is not shared by members of the lower class—who are lazy, drunk, and dirty—and

[31] Herbert Gutman's findings will soon appear in book form.

[32] The anti-culture-of-poverty theorists are strongest when undermining the contention of others. When they present their own views, their arguments become more problematic. Hannerz, Valentine, and Liebow simply assert, rather than prove, that lower-class black people accept mainstream values on an aspirational level. Hannerz does a good job of explaining *how* lower class people get enough exposure to standard American morality to make it their own, which the others do not; but even he is not totally convincing since, among other things, he assumes that mass media exposure to values means people accept them, despite the well-known phenomenon of viewers "tuning out" media ideas they do not find congenial—a point made quite well by Herbert Gans in *Urban Villagers*. Liebow goes to great lengths to prove the existence of only one American value system, but his own evidence points strongly to the existence of at least some alternative cultural patterns, especially relating to kinship ("going for cousins," "going for brothers"). Hannerz, who is in sympathy with much of Liebow's argument, feels that a real alternative value concerning masculinity may exist among the lower class—something Liebow unconvincingly attempts to psychoanalyze away. Valentine (pp. 141-147) appears to take a strong position on the universality of middle-class values among the lower class throughout his book until his conclusion, when he opens the door for other possibilities, thereby emphasizing that his proposition is more a useful hypothesis for questioning the orthodox view than a viable alternative.

if those middle-class blacks act in line with their perception, that is enough upon which to build a definition. One does not have to be certain that the middle-class blacks are right, nor agree with their moral judgments, as so many scholars seem to do. By using social perception as a guide, the black middle class can be studied as an actual social group with a minimum of discomfort despite our lack of knowledge about the lower-class life style.

The second approach contrasts the reality of lower- and middle-class behavior and values, but it requires only a limited factual comparison and avoids the sweeping allegations of value and behavioral difference that other theories assert. In this approach I maintain that the contrast between lower class and middle class is not necessarily a general value difference (e.g., the middle class believes in petty-bourgeois morality and the lower class does not); nor a general behavioral one (e.g., the black lower class has loose sex values and the middle class does not); but rather a very specific and limited difference: to the middle class, "respectability" is the highest value, and respectability is obtained by carrying out in *public* behavior standard American bourgeois morality. Those who act correctly are middle class, while those who violate the moral code in *public* situations are relegated to lower-class status. My contention is that the black middle class does carry this value out in practice and the black lower class does not. This value, and the behavior that flows from it, I believe objectively separates the black middle class from the lower class on the basis of real, not simply perceived or imagined, differences. My approach does not assume that the two groups actually differ in their ideal value systems, nor that the middle class necessarily acts in *private* differently from other people; it only maintains that public behavior does differ and that the middle class works to differentiate itself on this basis.

While other observers of black society have not emphasized public behavior to this extent, support for my conceptualization can be found in many other works. Hylan Lewis in *Blackways of Kent* creates the social categories of "respectable and non-respectable" that support my approach. Though Lewis's position appears similar to that of other researchers who believe in the existence of "class cultures," he does not emphasize value differences; instead, he emphasizes behavioral differences. And the behavioral variations are discussed less as general differences than as public ones. For example, he maintains, "In general, the respectable persons are defined by what they do not do. They are people who are careful of their *public* conduct and reputation: they don't drink whiskey in *public* or get drunk in *public*; they don't frequent the taverns; they don't get in trouble; and they are proud of their lack of contact with the law and the courts."[33] Elsewhere he points out that "Nonrespectable behavior tends to be more dramatic, unrestrained, and public, and therefore it looms larger in the public eye . . . the persons who practice it contribute more heavily to the over-all tone of the society than [the respectables]."[34] This second point helps explain the exaggerated perception of the black lower class which shapes both the white and black middle-class views of black society. St. Clair Drake and Horace Cayton in *Black Metropolis* also support my approach. While they appear to believe in general behavioral differences between the lower and middle classes (though they allow for a "respectable" lower class group and a "shady" middle class one, too), they *emphasize* a more selective difference: "There is a very sharp division . . . between those who value 'front'—who stress decorous *public* behavior and those who don't. . . . *The decisive measure of the man is how he acts in public.*"[35]

An emphasis on public behavior as the chief characteristic of middle-class status is very useful because it protects us from casting aspersions on the morality of the black lower class or assuming behavioral differences that remain unproved. It inhibits middle-class ethnocentrism. However, it lends itself to a potentially hostile view of the black bourgeoisie. The middle class's concern with respectability and "front" is often dismissed by unsympathetic observers as simple hypocrisy.[36] Hypocrisy, however, is an individual trait, not a class one. When an entire group acts in a uniform, socially-determined way, such a moralistic label is misapplied. Since the practice of

[33] Hylan Lewis, pp. 233-234. Italics in original.
[34] Hylan Lewis, p. 236. See p. 204 for his discussion of drunkenness as well.
[35] Drake and Cayton, p. 519. Italics in original.
[36] Drake and Cayton point out this tendency when they say "Because of the stress that the 'dicties' place upon correct *public* behavior they are often the target of the less sophisticated people who dub them 'hypocrites' " (Drake and Cayton, p. 519, italics in original). I would add that they are often the target of ultrasophisticated upper-middle-class white academics as well.

maintaining appearances is a crucial element in the process of social differentiation, and to be middle class by definition means making a commitment to maintain the aura of respectability above all else, this concern for "front" must be accepted as a legitimate group process, not dismissed as an individual pretension.

The black bourgeoisie's commitment to respectability as a defining trait is well illustrated by testimony in my research. During an interview with several Masons, discussion developed on the question of differentiating true Prince Hall Masonry from lower-class imposter organizations. The Masons noted that if a Prince Hall Mason commits an illegal act he will hide his Masonic pin even though he is safe from prosecution, and if arrested he will deny his association with the Order. If a lower-class member of a "bogus" Masonic Lodge finds himself in the same situation he will flaunt his Masonic status in the first case and try to use it to obtain leniency in the second. The differences in actual legal behavior may be nonexistent, but the differences in attitude and consequences are not. When people deviate from the ideal, the black middle class is concerned that the proper appearance or "front" be maintained in order to insure that the deviation does not become an acceptable model for behavior.[37] To call this attitude simple hypocrisy is both unfair and inaccurate.

My definition, even when it does not give rise to the accusation of hypocrisy, does tend to obscure a "heroic" side of middle-class respectability. Thus far I have discussed with approval the anti-culture-of-poverty position that lower- and

[37] A story that highlights the "humanness" of Masons and the socially differentiating importance of "front" was related to the author by a California Mason. For years men came to him asking that he propose their names for membership in his lodge, but since most of them were not "respectable" enough he felt obliged to refuse. Finally, he was asked by a man he deeply admired and he immediately put his name up for membership only to find the man blackballed by the Worshipful Master (WM). Knowing that the WM was a personal friend of the rejected applicant, he asked the WM why he had vetoed such a well-qualified man. The WM told him he was morally forced to act as he did because he was "playing around" with the applicant's wife—something he knew was wrong—but since it was not "common knowledge" and no one could say "you are dishonoring the fraternity and yourself," he could not stop. He blackballed the man he cuckolded because he could allow himself to cheat on a neighbor—but he would die before cheating on a brother! My informant thought the story quite amusing. "Men are men and sex is sex," he said, but if the WM's activities had been widely known, the outcome would have been less amusing. He would have been expelled from the Order in disgrace. (Name of informant withheld by request.)

middle-class people share the same value system and that the lower class fails to act out those values because of factors outside its control. The argument in favor of "macrostructural causation" is a very convincing one: change the larger society's behavior toward the poor and you will change the ghetto; provide the lower class with the economic resources to choose its life style freely and you will end antibourgeois behavior. This interpretation takes the blame off the victim and places it where it belongs—on white society. However, when the structuralist interpretation is applied to those who have with great effort risen above the structural restraints and have refused to adapt to what Hannerz calls "ghetto specific" modes of behavior, the explanation seems less than either appropriate or just.[38]

The problem with the structuralist interpretation, which denies lower-class free will and therefore culpability, is that while it avoids middle-class ethnocentrism, moralism, and cultural imperialism, it answers the question of why blacks are poor by ignoring the many blacks who are not poor. As long as one asks, "Why do blacks fail?, Why do blacks live in poverty?," the macrostructuralist interpretation is acceptable. But if the question is "Why do many blacks succeed?," difficulties in explanation arise. For if structure is the determinant of action, and the American social structure is and always has been antiblack, how did some—and not a handful but a substantial part of the black population—overcome structural obstacles while other blacks were forced to adapt to them? To even ask the question may appear as heretical since it implies an ethnocentric concern for those who "succeeded" over those who "adapted," but scholars have no right to sweep the nonpoor blacks under the rug of structural causation.

Put another way, the structuralists are correct in seeing poverty as a *necessary* cause of black lower-class behavior. They go on, however, to imply that structure is not only necessary but *sufficient* as the cause of black lower-class behavior. That this is untrue is proved by the significant number of blacks who have not "adapted." Exactly what variables intervene to allow some to rise is a complex problem, but attitudes, values, or commitments other than those created by structural restraints are certainly involved. This analysis

[38] Hannerz, pp. 36-37.

must allow some room for an appreciation of individual or group perseverance and determination. Without seeing those who do not rise as defective or morally deficient, one should be able to see those who do as worthy of additional respect.[39]

In the rest of this book I will use both methods of defining the black middle class that have been discussed here: I will demonstrate that the black bourgeoisie, as seen in Prince Hall Freemasonry, perceive themselves as different from the lower class in their values and behavior, and that they emphasize public performance of standard American morality as the key to social status. To the extent possible, I will supplement these approaches with economic and occupational material where it is available and will shed light on the "objective" characteristics of the black middle class.

One problem I still face in discussing the black middle class is to delimit its upper and lower boundaries. Given a "public respectability" definition, it is especially hard to differentiate between the black middle class and upwardly mobile lower-class individuals. I shall later present evidence that Masonry has drawn more heavily from the former than from the latter, but my ability to clearly distinguish the groups is unfortunately limited. Frazier in *The Negro in the United States* presents the problem succinctly:

Since the class structure in the Negro community is fluid, the upper layers of the middle class merge with the upper class, while the lower layers are hardly distinguishable from the lower class.[40]

[39] Of course, one should not overdo the amount of sacrifice and effort that the black middle class has had to endure, real as it has been. The middle class has created a social environment that forces conformity to respectable behavior, and for many it is easier to do as they are expected than not. Also, as Hylan Lewis makes clear in *Blackways of Kent*, to some extent the occupations and positions the black middle class occupies force the maintenance of a bourgeois life style: "[Relatively higher] education or economic status not only involves the voluntary assumption of different behavior standards but it also means having impressed upon one a definite role: since they are people who are going somewhere—or aspiring to—they should act like it" (Hylan Lewis, p. 234). Thus, the realm of free will which is the necessary basis for praise and blame is significantly lessened. However, while the middle-class life style is strongly facilitated by a man's economic and occupational position, it cannot be totally explained by it. Lewis himself points this out when he says that the type of jobs that promote "respectable" behavior are not achieved simply on an accidental basis, but are usually attained by those already demonstrating a propensity to such a life style (Hylan Lewis, p. 243).

[40] Frazier, *Negro in U.S.*, p. 301.

To the extent that upwardly mobile lower-class men have characteristics significantly different from the black bourgeoisie, my treatment of them as a single middle-class group could create a significant distortion. Fortunately, the harm done by not being able to emphasize their differences is severely reduced because the lower-class "strivers" are divisible into two separate groups, only one of which plays any part in Masonry, and that group of mobile individuals is close enough in its characteristics to the black middle class to make a unified treatment of the two strata reasonable.

One group of upwardly mobile men is composed of ambitious individuals who wish to move into the middle-class social network. They see a middle-class status-conferring organization such as Masonry as the means to enter middle-class society. Masonic membership will both proclaim their acceptability to the middle class and provide a meeting ground for socializing with would-be fellow class members. These people though lower class initially are committed to the public performance of conventional middle-class behavior. Their existing reputations reflect this orientation and thus they possess the key characteristic of middle-class status before they enter the fraternity. Their lower-class status results either from extreme poverty— since even in a generally poor group, with weak income differentiation, there is an income range, with those falling too far below the standard being designated a "poor but respectable" lower class—or from simple lack of associational ties with the "right" people. They do not need to be socialized into middle-class behavior after admittance and thus, in a fundamental sense, they are not *lower-class* strivers at all, but rather middle-class people trying to get official recognition of their "deserved" status. Only a minimum of harm is done by lumping this group into a single category with the black bourgeoisie.

The second type of upwardly mobile person is truly a lower-class striver. He aspires to social acceptance by the middle class but must change his behavior in order to be accepted. He does not possess the public reputation necessary for the status he desires but rather hopes his future conduct will make him acceptable and that obtaining middle-class associates will help him rehabilitate both his behavior and reputation. There are many middle-class organizations that accept such men gladly, that desire to resocialize "bad men" and make them "good."

In Hylan Lewis's study of "Kent," the Order of Elks proclaims just such a policy. Masonry refuses to perform this function.[41] It will not reform its adherents. Rather, it aims to make "good men better" and not "bad men good."[42]

While one cannot easily specify the percentage of solidly middle-class versus upwardly mobile lower-class men in Masonry, we can say that the Order is restricted to the type of lower-class man who is only nominally lower class to begin with. Given the growth of the black middle class and the growth of Freemasonry over the years, the "respectable" lower-class striver probably makes up a sizeable portion of the Masonic membership.[43] The other type of lower-class striver, those more deserving of the name, are not found in Masonry to any large extent.

There is also a problem in differentiating the middle-class from the upper-class elite since an intensive social analysis is necessary to pinpoint the elusive division between the top of one class and the bottom of the other.[44] As a result, my working definition of the black middle class will be more inclusive than I wish, but this is a minor distortion compared to the "under" inclusiveness of studies such as Frazier's *Black Bourgeoisie.*

Part 2. Masonry and the Middle Class

Prince Hall Freemasonry is the Afro-American branch of the worldwide Masonic Order. English Freemasonry, the parent of the Prince Hall Fraternity, was a creation of the eighteenth century, at least in the form we know it today.[45] The Order of "symbolic" Masons grew out of the organization of actual, "practical" masons in medieval England. In the Middle Ages

[41] See Chapters II and IV for examples of this attitude.

[42] Interview with Adrian Bridges, Secretary of an Oakland, California, Masonic Lodge, May 1970.

[43] As will be shown, the Masons tend to discriminate against the poorer members of this group, despite their adherence to bourgeois standards. The Order accepts only the economically better off lower-class striver. See Chapter II.

[44] When Drake and Cayton, p. 530, asked knowledgeable Chicago blacks how many of the Chicago blacks in *Who's Who in Colored America* were upper class, they were surprised that only a small proportion (31 out of 106) were so designated. Thus the upper and lower boundaries of the middle class must be left vague in the absence of intensive local study.

[45] The following discussion utilizes the essay "Freemasonry" by Mervyn Jones found in *Secret Societies*, edited by Norman MacKenzie (New York, 1971). His discussion is a judicious and balanced overview, though in a popularized form.

masons were an unusual occupational group. Unlike most laborers they were not employed in small domestic units with a master and a few journeymen, but rather in large groups. Since most dwellings were of wood, and masons worked with stone, they were chiefly employed in constructing large buildings such as cathedrals, monasteries, and castles. This type of work meant that masons were forced constantly to move over the countryside, on to the next big project. Large groups and constant movement, combined with the normal medieval practice of setting up craft guilds, created an exceptionally tight-knit group. It appears that while the masons were organized into local "lodges" they also belonged to a national assembly—though information on this is scarce. The masons operated under rules called the Old Charges, which were basically guild rules governing work but also contained "moral obligations regarding honesty, sobriety, piety, and loyalty to the king, which masons were bound to observe for the sake of their collective reputation."[46]

At some point the "practical" masonic lodges began to allow "honorary" members, those not actually skilled in stone work, into their associations. The initial attractiveness of the Order is not totally clear, except that the masonic groups had social, intellectual, and recreational as well as occupational functions. Some men may have been attracted by the hope of hidden wisdom, others by a desire for knowledge about architecture.[47] By the early 1700s many of the lodges were filled primarily with men not engaged in the building trades. These men "reformed" the Order, creating modern, "speculative" Masonry open to men interested in brotherhood and an understanding of the mysteries of life.[48] In the years before 1700 the members developed a system in which the tools and methods of practical masonic work were given a symbolic, primarily moral, meaning. In 1717 four London lodges came together to form the United Grand Lodge. The new Grand Lodge helped spread the Order throughout England and the American colonies; at the same time the Masonic fraternal concept was transported to Europe as well.

[46] MacKenzie, p. 133.

[47] Ibid., pp. 134-5

[48] Jacob Katz, *Jews and Freemasons in Europe, 1723-1939* (Cambridge, Mass., 1971), pp. 11-12.

During the eighteenth century, the English Order grew quickly. Membership in Freemasonry became very fashionable. It attracted members of the wealthy middle class and was eminently respectable. For most of its history it has been common for the Grand Master, the head of the Order, to be a member of the royal family. Both King Edward VII and King George VI were Grand Masters before mounting the throne.

English Freemasonry expounded the doctrines of intellectual free inquiry and religious tolerance. It was influenced by the Enlightenment and attempted to appeal to and harmonize as wide a range of religious opinion as possible. While members were required to believe in God, even a watered-down Deism fulfilled this requirement. The lodges were told to avoid religious and political controversy and they did so. During this period England led the way toward the modern bourgeois society and Freemasonry's ideals were in harmony with the coming order.

On the continent Freemasonry found itself in a far less hospitable climate. Free thought and religious tolerance were not looked upon kindly by most leaders (secular or spiritual) of the *ancien regime*. As one observer has said:

> As soon as men became Freemasons, they seemed to place themselves in opposition to both Church and State. In the first place, Freemasons devoted themselves to the spread of knowledge in its broadest sense. . . . Logic led them to the realization that their aims could be pursued only when free debate and the spread of knowledge were guaranteed. . . . The preconditions for the triumph of knowledge were freedom of association, of speech, and of the press; the abolition of censorship by State and Church. . . . All this amounted to a program for fundamental change, and to demands that authority would not concede unless it was forced to.[49]

As a result even when lodges stayed clear of politics—as they were supposed to—many of their members did not, and the Order's reputation with the authorities suffered.

In many European countries the evolution of Freemasonry diverged markedly from that of the Order in England. It became involved with or adopted many new and unusual doctrines—some mystical, others revolutionary. Its involvement with

[49] MacKenzie, pp. 141-142.

radical change was quite marked in Italy, where it was constantly at war with the Pope and his attempt to thwart Italian unification. In France, Freemasonry became identified with the pro-Republican, pro-Revolutionary elements of French politics and opposed to the Catholic, monarchist and reactionary ones.[50]

The fraternity also spread to the American colonies, where it became very popular among the elite. In keeping with the English tradition the lodges stayed out of politics, but their members (including George Washington, Benjamin Franklin, Paul Revere, John Paul Jones, and Alexander Hamilton) were quite active in colonial affairs. For them, Freemasonry stood for the Enlightenment ideas they hoped to put into practice through the Revolution.[51]

While the ideals of Masonry and its role in politics have been investigated, not a great deal is known about its social composition or the general social function the Order has played in the Western world. It is a secret organization, and what literature exists about it has usually been written to attack or defend the fraternity from the charge that it has been an international conspiracy. Because of the secrecy of the fraternity the records of Freemasonry are often inaccessible, making analysis even more difficult.[52]

One of the few scholars to attempt such an analysis is Jacob Katz in his book *Jews and Freemasons in Europe, 1723-1939.* Because of the Freemasons' official commitment to the ideal of universalism, to "the Brotherhood of man and Fatherhood of God," regardless of religious, racial, class, or national differences, the Order has been described by Jacob Katz as a symbol of and major instrument for the creation of the modern "neutral" society—a society in which the fixed statuses of the medieval world gave way to the needs of a changing and dynamic economic and social structure, where artificial and dysfunctional group distinctions are ignored and the individual

---

[50] Ibid., pp. 142-149. Also see the first half of Katz, *Jews and Freemasons*, passim. E. J. Hobsbawm, in his *Primitive Rebels* (New York, 1959), p. 163, has some perceptive observations on the relationship between Freemasonry and radical politics.

[51] MacKenzie, p. 143. E. J. Hobsbawm's *The Age of Revolution, 1789-1848* (New York, 1962), pp. 37, 106, 147 contends that Masonry was extremely popular with the rising bourgeoisie and the progressive elements in the aristocracy.

[52] Katz, p. 6. Katz found that the archives of the Grand Lodge of England were closed to him, though other Masonic libraries were quite cooperative. The present author found some black Masonic officials quite helpful while others forbade him access to the material.

is judged on his achieved rather than ascribed status.[53] While in the early years the Order had a decidedly aristocratic tone because of its ability to attract members from the European nobility, the aristocrats who joined were willing to associate with members of the rising middle classes and even with the upwardly mobile "social adventurers."[54] Its role in giving birth to a new society was witnessed by the fact that "Masonic membership in the Eighteenth Century was a sign of [either] marginal status in one's original social class or else a leading position in the general society." As a result of its socially diverse but prestigious character it functioned to bind the new classes together.[55]

During the nineteenth century the character of the fraternity changed. It became less aristocratic and more solidly bourgeois, taking on an aspect of middle-class respectability it has maintained since then. The loss of the ruling and intellectual elites and the exclusion of the social adventurers that eighteenth-century Masonry had included diminished its ability to mediate between classes. Instead, "the main function of the lodges consisted in providing peaceful [and respected community dignitaries] . . . with the opportunity to cultivate social and spiritual values in retreats far removed from the surrounding reality."[56] Masonry in the nineteenth century lost much of its "designs for change and revolution" and "gave evidence . . . of a secure and recognized status in the group [the middle class] constituting the central pillar of society as a whole."[57]

The Order's claim to universal brotherhood combined with its social prestige (aristocratic and/or bourgeois) proved attractive to the two major proscribed "racial" groups (Jews and Blacks) in Euro-American society as their members broke out of the social and cultural isolation of their folk communities. The rapid movement of large numbers of German Jews out

[53] Katz, pp. 210, 214. The ideal has not been the practice. The fraternity has been permeated by nationalism, classism, and racism. However, the incongruity between ideal and practice has created a dynamic tension within the Order straining toward a union of the two along the lines laid out by the more idealistic principles. It would be unfair to dismiss those fighting for justice in the Order simply because their fight has not always been an easy or successful one.

[54] Katz, p. 211.

[55] Ibid.

[56] Ibid.

[57] Ibid. In countries where the Order was not firmly established, especially non-Protestant ones, it maintained an anti-status quo aspect.

of "traditional Jewish society"[58] and their rise into the middle class worked to make Freemasonry appear an attractive "common social framework uniting them with non-Jews" which could facilitate their assimilation into European society.[59] The "Jews naturally desired to become integrated into the surrounding society, to become part of that group [the bourgeoisie] to which they would most likely have belonged, had no social discrimination stood in their way."[60]

The desire of the emerging secular Jewish middle class to enter European society was matched by many gentiles who saw the logic behind accepting them. As Jacob Katz puts it, "Any country wanting to compete with its neighbors in the economic, technological, or scientific fields, could hardly afford to deny those principles which constitute the very basis for development and progress. One of these principles was the universalist ideal of equality for all citizens under law."[61] The Masons represented that logic in institutional form, and the exclusion of the Jews belied Masonic ideals as well as social and economic logic. The failure of the Jews to win acceptance from the German Masons—as they did from the French and English—was symbolic of Germany's reluctance to fully accept modernity; the Nazi holocaust was the final outcome of that position.[62]

The free blacks of eighteenth-century America, like the Jews of Europe, were attracted to the Masonic fraternity, and for much the same reasons. Prince Hall and his followers saw Freemasonry as a meeting ground where notions of black and white did not exist. They also saw themselves as a black elite entitled to fraternize with white aristocrats and burghers on an equal level. The free blacks like the secularized Jews saw the Masons as representative of the social strata in the general society to which they should rightfully belong. Unfortunately, the white American Masons fought modernity (at least as it challenged racial ascription) as hard as the Germans did.[63]

[58] See Jacob Katz, *Tradition and Crisis: Jewish Society at the End of the Middle Ages* (New York, 1971).

[59] Katz, *Jews and Freemasons*, p. 3.

[60] Ibid. p. 211.

[61] Ibid., p. 214.

[62] Ibid., passim.

[63] Katz sees America along with England and France as the polar opposite of Germany because of their acceptance of the Jews—he probably would have seen it otherwise if he had known the white American reaction to the blacks.

The American blacks, like the Jews of Germany, found that Freemasonry as a worldwide organization could work to counteract the rejection and humiliation that local Masonic lodges exposed them to. Just as the German Jews looked for recognition from foreign Masonic bodies to bolster their self-respect and to force a liberalization at home, the black Masons in America looked to Europe (including Germany) for the same objective. Both groups received foreign acceptance and thereby, though "once removed," felt they had achieved a level of social acceptance in Western society.[64]

Part 3. Prince Hall Freemasonry and the Black Middle Class

The importance of Freemasonry for the black middle class can be understood only against the backdrop of discrimination and poverty and the limitations these placed upon normal social development. Because the occupational and income differentiation which is traditionally the basis for the creation of a clearly stratified class structure was long retarded among black Americans, those men and women desirous of claiming an elevated status were forced to emphasize, to a greater degree than whites, criteria other than economic to support their claim.

As was suggested above, the line of demarcation between those aspiring to middle-class status and the mass of black men became a visible adherence to bourgeois values and behavior (fortified, to the limited extent possible, by economic and occupational considerations.) The use of value and/or behavioral criteria for class differentiation was feasible because of the high visibility, among blacks, of those practicing alternative life styles. The aspiring black middle class, and white observers as well, assumed that blacks who purposely rejected middle-class morality made up the bulk of the Negro population.

To give reality to the perceived and real differences between the self-proclaimed middle class and the black majority, institutions providing social distance had to be created. Such institutions brought together men considered eligible for middle-class status, and excluded all others. They gave the members support in maintaining the moral and behavioral

[64] Katz, *Jews and Freemasons*, pp. 56, 217. See Chapter IX for more details of the black experience.

characteristics that were considered class defining. By enabling members of the new class to meet and interact, they helped form a socially cohesive and self-conscious group. Prince Hall Freemasonry has been one of the most important of those institutions.

Since its American founding in 1775 as a branch of worldwide Freemasonry, the Prince Hall Order has served as one of the bulwarks of the black middle class. It has worked to separate its members, both socially and psychologically, from the black masses. It has done so by encouraging its adherents to believe that they occupy an exceptional position in the black group, that they represent the finest of their race and possess outstanding abilities as leaders. Members of the Order have felt that only by the use of a rigid, exclusionary admission system—which screens initiates on the basis of public adherence to conventional bourgeois morality—can this exceptional status be maintained. To allow nonbourgeois men to enter would destroy the Order's ability to serve as a badly needed model for the race, weaken the resolve of the membership to maintain their life style, and destroy the Order's potency as a class-defining institution.

For the men admitted, the Order has provided the opportunity for a tight-knit social environment, working to separate them from the majority of blacks. Members have been able to spend their entire social (i.e., recreational) life within the confines of the Masonic social network, a network that includes not only the local lodge and its clubs, but Masonic Auxiliary Orders such as Shriners, Knights Templar, Royal Arch Masons, Scottish Rite Masonry, and the Order of Eastern Star as well.

In creating social and psychological distance between its membership and the majority of blacks, Masonry has not worked alone. Rather, it has been one link in a chain of mutually supportive organizations which perform similar roles. Many of these organizations, like Masonry, are fraternal orders (e.g., Odd Fellows, Knights of Pythias, and the Order of Elks). Taken as a network of interlocking and cooperative organizations, Masonry and its higher degree auxiliaries, allied fraternal orders, and the middle-class churches have formed an environment conducive to the creation, maintenance, and protection of a self-conscious, socially cohesive black middle-class community.

While Masonry has served this broad social function, it has also performed an important specialized role as well: the formation of a leadership group within the black middle class. Members of the black bourgeoisie have always thought of themselves as the natural leaders of their race, but Masonry as an institution has been concerned with changing that boast to reality by inspiring and training its membership in leadership roles. Through the fraternity, members have learned to perform many bourgeois social roles with which they have had limited or no prior experience. By teaching these roles, and by providing an arena for their enactment, Masonry has worked to bring the leadership potential within its membership to practical fruition.

The Order's community or class-building role has only been a part of its function, however. Masonry has also created ties between the black middle class and its white counterpart. Because of the severity of white discrimination within Masonry, the links have not been institutional or social (as they were, for example, for the deghettoized Jews of Europe) but ideological.[65] The Masonic fraternity has heightened the black bourgeoisie's consciousness of, and claim to, kinship with the white middle class. This linkage has had major ramifications in the black community. It has led to a marked degree of co-optation of black leaders and potential leaders by the whites and a significant amount of alienation of the black middle class from the black lower class. At the same time the constant rejection of middle-class blacks by their white class peers has fostered race consciousness, hostility to whites, and a sense of common destiny with the black masses.

The result of the conflicting pressures on the black Masons has been the heightening of racial discontent and protest simultaneously with the blunting of the Masons' ability to achieve political results. The ambiguous position of the black middle class, situated between the white bourgeoisie and the black lower class, has led to a love-hate relationship between the groups which has done much to dissipate the middle class's leadership potential and to retard the formation of a viable, unified black "community."

Though we are treating Prince Hall Freemasonry as a vital black institution, the consensus among scholars for many years

[65] This will be discussed in more detail later in this chapter.

has been that fraternities are a relic of the past, a predominantly late nineteenth-century phenomenon that has lingered into the twentieth. In *The Negro in the United States* E. Franklin Frazier says that fraternal lodges were important for the free Negro in the cities before the Civil War, but the real growth and heyday of the orders came in the period 1865-1900.[66] After that the secret societies suffered a severe eclipse, with the exception of the black Elks:

> The fraternal organizations [in the cities] continue to attract the less sophisticated urban Negroes. . . . Moreover, as the Negro acquired an education and a more secular outlook, these societies with their religious outlook have become less congenial.[67]

His position is supported by Allan Spear in *Black Chicago* where he maintains that in an urban center like Chicago the lodge declined by the first decade of the twentieth century because, "Geared primarily for small, relatively homogeneous communities, the lodges find it difficult to compete for membership and prestige in a city. . . ."[68]

Other observers have supported these interpretations, though the exact date for the beginning of fraternal decline varies greatly. While Spear sees the first decade of the twentieth century as a turning point, others place it later. St. Clair Drake and Horace Cayton, after asserting that the "traditional bulwarks of organized middle class life—the conservers of the traditions—have been the church and the lodge," state that fraternities were being replaced by more secular and urban institutions by 1920 or 1930.[69]

Though the differences in dating the decline (or demise) are not insignificant, there is widespread agreement that fraternities can be securely ignored at some point in the early twentieth century.[70] As a result of the unanimity on this point there has

[66] Frazier, *Negro in U.S.*, pp. 378-379.

[67] Ibid.

[68] Chicago, 1967, p. 108. Spear, unlike Frazier, specifically mentions Masonry as a declining organization.

[69] Drake and Cayton, p. 669. The authors at one place put the decline of the lodges 10 years before the study and in another place 20 years before. Gunnar Myrdal in *An American Dilemma* (New York, 1944), sees the Depression itself as the period of most severe decline.

[70] Drake and Cayton, p. 711, simply ignore fraternities when drawing up an organizational chart of the middle class. It is interesting to note, however, that when the authors asked which of the 106 Chicago blacks in *Who's Who in Colored America* were actually upper class rather than just "prominent" people, 50 percent of the 31 people picked

been no in-depth study of black secret societies and their role in the black community or the black middle class.[71]

Whether secret societies and lodges generally were eclipsed around the turn of the century one cannot say, but Prince Hall Freemasonry was not. In fact, black Freemasonry has been and is a remarkable long-lived and healthy institution. Founded during the American Revolution, it witnessed a marked expansion at the end of the Civil War and saw its greatest numerical growth after, not before, the turn of the twentieth century. From 1900 to 1930 the fraternity's membership exploded. States such as Texas which had 2,000 members in 1903, had 10,000 in 1919 and 20,000 in 1927. Alabama, with 264 members in 1904 reached 22,600 twenty years later. Georgia, with 6,500 in 1908 reached 24,000 by 1920; and California, with only 157 in 1900 reached 2,400 in 1929. The decade of the 1930s was characterized by a Masonic decline, especially in some of the large southern jurisdictions. Texas Masonry dropped to 8,000 by 1937. Georgia declined precipitously to 2,500 in 1932; giants like Tennessee almost ceased existence. However, with rising prosperity, recovery in Masonic membership occurred almost everywhere. Alabama, whose high point before the Depression had been over 22,000 members, reached 42,000 by the late 1940s. Texas regained its 1927 figure of 20,000 by 1947 and grew even further, reaching 32,000 by 1959. Taken as a whole, Prince Hall Freemasonry increased its membership from 46,000 in 1904 to well over 300,000 in 1955.[72]

---

out were Masons. Also, when giving the biographies of the two "representative" members of the "older" middle class, both were members of Masonic related organizations (Drake and Cayton, pp. 712-713). Even if Drake and Cayton are totally right about the Order's collapse, they nevertheless give evidence of its traditional prominence.

[71] Carter Woodson in *The Negro Professional Man in the Community: With Special Emphasis on the Physician and the Lawyer* (New York, 1934), presents evidence that Masonry was extremely attractive to at least two key professional groups around the same time the *Black Metropolis* study was undertaken. In his sample he found that 16 percent of the doctors and 25 percent of the lawyers belonged to the Masonic fraternity. The Masons attracted a higher proportion of lawyers than any other voluntary association—Woodson listed 20 different groups, including the N.A.A.C.P., PTA, and YMCA. The Masons were the third most popular group for doctors, after the Elks and Knights of Pythias who attracted 18 percent each (see Woodson, pp. 106-107, 115, 242-243, 179-180, for statistics on the different organizations).

[72] *Past Master Topics* [henceforth called *Topics* (Illinois)], Fourth Quarter, 1955. After a remarkable recovery from the Depression, Masonry has experienced a numerical decline in the 1960s compared to its height in the mid-fifties. It is too early to say how well the Order will weather the present social turmoil and change within the black community.

Masonry as an institution has not experienced a numerical decline in this century, nor has it experienced a proportional decline if one compares the post-1900 period with the period 1865-1900 or 1880-1900. Proportional decline becomes apparent only when one compares the Masonic membership as a percentage of the black population in 1925 and 1970. Masonry has grown—but not nearly as fast as the population has. This reflects a lessening in its attractiveness. But decline and fall are not synonymous. This type of decline is far less severe or crucial than Spear, Myrdal, Drake, or Cayton envisioned.[73]

There is another type of decline other than the one involving membership, absolute or proportional, to which Spear and the others have referred. This is a relative decline in the importance of Masonry and other fraternities in relation to other institutions in black society. Relative decline is indisputable. In the period 1865-1900, Masonry and the fraternities as a whole formed one major institution when there were few others. Black society was under-organized and lacked institutions, and thus a Masonic lodge with a few dozen members could easily be the second major social institution (next to the church) in a small town or even in a city like Chicago. With the growth of major black urban centers, and the creation of many civic and social organizations, Masonry had to become—no matter how fast it grew in numbers or wealth—one group among many.[74]

Masonry has suffered not only from being simply overshadowed but also from the direct competition for prestige, members, and resources that the new organizations generated. Modern specialized institutions such as professional societies, college fraternities, civil right organizations, social clubs, and charities have offered distinctive services and far greater social exclusiveness than Masonry, all of which have hurt the Order's

[73] The Myrdal and Drake and Cayton studies were done in the Depression when fraternalism, including Prince Hall Freemasonry, was at a low ebb. They assumed this situation was permanent and their analysis was shaped by this belief.

[74] Masonry, as well as other fraternities and voluntary organizations, has also been faced by competition from the products of cultural change. One finds continuous references in Masonic records in the period after 1930 to the competition for the attention of lodge members presented by the automobile, radio, movies and (later) television. In many ways these entertainment media have posed more of a threat to the organization than has the growth of business and professional associations, and social, welfare and political institutions, in the maturing urban environment. Indeed, those institutions have also been hurt by competition from the entertainment media.

ability to attract the elite of the middle class. For example, the Masonic proceedings have been full of laments over the competition created by college fraternities for men who at one time would have automatically entered Masonry. But the extent of the Order's difficulties has been significantly exaggerated by critics of the fraternities. The Masons noticeably lost ground among the upper-middle class (Frazier's elite group) after the Depression, but it did not suffer an eclipse among the black middle class as a whole.[75] In fact, despite its lessening attraction for the elite, as we shall see, in the 1960s it was still attracting a disproportionate number of prominent and successful black leaders.

To maintain, contrary to established opinion, that the Masonic Order among blacks has flourished in the twentieth century is not to claim that it has not suffered from significant problems. Prince Hall Freemasonry has been troubled by the rise of competitive social institutions, changing cultural values, and difficulties in attracting the most promising potential members. These are the problems, however, of a living and changing institution, not a dead one.

The beginning of black attempts to enter modern society through Masonry go back to 1775. In that year, Prince Hall, a West Indian mulatto of free status, and fifteen other blacks were initiated by a British Army lodge stationed in Boston.[76] From that group in 1776 came African Lodge No. 1.[77] The new lodge's bylaws embodied two ideas fundamental to the founders of Freemasonry among Afro-Americans. First, the Masonic promise of a new society was stated as: "All preferment amonge us is by Real Worth and Personal merit only. . . ." The second ideal, that black Freemasons were an elite, was incorporated

[75] The "decline" of Masonry as an organization where elite "individuals [can] symbolize their . . . struggle to get ahead" (Drake and Cayton, p. 662) probably started at the turn of the century when the Order began its rapid expansion, thereby becoming less exclusive than it had been in the nineteenth century, and less prestigious for the black elite. But that "decline" was the result of its popularity as a status organization for the growing black middle class.

[76] Harry E. Davis, *A History of Freemasonry Among Negroes in America* [published under the Auspices of the United Supreme Council, Ancient and Accepted Scottish Rite Freemasonry, Northern Jurisdiction, U.S.A. (Prince Hall Affiliation) Inc., 1946], p. 21.

[77] Davis. p. 21.

in "We [will] admit [no one not] having a tongue of Good
Reporte. . . ."[78]

Provisional African Lodge No. 1 ultimately became a full
Masonic lodge (African No. 459) when in 1787 Prince Hall
applied for and received a charter from the Grand Lodge of
England itself, the mother lodge of Freemasonry.[79] The blacks,
like their Jewish brethren in Germany, had not immediately
appealed to a foreign body for a charter. They had repeatedly
attempted to obtain a warrant from the white Masons of
Massachusetts, but the Americans had not responded favorably
even though Prince Hall was on "rather friendly terms with
a number of Boston's leading Masons."[80] As we shall see later,
the hope maintained by blacks that Masonry would afford them
the opportunity to enter the general society was fed not only
by the Grand Lodge of England's action but also by the
friendliness of a small but constant minority of American white
Masons.[81] This "saving remnant," which to a greater or lesser
extent ignored the color line, was important not only in 1776
but throughout the history of Freemasonry among Afro-Americans. This relationship between blacks and sympathetic whites
had negative as well as positive effects, not only on the black
Masons but upon the entire black population.

Prince Hall's efforts to open the Masonic fraternity to black
men was only part of his personal efforts to raise the status
of his race in America, to force the equal treatment of all men
according to their individual merits, not their ascribed characteristics. Prince Hall found that free Negroes in Boston were
severely oppressed. Emancipation brought a status above that
of slave but beneath that of citizen.[82] Free blacks were daily
subjected to insults and acts of discrimination. He set out to
both rectify this injustice and to fight for those still enslaved.
As a minister of the Methodist Church he used his pulpit as
a forum for influencing blacks and becoming acquainted with

[78] Ibid., p. 24. The desire to maintain a high tone to the lodge was apparently achieved;
at least the prominent white Mason, Dr. Belknap, writing in 1795, thought that African
Lodge No. 1 was noteworthy for the "care [which] is taken that none but those of
good moral character are admitted" (Davis, p. 26). Both propositions were basic to
the institution they created, from its founding to the present, as I shall show in the
coming chapters.

[79] Ibid., p. 39.

[80] Ibid., p. 67.

[81] For a discussion of this point see Chapter XI.

[82] Lorenzo Greene, "Prince Hall: Massachusetts Leader in Crisis," *Freedomways*,
1, no.3 (1962): 240.

powerful and sympathetic whites.[83] He was actively concerned
with ending external restraints upon blacks and with encouraging their self-improvement so they could effectively perform
as first-class citizens.[84] In behalf of his brethren in bondage
he was a leader in petitioning the legislature of Massachusetts
to end both slavery and the slave trade. In his petition he
"show[ed] a marked familiarity with the Revolutionary philosophy. Hall and his fellows . . . declar[ed] that they 'have in
common with all other men a natural right to our freedoms
without being deprived of them by our fellow men.' "[85] In
addition to asking the legislature to end slavery, Prince Hall
attempted to effect the same result by taking advantage of
the manpower shortage during the conflict with England:
"During the Revolutionary War Prince Hall requested [John]
Hancock and [Joseph] Warren [two Massachusetts leaders]
that they allow the slaves to enlist, seeing this a road to
freedom." Men who were allowed to fight for their country
could not be kept slaves within it after the war was won.[86]

While deeply concerned with aiding the slave population,
Prince Hall was just as anxious to help the emancipated blacks
raise their status. He was especially concerned that blacks be
offered the benefit of education, since without it black children
would be left in ignorance and this would put them at a
permanent disadvantage in life.[87] Hall fought to have the city
of Boston establish schools for black children. While Massachusetts had a public school law, blacks, free or slave, were
excluded. This exclusion was doubly unacceptable because it
not only deprived the children of a needed resource, but also
denied their parents the benefits derived from their taxes.[88]

Prince Hall was also a strong advocate of black self-improvement as a means of counteracting white hostility, and he saw
Masonry as the most important instrument for its accomplishment. The virtues he expected Masons to practice were those
that would establish them as the social equals of white men,
and leaders of the blacks. As Lorenzo Greene has pointed out:

[83] Ibid., p. 242-243.

[84] Ibid., p. 255-256.

[85] Ibid., p. 245.

[86] This comes from a discussion of Prince Hall and the fight for black rights in the
Proceedings of the Grand Lodge of Louisiana, 1958, as reported in the *Prince Hall
Masonic Digest* (California) [henceforth called *Digest*], 7, no.4 (1958-59): 3.

[87] Greene, p. 250.

[88] Ibid., pp. 249-250.

Hoping to change the community stereotype of the Negro, Hall
sought to instill in the members [of the Masonic fraternity]
acceptable personal habits. Thus he emphasized such necessary
traits as promptness, regularity, and reliability. Particularly did
he warn the members against drunkardness, gambling, and lewd
company, which would bring 'disgrace upon the Craft (Lodge).'
Those persons who came to the meetings drunk, Hall reminded
that their absence would be better than their company. He
further cautioned the brethren against boisterousness and a
display of temper which would destroy the harmony of the Lodge.
Instead, he admonished them to help each other, give good advice
where needed and help secure jobs for the unemployed.[89]

In all areas of black communal life Prince Hall showed himself
to be dedicated to the goal of achieving full citizenship for
the black man, full and equal participation before the law, and
an end to social discrimination, insult, and indignity.[90]

Despite Hall's efforts to establish a black Masonic lodge
under the Grand Lodge of England he still hoped to receive
a charter directly from the native American Masons. The
refusal of the white Masons of America to charter a lodge of
blacks under their jurisdiction led in 1791 to the founding of
Prince Hall Grand Lodge, from which black Freemasonry is
descended.[91] In addition to the first lodge founded in Boston,
the Order established branches in Rhode Island and Philadelphia. The Philadelphia lodge was composed of men "all of whom
had received their degrees abroad" and thus had all individually
experienced an important proof of white European social ac-

[89] Ibid., p. 255-256.

[90] See Harry Williamson, *Prince Hall Primer* (New York, 1946), nos. 10, 12, 13, 14,
and William Grimshaw, *Official History of Freemasonry Among the Colored People
in North America* (New York, 1903), ch. 8, pp. 67-84, for original Prince Hall petitions
and letters dealing with black rights.

[91] It was formed from African Lodge No. 459. Harry Davis accepts this date, though
other Masonic writers use 1808 as the founding year (Davis, p. 78). A word should
be said here about the Masonic structure: The Prince Hall Masonic Fraternity in
America has no national agency with supreme authority. Power is vested in a "Grand
Lodge" in each state. Each Grand Lodge is officially independent of all the others.
All the local lodges in a state owe allegiance to their state Grand Lodge, and
representatives of the local lodges make up the general assembly that constitutes the
state body. The Grand Lodge meets only once a year, but its elected head, the Grand
Master, has power year round. Prince Hall Masons did have a national Grand Lodge,
but only for a few years during the middle of the nineteenth century, as a means
of protecting themselves during the slave period. Today, the state leaders meet once
a year in an advisory, officially powerless, body called the International Conference
of Grand Masters.

ceptance.[92] The members of the Philadelphia lodge, like Prince
Hall himself, were exceptional men and leaders of free black
society. The most famous Philadelphia Masons were Absalom
Jones, founder of St. Thomas Episcopal Church, and Richard
Allen, founder and first Bishop of the African Methodist
Episcopal Church. They, together with William Gray, William
White, Caesar Cranchell, and Mark Stevenson, seceded from
St. George's Methodist Episcopal Church because of racial
discrimination. With Joseph Husten, Joseph Johnson, Nathan
Gray, J. Caton, and others (Masons, all), they founded the
Free African Society, one of the oldest mutual benefit associa-
tions and the seed from which St. Thomas and the African
Methodist Episcopal Church grew.[93] Five of these men were
ministers, and with the selection of Absalom Jones as first
Master and later Grand Master of Pennsylvania, the influence
of the church group in Masonry was affirmed. The early
Philadelphia lodge also claimed other men of high stature,
including James Forten (abolitionist) and Prince Saunders
(later Attorney General of independent Haiti).[94]

In the early years of expansion the fledgling Prince Hall
Fraternity, while still operating under the Grand Lodge of
England, founded a lodge in Rhode Island. Interestingly
enough, it became inactive soon after the turn of the nineteenth
century because "a number of its members emigrated to Liberia. . . ."[95] It was perhaps these men, or later Masonic emi-
grants, who founded Liberian Freemasonry. This branch of the
Prince Hall family became the most illustrious black Masonic
jurisdiction since Freemasonry as a sociopolitical institution
became one of the ruling elite's main instruments for the
solidification and maintenance of its identity and the perpetua-
tion of its power.[96] The position of Grand Master of Liberian
Masonry appears to have been held by the country's President,
Vice-President, or Speaker of the House of Representatives for
well over one hundred years.[97]

[92] Davis, p. 74. Indeed, between 1797 and 1818, fully 37 out of 106 members of African
Lodge of Philadelphia received their Masonic initiation outside America (Davis, pp.
290-291).

[93] Davis, pp. 292-293. And see Abram Harris, p. 20.

[94] Davis, pp. 292-293.

[95] Ibid., p. 83.

[96] See Chapter VIII for more details.

[97] Davis, p. 85, provides the oldest reference to the Liberian Masons I have seen
when he discusses an 1851 petition to the (white) Grand Lodge of Washington, D.C.,

Just as Liberia's elite actively used Masonry to maintain its political, social, and economic power, in the early nineteenth century many white Americans grew fearful that (white) Masons at home would use the secret society for undemocratic purposes. The result of white America's fears was the anti-Masonic agitation of the late 1820s and early 1830s. This political movement accused Freemasonry of possessing aristocratic pretensions and being an antirepublican conspiracy. The historian David B. Davis has categorized this hostility as a "scapegoat reaction" to social and economic changes that Americans could not understand.[98] Regardless of the motivation of its attackers, the Order among whites came close to disintegration. When it was revived in the 1840s, Freemasonry was more democratic and open, but still a solidly bourgeois organization.

While almost fatal for white Masonry, the agitation was harmless to the blacks. Apparently the anti-Masons did not see any danger to equalitarian democracy in the aristocratic pretensions of black free men.[99] Indeed, the hard times the whites experienced provided new opportunities for Prince Hall Masons. Some "unemployed" white Masonic degree instructors found jobs in teaching blacks some of the higher ritual of the Order, while others asked the assistance of blacks in carrying out their Masonic work when a quorum could not be raised.[100] Since no penalty in the way of political persecution or social proscription was attached, the charges of a worldwide aristocratic Masonic conspiracy probably made blacks feel rather proud of their fraternal ties. For a despised minority, accusations of hidden power do not hurt the ego.

In the early nineteenth century, Prince Hall Grand Lodge of Massachusetts lost its role as chief missionary for Masonry among blacks, and the Pennsylvania branch of the Order assumed that role. The Quaker State blacks took the lead in chartering new southern and western lodges. In 1846 Richard Gleaves (later Lieutenant Governor of South Carolina) was

asking for a charter by J. J. Roberts, President of the Republic, his brother Rev. John Day, and others. Thereafter, the Proceedings of Masonry are replete with references to the Grand Masters of Liberia—all of whom have also been high officials of the government.

[98] See David B. Davis, "Themes of Counter-Subversion: An Analysis of Anti-Masonic, Anti-Catholic, and Anti-Mormon Literature," *Mississippi Valley Historical Review*, 47, no.2 (September 1960): 205-224.

[99] Davis (all references to *Davis* are for Harry Davis, unless so specified), p. 174.

[100] Ibid.

made Deputy Grand Master and went west of the Allegheny
Mountains to work. Much of the growth of black Masonry
in Ohio was due to his zeal. One of the first flourishing lodges
was established in Cincinnati, where "a large number of . .
. [black men] had acquired education, property and personal
culture, which were the bases for fellowship among themselves
with others."[101]

Once established, the Grand Lodge of Ohio (with Gleaves
as one of its Grand Masters) took the lead in spreading the
Order into other free states before the Civil War and in the
reconstructed South after it. Simultaneously they agitated for
European and American Masonic recognition of the Prince Hall
lodges.[102] Between 1849 and 1869 Ohio was instrumental in
spreading the fraternity into Kentucky, Indiana, Louisiana,
Tennessee, Alabama, and Missouri, and later into others. This
was the key period in black Masonic territorial growth.[103]

Ohio's ability to spread the Order was facilitated by the
destruction of the slave system. Not only had the southern
elite prevented the masses of slave blacks from becoming
potential Masons, also the white governments had opposed the
spread of secret societies among free blacks. The South did
not like the idea of blacks meeting together without supervision,
and an organization such as Masonry appeared especially
dangerous to them. According to Harry Davis, an historian
of Prince Hall Masonry, King David Lodge No. 5 of Havre
De Grace, Maryland, was closed by the slave government and
its members arrested and fined, while Lamech Lodge No. 11
of the same state received much opposition because white
slaveholders feared this black secret organization.[104]

By ending slavery the Civil War opened the South to Masonic
activity, and political reconstruction provided specific opportunities for Ohio Masonic leaders to carry on their work. Richard
Gleaves, now an active Grand Master of the "National Compact" (a temporary unified organization of Prince Hall Grand
Lodges), went to South Carolina where he became Grand
Master of the new South Carolina Grand Lodge and also

[101] Charles Wesley, *The History of the Prince Hall Grand Lodge of Free and Accepted
Masons of the State of Ohio, 1849-1960* (Wilberforce, Ohio, 1961), pp. 30; see also Davis,
pp. 162-163.
[102] Davis, p. 94, and Wesley, pp. 36-38.
[103] Wesley, p. 49.
[104] Davis, p. 175.

Lieutenant Governor of the state.[105] Thomas Springer, also a Past Grand Master of Ohio (1849-50) settled in Mississippi and became Grand Master of Mississippi's Springer Grand Lodge.[106] Past Grand Master John Parson of Ohio went to Louisiana to be head of its Grand Lodge.[107]

While black Masonry spread south with leaders who were to become active in Reconstruction politics, it also migrated hand in hand with the black church—though politics and the church are not easily separable for analysis.[108]

One of the major links between Freemasonry and religion in the newly liberated South was Bishop J. W. Hood of the American Methodist Episcopal Zion Church. During Reconstruction Hood left the North wearing, as it were, three hats: Assistant Superintendent of Public Instruction of North Carolina under the Freedmen's Bureau; Superintendent of Missions for the A.M.E. Zion Church; and Superintendent of the Southern Jurisdiction of the Masonic Grand Lodge of New York. In North Carolina he helped establish both his church and large numbers of Masonic lodges. When both institutions were firmly established he became a Bishop of the church in 1872 (later rising to Senior Bishop) and Grand Master of the Masons of North Carolina (after it became independent of New York) from 1870 to 1883.[109]

Deeper in the South the alliance continued. The organization of Masonry in Georgia and the formation of the first African Methodist Episcopal (A.M.E.) Church were also closely related.[110] The first Worshipful Master of the first local lodge in

[105] Wesley, p. 39.

[106] Ibid., pp. 39-40.

[107] Ibid., pp. 40-41.

[108] Edward Palmer in "Negro Secret Societies," *Social Forces*, 23 (December 1944): 208, says, "Maryland, Virginia and Louisiana, the centers of the free Negro population, were the only southern states with Negro Masonic lodges before 1860." *Digest* (California), 7, no.4 (1959), lists the founding of state Grand Lodges as follows: Massachusetts, 1791; Pennsylvania, 1815; Maryland, 1845; New York, 1845; Washington, D.C., 1848; New Jersey, 1848; Ohio, 1848; Delaware, 1849; California, 1855; Rhode Island, 1855; Ontario, Canada, 1855; Indiana, 1855; Louisiana, 1863; Michigan, 1863; Kentucky, 1866; Missouri, 1866; Illinois, 1867; North Carolina, 1870; Tennessee, 1870; Alabama, 1870; Florida, 1870; South Carolina, 1872; Texas, 1873; Kansas, 1875; Virginia, 1875; Colorado, 1876; Mississippi, 1876; Arkansas, 1878; West Virginia, 1881; Iowa, 1887; Oklahoma, 1892; Minnesota, 1894; Washington State, 1903; Arizona, 1919; New Mexico, 1921; Wisconsin, 1925.

[109] See *Proceedings* (New York, 1920 and 1915); *Proceedings* (California, 1920), C.C.F.C. commenting on New York; *Dictionary of American Biography* (J. W. Hood).

[110] The African Methodist Episcopal Church is different from the African Methodist Episocpal *Zion* Church mentioned earlier.

that state was also Pastor of the first A.M.E. Church, and the first cornerstone laid in Georgia by a Masonic lodge was for the same church—Pastor Al Stanford bringing from the North both his faith and his fraternity. George H. Dwells, one of the three men to petition in 1871 for the establishment of a Masonic lodge, was one of the principal founders both of the A.M.E. Church and of Masonry in Georgia.[111] A similar role of fostering religion and Masonry was performed by Col. James Lewis in Louisiana; he helped establish schools for Negroes in the South in his capacity as Field Secretary of the American Missionary Association and served as Grand Master of the Grand Lodge of Louisiana from 1878 to 1880.[112]

In the spread of Prince Hall Freemasonry, one problem that plagued the leadership stemmed from an unsuccessful experiment with national unity. Because of internal black Masonic factionalism, especially in Pennsylvania, a group of prominent leaders decided to set up a National Masonic Grand Lodge, a body superior to the state Grand Lodges. They hoped to end internal dissent, create a nationwide Masonic communication network, and help present a united front of black Masons to the whites. Given the dangers to freemen from slave America, the argument for unity rather than local autonomy was compelling. The National Compact, as it was called, had no precedent in Masonic tradition, and the attempt by the national leadership to centralize power in their hands at the expense of the state leadership led to increased friction and disunity rather than harmony and strength.[113]

The National Compact was instrumental in chartering lodges throughout the country, but was relatively short-lived as more and more states withdrew from it and declared it an un-Masonic institution. It was officially pronounced dead in the 1870s. However, its disunifying effect did not disappear with its early demise. From the body of the National Compact arose "false" Grand Masters claiming legitimate Masonic power and setting up "bogus" lodges throughout America.[114] The social characteristics of this "clandestine Masonry" are unknown, but Prince Hall leaders have always contended that while some members of those lodges were "honest and well meaning citizens . . .

---

[111] Sol C. Johnson, "History of the Grand Lodge" (Georgia, 1920), pamphlet.

[112] *Digest* (California), 7, no.4 (1959).

[113] Davis, pp. 98, 101, 103.

[114] Ibid., p. 106.

too often their victims were among the ignorant class" which wanted, and could only afford, "cheap degrees."[115] Indeed, "The character and quality of some of its [the bogus lodges'] membership [has been] . . . such that it could not be healed [i.e., made legitimate Prince Hall Masons] and absorbed without corrupting the entire Craft."[116] Prince Hall leaders felt it required a struggle to maintain quality when forced to compete with unscrupulous money-grubbers.

In the years between Reconstruction and the turn of the century, Prince Hall Masonry was a solid, highly prestigious, relatively small fraternity. During the same time a multiplicity of fraternal orders were founded, flourished, and died, while Masonry continued on a stable course. While the Order has always been relatively exclusive and difficult to enter, this appears to have been more true in the years before 1900 than afterwards. It was in the twentieth century that Masonry experienced a rapid expansion of membership and a concomitant lessening of its extreme exclusiveness. Allan Spear's picture of Chicago in this period is probably typical for urban areas like it. Among the old black elite, "Most important [of the fraternities] were the Prince Hall Masons. . . ." The Order included many of the community leaders of later nineteenth-century "society" such as John Jones, Ferdinand Barnett, and Theodore Jones. Prince Hall "social affairs were events of community-wide interest; over two thousand of the 'best colored people' attended the Knights Templar Ball in 1900."[117]

In their attempt to maintain standards, the Masons were reluctant to add the type of insurance feature that other fraternities used to attract a membership. They did not want to appear to be competing for adherents, nor to be forced to lower their requirements in order to maintain the system. Ultimately, many Masonic jurisdictions did give in to the pressure but worked hard to prevent the subordination of their social functions to their insurance role.[118]

[115] Ibid. For evidence on the social characteristics of Prince Freemasonry's membership see Chapter II.

[116] Davis, pp. 106-107.

[117] Spear, pp. 107-108.

[118] Edward Palmer, p. 210, when discussing the Masons says "It is interesting that competition for members forced the Negro Masons in the South to add the insurance feature," with Arkansas the first to do so in 1892. He goes on to observe that "The northern Negro Masons have never had" such plans. Actually, some non-Southern

Due to the Order's selectivity and elite character in the nineteenth century, it had a strong "mulatto" caste to it. The pre-Civil War black population was heavily mixed racially, as were many of the elite-slave blacks who received privileges under the slave regime. As a result, the group from which Masonry chose its adherents tended to be light in complexion.[119] Intraracial "blackballing" by light-skinned blacks against darker ones was probably fairly widespread in the Order. Indeed, it continued to some extent well into the twentieth century.[120] The relative "democratization" of the fraternity, by the admission of middle-class, non-elite, darker blacks appears to have come after the turn of the century when thousands of new members entered.[121] The establishment of Masonic insurance systems in the South was probably one of the key factors in forcing a change in the standards of admission, though they weren't lowered enough to compromise the fraternity's claims to relative exclusiveness.

states did adopt Grand Lodge insurance—California, for example—but the Southerners were under greater pressure than the Northerners. The fears entertained by many Masons about insurance plans were not totally groundless. In states like Alabama and Arkansas, standards were lowered to get dues-paying members in. The Arkansas jurisdiction at the turn of the century became extremely large primarily due to its insurance plan. In the Great Depression some Southern states got caught in the financial squeeze because of their insurance features.

[119] Hard evidence for color factors within black Masonry are hard to come by since such things as color hostility are not mentioned openly. I have found that early twentieth century photographs of Masonic leaders show a very light-skinned group of men. Also, statements such as the following can be found in nineteenth century Masonic publications: "Brother William H. Parlam [of Ohio] . . . wrote, 'In objecting to the title "African," [that Ohio white Masons wanted blacks to call themselves before they would recognize them as Masons] we did so because our lodges are not made up of Africans. I cannot now recall to mind one brother in all these lodges of whom it can, with certainty, be said, "He is an African." "African descent," says one, "How about that?" So far as that is concerned . . . there is as much Caucasian as African [blood in the membership], if not a little more' " (Wesley, p. 69).

[120] In a 1969 interview with Royal Towns, a prominent California Mason, he said there was little such hostility now, but it did exist in years past. For the existence of such intraracial conflict in black society generally in the 1930s see William Muraskin, "The Harlem Boycott of 1934: Black Nationalism and the Rise of Labor-Union Consciousness," Labor History, 13, no.3 (Summer 1972), and "An Alienated Elite: Short Stories in the Crisis, 1910-1950," Journal of Black Studies, 1, no.3 (March 1971).

[121] The decline of Masonry that Spear thought he saw in early twentieth century Chicago may have been a reflection of the old elite's hostility to the Order's new, "lower" standards. Spear felt that the difficulty the Masons faced in 1906 in establishing a successful insurance plan was proof of the fraternity's inability to adjust to the city. Actually, since such a system would have attracted and required more members, many of those desirous of maintaining the Order's exclusiveness were probably opposed to it.

As was noted earlier, the Order flourished in the years before the Great Depression. Its numbers rose and its lodges grew wealthy and more socially active. However, the Order's attractiveness for the social elite, while remaining strong, nevertheless began to decline. At the same time Masonry attracted larger numbers of the growing middle class. After the Second World War the Order recovered much of the membership it lost in the late 1920s and 1930s; and, while the withdrawal of the black upper class continued, Masonry remained attractive for hundreds of thousands of middle-class black men. Thus the study of Prince Hall Freemasonry in the United States is the story of a major social foundation of the black bourgeoisie, an institution that allows us to better understand one of the key segments of black society.

Chapter II

The Membership of
Prince Hall Freemasonry

Middle-class morality has been an influential standard for black Masons. As I shall show in Part 1 of this chapter, the fraternity has successfully attempted to restrict entrance to those blacks who demonstrate a prior commitment to middle-class morality. In Part 2, I shall point to the efforts of Freemasonry to reinforce and broaden the membership's adherence to the bourgeois lifestyle. These prior commitments and strengthened adherences to the bourgeois moral code have in turn brought about estrangement and conflict between the middle and lower black classes. This conflict is discussed in Part 3.

Part 1. Selecting Initiates

In Prince Hall Masonry's efforts to create an environment conducive to the formation and maintenance of a black middle-class community separate from the majority of the black population, it carefully selects its potential members from the ranks of black men visibly committed to middle-class modes of thought and behavior. As a Grand Master of California said in 1909, "[W]e should closely guard the inner portals of our Fraternity. See that none enters whose character will not bear [the] closest scrutiny."[1] The major instrument to insure exclusiveness has been the local lodge Investigatory Committee,

[1] Whenever possible the entire reference for a Masonic Grand Lodge Proceeding will appear in the text without a separate footnote. When a state, a date, and a speaker (or committee) are cited, the reference is always to a Proceeding and should be read as this reference is: *Proceedings* (California, 1909), speech of Grand Master. The reference for the quote that follows this one should likewise be read as *Proceedings* (California, 1923), report of Investigatory Committee.

which screens applicants on the basis of moral behavior. In
1923 the California *Proceedings* included a sample question-
naire of one such committee:

> 2. Do you believe him [the initiate] to be of sufficient
> mental capacity to understand and appreciate the lessons
> of Masonry?
> 3. Is he a clean, right-living man, sober and industrious?
> 4. Has he any habits which tend to degrade his morals?
> 7. Does he live with and support his family as a husband
> should?
> 9. Is he likely to become a charge upon the Lodge?

The moral prerequisites for applicants to Masonry, as demonstrated in the records not only of California but of New York,
Georgia, Texas, and Alabama are designed to rigorously exclude
those who deviate from acceptable bourgeois behavior—a test
the Masons have felt would leave only a minority of the black
population eligible for membership.[2] In working to keep the
membership select and to exclude a sizeable number of blacks,
Masons have rigidly rejected anyone who has run afoul of the
law. As the Masonic Constitution of Georgia in 1924 stated:
"No subordinate lodge shall receive and initiate any person
who has ever been charged with and found guilty of any crime
or moral turpitude." The Grand Master of Texas reiterated
the Georgia pronouncement in a more sweeping statement on
the moral responsibilities of Masons: " 'Be ye temperate in
all things,' not only avoiding what is in itself improper, but
also whatever has the least or most remote appearance of
impropriety. . . ."[3] A man with even one legal mishap could

[2] Charles Wesley says of the growth of Ohio lodges in the nineteenth century: "Ohio
was thus engaged . . . in organizing the *selective, well-qualified few* among colored
Americans" (Charles Wesley, *The History of the Prince Hall Grand Lodge of Free
and Accepted Masons of the State of Ohio 1849-1960*, [Wilberforce, Ohio, 1961], p.
49, italics added. See also Hylan Lewis, *Blackways of Kent*, [Chapel Hill, N.C., 1955],
p. 260.)

[3] *Proceedings* (Texas, 1947). The Masons are very concerned that investigatory
committees take heed of the fact that "a man's reputation is not difficult to ascertain
and the reputation he has should be of vital importance to the committee" (*Digest*
[California] 11, no.2 [Jan.-April 1964]: 7). The same attitude was shown in 1910 when
the Chicago Masons expelled the leader of the South Side's gambling industry, Henry
"Teenan" Jones, because of his notorious "shady" activities (Allan Spear, *Black
Chicago* [Chicago, 1967] p. 77). This is not to say that Masonry does not have any
members whose businesses are less than legal. Many successful blacks have had to

not fulfill the requirement—and given the nature of American discriminatory law enforcement the number of blacks who have gone afoul of the law is quite high. The Grand Master of California in 1915 explicitly ruled on the problem of admitting a man into the Order who had served a sentence in prison by observing, "Freemasons represent the highest type of citizenship and its moral teachings which are so lofty that it would be entirely out of harmony with its exalted precepts to admit into its membership anyone below the standard."[4]

One area of conformity to bourgeois behavior with which Masonry has been especially concerned involves the initiate's marital relations. In 1919 New York's Grand Lodge added to the list of questions required of all petitioners the following:

> Are you married? Are you at present living with your wife? If not living with your wife, state cause for separation. Have you any children? Are you divorced? If divorced, were you named as being the guilty party?

The Texas Masons in their 1919 Constitution declared that no lodge could initiate a candidate who was married unless he showed a marriage certificate. A violation of this rule by members of the lodge involved a twelve-month suspension. The Masons have been very concerned that applicants conform to the standard American concept of a good father and husband, responsibly providing for his household. Their demand that initiates meet these requirements reflects their belief both that these values are good in themselves and that a large part of the black population can not meet them. In an interview with the present author, one local lodge secretary pointed out that it is important to thoroughly check the background of an applicant, especially his sex life. In order to do this, it is best to receive applications from married men, since it is possible to investigate their marriage and to discover from their wives if they are "good providers, good family men, good husbands." A single man is harder to investigate since

---

make their money in illegal or quasi-legal enterprises. When they have chosen to live respectable public lives in all matters save their occupations it has been hard, and perhaps unnecessary, to take action against them. The Masonic rules make no exceptions to their exclusionary policy, but there have probably been a fair number as long as the proper "front" has been maintained.

[4] *Proceedings* (California, 1915).

there is no one with whom to check his moral behavior.[5] C. L. Dellums, successor to A. Philip Randolph as head of the Sleeping Car Porters' Union and life-long Mason, stated in an interview that he was especially proud of the strictness of the investigatory committees. He emphasized that they went into the home, not just "the job situation," and refused to take anyone's word for the applicant's marital state without documentary evidence—"even if ten kids were running around." Because of this laudatory strictness, Dellums went on, if a man was accepted into the Order, it meant that "his background stood up" and he could justly feel his peers considered him a "first-class human being."[6]

In addition to the restrictive legal and marital requirements, the fraternity has further demonstrated its commitment to exclusiveness by forbidding lodges to "receive or retain as a member ... any man who is a common profane swearer, a reputed libertine, an excessive drinker, or one who is guilty of any crime involving moral turpitude or ... any demoralizing practice ... ,"[7] with investigatory committees to screen out non-conformists.[8]

Perhaps the most important questions that Masons ask of potential adherents, and the questions that ultimately are most restrictive in their effects, are the personal ones, those in which the full weight of class bias is able to come into play. Sometimes the question posed inquires, "Is this the kind of man I will enjoy sitting next to in a lodge? Will he enjoy talking with me about our common interests?"[9] More often, "Is he someone I can bring to my home; someone I can introduce to my wife and children?"[10] Or, when being very blunt, "Will you be ashamed to associate with him in public or private life?"[11] Unless the answers are an unreserved affirmative, the applicant is rejected. To make sure the prospective Masons meet all the standards, many investigatory committees institute rather inquisitorial type of investigations aimed at discovering "something [about] ... his social standing, who ... his company

[5] Interview with Richard Wilson, Secretary of Good Hope Lodge, Oakland, California, May 1971.

[6] Interview with C. L. Dellums, May 1971.

[7] *Constitution of Georgia Masonry*, 1924.

[8] *Proceedings* (California, 1913), report by C.C.F.C.

[9] *Digest* (California), 11, no.2, (Jan.-April 1964): 7.

[10] Interview with Adrian Bridges, May 1971.

[11] *Proceedings* (Texas, 1953), Grand Master's speech.

[is], his family relationship, *his real attitude toward society*, where he spends his idle hours, and something of his past history."[12] How many poor ghetto blacks can stand such scrutiny?

All of these requirements and regulations reflect the fraternity's long-standing demand that only "respectable" blacks, those who demonstrate by their public behavior their adherence to middle-class standards, be admitted—regardless of their economic standing. But Masonry has not only tried to exclude a substantial portion of the black population on moral grounds, it has also endeavored to limit candidates by its economic requirements. For if adherence to bourgeois behavioral standards alone were used, a substantial part of the lower class would be eligible for Masonry. According to Drake and Cayton in *Black Metropolis*, "a decided minority within the larger lower class" is made up of "respectable lowers," people who try to live by middle-class codes of conduct.[13] This group differs from those who are admitted into Masonry by their poverty. Even within a poorly developed system of economic stratification, some blacks have been poorer than others, and their poverty has been such that even a bourgeois life style has not been enough to make them "middle class." Their poverty has forced them to struggle, often unsuccessfully, simply to maintain their value code, let alone acquire any of the social graces and manners that the Masons have expected of their initiates.[14]

There has always been an economic bias built into Masonry's

[12] *Proceedings* (Georgia, 1922) where Foreign Correspondent quotes from *Proceedings* of Indiana, 1921. Italics added.

[13] According to St. Clair Drake and Horace Cayton, *Black Metropolis* (New York, 1962), p. 612, most of the black "poor but respectable" strata have not been men (and thus eligible for Masonry) at all, but church-oriented women, women often married to men who have not supported their life styles. Also, this group's economic instability has made lapses from "acceptable" behavior frequent.

[14] The Grand Master of New York in 1921 pointed out that Masonic standards require more than avoidance of illegal or immoral acts: "Masonry approves of no trickery or chicanery, no double dealing, no unmanly or ungentlemanly acts or words. Masonry does not accept as its votaries, the gambler, the drunkard, the libertine, the man who in any manner violates the laws of the land or *the rules of polite society* . . ." (Italics added). The Grand Master of Texas in 1947 also pointed out that as important as prudence, frugality, and temperateness in behavior are, they are not enough to make a Mason. A man must have the "social graces" as well as live a moral life style to be worthy of the Masonic honor. In addition, see the biography of nineteenth century Grand Lodge official Rev. John Peterson, by Masonic historian Harry Williamson in *Proceedings* (New York, 1921), for a suggestion of the importance of "good manners" to Masons.

"moral" and "behavioral" requirements. To successfully perform the role of responsible father and husband has required
that a man at least have a steady job. Thus the Masonic demand
for faithfulness, in practice rather than in intentions, to bourgeois values has discriminated against those lacking a minimum
of occupational and income security. This has been compounded by the expensiveness of Masonry.

It is, and always has been, costly to become a Mason. A
man must pay for initiation into each of three separate steps
that create a "Master" Mason. The fees are explicitly used
for the purpose of excluding undesirables (i.e., "respectable
lower") recruits. The Chairman of the Committee on Foreign
Correspondence of Georgia in 1922 put the matter bluntly,
reporting approvingly the rise in cost of initiation in the
Minnesota Lodges from $20 to $25: "This sum is not a bit too
much. Masonry is not intended for the rabble, in order to
appreciate it, applicants should pay a proper fee." Not infrequently Grand Masters have been asked or forced to give
dispensations temporarily lowering the fees in order for smaller
local lodges to obtain needed members. However, they have
generally been opposed to "cheap Masonry" and felt that to
lower the fee is to lower the quality of the membership.[15]

The expensiveness of initiation can be easily ascertained from
the Grand Lodge proceedings of the different states. In 1873
the Jurisdiction of Alabama charged a uniform $50 for initiation
into the Order. A year later, in order to meet the wants of
the "horny-handed laborer," the Grand Lodge saw fit to require
its subordinate lodges to reduce their fees and charge "only"
$40 for "city" and $20 for "interior" lodges. How long these
rather high fees lasted cannot be ascertained, but they show
what the Alabamians expected in the way of wealth from their
members. By contrast, a local lodge in New York at the time
required only $15, which was still a substantial sum.[16] In the
early twentieth century states like Louisiana, Georgia, and
Texas were charging from $15 to $25.[17] When the Grand Master

[15] *Proceedings* (New York, 1906). This is true outside America, too. In the Masonic
lodges of Sierra Leone, West Africa, the Order is so expensive that only a minority
within the Creole elite can afford it (Abner Cohen, "The Politics of Ritual Secrecy,"
Man, 6, no.3 [1971]: 435).

[16] *Prince Hall Masonry in New York State*, Harry Williamson, vol. 1 (Manuscript),
Schomburg Collection. The lodge is discussed under the heading "1876."

[17] *Proceedings* (Georgia, 1908), C.C.F.C. reports that Louisiana's Grand Master
wanted fees raised from $20 to $25; Georgia herself charged $15; Texas in its Constitution

of the State of Iowa in 1914 recommended that fees be dropped from $20 to $15, the Foreign Correspondent of California was appalled and deprecated this "progress in the wrong direction." By the early 1920s various Masonic jurisdictions were raising their fees even higher. A New York official recommended that initiation fees in the most populous districts of New York be raised to $50.[18] Soon after some California lodges reached the $75 level.[19] At least one state, Michigan, in 1920 explicitly raised its fees from $30 to $45 for the purpose of stopping the flood of applicants occasioned by the rapid growth of the state's black population.[20] Initiation into the fraternity has been expensive, often by design; and, even without conscious intent, the high initiation fees have effectively excluded poor blacks.

The Depression affords an opportunity to view in microcosm the fraternity's use of money as a device for exclusion. Sometime in 1934-5 the Masons of Ohio sent a letter to California informing them that in order to fight the economic slump, they had instituted a campaign to reinstate Masons "regardless of their worldly standing or financial condition"; if a brother needs charity it is certainly during times like these. The reaction of California's Foreign Correspondent was one of sharp disapproval, for while generosity was laudable, he said, a total disregard for the financial standing of members was foolhardy. Not even the greatest depression in history and the extent of black destitution throughout the country could shake this Mason's commitment to keeping the rabble—economically defined—out.

Once economic conditions improved, the fees mounted. By 1958 at least one lodge, a local in New Brunswick, New Jersey, went so far as to charge $100 for the first degree (out of three necessary for initiation) alone. This was indeed an effective barrier for a substantial part of the black population.[21] Around

---

of 1919 specified that no fees could be lower than $15 or higher than $25.

[18] At the time of his recommendation one local lodge did raise its fees to that sum and another to $40 (see *Proceedings* [New York, 1920]). However, the average fee was probably around $25 (see *Prince Hall Masonry in New York State*, vol. 3, under heading "1924-1925").

[19] *Proceedings* (California, 1921). The Foreign Correspondent of California mentioned that the Grand Master of Georgia was annoyed by such high fees in California. Georgia once had $25 fees but felt compelled to lower them to $15. See *Proceedings* (Georgia, 1922).

[20] *Proceedings* (California, 1920), C.C.F.C. reporting on Michigan.

[21] *By-Laws of Progressive Lodge No. 17*, New Brunswick, N.J.

the same time a local Georgian lodge decreed that no applicant would be acceptable to them that did not possess a $500-insurance policy or $500 in the bank before joining.[22]

Masonry has placed many other financial burdens upon its membership which have reinforced its initial restrictiveness. Masons have been required to contribute regularly to the local and Grand Lodge Relief (burial and/or charity) Funds, Building Fund, and other special causes that the state organization might determine (e.g., the N.A.A.C.P.). While the total of these fees has rarely been prohibitive, the need for regularity has placed both financial and psychological requirements on the Masons that a large part of the black community has been unable to meet.[23] In 1964 a local California Masonic leader advised the Order that the economic condition of applicants was of the utmost importance, especially their spending habits:

> The financial position of an applicant should be ascertained. Can he afford the fees? Can he afford the dues? Here again the presence of the wife at an interview is suggested as wise. Masonry is injured, not aided, by members whose income and outgo are so nearly balanced that lodge dues become a hardship.[24]

It is important to Masons that a prospective member be financially able to afford the proper life style of Masonry without monetary embarrassment. As a result, the Fraternal Columnist for the New York *Age* was correct in 1935 when he wrote, "Let us frankly admit that Masonry is a luxury; that its members are . . . capable of supporting themselves and families, and that with proper care exercised, but few, comparatively, will need [Masonic] charity."[25] Because of the economic and moral requirements Masonry has imposed on its members it is probable that the fraternity has drawn a disproportionately large percentage of its members from the most economically secure segments of the "behaviorally" middle class, drawing only lightly on poverty-stricken "respectable lowers" who,

---

[22] *Proceedings* (Georgia, 1956); This is part of the minutes of the Grand Lodge, not an official's report. The lodge protested vehemently that this was not "class legislation" but protection against the expense of burying the man if he died soon after entering tle lodge.

[23] The attitude of the membership to some of these fees will be discussed in Chapter XIII.

[24] *Digest* (California), 11, no.2 (Jan.-April 1964): 7.

[25] New York *Age*, Bertram Baker's Column, January 26, 1935.

because of their adherence to bourgeois values and behavior, might be considered part of the black middle class.

Masonry protects itself from "undesirables" not simply by moral and economic restraints but by discriminating against certain specific "unrespectable" groups as well. For example, it does not attract or accept as members recent migrants into the cities, a group that has been important in swelling the size of the black poor.[26] The Order's investigatory committees are interested not only in "how they [the applicants] live, [and] what kind of work they do" but "how long they have been working, how long they have been in the community."[27] Since Masonry wants stable, respectable men of good reputation, recent migrants are at a great disadvantage. Besides this, the poor migrant himself often avoids the Order until he has achieved a minimum stability in the community. It is only after he has established himself that he will be concerned about associating with "respectable people."[28] The desire for respectability, and the need to find "safe associates" within the black community is of crucial importance in the Order's ability to attract the most successful and adjusted black migrants.

It is not only recent migrants which the fraternity keeps at a distance. The Order also repels men (migrant and native) below the age of 30. As the secretary of a local Oakland lodge put it recently, young men are too distracted by "life in the streets" to be either interested in, or acceptable to Masonry. It is only when "their running days are over," they finally marry, have children, take on responsibilities and wish to "establish themselves" in the community that they may join the Order.[29]

In attempting to evaluate Masonry's success in attracting the restricted clientele it has desired, there are a number of possible approaches. One is to examine the views of Masonic leaders themselves in their addresses to their constituencies. Though there is a danger that these speeches contain exaggeration, flattery, or even outright lies, ultimately the knowledge that the audience, as well as the official speaking, knows the

---

[26] Unless the migrant was a Mason in his home state, or is quite exceptional in his social characteristics.

[27] Bridges interview, May 1971.

[28] Bridges interview, April 1971.

[29] Bridges interview, May 1971.

"truth" helps set reasonable limits to the range of possible distortion.

In their speeches, Masonic leaders refer to the founders of their state lodges, with particular reference to their social standing. Grand Secretary Sol C. Johnson of Georgia (a prominent black leader in his own right as editor and publisher of the Savannah *Tribune*) in his "History of the Grand Lodge" spoke approvingly of the founder of the first three lodges in Georgia as "the most prominent men of their respective communities." He went on to prove this by pointing out the close links between the fraternity's founders and those of the African Methodist Episcopal Church in Georgia (they were the same men).[30] The founders of Georgia Masonry were prominent not only in the church but in politics and business as well. The second and third Grand Masters of Georgia, L. B. Toomer and John H. Deveaux, were both active Republicans during Reconstruction, the former a justice of the peace and the latter a state senator and federal appointee. Deveaux was also the editor and publisher of the *Colored Tribune*, which later became the Savannah *Tribune*. A history of a local Cleveland lodge presents a similar claim concerning the importance of its founders: "The early rosters of our lodges here show that they comprised most of the founders of our 'old' families."[31] And while claims like these may sound like the normal self-congratulation of any group, they receive much support from lists of prominent individual Masons whose identities are known.

A striking example of outside support for Masonic claims about the importance and prominence of their founders can be found in Herbert Aptheker's *The Negro in the Abolitionist*

[30] Speech given in 1920.

[31] *History, Constitution and By-Laws of Excelsior Lodge No. 11 Free and Accepted Masons* (Cleveland, 1926). Charles Wesley, as mentioned earlier, supports this estimation when he says the Masons could draw upon the flourishing black community of Cincinnati in the 1840s since "A large number of them [black] have acquired education, property and personal culture, which were the bases for fellowship among themselves . . ." (Wesley, p. 30). He also mentions a 1906 history of Ohio Masonry which made note of the Order's appeal in the early years, i.e., 1873, to black teachers. In that year the Grand Lodge decided it had to move its meeting time to August from June in order "to accommodate teachers of the public schools . . . as there was a large number of them prominently and actively interested in the affairs of the Grand Lodge at that time" and June interfered with their school term. For the general elite quality of Ohio Masonic leadership (including their high occupational achievement) during the nineteenth century, see Wesley, passim.

Movement.[32] The book reads like a "Who's Who in Black Masonry," though Aptheker chose the men solely on the basis of their abolitionist activities: Peter Ray (Grand Master of New York), John De Grass, Lewis Hayden (Grand Master of Massachusetts), Absalom Jones (Grand Master of Pennsylvania), Thomas Dalton, Moses Dickson (Grand Master of Missouri), Patrick H. Reason (Grand Master of New York), James T. Hilton (Grand Master of Massachusetts), James Forten (Senior Warden of the second black Masonic lodge in America), Theodore Wright, and Major Martin Delany (noted Masonic author). This is only a partial listing for pre-1860 abolitionists. The names of major Reconstruction black leaders, like Lieutenant Governor of Louisiana Oscar Dunn (Grand Master of Louisiana), Lieutenant Governor of South Carolina Richard Gleaves (Grand Master of the National Grand Lodge), Congressman Robert Small of South Carolina, Senator Hiram Revels and Congressman John Lynch of Mississippi, would extend the list considerably.

If Masonic leaders are laudatory about their founding fathers, they are no less so about their current membership. Whether it is the Grand Master of Alabama in 1939 telling his brethren that "You represent the most fortunate group of the various communities from which you come"; or the Grand Master of Georgia in 1908 boasting that the fraternity was "largely made up of some of the best and most law-abiding colored men in this state—men who have made themselves part of the communities in which they live by owning their homes and living honest and respectable lives"; or the leader of Texas Masonry in 1919 proclaiming that "The best men of every community, town or city, are members of the Masonic lodge," the leaders of all the jurisdictions have agreed that being a Mason has always been "an honor and testimonial of character and standing."[33] Not only have they claimed that the membership has been composed of good men, but that they have been

[32] New York, 1941. It is very difficult to obtain information on Masonic affiliation of individuals from secondary sources. One of the few biographies to provide it is Victor Ullman's study, *Martin R. Delany, The Beginnings of Black Nationalism* (Boston, 1971). Ullman emphasizes that Delany found the Masonic bond a "source of strength and comradeship" and an added link tying him to his co-workers fighting for black freedom. Whether he was in Pittsburgh or Canada he found the Masonic fraternity a place of warmth and community with other blacks. See especially p. 193.

[33] *Proceedings* (California, 1930), C.C.F.C. reporting on Texas.

the "natural leaders" of the communities in which they live as well.

Masonic claims for the distinctiveness and importance of its adherents in the twentieth century receive objective support from the pages of the Masonic records. The Grand Lodge *Proceedings* and journals contain the names of hundreds of easily identifiable black community leaders. The comparatively small jurisdiction of New York includes a significant segment of the elite of New York's black community. A listing of prominent New York Masons appeared in the *Prince Hall Sentinel* in 1954: "We of New York are indeed fortunate in having in our Craft such noted brothers as Rev. A[dam] Clayton Powell, Jr. (Congressman), Francis E. Rivers (Judge), Julius A. Archibald (Senator), Arthur T. Giddings (Civil Engineer), Matthew Henson (Explorer)[,] Rev. Elder Hawkins (Social Worker), Elmer Carter [Head of the Civil Rights Commission in New York State] (Anti-Discrimination), Rev. John H. Coleman (Board of Education), Doctors, Lawyers, Politicians, Business-men and others who combined, could aid not only our jurisdiction but the whole Negro race in general. . . ."[34] This list could easily be extended to include such men as Percy E. Sutton (Borough President of Manhattan), Rev. Milton Galamison (civil rights leader), Joseph E. Davis (president and founder of Carver Federal Savings and Loan Association), J. Daniel Diggs (councilman of New York City), Rev. E. S. Callander (Executive Director of the New York Urban League), Justice Oliver Williams (Justice of the Supreme Court of New York), Arthur Schomburg (bibliophile), and Adam Clayton Powell, Sr. (religious leader).[35]

The situation in other states is remarkably similar. Masonry has claimed the adherence of Oscar DePriest (Congressman from Illinois, later Grand Master of Illinois), William Dawson (Congressman from Illinois), Harry Davis (state senator, Ohio), Edward T. Powsor, Sr. (assemblyman, New Jersey), and Thurgood Marshall. A perfect illustration of the type of men Masonry attracts appears in the Third Quarter, 1968 issue of the *Prince Hall Sentinel*. An article in that issue reported the initiation of Mayor Carl Stokes of Cleveland into the fraternity.

[34] *Prince Hall Sentinel* [henceforth called *Sentinel* (New York)], 10, no.5-6 (May-June 1954): 11.
[35] *Sentinel* (New York), 19, no.4 (Oct.-Dec. 1966): 8-9.

At his "raising" a number of other members of the Craft were present: Judge F. M. Coleman, Judge Perry Jackson, Councilman Charles V. Carr, Civil Service Chairman J. B. White (of Cleveland), and J. F. Ryne, city councilman of Alliance, Ohio (Junior Grand Warden of the Grand Lodge of Ohio). Names such as these, and they are only a sampling, give much support to Masonic claims that the fraternity attracts not only men of high quality and ability, but the leaders of the black group. What the few available records reveal about the composition of the general membership also lends credence to Masonic claims. For example, the editor of the non-Masonic *Fraternal Review* said of the Prince Hall Square Club of New York in 1931, "This club, composed of men employed in the Federal, State and Municipal Governments, and who are Prince Hall Masons, is one of the leading and most popular clubs in the city. It has a limited membership of 130, and has proven a credit to the community, because of the excellent work it has done, modestly and quietly, in aid of charity, and in helping promote the best interests of the Negro in all spheres of life."[36] Elsewhere, references are made to the erection of a local lodge restricted to men employed by the New York Post Office,[37] and to the mass initiation in another lodge of 17 new members "all railroad employees."[38] An article in the *Proceedings* of New York in 1941 proudly states that an upstate local lodge "continues to hold an important position in the community life of Rochester, and many of its members are to be found on the boards of several churches, the Y.M.C.A. and other organizations." One of the most interesting types of evidence that abounds in the Masonic records is the prominence of black pioneers listed in the membership. One finds constantly reports of local lodges giving honorary dinners for members who are "the first" among the black race to reach high levels of achievement in their profession. A typical example was the dinner given Lieutenant Battle of Mt. Oliver Lodge, New York, to pay homage to the fact that "Bro. Battle was recently promoted to Lieutenant in the Police Dep't of New York City, the first Negro to be promoted to such a coveted office."[39]

[36] *Fraternal Review* (New York), 10, no.1 (January 1931) n.p.

[37] *The Story of Carthaginain, 1904-1947*, Harry Williamson, 1949 Carthaginian, (pamphlet).

[38] *Sentinel* (New York), 1, no.6 (May 1944): 1.

[39] *Proceedings* (New York, 1935).

The Masonic records contain one final source of evidence concerning the nature of the fraternity's membership. In both 1936 and 1958 the Masons of California reprinted articles by white Masons who had investigated the Prince Hall fraternity in an attempt to decide if the black organization was legitimate. In both cases the white investigators recommended against recognition—for extraneous reasons. Nevertheless, they had some very favorable comments on the type of blacks who belonged to the Order. The first observer said of the California jurisdiction, "This Negro grand body has appealed to the better situated Negroes. It has been very active in the communities where they are organized in promoting fraternal and material assistance."[40] The second, commenting on the entire Prince Hall Family, proclaimed that "The membership is one of the highest type Negro men in the land. The mothers, sisters, daughters, and wives are in affiliated ladies societies, and of course, are of just such high type folks as are the men. These lodges are prosperous and respectable and fill an important need in the Negro communities of the land."[41] Both views lend support to the picture the Masonic leadership itself creates.[42]

If we leave the black Masons' own records and look for confirmation of their claims in other sources, we again find important evidence. A perusal of the 1930-32 *Who's Who in Colored America* shows that over 50 percent of the men listed in the volume were members of the Masons, despite the fact that the Order contained only a small fraction of the black adult male population. The *Who's Who in Colored America* for 1950, with approximately 33 percent of the men being members, shows the Masons still attracting a disproportionate number of prominent black men into the Order. If we turn

[40] *Proceedings* (New York, 1936).

[41] *Digest* (California), 7, no.1 (1958): 3.

[42] The praise Masonry received from white observers was more than matched by that given by W. E. B. Du Bois. In a *Chicago Defender* article in the late 1940s he said that as a result of discrimination blacks had to establish their own organizations. These were usually markedly inferior to their white counterparts. Black Freemasonry, however, was a striking exception. It operated as efficiently and effectively as the white branch. While Du Bois attacked those who wanted segregation for its own sake, he had only encouragement for those who established excellent separate organizations until integration was possible (cited from W. E. B. Du Bois, "The Winds of Time," *Chicago Defender* 2, 1946), in *Prince Hall Masonic Review* [henceforth called *Review* (Georgia)], 11, no.1 [Jan.-March 1947]: 6, 17). Du Bois had been made a Mason in 1910, but it is unlikely that this effected his judgment 37 years later.

from the national to a state volume, we discover a similar situation. The *Negro Who's Who in California*, 1948, reveals that out of 150 men listed, 43 of them, or 26 percent, were adherents of Masonry. Similar results come from a perusal of a local guide to black businessmen in northern California published in 1930. *Thompson's East Bay Directory* (dealing with Oakland and Berkeley, California) shows that at least 26 percent of the men listed were also identifiable as Masons. And, of even greater interest, when we take the 40 Masonic businessmen listed in the directory and compare them to the membership lists of the East Bay Lodges we find 10 percent of the enrollment to be black businessmen.[43] A similar list compiled two years earlier than the *Thompson Directory* by a graduate student at the University of California, Berkeley, included 11 additional names of Masonic businessmen; and even that list was certainly not exhaustive.[44] Information such as this, while fragmentary, does provide support for our contention that Masonry has been successful in its desire to attract an exclusive part of the black population;[45] more detailed evidence will be presented later which reports our findings from an intensive study of the lodges of Oakland, California.

Part 2. Bourgeois Morality and Responsibility

Once Masonry has selected its initiates it works to solidify and extend the differences, real and supposed, between them and most blacks. It strives to reinforce the membership's commitment to bourgeois values and behavior, to keep the "faithful" from slipping into nonbourgeois practices. Masonry attempts to perform what Ivan Light considers the ideal function of churches and fraternal orders:

[43] It must be pointed out that the term "businessmen" is used rather loosely by the compiler, who includes some clergymen and some professional men such as dentists and doctors under this heading. However, the actual percentage is probably considerably higher because the directory is quite incomplete.

[44] The number of men who went into and out of business quickly would also swell the percentage of "businessmen types" who were Masons. For example, 10 Masonic businessmen who advertised in the 1922 Grand Lodge Proceedings do not appear in either the 1930 or 1928 listings. Other 1920s' volumes probably all had their share of ill-fated black Masons venturing into and out of business.

[45] While academic observers have not paid much attention to Masonry since they have prematurely thought it dead, they have all commented on its prestige as a relatively exclusive fraternity. This is the case for Allan Spear, St. Clair Drake, Hylan Lewis and Edward Palmer.

Both church and fraternal order tend to institutionalize a moral community. These organizations were, first of all, moralistic in that they stressed ethical conduct on the part of the membership. Membership ... formally involved public commitment to a set of moral or ethical ideals. ... Church and fraternal order also encourage active membership participation and a public way of life. Active participation usually involved a fusion of institutional and extra-institutional roles.... The public way of life... resulted in peer group scrutiny of daily conduct and increased the social pressure on an individual to conform to the standards of his membership group.[46]

Light found that the degree of intensity and success achieved by such organizations varied greatly. The evidence shows that Masonry has been one of the more successful black organizations in creating a moral community, though within significant limits.[47]

The formation of a middle-class peer group such as Masonry is especially important because it provides a supportive network which directly helps maintain the middle-class value system and life style. First, it affords spatial and social separation from the lower class while the membership engages in recreational activities. Second, it lowers the danger of physical harm to middle-class blacks caused by association with members of the lower class. Third, it prevents the membership from forced interaction with people whose behavior offends their moral code. Fourth, it protects the middle class from having its reputation damaged and its respectability called into question by reason of "guilt by association." Fifth, and most important, it protects its members from "contamination" by the attraction of alternative life styles.[48]

[46] Ivan Light, *Ethnic Enterprise in America* (Berkeley, 1972), p. 130.

[47] See Chapter XIII for discussion of these limits.

[48] The problem of life-style contamination is easily lost sight of once we accept the anti-culture-of-poverty argument that no lower-class value system exists and the lower class is prevented by forces outside its control from acting out standard American morality. One of the major implications of the macrostructuralist argument of Charles Valentine (*Culture and Poverty* [Chicago, 1969]) or Elliott Liebow (*Talley's Corner* [Boston, 1967]) is that mainstream ideals are so attractive that, given the chance, every lower-class black will immediately conform to them. Since these theorists posit no major value or cultural obstacles to prevent the lower class from becoming middle class when structural restraints are removed, they of course see no danger that those who have already "made it" might reject their life style. This view ignores the strain that active conformity to middle-class morality entails for the black bourgeoisie. While the lower class may lack a distinctive value system, to the middle-class black Mason

In addition, Masonry attempts to give the commitment an added dimension: to make its adherents aware that the bourgeois life is worthwhile not only because it is "morally good" but because it brings concrete material and social rewards. By emphasizing the benefits, it hopes to inspire its followers to a more dynamic and diligent exercise of virtue than "morality is its own reward" provides, thereby giving more substance to the Masonic claim that its membership occupies an elite status in the black group. -

For Masonic leaders middle-class values and behavior are important not only because they are valuable in themselves, useful for social differentiation, and bring material rewards, but also because adherence to them is highly regarded in the white community. The Masons are acutely sensitive to what Caucasian Americans view as noble and ignoble. And to whites, bourgeois behavior is a moral imperative. The Masonic leadership's emphasis on rigidly maintaining a middle-class style of life has been strongly influenced by their sensitivity to the white charge that blacks neither practice nor are capable of practicing bourgeois morality and, therefore, are an immoral and inherently inferior race. The Masons have fervently desired by their conduct to disprove the charge; though by their own view of themselves as different from most blacks they demonstrate an acceptance of the white stereotype at least as it pertains to the black masses, while rejecting it for the race (i.e., themselves) as such.

---

he *appears* to live by such a code, and that different value system is anything but totally repellent. If the black mainstreamers did not form their own social group, with the black lower class as the major negative reference group, they would be hard pressed to resist the temptations of the alternative life styles around them. The problem posed for the black bourgeoisie is not very different from that of the white middle class. Observers of white society have long taken note of the attraction-repulsion which middle-class people feel toward out-groups that appear to enjoy life more than they. The extreme hostility of the white bourgeoisie to "bohemians" is partially motivated by the obvious envy and fear of succumbing to temptation that many solid white burghers feel. The argument that there is nothing pleasurable about being poor and oppressed overstates the facts—at least insofar as lower-class "adaptation" has its good points *in the eyes of the middle class*. Or, more important, the middle-class life style has so many inherent problems that almost anything different looks good. We are not concerned with whether or not large numbers of black Masons would actually desert their life style (or even psychologically *could*) but with the anxiety that exists. Masonry provides its membership with both peer group support and verbal admiration of their continual struggle against temptation. It also brings to bear social constraints against any deviation from accepted middle-class norms.

In Masonry's efforts to reinforce and broaden the members' appreciation of middle-class values and behavior, the idea that receives the most persistent reiteration is the duty of Masons as individuals, and the Masonic Order as an institution, to obtain property. An excellent summary of this idea is found in the *Proceedings* of the California Grand Lodge for 1914 in which the Chairman of the Committee on Foreign Correspondence reports:

> It is a fact worthy of note that Masonry is teaching more than signs, grips and passwords. That it is teaching men the practical lessons, how to live, how to economize and the worth of the dollar. . . . [I]t is . . . laudable, and a . . . duty for husbands and fathers to build a home for the comforts of loved ones. . . . Let the habit of acquiring great responsibilities be carried through Lodges, grand and subordinate, to the individual members, till it results in the Negro acquiring large land holdings and managing great businesses for himself, and then the leopard will have done much to change his spots and the Ethiopian to change his skin.

The ownership of property for the Masons possesses greater importance than simply its ability to create a higher standard of living. More important, it has major psychological and symbolic significance. Material success is a "source of pride and inspiration for the entire Colored Race" which for the fraternity is of key importance.[49] As the head of Texas Masonry said in 1930:

> Brethren we should set the example for our people. There is little excuse in this day and time for a man not to own something. Every man should at least own his own home . . . ; let it be a cabin, yes a log cabin, if nothing else, but let it be your own.

The size of the property is not important, anything will do, as long as it demonstrates the black man's willingness to start at the bottom and by sacrifice work his way up. The Grand

---

[49] *Review* (Georgia), 1, no.5 (February, 1938): 19, reporting on Alabama. The authors of *Black Metropolis* point out that "To former sharecroppers and the descendants of chattel slaves, real estate is a potent symbol of stability and respectability." The home is of vital importance for the black middle class (Drake and Cayton, p. 663). The concern among Masons for property goes back to the very beginning of the fraternity. Lorenzo Greene in "Prince Hall: Massachusetts Leader in Crisis," *Freedomways*, 1, no.3 (Fall 1962): 242, says that Prince Hall himself, in response to the "sneers" and "insults" heaped on free Negroes and slaves alike, "through diligence and frugality ... became a property owner, thus establishing himself in the eyes of white persons as well as Negroes."

Master felt a good example had to be set by the Masons since too many black people thought they could start at the top, refusing to learn how to crawl before they learned to walk. In this case, as in so many others, Masons have seen the majority of blacks in the same way whites have: blacks lack the Protestant ethic and need guidance from above to learn it.[50]

In addition, the ownership of property provides a way of proving to whites that blacks are not an inferior but rather an equal race, worthy of respect and admiration. As a Grand Master of California put it, all of his efforts were "endeavoring to show that our people measure up favorably with other races, in proportion to their number and ability in the acquirement of property and homes," and this was of great importance for the race's image because "Property owners as a rule are considered among the most desirable citizens . . . ."[51]

In order to truly impress the dominant race, and inspire the rest of the black community, the Masons have wanted black property to be as well kept and cared for as possible. As the Grand Master of Texas expressed it in 1947, lodges, schools, parks, and streets must be lovely to look at, since "Our unsightly homes, our broken down fences, our dilapidated lodge buildings" work against us in our attempt to get decent treatment from the white population. Because of Masonic preoccupation with white opinion, Masons have been overly conscious of problems of cleanliness and neatness in the black community. By being made hypersensitive to these problems, they have tended to accept many of the whites' negative stereotypes of the black masses.

Many a Masonic leader over the years has attempted to motivate his followers to acquire property by collecting information demonstrating the financial success already achieved. In 1915 the Grand Master of California Masonry received

[50] *Proceedings* (Texas, 1930). The Grand Master uses Peter Cooper as the hero of a Horatio Alger-type story to illustrate what blacks should and can accomplish. The idea he stresses is: start at the bottom and work up, don't expect to begin at the top. The belief that the black masses lack bourgeois virtues and need to be taught them by right-thinking and right-acting Masons is found throughout Prince Hall records. See, for example, *Proceedings* (Texas, 1919) and *Proceedings* (California, 1931). In the latter, the Chairman of California's Committee on the State of the Country said "The race must be taught that a people who won't live right and behave themselves in a room ten feet square here on earth, can never live in a big place like Heaven."

[51] *Proceedings* (California, 1915), Grand Master's speech.

reports from most of the local lodges and proudly announced
that of 760 Masons in the state fully 50 percent were property
owners and 20 percent were in the process of buying property.
In 1920, the Grand Master of Georgia, Dr. H. R. Butler, as
was his custom, asked the members of the Grand Lodge how
many of them owned their own homes and was gratified that
90 percent raised their hands, with the other 10 percent promising to strive to do likewise. A few years later the head of
Oklahoma Masonry boasted that 2,500 out of 4,000 Masons
in his jurisdiction owned their own homes.[52] Masonic leaders
throughout the country have been concerned that blacks "be
not content to remain a floating part of the population" but
acquire homes, and businesses, thus making a favorable impression in the larger black and white communities.[53]

Masonic leaders have desired more than that individual
members obtain property. They have demanded that the fraternity as an institution grow and prosper, thereby proving
to the "dominant race" the Negro's worth. The Grand Master
of California in 1927 put the issue succinctly when he pointed
out to his brothers that "owning your own lodge homes insures
respect and takes us out of the pauper class." When local lodges
have bought or built their own lodge halls, Masonic spokesmen
from New York to California have been quick to applaud their
efforts. When a lodge accomplished this laudable goal by the
use of sophisticated business practices, such as setting up a
stock company, it has provided even greater cause for rejoic-
ing.[54]

Masons have been very active in emphasizing the idea that
obtaining property is a virtue, and from that virtue many, if
not most, benefits flow. One of the most important benefits,
at least in theory, is that through property ownership "the
leopard will have done much to change his spots and the
Ethiopian his skin," that possessions speak louder than race.
One Grand Master addressing this issue argued that when
anything had been done for Negro rights it has not been done
out of love or humanitarianism but because "We have acquired
property rights that *could not be ignored*."[55] The lengths to

[52] *Proceedings* (Georgia, 1926), C.C.F.C. reporting on Oklahoma.

[53] *Proceedings* (California, 1915), Grand Master's speech.

[54] See, for example, *Proceedings* (Georgia, 1920), Grand Master's speech.

[55] *Proceedings* (California, 1929), italics added.

which some Masons have gone in their concern and respect for property can be seen in the speeches of one Grand Master of Georgia, Dr. H. R. Butler. It was his habit to calculate for the Grand Lodge the financial losses borne by the fraternity, the black community, and the state by the death of Masonic members during the year. He elaborately listed the number of dead Masons and how much was lost in wages, medical expenses, funeral costs, membership dues, insurance payments, taxes, etc. The importance and uniqueness of the individual was totally obscured in the mountain of financial data the Grand Master poured out. Such a materialistic view of the "dear departed" was not out of keeping with the Masonic commitment, bordering on idolatry, to bourgeois values.[56]

Another virtue that the Masonic Order has tried to reinforce and expand upon has been faith in the importance, honor and dignity of work.

> [Masonry] teaches those who frequent its Temples, that the nobility of human nature is displayed in WORK. . . . Work alone enobles [sic]; work, not meant by us to benefit ourselves alone; for that does not enoble [sic]. [We must] help the less favored of our race-not alone our children, or neighbors, but those remote from us. . . .[57]

This emphasis on the dignity of work is combined with a belief that the black masses lack the desire to engage in honest, hard

---

[56] *Proceedings* (Georgia, 1922). The Grand Master provided the membership a chart demonstrating that "it is a costly matter for a man or any human being to drop into the sea of death":

. From an economic viewpoint the estimated value of the year's labor of these members

amounts to some	$214,718.00
Estimated cost of funerals	$ 25,000.00
Estimated doctor's bills	$ 3,500.00
Estimated cost of medicine	$ 1,700.00
In the death of these brothers the G.L. [Grand Lodge] loses G.L. tax	$ 80.00
In their death the Orphan Home losses, estimate	$ 138.00
In their death the Home cost [? illegible in text] estimate Dormitory Fund	$ 345.00
Donations during sickness, estimated	$ 3,000.00
Time lost by bros. attending funerals, estimated	$ 3,000.00
Given to relatives by the Grand Lodge thru the M.R.A. [Masonic Relief Association]	$ 70,083.33
Total	$321,551.33

[57] *Proceedings* (California, 1933), Grand Master's speech.

labor; in this the Masons see the situation in the same way as do whites. In 1951 the Grand Master of South Carolina told the International Grand Masters' Conference that the local lodges had an obligation to the larger community to produce worthy citizens who "accept that part of their responsibility which provides that they must be able and willing to work" because only "The worthy citizen is a producer . . ." and it is Masonry's job to help create more of them.[58] Almost a hundred years before this speech, a leader of New York's fraternity had made a similar point when he said a Freemason must be a good and upright man; which meant that he had to be "particularly industrious in his vocation . . . [and] have good natural endowments with an estate, office, [or] trade . . . or some visible way of acquiring and [sic] honest livlihood [sic] as becomes a member" of Masonry.[59] The extent to which the black Masons have gone in praising work can be seen in the words of the California Grand Master in 1932:

> [O]f deeper signilcance [sic] if possible, than equality before the law . . . is equality of industry. . . . He who earns his bread by the sweat of his brow is, in our teachings, as much entitled to respect and honor as he . . . who rules an empire and enjoys with him an equality of fraternity, friendship and recognition.

The Masons have emphasized the nobility of labor not only as a means of differentiating themselves from the mass of blacks but in order to counteract the ego and status problems of their own restricted economic postion. The Masonic author who recently praised the teachings of Prince Hall was as much concerned with providing moral support for his fellow Masons as he was instructing lower class blacks:

> On the matter relating to the Dignity of Labor, Prince Hall made his greatest contribution. . . . Upon striving toward perfection, one lends purpose and *dignity* to his labor *no matter what* the assignment may be.[60]

In addition to an emphasis on the dignity of work, Masonry has been concerned with the importance of charity. The question of charity and communal cooperation has been one that

---

[58] Quoted in *Review* (Georgia), 15, no.2 (April-June 1951): 19.

[59] *Prince Hall Masonry in New York State*, Harry Williamson, vol. 2; see the heading "1856."

[60] *Digest* (California), 7, no.1 (no month 1958): 4. Italics added.

has long concerned the black middle class. They have been sensitive to white accusations that Negroes do not help each other, a failing witnessed by the prominent lack of institutional philanthropy. The Masons have accepted this censure as legitimate, thereby ignoring the tradition of nonorganized charity common in the black lower class.[61] By accepting the view that institutional almsgiving is of fundamental importance in judging a race's philanthropy, the Masons have been compelled to feel ashamed at their race's deficiency. As an Order, Masonry has long dedicated itself to create a tradition of charity in the black community.

Within the Order the tradition is a long one. The Grand Master of Alabama emphasized to his recently formed Grand Lodge in 1875 that charity is a virtue inseparable from Masonry and requires that the brethren never turn a deaf ear toward others. Masons have a duty to act at the first sign of distress and not wait "until squalidness shall plead and destitution drive to crime . . . [or] until shrunken forms and shrunken eye shall meet your charity . . . ." Grand Lodge proceedings constantly stress the obligation of Masons to provide charity to their brothers or the general community. In their attempts to inspire blacks to acts of charity, it has not been uncommon to find a Grand Master lauding the achievements of white Masonry in setting up such benevolent institutions as hospitals, both in America and in England. Such examples are designed to strengthen black commitment to charity both by providing a good example to follow and by stimulating competitive energies.[62]

The Masonic emphasis on charity has served innumerable purposes; one of the most interesting has been its role in creating race pride by providing blacks with the satisfaction that they are living up to their manly responsibilities. The Grand Master of Georgia in 1933 expressed this sentiment when he noted proudly that the Masonic Orphans' Home of his jurisdiction was paid for solely by black people, without "one cent of aid from whites." A noted New York Mason made a similar point when he said a local old age home (non-Masonic

[61] Such aid is manifested in the "adoption" of stray children by distant relatives and strangers in the rural South. The tradition of lending money to friends whenever one gets it is common among lower-class urban blacks. See Liebow, *Talley's Corner.*
[62] *Proceedings* (Georgia, 1934).

but with many Masons actively involved in it) which a few
years before was almost totally supported by whites was now
funded only by blacks. He felt no ingratitude for white aid
in the past, but was filled with pride because the black man
was finally doing things for himself.[63]

While Masonry has lauded charity as one of its highest ideals
it has set some very specific limits to how and when it should
be dispensed. For Masons charity and middle-class morality
go hand in hand; one without the other is unacceptable. Charity
must go to the "deserving poor," and to no one else. As the
Grand Master of Texas instructed his colleagues in 1918, never
give charity indiscriminately but only in regard to real needs
and "real merit."[64] A misplaced benefit creates more harm than
does no charity at all. This belief was shared by other Masonic
leaders of his jurisdiction and given practical application in
the Masonic Constitution of Texas passed in 1919. In that
document specific regulations were laid down for cases in which
the normal beneficiary of the Grand Lodge "insurance" fund
would not be paid: "No father of a Master Mason who is a
habitual drunkard, a gambler, or who runs an illegal place of
business shall" derive any death benefits from a dead Masonic
son. Also, "No child of a Master Mason who lives a life of
shame or debauchery or who is a gambler, or a drunkard or
a harlot shall" receive such charity. No financial aid of any
kind was to be given to a living and destitute Mason who was
guilty of committing any crime. Thus Masons, even if they
paid their dues regularly and obeyed all the technical requirements of the Order's quasi-insurance fund, were rightless if they
transgressed the moral precepts of the fraternity.[65] Texas was
by no means unique in its attitude, as witnessed by the Grand

[63] New York *Age*, Bertram Baker Column, September 19, 1931.

[64] Prince Hall, in addition to founding black Freemasonry, also helped establish the
African Benevolent Society (1796), an organization pledged to help blacks in Massachusetts become self-supporting. According to Lorenzo Greene, "In addition, the Society
sought to improve the morals of ... [black] people. Therefore, certain restrictions
accompanied any assistance .... The Society would assist a widow and her children
only 'so long as she behaves herself decently ...' " In addition, no one suffering from
distress caused by intemperance would be aided (Greene, pp. 256-257).

[65] Two other clauses are interesting: "No relief shall be extended to the mother of
a Master Mason who runs a bawdy house or who lives a life of prostitution, or who
lives with a man without being legally married to him," and "Master Mason's wives
who separate, quit and live lives of prostitution, shall not be granted ... relief ...."
Requirements like these not only point up the close tie between charity (even of a
quasi-legal insurance type) and morality but also illustrate to what extent the Order

Master of Alabama's threat to the fraternity in 1925 that "we require each member to lead clean and pure lives . . . [and] do not intend to pay one cent to men who live otherwise and lose their lives in a disreputable manner."

Very closely related to the ideas of charity and property ownership is the idea of thrift. Thrift is one of the most basic of all bourgeois values and one that the Masonic leadership has been most determined to strengthen in the membership. The leader of Texas Masonry in 1947 put the matter as strongly as he could when he proclaimed, "Frugality . . . is highly necessary to the supporting of every desirable character [,] to the establishment of every society [,] to the interests of every individual in the community. It is a moral, it is a Christian virtue." Thrift is the obvious foundation for almost all the virtues that Masonry preaches. Without it, very little in the way of charity, property ownership, business, or upward mobility would be possible.

The extreme to which dedication to thrift has forced Masons is nowhere better illustrated than in a speech presented by the leader of Texas Masonry in 1934, during the Great Depression, when economic conditions looked desperate. As bad as things were, he foresaw a greater catastrophe. Ultimately the world would suffer a universal cataclysm which would culminate in the exhaustion of all natural resources and probably the destruction of Western civilization as well. What, he asked his brothers, should black Masons do in the short time before the terrible event struck? Save! Masons, individually and as a group, should put aside resources so that they, though no one else, would be prepared. This is "saving for a rainy day" carried to its most illogical conclusion.

Just as Masons have seen success in material pursuits and thrift as the key to acceptance in the larger society, they have seen education as the means for obtaining that initial economic prosperity. Their records are full of exhortations for Masons and non-Masons alike to dedicate themselves to obtaining a good academic background. A classic example of this philosophy was given by the Grand Master of New York in 1921 when he told the Craft that "Most of our time must be given to education, if we would take our place in the procession of

---

felt it had to fight to keep its members on the straight and narrow path of middle-class virtue when surrounded by lower-class influences, even in their immediate family.

progress." This is especially true since "our race with but few exceptions are [sic] willing to let well enough alone, while wast-[ing] the time in pleasure or pursuits less qualified to prepare themselves to take their rightful places in the world of litera-ture, finance and science." It is only through education and the benefits it brings that black men can compete successfully "in the fields of labor as well as science and industry with the supposedly superior race. . . ." Black Masonic leaders like the Grand Master of New York have seen education as a virtue that must be impressed on the entire race, not just on their own followers. The lack of concern shown by many parents for education is a major reason, they argue, for the failure of blacks in the past. As a high-ranking Masonic official of Califor-nia said, while education is the key to upward mobility "Too many of our boys and girls quit school in the grammar grades. They are allowed by parents to quit school and drift with UNTHINKING and IDLE elements of the race." And such an attitude does inestimable damage not only to the boy or girl but the race and nation.[66] If there is one thing Masons have always deplored it is the contamination of youth by lower-class black behavior. The protection of the children of Masons has been one of the rationales for the existence of the fraternity, though Masons have also hoped that the education-al values they support would extend further than their own children and affect the entire black population.

All these values are part of the general Masonic commitment to the ideal of self-help. Black Masons have believed that the race has to be taught to look after itself and not depend upon others to aid it; white paternalism even where well intentioned is not acceptable. A committee of the Grand Lodge of Texas in 1934 expressed this Masonic commitment when it comment-ed upon the effects of the New Deal in helping the country fight the Depression. While the federal government had "done wonders" for the American people, such aid "is not like that help that comes from our own efforts, that help that comes by our being willing to work hard, as our forefathers did, husband our resources and lay aside a part of our earnings for that rainy day that never fails to come." Self-help is important not only as protection against disaster, but in build-

[66] *Proceedings* (California, 1931), report of the Chairman of the Committee on the State of the Country.

ing morale in the individual and the race. Masons have believed that insofar as the fraternity teaches self-help, it does an inestimable service for black people because "it instills into men personal pride and independence to ask no favor or help so long as one is able to help himself"; it thus puts an end to the "un-Masonic" and unmanly practice of "begging help" from others.[67]

The Masonic fraternity leaves very few of the classic petty-bourgeois mores unattended. The Grand Master of California in 1915 pointed out that Masonry shows "how to avoid intemperance in drinking, eating and speaking." The Temperance Committee of the Texas Grand Lodge went further and said Masonry is concerned with temperance in all things, including dress, "the expenditure of money . . . the making of bills," and sex. Indeed, for Masonry "Temperance is a restricting factor for our affections, appetites and passions" generally.[68] While strong drink has been the area given greatest attention by the Masons, the desire to control drinking has been symbolic of the fraternity's dedication to cultivate general individual repression of "disruptive" desires. The type of temperance the Masons have advocated is mandatory for the existence of the whole petty-bourgeois life style they have stood for. The Masonic leadership has also seen temperance on the part of the membership not only as a benefit to Masons, as individuals, but as a model for the non-Masonic black community to follow.[69]

[67] *Proceedings* (Oklahoma, 1925), Grand Master's speech.

[68] *Proceedings* (Texas, 1918).

[69] *Proceedings* (Georgia, 1926), Grand Master's speech. "Temperance" in its broader usage has been seen as the foundation for maintaining the Order's good reputation. If that were lost through ill-advised admissions or activities the fraternity would lose its reason for existence. The Grand Master of Texas in 1947 warned against letting "loose" men into the lodges, men who think the Order exists for entertainment and by their actions would give the lodges a bad reputation. He counseled his followers on the need for: "rejecting all who are not of good repute, sound morals, and competent understanding . . . . On sobriety your pleasure depends, on regularity your reputation and not our reputation only, but the reputation of the whole body . . . , no [one] . . . contribute[s more] to the desolution [*sic*] of a Lodge, than do great number[s] of member[s] indiscriminately made; for the want of regulation in their expenses and keeping unreasonable hours [*sic*]. To guard against this consequence, we shall do well to cultivate the following virtues, viz: *Prudence, Temperance,* and *Frugality.* These virtues are the best support of every community." See also the Grand Master's speech, *Proceedings* (Texas, 1949).

The Grand Master of New York three decades before (1920) also pointed out the role of temperance in making Masonry attractive for respectability-conscious

Cleanliness is another virtue extolled in Masonic literature
and is yet another way in which Masons demonstrate their
acceptance of middle-class standards. The emphasis on cleanliness also serves to highlight the black middle class's sensitivity
to white charges that blacks as a race are unclean in their
persons, a charge the Masons are determined to disprove by
their behavior and appearance. However, to the extent that
they believe that cleanliness is a virtue that the mass of blacks
must be taught, they show that they accept a large part of
the white stereotype.

The importance of cleanliness can be seen in the words of
many Grand Masters. The Grand Master of Georgia in 1922
pointed out that one "encouraging thing about the Lodges .
. . is the great amount of interest being displayed by the young
men in their endeavor to elevate themselves and their Lodges
by their clean, gentlemanly deportment, both in and out of
the Lodge." His enthusiasm for such behavior was not fleeting
since Masonry intentionally has tried to "impress upon the
members . . . the great necessity of being sober, clean and honest

blacks: "Let other organizations parade the necessity of a big time, how much liquor
can be drunk by the members thereof, and how much noise they can make, it is our
place to be so temperate in all that we do that we may be the criterion by which
they regulate their being." It should be noted that all these remarks on temperance
not only reflect the image Masons had of their Order's proper function, but also the
dangers and temptations facing it. The Masons have always tried to select their
membership for the qualities they value, but, of course, they have never totally
succeeded—especially in periods of very rapid growth, or when standards have been
lowered in order to obtain more members for their insurance plans. Masonry has always
had to weigh the attractions of quality versus quantity.

As we have emphasized before, the importance of "respectability" derives from
both the internal process of class differentiation within the black population, and the
external pressure exerted by the white middle class. This second factor is very prominent
in both the 1908 speech of the Grand Master of Georgia and in a letter he released
to the white newspapers (the text of which was read by him during his speech to
the Grand Lodge). In that year Georgia race conflict reached a point at which whites
were bombing Masonic meeting halls and killing lodge members. In an attempt to protect the Order, the Grand Master both informally contacted prominent white leaders
and attempted to use the mass media to sway general white opinion by sending out
a public letter defending the Masonic membership. In discussing the letter and the race
conflict generally before the Grand Lodge the Grand Master pointed out that there
were "legitimate" reasons for "so much antipathy on the part of our [white] friends
against our secret orders in the jurisdiction." They have a right to be angry that:
1. meetings occur in the same hall *every* night; 2. meetings last all night; 3. lodge
halls owned by Masons are rented to all types of small secret societies—some "disreputable"; 4. some of the small secret societies that use the Masonic halls hide criminals;
5. some societies use indiscriminate language; 6. some Masons who attend meetings
stay up all night and are not in condition the next day to work, which justifiably

men themselves and to transmit that something to their families and neighbors. . . ." When members live up to such requirements of the fraternity Masons have believed that the effect is far-reaching, operating for the benefit of many besides themselves. The Grand Master of California in 1919 testified personally to the fact that "by reason of the dignified, clean cut position maintained by the Craft men have in many instances changed their mode and manner of living." The Grand Master of Georgia in 1908 pointed out that cleanliness and neatness not only aid individuals but the reputation of the entire race. He singled out one local lodge because "Their hall has the reputation of being one of the cleanest meeting places for colored men in that county, and the white citizens were very loud in lavishing praise on the behavior of the brothers of that city." In Prince Hall Masonry, cleanliness is always linked to the highest virtues. The leader of Illinois Masonry in 1916 put quite succinctly the ideal when he said "My brethren, you need backbone, cleaner lodge rooms . . . [and a] cleaner membership." One can best sense the importance

creates hostility among employers. The Grand Master in his public letter to the whites emphasized that while the Masons have made mistakes in not screening the societies that rent their buildings carefully enough, they themselves are strictly law-abiding, hard-working, thrifty middle-class black men: "[Masonry is] largely made up of some of the best and most law-abiding colored men in this state—men who have made themselves part of the communities in which they live by owning their homes and living honest and respectable lives." Such men should not be confused with unrespectable, lower-class blacks. He at the same time (in his speech) admonished his Masonic brethren to be more careful, not only of whom they rent to, but to whom they allow in their lodges: "Never take any part in hiding crime or criminals, neither take them in your lodge if you know it . . . , under no circumstances must an applicant for the degrees of Masonry be or have at any other time been connected with any crime." To violate this requirement is not only to retard black class formation but to lose the respect (and protection) of the whites. The Grand Master's attitude demonstrates an acceptance of many anti-lower-class-black prejudices. It does not mean that he was servile or lacking in race pride. Like so many Masons, he had mixed feelings about both whites and lower-class blacks. After World War I the same man makes quite clear his hostility to the white race's hypocrisy in promising decent treatment to those who live the bourgeois life style and then refusing to fulfill it. Even in 1908, in his letter, he mixed his plea for white understanding and protection with a threat: "[It is an error to destroy the Masonic halls of] these poor struggling men . . . It is a serious mistake to destroy the property of any people. They become dissatisfied, suspicious of their neighbors, lose confidence in the law and its officers and will finally move away, thus creating a labor panic. A dissatisfied people, a people suspicious of their neighbors, a hopeless people, are a dangerous people." Though by "people" he meant property-owning men like the Masons, not the average black. (For a discussion of black middle-class ambivalence to both whites and poor blacks see the end of this chapter and Chapter XI.)

and pervasiveness of the value of cleanliness for black Masons in the 1920 report of Georgia's Matron of the Orphans' Home and School:

> The girls clean and dust their rooms daily; chang[ing] wash and bedding weekly. The rooms are well ventilated at all times. The kitchen, dining room, and pantry are daily cleaned . . . the girls [work at] . . . cooking, canning . . . wash[ing] and iron[ing], also clean[ing] the yards.

The Masonic Orphans' Home of Georgia, where the girls were enabled to keep busy cleaning, "cooking, canning, . . . sewing, dressmaking . . . washing and ironing" and otherwise living up to good Puritan requirements also served another important function for the fraternity. It helped demonstrate that for Masons "Female protection is her great pride and glory . . . [and] each Mason is a sworn protector of womanhood."[70] It also made a moral demand upon the Georgian Masons that many jurisdictions saw as one of their highest duties—the protection of the children of dead Masons from the dangerous influences of black lower-class life:

> So many are the temptations that surround our bodies in their period of life when character is being formed; so many are the snares and pitfalls that beset the young girl when she is approaching womanhood, that constant guardianship, unceasing admonition and watch-care is necessary, less they be misled. Do we not owe something to these Masonic kindred?[71]

The Masons not only have wanted to protect their children and themselves from the corruption of other life styles, but to help save the larger black community itself. For example, the Texas Masons recommended strict regulation of night clubs, supervision of youth, and prohibitions against the carrying of weapons—rules obviously directed at the black lower class.[72] Not only the Masons but the race generally was challenged "to meet their responsibilities as men in the advancement of their children and women."[73]

---

[70] Grand Master of South Carolina quoted in *Review* (Georgia), 2, no.4 (Oct.-Dec. 1939): 3. The Grand Master put respect for womanhood as the first requirement of a good Mason—the other requirements were living an upright moral life, obedience to the laws of God and Country, helping a Masonic brother's widow and orphans, helping a brother who was physically attacked and vindicating a brother who was slandered.

[71] *Proceedings* (Texa., 1912), Grand Master's speech.

[72] *Proceedings* (Texas, 1934), Grand Master's speech.

[73] *Review* (Georgia), 1, no.2 (November 1937): 7.

One finds the theme "We are *men* and Masons" who must assert the responsibilities of "Manhood" as a constantly reoccurring one in the Masonic records, and one which most of the preceding discussion of values suggests as well.[74] The Masons have wanted adherents who possess all the middle-class virtues, do all the right things, and as a result can boldly and virilely lead themselves, their families, their fraternity and their race to success; as the Grand Master of Georgia put it, "It is a wonderful privilege to be a real man—not a mere wearer of breeches—not a whiner, not a hanger-on—not a male being with no vision, but rather a real man with nerve, vim, vision and . . . determination. . . ."[75] The Order has hoped that it has

[74] *Proceedings* (New York, 1920), Grand Master's speech. Italics added.

[75] *Proceedings* (Georgia, 1922). The importance of Masonry for *male* pride (as well as *black* pride) is very marked. A Grand Master of Missouri put the matter quite clearly: " 'I am a Freemason because it gives me a greater opportunity to work with men. So many of the tasks of society have been left almost entirely to the women. . . . Freemasonry finds many a man whose talents otherwise would be lost. It helps men to guard their morals and their speech, and to cooperate, one with another, without rancour or jealous[y].' " *Topics* (Illinois), 14, nos.4-6 (April-June 1951): 18.

Drake and Cayton point out in their study, p. 688, that in middle-class "society" fully two-thirds of the clubs were composed of women only. Abner Cohen in a study of Freemasonry in Sierra Leone ("The Politics of Ritual Secrecy," *Man*, 6, no.3 [1971]: 434) observes another aspect of the same phenomenon. He discusses the importance of an all-male Order in providing distance between men and women, reducing intramale sexual competition, and in weaning men from their wives. (This study will be discussed at length in a later chapter.)

The reduction of sexual competition is important in America too. The Masons are very concerned about public sexual conduct. But they are aware that in private, monogamy is more honored in the breach than the observance. They are desirous that Masonry form a bond of fellowship that at least protects their own wives, even if not all wives, from improper advances. We have already reported one incident in which a Mason blackballed an applicant on this very ground—he was cheating with the man's wife and did not want to harm a "brother." Also see Lewis' *Blackways of Kent*, p. 270, for a discussion of the meaning of "brotherhood" to Kent Masons. Of course, sex being sex, even "fraternal" protection is not always effective, but when the lodge finds out that the bond has been broken, drastic action is taken; see *Proceedings* (Texas, 1918), for a representative example. When the sexual misconduct does not involve the betrayal of a brother there may be greater reluctance to take action against the wrong-doer, especially if he is very popular; but action will be taken. For example, in the *Proceedings* of New York, 1912, the Grand Master investigated the charge of adultery against a prominent Mason and personal close friend: "My obligations to the fraternity were far more sacred than my personal friendship with the individual. As reluctant as was the Lodge to try the brother, it found him guilty by a unanimous vote after trial . . . ." and expelled him for 99 years. (Actually, the local lodge did not want to try him and they voted to dismiss the charges. The Grand Master overruled them and admonished them to be just and honorable about the problem.) When popular lodge officials commit transgressions, higher level authorities often have to intervene to maintain the Order's rules and protect the respectability of the lodge.

been able to create such men in its lodge halls. To the extent that it has been successful, Masonic leaders have felt they have aided the race by exhorting their followers to "go forth into the field and work for the saving of our people, teaching them to observe all things, to live right, to be honest, to be frugal, get homes, respect their families and those of their neighbors. . . ."[76]

Insofar as Prince Hall has been effective in teaching and reinforcing the values and behavior it stresses, the fraternity has performed a number of significant psychological and social functions. It has helped create an integrated self-image for the individual black Mason as an upstanding American citizen; it has helped psychologically bind the black Mason to white society by enabling him to identify with the Caucasian middle class; it has created a haven within the larger black society where bourgeois Negroes have received protection from the life style of the nonbourgeois blacks who surround them; and while having helped to create a positive sense of community among its middle-class adherents, it has served to estrange them from the mass of black people.

Part 3. Intra-Black Class Conflict

The estrangement of the Masons from the black lower class is a shattering side-effect of its efforts to bind middle-class blacks together. The Masonic proceedings are permeated by a class consciousness that demonstrates how alienated the membership has been from the mass of blacks, an alienation strongly influenced both by a concern for white opinion and an acceptance of white stereotypes. When the Foreign Correspondent of Georgia in 1957 pointed out the limits of organized social protest to achieve equality, he implied a great deal about his vision of the majority of black men:

> Thrift, morality, marital integrity, cleanliness, good manners, voting and education to a large degree, are personal and individual matters—all of which play an indispensable role in determining social, political and economic *acceptability*. It is in this area that courts and our leaders can do very little.[77]

[76] *Proceedings* (Texas, 1919), Grand Master's speech.
[77] *Proceedings* (Georgia, 1957), C.C.F.C.'s report.

In the eyes of Masons like him, the majority of blacks were noticeably lacking these "personal and individual matters." The attitude evidenced in this statement is completely consistent with the view expressed 25 years earlier by the Grand Master of Georgia when he succinctly spelled out the class bias inherent in Masonry throughout its history:

> I have faith . . . the day will come when the Masons of any race will understand the . . . principles of Masonry to the extent that they will be willing to shake hands with a black Mason of the type of Robert Russa Morton, Principal of Tuskegee Institute, and call him Brother.[78]

The day Masons of any race were willing to shake hands with George Washington Jackson, Ditch Digger, was not of intimate concern to Masons in 1933 or 1958. The pervasiveness of class bias in the fraternity probably cannot be more revealingly shown than in the extremes to which some Masons have gone to interpret black history along class lines. In 1958 a California Mason attempting to promote race pride wrote an article praising the black hero Frederick Douglass. In that article he pointed out that:

> His mother, a slave, was Harriet Bailey. . . . The mere fact that she possessed a surname is evidence that they were one of *the oldest and best class of slave families* in Maryland. . . . The superiority of the mother over the majority of her race at that time is further attested by the fact that she was the only person in the whole village who was able to read.[79]

A black hero, even a slave, must not be confused with members of the lower class. Attitudes such as these could do nothing to bind the black middle and lower classes together.

While the Masons' hostility to the black lower class comes partially out of the natural need for the aspiring black middle class to create social distance in order to solidify their claim to status, it also seems to spring from another, less organic source as well. There are those who maintain that the general black bourgeoisie's commitment to and interpretation of middle-class respectability has an alien, externally fostered aspect to it. Among the major proponents of this idea are many

[78] The 1933 address by the Grand Master of Georgia.
[79] *Digest* (California), 8, no.1 (May-July 1959): 7. Italics added.

Afro-American nationalists and some of their white radical allies.[80] This idea is ubiquitous in speeches, articles and books by militants. The position has become so widespread that the present author received an essay from a moderate middle-class black student which read:

> For the most part, Afro-American social scientists, professional ... and so-called 'middle class Negroes' are using the wrong methods to understand themselves and their Afro-American brothers and sisters. Using 'white' values, and 'white' culture, 'white' religious and political systems, and 'white' success models are the wrong measures to use in understanding what it means to be black in a foreign land.

Many liberal observers have responded with indignation to this line of argument. To say that bourgeois values and behavior are in any sense "white," they contend, is basically racist. These values have not been the sole property of Europeans but have been developed independently by the Japanese, Hindus, West Africans, and other cultures whenever their economic and social structures have reached a stage of development necessitating their creation. Not only are such values possessed by nonwhites, but to say that hard work, thrift, cleanliness etc., are "white" implies that blacks if left without such alien values would be dirty, lazy, and prodigal.[81] This type of reasoning, by liberal academicans, is a persuasive one.

Nevertheless, to contend that the middle-class code of ethics and respectability is to some extent alien to the black community, and that the negative stereotyping of the lower class is exaggerated thereby, seems to me fundamentally correct, though only after certain modifications of the term "alien" are made. The fact that nonwhite groups and, indeed, black groups

[80] It is also a widespread idea among academicians, though they usually espouse it without giving any logical argument to prove its truth.

[81] This last argument is more effective as a rhetorical device than as a logical position. While apparently aimed at the use of the word "white," if true the argument would destroy the whole notion of bourgeois values. For if the term "white middle-class values" implies that blacks are lazy, etc., it also implies that lower-class or working-class whites are as well. But it does not. Rather, the term refers to very specific class- and culture-bound interpretations of what cleanliness, thrift, etc. mean and to the extent that lower-class white or blacks violate those specific meanings (whether for macro-structural reasons, or because of rival cultural values, or because the middle class interprets the values in such a way that normal human beings can't live up to them) they are indeed, from the bourgeoisie's standpoint, deviant.

in Africa have developed bourgeois value codes on their own is irrelevant to the Afro-American community. It simply proves that under favorable circumstances, as their economic and social institutions matured, blacks in America could have developed values and behavior supportive of an indigenous black bourgeoisie. But American blacks did not produce such codes because they did not live in isolation but rather among another people who already had such a life style. For blacks in the United States, the originators of, models for, and interpreters of bourgeois respectability were white men. If we modify the following observation by Eugene Genovese to apply primarily to bourgeois culture rather than to all culture, he is correct when he contends:

> If enslavement in the United States destroyed most of the African family structure, religion and general culture, then the slaves [who would be bourgeois] had to aspire to the master's civilization or to none .... The fact remains that the prevailing standards of decency and morality, as well as most of the scientific and artistic accomplishment, necessarily came from above.[82]

The nature of the black man's coming to America, the slave system he lived under, and the presence of a surrounding white bourgeois society determined that at least the origin of the middle-class worldview would not be indigenous.

Of course an alien origin for a group's cultural values does not mean they will remain alien. Once the ideals were accepted, made the basis of a segment of the black population's life style (such as the Masons), and passed on by them to their children, the values were in a real sense no longer foreign. Rather, those black men who lived them became models for middle-class conduct and, to children learning from them, the moral codes appeared comfortably "native." This is obvious when we consider the ways middle-class blacks work through institutions such as the family, church, and fraternities to perpetuate *their* standards within black society.

Thus, logically, the existence of a middle-class life style among blacks could be considered "native" rather than merely

[82] See *Studies on the Left*, 6, no.6 (1966): 61. Genovese may have overstated his case by not allowing for the possibility of a slave culture among blacks. But the culture and morality they might have created did not include the virtues that comprise bourgeois morality.

borrowed. This argument would be persuasive if the Afro-
American bourgeoisie after slavery had lived in isolation from
whites. But they did not, and do not, live apart. The whites
are present and because of their social and economic power
have maintained themselves as "high priests" of bourgeois
morality and respectability. Black men who followed mainstream values and behavior always have had to look over their
shoulders (black models notwithstanding) to see what position
whites have taken toward their conduct.[83] Since whites insisted
that blacks could not live up to moral standards as whites
defined them, blacks have not been able to be oblivious of white
opinion but have always had to justify their actions.

Not only have bourgeois standards been less than comfortably "native" because of the white presence but, since the
values were practiced by a minority of the black community,
they severely alienated the practitioners from their fellow
blacks. The ambivalence of middle-class blacks toward the
lower-class blacks has been the inevitable result. In sum, the
bourgeois code of ethics has been simultaneously native and
alien to the Afro-American community, but the foreignness
has tended to exaggerate the normal estrangement of a forming
middle class from the lower class.

A good example of the paradoxical "blackness" and "white-
ness" of middle-class morality and the way this ambiguity
operates to co-opt black leadership and maintain white hegemony is found in the life of Major Martin Delany, prominent
Prince Hall author, abolitionist, black leader, and classic model
for the pride and prejudice of the black bourgeoisie.[84]

Delany, who in recent years has been proclaimed widely as
the father of black nationalism, was an exceedingly proud black
man. Frederick Douglass once said in reference to him: "I thank
God for making me a man simply; but Delany always thanks
Him for making him a *black man.*"[85] His race pride was striking
enough and his disdain of white men great enough to make

---

[83] Drake and Cayton, p. 519, note the importance of the whites for black middle-class
behavior when they observe: "The 'respectable,' 'educated,' and 'refined' believe in
'front,' partly because it is their accustomed way of life and partly *in order to impress
the white world.*" (Italics added.)

[84] Delany was the author of *The Origins and Objects of Ancient Freemasonry, Its
Introduction into the United States and Legitimacy among Colored Men* (Pittsburgh,
1853).

[85] Quoted in Frank A. Rollin, *The Life and Public Services of Martin R. Delany*
(Boston, 1883), p. 19. Italics in original.

one acquaintance proclaim, "I do not believe Delany considers any white man as good as himself."[86] Delany made no attempt to hide his hostility to the oppressors of his people, one of the manifestations of which was his championship of emigrationism during the 1850s. Emigrationism envisioned the exodus of American blacks to a new homeland outside the boundary of the continental United States. In support of his views, Delany wrote a number of pamphlets, two of which—"The International Policy of the World Towards the African Race" and "The Political Destiny of the Colored Race on the American Continent"—are quite astonishing in their modernity, perceptiveness, and radicalism.[87] They provide firm support for Delany as a hero of modern black nationalists.

And yet, in a most crucial sense Delany was not a radical at all, despite his pride in blackness and his apparent hostility to the white race. When he talked of the Negro people and their future he measured their glory, achievements, and prospects in white terms. In praise of his race he said:

> That the colored races have the highest traits of civilization, will not be disputed. They are civil, peaceable, and religious to a fault. In mathematics, sculpture and architecture ..., commerce and internal improvements ... the white race may probably excel; but in languages, oratory, poetry, music and painting ... and in ethics, metaphysics, theology, and legal jurisprudence ..., in the true principles of morals, correctness of thought, religion, and law or civil government, there is no doubt but the black race will yet instruct the world.[88]

However, Delany's own "true principles of morals" were not those of the African peoples but rather a mirror reflection of mid-nineteenth-century Anglo-American morality. And he demonstrated his loyalty to that ethical code in practice as well as theory, to the detriment of his own race.

After the American Civil War Delany went to South Carolina to work in the Freedmen's Bureau, and while there he was instrumental in reconstructing relations between the ex-slaves and their ex-masters. One clause in the labor contracts he composed readily demonstrated his moral commitment:

[86] Ibid., p. 20.
[87] Ibid., pp. 303-367.
[88] Ibid., p. 335.

And all dwellings and immediate premises of freedmen must be kept neat and clean, subject to inspection and fine for neglect by such sanitary arrangements as the government may make .... No sutlet stores will be permitted on the place ... [so] that no inducements may be given for spending earnings improperly. Spirituous liquors will not be permitted.[89]

What Delany meant when he talked of the glories of the black race was that the Negro could "out Anglo-Saxon the Anglo-Saxon." When actually tested, when brought face to face with newly freed men, men who were not middle-class white men with black skins, Delany's moral attitudes were not conducive to feelings of empathy with his oppressed brothers. His reaction to the ex-slaves was so negative, and his censure of them so strong, that it drew a heated response from Frederick Douglass who, despite his own middle-class loyalties, was shocked to see Delany's bourgeois commitments so nakedly revealed. Douglass wrote:

As to destitution of political knowledge among the newly emancipated class—what else could have happened? ... Doomed to ignorance for ages, the Negro could not be expected to cope with the white men about him at the start ....

I cannot agree with you in denouncing colored men for going armed to political meetings in South Carolina, nor can I agree with you that the practice is an imported one .... I may be wrong, but I had supposed that this practice on the part of the newly enfranchised class at the South had been impelled by a dire necessity. It is a bad practice, and one which cannot be commended in a truly civilized community, but everything ... is relative. ...

One other thing: I hardly think you are quite just in what you say of the changed manners of the colored people .... It does not seem to me that their degeneracy is so complete as you describe it to be. Were you not M. R. Delany, I should say that the man who wrote thus of the manners of the colored people ... had taken his place with the old planters. You certainly cannot be among those ... who prefer the lash-inspired manners of the past. I know too well your own proud and independent spirit, to believe that the manners of an enslaved and oppressed people are more to your taste than those which are born of freedom and independence.[90]

[89] Ibid., p. 261.
[90] Philip Foner, *The Life and Writings of Frederick Douglass*, vol. IV (New York, 1955), pp. 277-278.

But Delany wanted neither the "lash-inspired manners" of slavery nor the rude, spirited ignorance of a newly freed population. He wanted and expected to find black Anglo-Saxons with the manners, gentility, and political sophistication of free born white men.

In keeping with Major Delany's commitment to mid-nineteenth-century Anglo-American morality and bourgeois respectability and his complementary alienation from the aspirations of black freedmen, was his plan to solve the problem of economic relations in the post-Civil War South. His solution was to create a combination of economic forces:

> Capital, land, and labor require a copartnership. The capital can be obtained in the North; the land is in the South, owned by the old planters; and the blacks have the labor . . . , the net profits being equally shared between the three,—capital, land, and labor, —each receiving one third, of course.[91]

A plan somehow less generous to the laboring class than one might expect from a champion of the black race.

In his biography of Delany, Frank Rollin tells us that in South Carolina the Major was treated by the ex-master class in a way that no black man had ever been before.[92] Planters from all over the area flocked to his office to have him arrange contracts with the ex-slaves. The journal *New South* on more than one occasion heaped praise upon him for his work, saying: "He tells them to go to work at once; that labor surely brings its own reward; and that after one more good crop is gathered, they will find their condition much better. . . . And he tells the planters they must be kind and just to their laborers . . . ."[93]

Needless to say, the good Major's fraternization with the planter class could only create suspicion among the freedmen. On numerous occasions Rollin goes out of his way to "disprove" the recurrent rumor that Delany had "sold out."[94] Certainly for Martin Delany to consciously sell out to whites was impossible. But his ideas about respectability, morality, manners, economics, and politics were such as to make him a stranger in the world in which the ex-slaves lived. His attachment to the Prince Hall Masonic fraternity was totally in keeping with

[91] Rollin, p. 242.
[92] Ibid., p. 250.
[93] Ibid., p. 263.
[94] See, for example, Rollin, p. 267.

his faith in himself and his race, and with his commitment to the ideals, values, and behavior of the Anglo-American middle class.

Once the alien aspect of the bourgeoisie's life style is recognized, it is possible to see yet another function Masonry has served in the black community. In addition to its many other roles, the fraternity has been an important agent of acculturation. As Edward Palmer has pointed out, "A careful study of the Negro secret society as an institution will throw much light on the processes of acculturation," and this is especially true of the Prince Hall fraternity.[95] Freemasonry in the nineteenth century was a prominent representative of white middle-class idealism on both a moral and social level. Its acceptance by blacks was part of an attempt to further their assimilation into and acceptance by American society. It was not coincidental that blacks found the most prestigious Euro-American fraternity the object of their desires rather than an Afro-American fraternal organization.[96]

The Order they and their descendants accepted was not a primary agency of acculturation. Rather, the values Masonry emphasized were first presented to the membership in their families and churches where the work of acculturation was initially undertaken. Masonry functioned as a secondary, adult, acculturative institution, teaching new values and roles that the family and church had been unable to transmit, and reinforcing commitment to those already learned, while helping to prevent the acceptance of lower-class black behavior with which the membership was in constant contact.

[95] Edward Nelson Palmer, "Negro Secret Societies," *Social Forces* (December 1944): 207. Palmer, p. 208, says "Freemasonry is the oldest and most respected secret society among Negroes in the United States."

[96] Palmer, p. 209, takes the same position when he says, "There is no evidence that free Negroes or slaves ever attempted to set up African secret societies or their reasonably exact facsimile. On the contrary, they went to great lengths to associate themselves with Europe's most distinguished secret orders and with the only American order which permitted them." The Afro-American's whole-hearted acceptance of Freemasonry and its ideals can be contrasted with the attitude of some Chinese-Americans as reported by Stanford Lyman: "The [Chinese secret] societies . . . seeking to preserve their secrets and under pressure from both revolutionary and commercial interests to give up their lawless ways . . . accommodated their organizations to changing conditions. Many of the societies adopt innocuous names, styling themselves as merchants' associations or, on discovering the favorable imagery of masonry in the Occident, calling themselves 'Chinese Freemasons'. . . ." (Stanford Lyman, *Chinese Americans* [New York, 1974], p. 45).

This role in cultural transmission has an important bearing upon a discussion I shall take up later on the urban nature of the Order. Masonry was created in the city from an Anglo-American model and then spread to the countryside. Once established in the small towns and rural areas the fraternity helped compensate for the lessened contact between whites and blacks which the end of slavery created. Masonry was important in spreading Anglo-American cultural values and behavior to areas where post-Reconstruction racial segregation was most severe and the acculturative process most retarded.

Masonry helped reduce the divisions between urban and rural areas, though simultaneously magnifying class divisions within the black community. Middle-class life styles and values split black from black by creating links between members of the minority community and the white majority. What this has produced is a situation in which whites have been able to co-opt black leadership and maintain hegemony over the oppressed race. As Genovese noted in an article on the Marxist theoretician, Antonio Gramsci, "The success of a ruling class in establishing its hegemony depends entirely on its ability to convince the lower classes that its interests are those of the society at large—that it defends the common sensibility and stands for a natural and proper social order."[97] This is what acceptance of bourgeois standards of respectability and morality by the black middle class has meant.

The fact that the black middle class adheres to a code of conduct and morality over which the dominant white race has the final power of interpretation has had very negative effects both on black solidarity and on the psychological security of the black bourgeoisie itself. Yet the dysfunctional effects of middle-class standards are even more pronounced than the existence of this "big brother" syndrome alone should have produced. Built into the foundation of middle-class ethics are philosophical assumptions that are in and of themselves destructive of black class cooperation. The bourgeois ethic is designed for dynamic economic change. It is highly functional for mobilizing and channeling individual abilities and aspirations toward sustaining social and economic change. Part of that ability comes out of its emphasis on human capacity, re-

[97] Eugene Genovese, "On Antonio Gramsci," in *For a New America*, edited by James Weinstein and David Eakins (New York, 1970), pp. 300-301.

sponsibility, and free will.[98] The ethic assumes that a man can control his destiny, especially economic, by conscious effort. Those who adhere to the code and succeed are praiseworthy and those who do not are blameworthy. The idea that man is shaped by outside forces (i.e., fate, nature, the social or economic system), and therefore is not morally culpable for most of his behavior, is anathema to this worldview. To the extent that black men, or any men, adhere to a doctrine of social activism such as this and emphasize personal responsibility, there is a strong tendency to be hostile and unsympathetic to those who fail to achieve. This attitude is built into the ethic, and its effect on a group with exceptionally limited freedom (such as the blacks) is bound to be destructive.

The fact that the so-called Protestant ethic's assumptions are not totally false even for blacks—that a minority of blacks can by their conscious effort achieve a measure of success within the system—has enabled it to maintain its hold on the black middle class, especially on the members of the Masonic Order. It is the ethic's inherent bias against the poor, combined with a self-justifying attitude of "I succeeded against great odds why can't you," that is most detrimental to black unity.[99] It is this divisive moralism more than bourgeois values per se that is so disruptive of black solidarity.[100]

In this chapter I have attempted to explain how Prince Hall

[98] We are talking about the Protestant Ethic when stripped of its original Calvinistic determinism.

[99] This negative consequence is the reverse side of the "heroism" we commented on in Chapter I. However, unlike the free will sacrifice expended to obtain middle-class respectability, the black bourgeoisie's hostility to the lower class is not primarily the result of free choice but a "determined" response, flowing naturally out of the ethic they espouse and the requirements of class maintenance.

[100] This is not to deny that some of the values are in and of themselves disruptive of group cooperation. The middle-class ethic is strongly individualistic under the best conditions, and even for groups more fortunate than the American blacks, social cooperation is impaired. Abner Cohen, p. 443, when speaking of Sierra Leone says, "Like the middle classes in many countries, the Creoles are in general notoriously individualistic and no sooner does a leader begin to assume leadership than a number of other men begin to contest his claim in the spirit of 'why . . . not me?' " Prosperous middle classes, however, usually overcome their intraclass divisions when facing other groups, and normally do not have to worry about controlling their hostility to lower-class people. The Afro-American bourgeoisie is not so fortunate. It is not able to ignore the black masses or (as we shall see later) overcome its intraclass conflicts. Ulf Hannerz, Soulside (New York, 1969), p. 197, also comments on the importance of middle-class individualism, as opposed to bourgeois morality per se, in dividing the black population.

Freemasonry creates an atmosphere favorable to the development of the black middle class and encourages its members to practice many of the highest ideals of American society—ideals whose accomplishment allow a man to develop self-respect and win the admiration of others. Freemasonry attempts not only to aid the individual, but to further the process of group differentiation within black society. It seeks to create a middle-class social environment in which the individual can receive group support for his way of life.[101] In the process of achieving these laudable goals a situation of class conflict is created. The black Mason as black bourgeois finds himself alienated from the majority of lower-class blacks. To affirm his lifestyle is to denigrate theirs; to bolster his self-respect is to lower theirs. The good moral life can only be achieved at the price of estrangement from, and lack of empathy for, his fellows. In this contradiction between the needs of the aspiring individual (and his class generally) and the needs of the larger social collectivity (i.e., the black race) lies the basic tragedy of the black bourgeoisie.

Here I have dealt with the subjective values and ideas of black Freemasons. The "objective" economic condition of the membership has been touched on only in passing. In the next chapter I will take a closer look at the economic characteristics of the Masons in one fair-sized American city during the twentieth century.

[101] The Prince Hall Fraternity has enabled its followers to live most of their recreational lives within the boundaries of the Order if they desire. This is well illustrated by a letter to the editor of the *Sentinel* (New York) in 1954. The writer points out that a "typically" committed Mason attends his regular lodge meetings, the meetings of his lodge's club (which raises funds for the lodge), participates on at least one lodge committee, if not more, goes to a Degree School where he becomes more proficient in the Masonic ritual, helps with and attends various Masonic entertainments (e.g., dances, Christmas charity, boat rides), joins one or more "higher degree" Orders of Masonry, and engages in their fraternal, ritual, recreational, and administrative programs too. (*Sentinel* [New York], 8, no.1-2 (Jan.-Feb. 1954): 10-11).

Chapter III

The Economic Foundations of Prince Hall Freemasonry— Oakland, California, as a Test Case

One of the problems in studying black Freemasonry is the lack of information about the economic level of its membership. I have utilized the impressionistic sources available to fill this gap in knowledge, but while the material is highly suggestive, it cries out for more substantial, quantitative confirmation— even though objective criteria are hard to come by, and less useful than it would be for whites. Nevertheless, in order to meet this need as best I could, I undertook a study of the black Masons in one large American city. The evidence will show that the Masons of Oakland, California, have always had a secure, occupational basis for their claim to middle-class status. While they have not always been middle class by white economic standards, they have possessed the minimum of financial and job security necessary to maintain a bourgeois lifestyle. The regularity and predictibility of their income has objectively set them off from most blacks.

The city of Oakland, California, lies across the bay from San Francisco. Among its many distinctions, it is the birthplace of the Black Panther Party. Oakland is fairly well segregated along geographic lines, with whites occupying the hilly areas and blacks living in the flatlands. While the majority of blacks who now occupy the flatlands arrived after the Second World War, there was a significant black community for at least forty years prior to 1945. Oakland, not San Francisco, was the second major center of black population in California (after Los Angeles) primarily because the railroads had their terminals in the East Bay, offering nonwhites an important source of employment. Oakland has not only surpassed San Francisco in black population during the twentieth century, but, of greater importance, it has maintained a much more developed black institutional and cultural structure.

As an area for research, Oakland has the advantage of being a large enough urban center in total size and black population to make investigation fruitful, but is small enough to make it practical. It is a northern metropolis and, like most such cities, has experienced a period of great black migration. While it is not a typical city (for example, its major influx of blacks did not occur until after World War Two and its black population has been more prosperous, on the whole, than those of eastern big cities), many of its features are suggestive of conditions throughout the United States simply because the range of variation within black ghettos has been fairly limited.

For purposes of in-depth study, I investigated one unit of Masonry in Oakland, the Good Hope Lodge. This is the largest black Masonic lodge in Oakland and the third oldest in that city. While I considered focusing on Acacia Lodge, the oldest, I finally chose Good Hope because its larger membership made it more useful. Since Good Hope was not formed until World War I, and there is no detailed membership information for the years before 1923, I will supplement my discussion with material from Acacia and Adonis (the two founding lodges) for the earlier years. For use in this study I have collected occupational information on the lodge(s) at roughly five-year intervals from 1906 to 1970.[1]

In studying Good Hope Lodge it was my aim to provide empirical support for my often expressed belief that the Masons are a middle-class group, both economically and behaviorally. However, the sources of information to confirm the socioeconomic status of Good Hope's membership are quite restricted, and must be used with care. Except for the years 1970 and 1941-43, only occupational and residential information are available; education, income, and home ownership statistics (except in the forementioned years) are not available. As a

[1] The intervals are uneven because of the appearance of a Masonic street directory which required using 1923, the availability of home ownership material which made 1941-43 mandatory, and the lack of city directories between 1943 and 1967.

result, I face the problem of determining "objective" class position within the black community by using occupation data alone. In many cases it can be easily determined; in some it is extremely difficult, if not impossible.

The limited amount of occupational differentiation within the black group means most people have jobs that can be classified under a small number of headings, headings that hide more information than they reveal. Titles such as "janitor," "porter," or "waiter" are broad, apparently bottom-of-the-ladder job categories; but actually they hide a host of gradations and differences. Part of these differences come from the kinds of people who staff the jobs. The college-educated janitor, Pullman porter, or Red Cap are well-known types in the history of black people. Aside from the individuals who fill the positions, many of the jobs themselves differ markedly in their pay, prestige, security, and difficulty of obtainment. For example, in Oakland many Masons were janitors for public buildings. To obtain these jobs the applicant had to pass a civil service examination as well as exercise political pull, albeit of a minor nature. As a result, these positions were rather good ones, particularly because of the security they provided. In a fair number of cases we know that janitor-Masons were employed by the city, but there is good reason to believe that many men who appear in city directories simply as "janitor" may also have belonged to this special category.

In a more critical (for my investigation) example, to be employed as a waiter on the Southern Pacific Railroad Company (S.P.) was a position far superior to that of restaurant waiter, but the distinction is usually lost in the records. The same holds true for porters and cooks. Even if more information had been provided, such as the employer's name, socioeconomic distinctions within job categories would still be missing. Among those employed by the railroad, the different job categories contained a number of steps with different income, power, and prestige in the community.

If one accepts the job classifications as they are given in the records it is still difficult to place them in usable categories. What exactly *is* a middle-class job within the black community, and how does it change over time? This is not easy to ascertain since there is no standard against which to measure. If we use the white community's evaluation of the job status, almost

all blacks would be lower class, obscuring all internal class
distinctions. But no obtainable black standards exist. In Oakland before World War II many of the best occupations in
the black community were with the railroad—and railroad men
formed the backbone of Masonry. Unfortunately, the kind of
information necessary to differentiate between the middle- and
nonmiddle-class element in railroad occupations—which require
knowledge of specific railroad rank, education, personality,
background, etc.—is lacking. There is only limited information
about the general characteristics of railroad men as a group.

A brief discussion of the relationship between railroad work,
middle-class status, and Masonry may help illuminate the
problems of classification. The Pullman Company and the
Southern Pacific Railroad Company were the two main sources
of jobs for blacks in Oakland in the early decades of the century.
One commentator has noted that "In 1930 the Pullman Company represented the largest single source of income for the
Black community . . . . the Southern Pacific followed closely
. . . . The combined figures represented sixty per cent of the
resources of the black community."[2] The railroads were especially important because of the lack of alternative employment.
Until very recently East Bay trade unions have been generally
closed to blacks, and many a skilled black migrating from the
South to Oakland has found his old profession denied him.
As a result the railroad jobs have attracted a fairly talented
group of black employees. According to Fire Department Lt.
Royal Towns, an important California Mason, S.P. waiters in
the 1920s were a very special group:

> Waiters were men that couldn't utilize their education, men that
> had degrees in various subjects. In fact, that was one reason
> that I was glad I railroaded because I met many men that were
> working just to get enough money to go into business . . . or
> to school. They were very fine men.[3]

If they used the income from their jobs carefully, men such
as these could easily become solid members of the black community. The same was true of Pullman porters and S.P. cooks.

[2] William Brown, Jr., "Class Aspects of Residential Development and Choice in the
Oakland Black Community" (unpublished Ph.D. dissertation, University of California,
Berkeley, 1961), pp. 82-83.

[3] Interview with the author, November 1968. (Towns was editor of California's
Masonic magazine for many years.)

Indeed, these two occupations were highly respected jobs, and many of those who held them owned their own homes. Pullman porters were considered the railroad elite, often owning fine Victorian homes, and were well represented in the social notes of the black press.[4]

The chief problem with any generalization about the class position of railroad men is that differences of life style within each occupation were tremendous. Royal Towns points out that while waiters were an exceptional group and made enough money to support a decent life style, their job discouraged personal economy. Waiters were in constant contact with rich white men who frequently showed off their status by extravagant tipping. Many waiters were deeply impressed by this upper-class style and proceeded to act the same role in their own lives. Towns feels that porters and cooks, however, were protected from this kind of influence by the nature of their positions.

Another problem in class analysis is that while the Pullman porters may have been a social elite and the backbone of the black community's middle class, in 1920 there were 520 such porters out of a total male work force of 2,500, too many men to fulfill the status that Brown and Towns feel they attained. Many of the black elite came from their ranks; but these men must have been a minority, and exactly who they were is not discernible. Since railroad men in Good Hope Lodge form about the same percentage as they do in the general black population it is best to simply note their numbers and the fact that they are probably from the more respectable parts of their occupational group. The important thing is that railroad jobs did provide the economic potential for a man to attain middle-class status.

While railroad men do not lend themselves to easy classification, the same cannot be said for the rest of the lodge. Many occupations which are obviously "better" ones are significantly overrepresented, while those apparently lacking status (and again they may be more than they appear) are underrepresented, compared to the black work force as a whole. When we examine the percentage of Good Hope Masons in given occupations as compared to the entire black community, there is

[4] Brown, pp. 93-94.

support for my thesis that Masons form a black middle class.[5]

Since Good Hope Lodge did not exist before World War I, the first available membership material (1906) comes from the only existing lodge, Acacia. In that year Acacia had twenty-three members, eighteen of whom were identifiable by occupation:[6]

Category	Number	Description
Professional and Manager	3	1 realtor, 1 attorney, 1 physician
Skilled Labor and Small Businessmen[7]	7	3 barbers, 1 carpenter, 1 bricklayer, 1 gardener, 1 tailor
Railroad, City or Quasi-Public Employees	7	2 S.P. porters, 1 S.P. cook, 2 city office janitors, 1 transit car operator, 1 Chamber of Commerce janitor
Others	1	1 cook

Given the limited occupational structure of Oakland's black community, this is a remarkable group of men!

[5] Since there is only a census breakdown by occupation for Oakland, I have subtracted the few Masons living in neighboring Berkeley from the calculations.

[6] Unless otherwise noted, the sources for each year given are from membership lists of the lodges for that year and the *Oakland City Directory* for the same year (in this case 1906).

[7] The City Directory for 1906 does not enable us to tell if these men were skilled workers, private entrepreneurs, or both.

The situation was quite similar in 1915, by which time Acacia Lodge had grown to fifty-one members. Because of the abbreviation of first names in the Masonic membership lists and the commonness of many black names only twenty-one of these men could be identified in the city directories:

Category	Numbers	Description
Professional	2	1 attorney, 1 physician
Businessmen and Managers	5	1 saloonkeeper, 1 tailor, 1 billiards operator, 1 cigar storeman, 1 hostler
Skilled Craftsmen	5	1 gardener, 1 barber 1 printer, 1 painter, 1 bricklayer
Railroad men	5	5 S.P. porters
Others	4	1 cook, 1 chauffeur, 1 steward, 1 janitor

The members of Oakland Masonry in these years were among the black elite of the time. Even on the basis of occupation alone one can recognize this, though the official occupation understates the reality. A perusal of the black press in 1915 shows that many Oakland Masons were prominent socialites, despite such listings in the city directories as "janitor" or "elevator operator." Being an elevator operator in the right hotel, employed by the right people or with the proper family background was of crucial social importance.

The year 1923 presents the first detailed information on the membership of Good Hope Lodge itself. In that year the lodge had ninety-three members, of whom seventy-three were identifiable in the city directory, presenting the following breakdown:

Category	Number	Description
Businessmen	9	3 restauranteurs, 2 realtors, 1 barber, 1 bootblack (business), 1 undertaker, 1 gardener (business)
Skilled Labor	7	2 carpenters, 3 plasterers, 1 tailor, 1 machinist
White Collar	3	2 clerks, 1 insurance agent
Public Employees	7	1 post office, 2 firemen, 2 city janitors, 1 library guard, 1 city street laborer
Railroad men[8]	31	12 waiters, 5 cooks, 1 car cleaner, 13 porters
Unskilled Labor	15	8 laborers, 4 stevedores, 2 janitors, 1 chauffeur (the eight laborers unspecified)
Others	1	1 trainer

[8] We know that *all* of the porters worked for the railroads since there were no black porters in Oakland stores at the time (interview with Royal Towns, May 1968). We cannot be sure that all of the waiters or cooks worked for the railroad; some probably did not, though most probably did.

We can get an idea of how unusual this occupational breakdown is by comparing the Masons with the general black labor force in Oakland in 1920. Among the better occupations Masons were strikingly overrepresented:

Category	Percentage of Male Black Work Force[10]	Percentage of Good Hope Masons
Carpenters	1	3
Plasterers	0.6	4.6
Firemen[9]	0	3
Restauranteurs	0.1	4
Realtors	0.1	3

While these and like job categories were overrepresented, the key undesirable occupations were underrepresented: 16 percent of the male black labor force were laborers (excluding city workers,) while 10.7 percent of the Good Hope Masons were laborers. The one category of unskilled work which is highly overrepresented among Masons is that of stevedore (0.5 percent of the male black work force and 4.6 percent of the Good Hope Masons), but this is a special case. The waterfront area was one of the few places where unionization meant integration for blacks. Ultimately the black stevedores were in an exceptionally enviable economic position in comparison to their black brethren.[11]

---

[9] Obviously, the 1920 census figure is inaccurate by 1923. However, there were at this time no more than a dozen black firemen in Oakland, and all but one were Masons (interview with Royal Towns, December 1968).

[10] "Male Black Work Force" statistics from census for year noted—here 1920.

[11] San Francisco lodges in the early 1950s showed a substantial number of longshoreman and stevedores as members, almost all of whom owned their own homes.

By the 1930 census the situation in Good Hope Lodge had changed in some important respects. There had been a noticeable but not overwhelming drop in membership because of the Depression. Of the members whose occupation could be determined (fifty-four out of seventy-nine) a sizeable minority lived in the neighboring community of Berkeley rather than Oakland. The occupational breakdown shows a remarkable similarity to that of 1923:

Category	Number	Description
Public Service Employees	7	2 firemen, 4 postmen, 1 city employee
Skilled Labor	5	2 carpenters, 1 plasterer, 1 hod carrier, 1 barber (not owner)
Businessmen	7	1 mortician, 1 gardener, 1 shoe repair, 2 realtors, 2 barbers
White Collar	3	2 clerks, 1 accountant
Railroad men	20	8 waiters, 7 porters, 4 cooks, 1 car cleaner
Unskilled Labor	12	6 laborers, 4 janitors, 1 chauffeur, 1 steward

This breakdown reveals a stability in the absolute number of those with easily identifiable good jobs, despite the loss in membership. A similar stability reveals itself in the lowest occupations (but, as we shall see, men with such jobs were living in the better residential area of Berkeley rather than Oakland). The major drop came in railroad occupations.

The 1930 figures, like those for 1923, show marked overrepresentation in better occupations:[12]

Category	Percentage of Male Black Work Force	Percentage of Good Hope Masons
Postmen	0.7	8
Firemen	0.4	5.4
Realtors	0.5	5.4
Barbers	1.8	8
Carpenters	1.5	5.4
Clerks (primarily non-store)	2.6	5.4

The situation among railroad employees in the lodge changed rather noticeably, especially among waiters:

Category	Percentage of Male Black Work Force	Percentage of Good Hope Masons
Waiters	14.6	5.4
Railroad Porters	12.6	10.8

[12] Because of the increase in the number of members living in Berkeley a problem arose in checking the lodge against the 1930 census. For example, while there were eight waiters in the lodge (better than 14 percent of the membership) only two lived in Oakland (5.4 percent of the Oakland membership). Fortunately, most of the Berkeley members were in railroad occupations. Nevertheless, for purposes of checking membership against the census it has been necessary to use only the Oakland figures since there is no census material for Berkeley.

It is interesting that the number of cooks in the lodge (most of whom were railroad employees) grew to 10.8 percent of the Oakland membership. Unfortunately, this occupation was not listed in the 1930 census. The one noticeable adverse change was the growth of men in the lowest occupations, especially laborer and janitor:

Category	Percentage of Male Black Work Force	Percentage of Good Hope Masons
Laborers	15.3	13.5
Janitors	5.7	2.7

But the increase among Masonic laborers was comparatively slight.

Given the period, the situation in 1935 was both unusual and significant. The number of Masons in the lodge showed a marked *increase* over 1930 despite the worsening of the Depression. Most of the new members were employed as skilled workers, thus exaggerating the middle-class nature of the lodge. Of the ninety-one men in the lodge, the occupations of sixty-seven are known:[13]

Category	Number
Small Businessmen	7
Skilled Workers	10
City and Government Employees	9
White Collar Workers	5
Railroad men	25

Fully fifty-seven of these men occupied jobs easily classifiable as black middle class, leaving only ten men in the less desirable occupations.

[13] Because there is no census to compare this with, I am giving figures for both Oakland and Berkeley.

With the advent of the war, the economy began to expand, and Masonry, like many other voluntary associations, benefited from the increased supply of money. By 1942, the lodge membership had risen to one hundred-seventeen, eighty-three of whom are identifiable.[14] None of these men came as part of the great migration of southern blacks who started to enter Oakland the previous year. A check of the Oakland city directory for 1940 and 1939 shows that all of the Masons listed in 1942 were Oakland residents previous to that year. It is important that only three men were employed in war-related work. This, coupled with their occupational stability (at least from 1940), suggests that we are not dealing with a temporarily war-inflated occupational level. The creation of a black pseudo-middle class as a result of war work does ultimately affect Good Hope's membership, as I shall show, but it does not manifest itself until after 1942. In that year the composition of the expanded lodge was very similar to that of earlier years—which is to say it was impressive.

Category	Number
Small Businessmen	10
Skilled Workers	13
Public Servants	11
White Collar Workers	4

[14] Because of home-ownership information available for 1941 and 1943 (there is no 1942 directory) I used figures from these years, not from 1940. However, a check of occupations in 1940 compared to 1941-43 showed almost no changes.

[15] The kind of comparison we have made between Oakland Masons and the censuses from 1910 to 1930 cannot be made in 1940 because, unlike earlier, the membership is divided into too many categories, often with only one member listed in each. Also, one of the most important groups, railroad porters, is no longer included in the census. The only comparable categories are postman, fireman, waiter, and laborer. In the first two the Masons are highly overrepresented, in the waiter group they are underrepresented, and in the unspecified labor category there is exact parity with the male black work force (19 percent).

Railroad men	26
Unspecified Laborers[15]	16

The 1941 and 1943 East Bay city directories provide additional socioeconomic information. They indicate home ownership, a significant barometer of class. The major problem with the directories is, however, that they are often inaccurate on this point, almost always understating the extent of home ownership.[16] Often men listed as homeowners in 1941 were not so listed in 1943, or vice versa. In both cases there is strong impressionistic evidence that no change of status occurred. These people continued to live in the same houses for years, and to hold the same jobs. Since we found listings for a large percentage of Good Hope's membership in only one of the two years, many owners who appeared by error in the renter category in 1941 did not have the opportunity to be correctly listed two years later. They, therefore, had to be considered renters for both years.[17] Nevertheless, though the ownership percentage is decidedly understated, the directories do give some indication of reality.

Of the eighty-two identifiable men, forty were homeowners according to city directories in either or both 1941 and 1943. This is a rather substantial figure (49 percent) which, if corrected to the true level, would be even more striking. Of greater interest than general lodge home ownership is the breakdown of ownership by occupation. Here, for the first time, one can get some idea of the actual economic status of many of the less desirable occupations. In arranging ownership by occupation one finds:

[16] This fact was discovered by comparing the 1969 directory against the 1970 tax assessor's lists. In almost every case in which the directory attributed home ownership to a Mason, this was borne out in the tax records. In the majority of cases in which the directory did not attribute ownership, the tax records contradicted it. In some of the cases the directory was obviously in error—a number of rich black businessmen were supposedly not owners. However, most of the errors were for men whose occupations were not listed either, indicating that directory surveyors were unable to interview the resident.

[17] The lack of a homeowner symbol had to be taken as signifying renter status.

Occupation	Owners	Not Listed As Owners
Railroad Porter	6	3
Railroad Waiter	5	2
Railroad Cook	5	2
Unspecified Laborer	5	8
Janitor	2	0

The railroad employees are predominately home owners. Of greater significance, all janitors and a high minority of laborers are in that same category. The situation is actually better among the less desirable occupations than it is among the more prestigious ones:

Occupation	Owners	Not Listed As Owners
Postman	4	1
Fireman	1	2
Business/Professional	4	6
City Janitor	1	2

The rather weak showing of small businessmen suggests two possibilities. First, the amount of error may be quite high. At least two of the non-owning entrepreneurs (a mortician and a liquor store owner) were almost certainly incorrectly listed. Second, it is possible that businessmen were forced to put most of their capital in their enterprises rather than in homes. However, it should be pointed out that most of these businesses were not fly-by-night affairs but existed for decades—the two mentioned above generating considerable wealth.

No East Bay directories were published between 1943 and 1967. As a result, no occupational information for those key years is available. According to Richard Wilson, the present secretary of Good Hope Lodge, there was great membership expansion during and immediately after World War II, made up largely of migrant southern blacks who obtained employment in Oakland and Berkeley. These newcomers were strongly motivated to join Masonry because of its high prestige at home; and as a result of the high salaries of war work, they were able to do so for the first time. The Order, according to Wilson, let down its normal standards temporarily and allowed in men who, once the war-induced prosperity died, were increasingly unable to maintain themselves in the fraternity. The result was a steady decline in membership during the 1950s.

For the period 1967-1970 there exists the most abundant supply of information on Masonic members of any period. By use of the 1967 and 1969 Oakland directories, the 1970 voter registration records, and the tax assessor's lists, one can draw a more accurate picture of the membership than ever before.[18] By 1967 (the date of the only membership list available) Good Hope, the largest lodge in Oakland, had 299 members. Of this number, some information is available on 232, occupational information on 170. The breakdown for the 170 for whom occupation is known suggest the lodge's middle-class character:

Category	Number
Small Businessmen	19
Skilled Craftsmen and Industrial Workers	23
Government:	29
Post Office	[7
Professional Military	3
City Workers	7
Federal Employees (armed forces bases)	12]
White Collar (includes 2 union officials)	8

[18] The new city directories, unlike previous ones, deal only with Oakland, rather than Oakland and Berkeley; voter registration provides occupational information for many residents of Berkeley who would otherwise be unknown—unfortunately for some who have not moved or changed party allegiance the information is very old, of ten from the 1940s; property roles are open to the public and give the value of both the land and improvements for each piece of property located in Alameda County—the county in which both Oakland and Berkeley are situated.

Retired	28
Transportation:	31
Railroad	[13
Longshoremen	6
Warehousemen	9
Truckers and Bus Drivers	3]
Others:	9
Security Guards,	[3
Custodians, Janitors or	
Maintenance Men	6]
Low-Skill:	4
(e.g. hospital porter,	
mortuary attendant,	
unspecified laborer)	
Miscellaneous	6
(e.g., safety servicemen,	
packer,	
stockman, etc.)	

The high status of the businessmen, skilled workers, post office employees, white collar and city government employees (total: sixty-four men) needs no explanation. Of the twelve men employed at the armed forces bases, most possess middle-class jobs. While two are listed simply as "employees," five rank as either supervisor foreman, electrician, or machinist. Of the other five, three are craters, one a stevedore, and only one a janitor; but even these jobs benefit from the fact that they are civil-service and hence have a higher degree of security than comparable jobs outside government. Many of the men who work at these bases have been there for over a quarter of a century. While black men often occupy the lowest positions in the federal establishment (few of these positions can be so characterized), even the worst provide a firm economic base for membership in the black middle class. Not only in Good Hope, but in lodges throughout the San Francisco Bay Area military bases provide employment for a significant proportion of Masonic membership.

The ten men who are employed as construction workers or longshoremen are among the fortunate black men in the ranks of organized labor. The powerful longshoremen's union was one of the few Bay Area unions to welcome blacks as members; the construction trades have been traditionally unfriendly, and thus those Masons who gained entrance have been all the more fortunate. The position of railroad workers has been discussed previously; especially since the growth of their unions into powerful national organizations, these members have benefited economically. Most of these men are part of the older generation, however, and when they retire or die few black men will replace them. The custodians and janitors, also usually in the employ of large public and private institutions, receive benefits in wages and security which mean a job better than the title implies.

Not only is there occupational information for this lodge, there is also evidence concerning ownership of real property (both homes and investment real estate) which even more strongly than occupation demonstrates the middle-class character of Good Hope Lodge. According to the tax assessor records for 1970, 83 percent of the lodge membership (193 men) own real property.[19] As high as this number is, it actually *understates* the middle-class nature of Masonic membership when compared with other Masonic lodges. A detailed study of home ownership among Acacia and Adonis Lodge membership showed almost 95 percent owning real property. Both of these lodges are older than Good Hope, but in a third study, of a small post-World War II lodge, the same figure emerged. By choosing Good Hope Lodge, then, I have not weighted the evidence in favor of my thesis.

Not only do 83 percent of the members of Good Hope Lodge own property, but of those who own, fully 25 percent own more than one piece of real estate. When ownership of real property is matched to occupation it illustrates how deceptive many of the "less desirable" job categories are as an indicator of class status. The list below gives a breakdown of occupation and property ownership:

---

[19] For purposes of calculating the percentage, 57 men were excluded, including 45 men living outside Alameda County and 12 men who were not identifiable.

Occupation	Number	Property Owner
Businessman	19	18
Skilled Laborer	23	21
Retired	28	21
Longshoreman	6	5
City Employee	7	6
Warehouseman	9	7
Employee, Armed Forces Base	12	12
Construction Worker	4	4
Railroad	13	12
Custodian or Janitor	6	6
Unknown Occupation	62	47

Masons employed in the "less desirable" occupations are not only predominately property holders, but many own more than one piece of real estate. Not exceptionally unusual are: the hospital custodian who owns his home worth $27,000 and another residential property with four rental units valued at $19,000; the hospital janitor who owns his home worth $17,000 and another property valued at $18,000; the supermarket clerk with a $16,000 home and a $17,000 second residence; the "unspecified laborer" with a $12,000 home and a $7,600 piece of industrial property. Even in cases in which a man has not raised a large sum of capital, his investments often show his level of aspiration. For example, one city janitor in Good Hope Lodge, while not owning his own home, owns two unimproved pieces of real estate.

If many members with less desirable jobs have been able to acquire considerable property, some men with only slightly better jobs have done phenomenally well. Certainly outstanding is the professional Navy man who owns two pieces of real estate: a $25,000 home and a $69,000 apartment house; or the railroad freight car man who owns three pieces of property: an $11,000 home and two houses worth $18,000 and $19,000; or the electrical mechanic whose total real estate is valued at $175,000![20]

Not unpredictably, the greatest success is found among those Masons in business. Perhaps the richest man in Good Hope Lodge is a businessman with real property assets of $310,000. He owns five pieces of property (two apartment houses and two commercial establishments) but lives in a modest $19,000 home. His nearest rivals, other than the electrical mechanic, are a businessman with ten pieces of property valued at a meager $130,000 and an entrepreneur worth $170,000.

While a large minority of Masons place their savings in income-producing rental property or business, as well as in their own homes, the majority possess only the latter. The ownership of one's home is a goal which for decades has been urged upon the membership, though in recent decades it is usually those who have already purchased property who enter the Order. Significantly, the property records also show that the Masons' homes are not crumbling or deteriorating structures, but are well-kept, respectable small homes valued slightly above or below $18,000.[21]

When one is finished reviewing the property and occupational records of the membership of Good Hope Lodge, one cannot help but feel that these men are not among the "dispossessed" of America. In a very real, material sense, they have made it in a way that most blacks have not. To a large extent, I believe that these findings from Good Hope (and Acacia, Adonis, and other) Lodge(s) are representative of Prince Hall Masonry throughout the United States.

Of course Oakland, California, is not every town. At the least,

[20] This man's occupation is from 1964 sources and property listing as of 1970. This discrepancy in time is one that occurs frequently because of the scarcity of source material.

[21] Oakland and Berkeley homes are less expensive than their Los Angeles or New York counterparts.

the black population of California generally has been better off economically than the Afro-Americans of most states. Some distortion must result from using one city or one state as a test case. However, since the material is consistent with a large amount of impressionistic information found elsewhere, I believe that the effect of Oakland's unique characteristics is limited. Indeed, while the study of Good Hope Lodge may exaggerate the economic level of the membership somewhat, it simultaneously understates the presence of the black elite. We do not find in Good Hope professional men—doctors, lawyers, teachers and professors—or political leaders, who by virtue of their occupations and income are "absolutely" middle class by white standards. Rather the members are a solid "ghetto" middle class, who form the backbone of respectability in the black community, but who are not rich enough, educated enough, or integrated enough to leave the ghetto behind entirely. While the Masonic Order has had difficulty in recent decades in attracting the college-educated black elite that once flocked to the fraternity, the names of prominent politicians, community leaders, and businessmen are still conspicuous in state after state. Such people even today are markedly overrepresented in Masonry. Good Hope lacks such people. The distortions in the case study tend to counteract each other.

Given all the evidence, I believe that the basic pattern of the Oakland lodges holds true for the Order as a whole. Compared to the average black man, Masons have been and are more likely to be relatively prosperous, to hold a better, more secure job, and to own rather than rent a home.[22] As a result the black Masons have been able to pay the financial price of a bourgeois lifestyle. Living according to the middle-class ethic is not simply a matter of money—witness the many poor people who are faithful to it and the many rich who are not—but it helps. Prince Hall Masonry assumes that its members are economically better off than most blacks, and this assumption appears to be correct.

In the next chapter I will focus less on the individuals in Masonry than on the institution itself. There has been a long-standing debate over whether fraternal organizations and their membership are worth studying at all since they are inherently rural rather than urban, and thus not relevant for

[22] This is true if single-family dwelling units are available in the city limits.

understanding the modern black middle class. I will show that Prince Hall Freemasonry is both a rural and urban institution, healthy in both areas. I will also point out the urban origin and bias of black Freemasonry and present a detailed study of the demographic history of Prince Hall in Texas to confirm my position.

Chapter IV

Town and Country

Black fraternal organizations are usually thought of as rural institutions whose importance to the black community was confined to the period before the urbanization of the Afro-American. The designation and subsequent dismissal of fraternities as a "rural phenomenon" has been much less the result of empirical findings than of theoretical speculations. For decades anthropologists and sociologists have developed theories of a rural-urban continuum and fraternities have been neatly pigeonholed at the "rural" end. To be so termed in a rapidly urbanizing environment is the social scientist's kiss of death for any institution; once an organization is so labeled it can be confidently ignored since it has no place in the academic's vision of society's future. If the outmoded form should refuse to die on schedule, so much the worse for it.

Since we have no crystal ball and cannot say which social structures will live and which will die, we will not use the terms "rural" and "urban" as shorthand for "healthy" and "dying." Rather, they simply designate two different social environments. The most striking characteristic of Prince Hall Masonry is that it has existed for two hundred years in *both* rural and urban areas, and in a healthy state at that. It has struck roots in both communities and answered a need for its services in each. The organization is worthy of study in both social settings as an interesting present-day phenomenon, regardless of its supposedly bright or cloudy future in either area.

Our source material does not allow a detailed discussion of the similarities and differences between the rural and urban Masonic lodges. The information found in the Masonic records comes almost entirely from the cities. Given the need to counteract the rural stereotype of black fraternities, this urban emphasis is probably all for the best, though ultimately research on small town and rural lodges is mandatory. For the moment, however, I will look at some of the ways that Prince Hall Masonry, even in the countryside, has been influenced by the city. I do this not in order to prove the organization totally urban, but rather to show the shortcomings of the usual, either-or, urban-rural, conceptual categories.

In origin, Prince Hall Masonry was a creature of the cities. It was born in the urban black communities of the North in the late eighteenth and early nineteenth centuries, and was nourished in that environment until the end of the Civil War when it was exported to the cities of the newly liberated South. In Texas, for example, the first seven lodges were established in San Antonio, Austin, Houston, Galveston, Marshall, Waco, and Dallas. When the Grand Lodge was established it was from Galveston, Austin, Houston and Brenham that the officers came. This pattern was repeated in Georgia (where the first lodges were established in Savannah, Augusta, Atlanta, and Darien) and throughout the South. In Texas, the city of Fort Worth was made the permanent headquarters of the Order in 1906, while other states achieved the same results unofficially by simply building their Grand Lodge Temples in their largest city. When we compare the 1860s and the 1960s we find that the predominance of city dwellers among the Masonic leadership is as strong today as in the past, with Texas leaders, for example, coming primarily from Fort Worth, Houston, San Antonio, Dallas, and Galveston, and Georgia officers from Atlanta and Savannah.

Once established in large communities such as New Orleans, Savannah, and Montgomery, "missionaries" were sent out to convert the rural hinterland. The spread of Freemasonry to the rural areas was so successful that ultimately the majority of Masons in many states were country rather than city dwellers. This was the result of the growth of the Order in the country, not of its weakening in the city. Once in the countryside, Masonry served the rural members as an extension of the urban, outside world, and thus, to a significant extent, the country lodges were not purely "rural."

The power of the city over the country Masonic lodges can easily be seen from both Masonic organizational structure and Masonic literature. We have already pointed out that the rural

lodges are subordinate to urban-dominated Grand Lodges. This
is the natural result of a statewide rather than locally focused
institution. The individual lodges are forced to turn outward
to the fraternal center which, of necessity, is placed in areas
of sizeable black population where service facilities, wealth,
and potential leadership are concentrated.

Perhaps of greater importance, the city influences rural
Masonry by bringing into the countryside a glimpse of the
outside world. One cannot understand the significance of the
Order and organizations like it unless one realizes that through
it thousands of country and small-town blacks have been
initiated into the mysteries not simply of a fraternity but of
Western civilization. They have been made aware, in a personal
way, of the existence of a world of ideas with which they had
no previous familiarity. Intellectuals may dismiss Freemasonic
philosophy as pseudophilosophy, its literature as a pseudoli-
terature, its intellectuality as pseudointellectuality, but for
many men (white and black) it has been their *only* taste of
literature and philosophy.

In Masonry, the initiate is told of the importance of learning,
of history, and of science. He is taught that the Order is
dedicated to the maintenance of the liberal arts, to the furth-
erance of mathematics, rhetoric and music. Masonry, he is
informed, not only supports these intellectual pursuits, but its
history is intimately linked with their creation; Masonry actually invented "culture." The achievements of Freemasonry,
black and white, may be infinitely below its claims, and in
practice Masons may encourage rhetoric more than any other
liberal art, but this does not nullify the Order's power to widen
the intellectual horizons of its followers. Within one institution,
secular intellectuality and religious enthusiasm coexist together, helping to reunite the two traditions which broke apart
in America when Puritanism disintegrated into Unitarian
"mind" and Baptist "heart." These functions have been characteristic of Masonry everywhere, but especially in the rural
districts where intellectual sophistication has been most lacking.

The philosophical ideas of Masonry may not superficially
seem particularly urban. Rather, they are simply the values
and ideals of Anglo-America, urban and rural. But for the
isolated black population of the South, Masonry's attack on

parochialism has constituted a major cultural intrusion into rural life. A man who could cope with the intellectual challenge of Masonry, whose horizons were broadened by contacts with it, was far better able to adjust to the demands of an urban society than those who lacked such exposure. Even if we forget the broadening nature of Masonic ideology and emphasize only Masonic structure, we find a member of the Order forced to look outward from his parochial home community toward the state Grand Lodge and the Grand Lodges of other states and of other nations in order to find both leadership and "brethren."

While we have no qualitative material to provide insight into the varying characteristics of rural and urban lodges as such, we do have quantitative material to illustrate the actual distribution of the membership over time in different demographic areas. These statistics come from the membership lists of the Texas jurisdiction. Unfortunately, the material is limited, both in quantity and content. We have access to no individual town or city information except the total membership per living area, the total population of that community, and the total black male population twenty-one years of age or over. This allows us only to organize living areas of Texas into crude categories of rural, urban, small town, large city, etc., and to determine the distribution of the Masonic membership into these groupings over time. Since we have no additional information we cannot take into consideration the general prosperity or poverty of the areas, the peculiarity of each city or town, or any factors other than population size as a possible determinant of Masonic presence. Nevertheless, some interesting relationships emerge.[1]

The 1899 membership figures are the earliest available for the Masonic Order in Texas. At that time there were 1,500 adherents. We do not have a lodge-by-lodge breakdown for that year, nor for any year until 1912. By that time the Order had grown to 5,400 men, which represented a little less than 3 percent of the total black male population twenty-one years or older. While the 1912 Masonic membership is almost evenly

[1] Texas was chosen as the model state because it possesses a number of important features. It has the largest membership of any Masonic jurisdiction. It is a Southern state (where most Masons are located), but unlike most Southern states it has a large number of major urban centers. Many Southern states have so few cities that a study of rural vs. urban residency is unfairly weighted. In the North the problem would be just the opposite. All of the figures in this chapter come from the membership lists (by lodge) found in the *Proceedings* of the Texas Grand Lodge.

divided into urban and rural populations (using the census definition of 2,500 or above as urban) the Order was actually considerably stronger in urban than rural centers. The Masons attracted 4.5 percent of the eligible black males in cities and only 2 percent of their rural counterparts.

If we refine the term urban into more meaningful categories, such as big cities (i.e., San Antonio, Austin, Houston, Dallas, Waco, Fort Worth, Corpus Christi, Beaumont, El Paso), medium-sized towns (i.e., 10,000-20,000), and small urban centers (i.e., 2,500-10,000), we find that Masonic strength varies considerable among these areas:

Category	Percentage of Males 21 or Over in Masonry in 1912	Percentage of Masonic Membership in Each Living Area in 1912
Big City	4.5	26+
Medium-Sized Town	9	10
Small Urban Center	4	11
Rural	2	53

The areas with the highest percentage of Masons out of eligible black populations in 1912 were the medium-sized towns. In those areas 9 percent of the eligible blacks were Masons. Both the big cities and the small urban centers averaged around 4 percent. However, despite the greater attraction of Masonry in the medium-sized towns, the average urban Mason in 1912 lived in a big city: more than 26 percent in big cities, 10 percent in medium-sized towns, 11 percent in small urban centers. These figures are quite consistent with the observation that Masonry was originally an urban institution that spread to the rural hinterland yet continued to flourish in its original setting. It is also proof that Masonry was not simply a nineteenth-century institution that died at the turn of this century.

The most outstanding feature of Texas Masonry between 1912 and 1926 was its phenomenal growth. From 5,400 members it grew to 21,500. This was not only an absolute, but a significant percentile increase as well. While Masonry in 1912 could claim

less than 3 percent of the adult black males over twenty-one,
fourteen years later it could boast 9 percent of that same group.
The absolute number of Masons in rural as compared with
urban areas was approximately the same in both years. This
meant that the urban Masons claimed fully 10 percent of the
eligible black population, and the rural Masons 8 percent. The
urban part of the Order was still more attractive than the rural,
though the ratio was much closer to parity than it had been
in 1912.

The 1926 figures, when compared with 1912, also show an
increase in all urban categories:[2]

Category	Percentage of Male Population in Order in 1912	Percentage of Male Population in Order in 1926
Big City	4.5	8
Cities 20,000 + (excluding Big Cities)	Didn't exist	13
Medium-Sized Towns	9	11
Small Town	4	17

The great strength of the Masonic Order in the big cities
well into the third decade of the twentieth century makes it
impossible to argue for the uncongeniality of urban centers
to the institution. The closest one can come is to note that
during the 1912-1926 period the Order began to spread among
the small urban centers at a much higher rate than among
the larger ones. However, the growth in importance of the small
urban centers was not at the expense of large cities but rather
of the rural areas.

The rapid growth of Masonry throughout the United States
was cut short by the Great Depression. Texas Masonry, like
most states, underwent a severe loss of membership during the
1930s.[3] Most observers assumed that the Depression debacle

[2] The 20,000 + category (excluding big cities named earlier) is a new one owing to
the rise in number of cities over 20,000 population.

[3] Some of the large Southern jurisdictions started a slow decline in the latter part
of the 1920s because of the arrival of the agricultural depression.

came at the end of a long-term decline of fraternities and that
the situation was permanent and irreversible. In 1939, membership in the fraternity was certainly not satisfactory—though
the Texas Order was far from defunct. In that year the brotherhood could claim only 8,327 members, a sizeable decline from
over 21,000. The rapid decline of Masonry occurred equally
in almost all geographic areas; the rural areas did not decline
faster or slower than the urban; the big cities fell at the same
rate as the small towns.

The only evidence for the nonurban nature of the Order can
be found in the fact that the rural areas, despite declining
population, continued to provide about half the Masonic membership. In 1939 they accounted for 49 percent as compared
to the urban 51 percent. In earlier years the rural Masons had
made up more than half, and thus 1939 represents a positive
decline in percentage, but this is offset by the greater relative
decline of rural to urban population in Texas generally. What
this means is that while in earlier years the overwhelming
majority of blacks were rural and they supplied only slightly
more than 50 percent of the membership, now, with the rural
and urban areas having an equal number of males twenty-one
and over, rurals were able to maintain their position. This
demonstrates not that the urban lodges declined but that rural
areas were, for the first time, supplying the percentage of
members equal to their population percentage.

That the Depression did not destroy Texas Masonry is clearly
proved by the 1947 membership figures. By that year the Order
had increased its membership to approximately 20,000, an
equivalent of 7 percent of the eligible population. By 1947, also,
the division between rural and urban members had changed
dramatically, with 60 percent of the Masons living in urban
areas. Within the urban category the distribution remained
remarkably similar to earlier decades:[4]

---

[4] We were unable to trace 2.5 percent of the Masonic population to a geographic
area.

Category	Percentage of Masons in Each Area in 1947
Big City	26
20,000+ Cities (except Big Cities)	7.5
Medium-Sized Towns	7
Small Towns	17
Rural	40

By 1947 Masonry again was strong in all areas but, with the decline of rural population, the ratio of Masons to the eligible black population in rural areas was greater than in cities—a situation unlike 1912, 1926, or 1939. In 1947 urban Masons were 6.5 percent of the black population twenty-one and over, while rural Masons were 8.5 percent. As I shall show, this difference is not temporary but has continued in recent years.

The last available membership lists are for 1964 when the total Masonic population of Texas was 28,500, representing 9 percent of the eligible population. Sixty-eight percent of these men live in urban centers and 31 percent in rural areas. When the urban category is broken down, we find:[5]

Category	Percentage of Masons in Each Area in 1964
Big City	29
20,000+ Cities (except Big Cities)	16
Medium-Sized Towns	5
Small Towns	16
Rural	31

[5] Two percent once again cannot be traced to a geographic area.

Though the Order is healthy everywhere, the rural sections still show a higher percentage of eligible population in the Order than do the urban (11 + percent and 8 + percent, respectively).[6]

The general health of Texas Masonry in all residential areas, particularly the largest cities, is incompatible with the hypothesis that Masonry in the twentieth century is either dead or dying, or with the assertion that it is a rural and small-town rather than an urban institution. The only substantial evidence that might appear to support that contention is the continued rise in the percentage of black population in rural areas that join the Order. This, however, can be explained in a way having little to do with the supposed rural or urban character of Masonry.

First, the rise in the attractiveness of Masonry in nonurban areas is not a traditional phenomenon. Until at least 1939 Masonry showed the urban lodges attracting a larger proportion of the total eligible black population than their rural counterparts. The assertion that fraternities are a rural phenomenon because they thrive only in homogeneous, parochial environments does not hold, either, because it was precisely during the years that preceded 1939 that rural areas and small towns were most cut off from the outside. Masonry was, in fact, weaker in rural areas then than now, when contacts with the outside world are on the increase.

Second, much of the explanation for the relative changes between rural and urban Masonry in recent years can be explained as the result of demographic changes. The rural areas, and small urban centers as well, are migrant-producing areas. These areas witness large-scale out-migration of young men and women who flood the cities. The size and importance of this phenomenon is witnessed not simply in the general decline of the rural population but, more importantly, in the decline of specific age groups. If one compares the proportion of black males twenty-one years of age or older in rural and urban areas,

[6] The key fact in these statistics is not that 29 percent of the Masons live in big cities, but that 8 + percent of the eligible black population is in the Order. The former figure, which is only slightly higher than the 1926 one, would seem to be a decline since the black population was far more urbanized than it had been and thus the big city figure should have risen steeply. But the second figure, a healthy 8 + percent, which is quite as good as the 1926 one, shows that 29 percent is artificially kept low—not because Masonry is sick in the big cities, but because it is overly healthy in the small towns.

one finds only 50 percent of the former are over twenty-one, as compared to fully 65 percent of the latter. This means that the "potential pool" of Masons is greatly decreased in the rural areas and increased in the urban. But this mass of *young* men (and that is what they tend to be) in urban areas are only in theory a potential pool for Masonry. In actuality they are too immature, unsettled, and footloose to join Masonry in any area. As we have seen, Masonry draws from the respectable, established family elements of the community and tends to exclude men in their twenties and early thirties. It is not until they settle down and finish "sowing their wild oats" (as one Oakland, California, lodge secretary put it) that they are Masonic material. However, because of their age it is necessary to count them as part of the eligible population, and insofar as they are found primarily in large cities they artificially swell that population and artificially decrease the one in rural areas. Thus, while the migration continues, the urban Masonic membership appears relatively weaker in drawing power than the rural.

This demographic explanation does not mean that there are no other reasons more specifically related to a rural-urban continuum which might not also operate. The statistics point strongly to such additional factors. For instance, one of the most striking features of Masonic membership distribution is the tendency for the percentage of Masons living in urban areas to rise as the size of the population decreases. This is apparent when one divides the urban centers into the four categories we have been using. Except for 1912, when the largest cities had a slightly higher percentage of members to population (4 + percent to 4 percent), the smaller towns have had a higher rate of Masonic membership:

	1926	1939	1947	1964
Big City	8%	2%	5%	5%
Small Town	17%	5%	12%	20%

The moderate-sized cities have been somewhat erratic in their attractiveness but are basically supportive of this trend.

Some of the demographic factors mentioned earlier apply here as well—the small urban centers have been population-exporting areas to the larger cities—but it seems unlikely that they can explain the entire configuration. Rather, many of the traditional ideas about fraternities have a degree of application here. The smaller urban centers (and the larger, unincorporated "rural" hamlets) have almost no recreational activities or service agencies. They are quite isolated and dull. As one Mason put it, they close down all week except Saturday night. For a large proportion of the black population the Masonic Order does provide services that can't be obtained elsewhere, and there is little institutional competition to the Order since the church is a complementary institution. These social factors, which lead to increased membership in the small communities, are less operative in larger cities. However, as this study has tried to demonstrate, factors such as these are *in addition to* other attractions of the Order in any geographic area. The other roles that Masonry performs explain why, when the added advantages (for gaining membership) of isolation, lack of competitive institutions, etc. are removed, big-city Masonry has refused to fade away, and instead has remained quite strong.

As was noted at the beginning of this chapter, the sources available have forced this discussion to emphasize Masonry in the cities. I must note at this point, however, that the fraternity probably fits into small-town and rural social structure in ways unlike its city role. While Masonry in cities has claimed a sizeable enough minority of the black adult male population to make the Order an important element in black society, in many individual towns and villages it has included so large a proportion of the eligible population that Masonry has become a *crucial* element in the social structure. The existence of many small towns with extremely high percentages of Masons to eligible population, often 35 to 40 percent, has been left unsurveyed in this discussion until now.[7]

The exceptionally high proportion of Masons to eligible population in these towns suggests questions about the general picture of Masonry drawn here in earlier chapters. If Masonry is a middle-class organization and helps differentiate the middle

---

[7] Most often these are small urban centers (2,500-10,000), though some larger cities (e.g., Tyler, Texas, with over 20,000) also have large Masonic percentages.

from lower class, why do some towns have 30 or more percent of the adult black male population in the Order?[8] And more important, how can small towns, just barely (and only by the liberal census definition) urban have such high percentages while big cities, with greater wealth and specialization, have much lower ones? Since our information on individual lodges is sparse, one cannot easily answer these questions, though one can make plausible speculations.

First, the existence of 30 to 40 percent of the adult black male population in a Masonic lodge *is* compatible with my contention that the Order differentiates the *respectable* from the *unrespectable* segments of the population. Indeed, that is one of its major social roles in small towns. Obviously, insofar as such a large part of the population is in the Order, it cannot make the finer social distinctions that it does in larger urban centers where between 5 and 10 percent of the eligible population are members. However, small towns are areas in which class distinctions are generally blurry because of the lack of specialization, limited economic opportunities, etc. Earlier I noted that Masonry attracts not only those who publicly practice bourgeois morality, but the economically middle class as well. This general view may now have to be qualified and its applicability restricted to the larger cities, where there is a large enough economically middle-class group to make such selectivity possible.

This analysis of the situation in small towns is based on a logical projection of the knowledge of Masonry in large centers. Proof requires in-depth research. However, another researcher lends significant support to my hypothesis. Hylan Lewis' *Blackways of Kent* not only discusses Masonry but provides a breakdown by occupation of two local lodges. According to Lewis, the black community of "Kent" is divided into those who abide by conventional morality in public ("the respectables") and those who do not ("the nonrespectables"). Masonry is one of only two organizations in the town that attempts to include only "respectable" people.[9] This goal is extremely hard, if not impossible, to achieve because "It is difficult in this small society for a person to confine his contacts

[8] Whether or not these small towns draw solely from their own populations or from both town and surrounding rural areas is not clear from the available material.

[9] Hylan Lewis, *Blackways of Kent* (Chapel Hill, North Carolina, 1955), p. 259.

or associations solely to respectables without suffering extreme isolation. ...."[10] Indeed, Lewis maintains that Masonry tries but fails in its attempted exclusiveness and that "the membership nearly runs the gamut of the status scale—only the extreme nonrespectables are not represented."[11] However, on second reading, it appears that Masonry was far more exclusive than Lewis realized. There were two Masonic lodges in Kent, and his view of the Order came from treating the two as a unit. One of the lodges was apparently a Prince Hall lodge, the other certainly a bogus one. The second lodge was set up in protest at the exclusiveness of the older one. It claimed a charter from a *white* lodge of Master Masons—a sure sign of its bogus nature—a situation that led the older lodge's membership to accuse the renegade founder of the second lodge of acting for reasons of personal gain and power. Lewis points out that "Some members of the older group of Masons made invidious comparisons between the groups, pointing out ... that the younger group was not discriminating in its membership."[12]

The higher quality of the older lodge membership is reflected in Lewis' belief that they were "men who are older, more established in the community by virtue of age, longer residence, and the families they have raised." The lodge contained "the principal of the school, three ministers, a tavern-store operator, a filling station operator, an auto mechanic, two farmers, a carpenter, two truck drivers, three mill workers, a barbershop porter, and a numbers writer."[13] Of the seventeen men, six were on Lewis' "nice house" list of better-off Kent blacks.[14] Even the bogus lodge had a more exclusive membership than most Kent organizations, but one which was still inferior to the Prince Hall lodge.[15]

Given the difference between the two lodges, if one does not treat them as a unit, the older one is basically *successful* in its attempt at exclusiveness. The two lodges together may only

[10] Ibid., p. 236. About 40 percent of the population are "nonrespectables."

[11] Ibid., p. 260.

[12] Ibid., p. 272.

[13] Ibid., p. 272-273. As exclusive as it was, it was not perfect.

[14] Ibid., p. 272.

[15] Lewis, pp. 272-273, says the two lodges had "similar" occupational profiles, but the differences seem fairly significant to this writer: "The newer Masonic group has as its nucleus eight persons whose regular employment is in the mills; with the exception of the fact that this group has but one minister, the distribution of occupations is about the same .... Only two persons of this group are on the 'nice house' list."

"aspire" to selectivity, but Prince Hall achieves it.[16] When Lewis compares the Masons (both lodges) and their affiliate, Eastern Star, with other groups, he points out that Masonry "indicates a greater emphasis upon persons of some stability as represented by steady jobs and upon persons with good community reputations."[17] Masons don't attempt to take in men needing moral reform as other uplift organizations do. For example, Lewis says, "A leader of the local Elks pointed out ... that the reason his organization took so many men in was because they thought they 'could do something with some of these fellows who drink and carry on so, and don't know how to act.' "[18] Masons reject such a role out of hand. Lewis admits that despite its "problems" in achieving exclusiveness, Masonry and Eastern Star "are probably the only organizations, with the possible exception of [a ladies' group], to which persons actively aspire and with reference to which the investigator has heard a person express regret at his inability to 'make it.' "[19] The picture of Kent Masonry, especially when carefully analyzed, is supportive of my basic contention concerning Prince Hall Masonry's social characteristics and function, even to the greater than average economic status of its membership.

While we have no direct testimony about the characteristics of Masons in rural areas we do have some observations on rural fraternities in general. During the depth of the Depression, Arthur Raper studied two rural counties in Georgia. In his book *Preface to Peasantry* he notes that the farmer, as opposed to the nonfarmer rural population, joined the less expensive lodges.[20] The three national fraternities in the counties— Masons, Knights of Pythias, and Courts of Clanthe—all had proportionately fewer farmers than the state or local organizations. Most lodges of national fraternities owned their lodge halls, unlike the local organizations. Among the farmers, a much higher proportion of owners and tenants (the highest

[16] The quotations Lewis uses to deflate Masonry's claim to successful exclusiveness can be discounted since they probably pertain to the bogus lodge: "they take in most anybody" and "members are not supposed to have more than one wife but I know at least three who do have." He does say, however, that for both lodges, men with a prison record are not acceptable (Lewis, p. 260).

[17] Ibid., p. 273.

[18] Ibid., p. 260.

[19] Ibid., p. 269.

[20] Chapel Hill, 1936.

status farmers) joined lodges than did croppers and farm laborers, and even more frequently appeared as lodge officers. From Raper's study one can conclude that in rural and small town areas the relatively more prosperous have been dispropor-tionately represented in the lodges of any type, and even more disproportionately in the national fraternities. This position is supported by E. Franklin Frazier's observation that in rural plantation areas, where the majority of blacks were not owners, it was the prosperous farmers who maintained stable families and who supported the churches and lodges.[21]

If this has been the case in the rural areas, it increases the likelihood that the same has been true of small urban centers as well. Thus I may not be far off in saying that the Masons in all ecological areas have been relatively better off economi-cally than their neighbors. Our only problem, again, is the tremendous size, proportionately, of Masonic membership in these areas, for which nothing in either Raper or Frazier prepares us. It is ironic to note that the absolute size and continued growth of small town Masonry shows the folly of those who have felt that by labeling fraternities "nonurban" they could safely ignore their importance after 1900.

In this chapter I have tried to demonstrate the basic health of Freemasonry in both rural and urban areas. The fraternity is not a creation of the rural black folk. It is an urban and rural organization, with strong historical roots in city life. Its ability to meet the needs of people in a rural or an urban environment has made it an important institution in black society—and, specifically, in black middle-class society.

I have maintained throughout this work that Masonry fulfills certain needs of the black middle class. Space already has been given to a discussion of those needs—especially those relating to the maintenance of a middle-class lifestyle. In the next chapter I will deal with the desire of black Masons to play a variety of social roles which American society values but which it bars blacks from enacting. I will further suggest that by providing these opportunities for its members Prince Hall has helped train men capable of leading not only the fraternity but the black group as a whole. The Order by its own actions thus strengthens its claim to contain within its ranks the cream of black leadership.

[21] E. Franklin Frazier, *The Negro in the United States*, (New York, 1957), p. 279.

Chapter V

Social Roles

Besides teaching and reinforcing middle-class values and behavior, Masonry also instructs its black adherents in a variety
of important social roles which until recently have been forbidden to blacks or severely restricted.[1] To the extent that Masonry has been able to teach and provide a stage for the performance of these social roles, it has created both a major outlet
for the sociopsychological needs of its membership and produced a large reservoir of experienced leaders for the entire
black population.

Observers of black society have often talked about the
importance of social clubs or fraternities as an outlet for
psychological frustrations of blacks. People who are denied the
opportunity to "be someone" are able to adopt fancy names,
glamorous gowns, and compete for long-winded titles as a way
of compensating. Many authors have gone so far as to postulate
certain "human needs," such as the need to play politics, and
have assumed that when such needs are frustrated in one area
they must come out in another—such as the fraternity.[2]
Whether or not there exists such universal human needs, there
are in America a whole host of specific social roles whose
desirability all Americans have been taught but which have
been traditionally available only to whites. A fraternity like
Masonry is important in allowing an outlet for these culturally
created needs, and by so doing simultaneously helps broaden
the membership's ability to perform social roles necessary for
the functioning of society. This chapter will discuss the oppor-

[1] The church is another black institution that allows blacks to play roles they are
forbidden to play in the larger community. The two institutions differ in that the
Masons provide a larger repertoire of roles.

[2] Raper in *Preface to Peasantry* (Chapel Hill, N.C. 1936) gives this interpretation,
pp. 373-383.

123

tunities the fraternity offers for Masons to act the part of judges, jurors, prosecutors, legislators, businessmen, and publishers rather than the more fanciful escape-oriented roles that most observers of the fraternities have emphasized—though we are not denying this other area has significance.

The most important roles Masonry allows its adherents to play are concerned with self-government. As a Georgia Mason noted, the original local lodge rules written by Prince Hall and his followers in the late eighteenth century were "the first set of regulations drafted by colored men for self government in the United States,"[3] and Masonry ever since has striven to teach its members "the fundamentals of collective government"[4] which are the basis of American life. To some black observers the right of self-government that Masonry has afforded the Negro is too great a blessing to have been an accident; rather, "It is a remarkable fact that Prince Hall Masonry had its beginning in the same era which witnessed the birth of American Democracy .... The circumstances seem to have been wisely designed for some 'increasing purpose' ... to have been adapted to the intention [that] the men of Hamitic extraction should not lack the means of preparing and qualifying themselves to exercise the rights and perform the duties of good citizenship in a Republic."[5] And while throughout most of our national history blacks have not been allowed to use that training in the larger society, they nevertheless have taken great pride in exercising self-governing roles within the halls of their fraternity.

The black Masons' success in managing their own internal political affairs has been important for the self-esteem of the membership. It has proved in their eyes and, they have hoped, in the eyes of unprejudiced whites, that black men are equal to the "dominant race" in their abilities. The Chairman of the Committee on Foreign Correspondence of California was not an exception when he saw the significance of the 113th birthday of the Grand Lodge of Pennsylvania as "proof of the Negro's ability to govern."[6] The successful careers of the almost forty other black Masonic Grand Lodges provided overwhelming evidence of that truth.

[3] *Review* (Georgia), no vol., no.3 (July-Sept. 1940): 9.
[4] *Review* (Georgia), 1, no.1 (Oct. 1937): 9.
[5] *Sentinel* (New York), 1, no.6 (May 1944): 2.
[6] *Proceedings* (California, 1929).

One of the most important social roles in the American system of self-government is concerned with the judicial process, specifically with the jury trial; and it is in the area of conducting Masonic trials that the fraternity performs one of its most significant functions. The Order is based upon an extensive body of laws and regulations; and in the interpretation of these laws, members of the fraternity learn to play the role of judge, juryman, advocate, prosecutor, and witness. Through this activity Masonry compensates for the lack of knowledge in the black community about how to administer justice. As the Grand Master of Illinois lamented in 1916, "The average Mason has but little practical knowledge of the simplest form to be employed, or of the application of the provision of the law . . . . The officers and members of the various Masonic lodges with no previous technical training in matters touching execution of the law, relative to disciplinary procedure, when called upon suddenly to conduct a Masonic trial or participate in the prosecution or defense of an accused Brother Mason, find themselves at sea and hesitate on account of uncertainty as to the details of procedure." Masonry has done everything it could to rectify this situation.

The first lesson the fraternity tries to impress upon the minds of its adherents is that a man's right to a fair and impartial trial is his most important possession, the cornerstone of Masonry, without which it would cease to exist. To make sure that local and Grand Lodges conduct trials in the correct manner, the Grand Lodges have set up committees to adjudicate legal problems when they arise. Such a committee is usually termed the Committee on Jurisprudence or the Committee on Grievances. While the committees often examine Grand Lodge actions, they tend to concentrate upon local lodge trials; and Masonic records demonstrate that these review bodies have not been reluctant to overturn lower level verdicts. For example, the Grievance Committee of the Grand Lodge of New York in 1880, after receiving the complaint of a local lodge member and "having had the matter under careful consideration, and hearing the history of the transaction . . . as well . . . [as] our examination of all papers and documents bearing upon the case presented to us . . . ," found the lodge in violation of Masonic law. Often these appellate hearings are quite elaborate, involving a multitude of roles. Typical of many cases in Masonic proceedings was a 1916 New York Commission established to examine charges arising out of an altercation between a Mason and his lodge leader. The commission consisted not of one, but of a panel of judges and a defense counsel; it called numerous witnesses and took a great deal of testimony before making a decision. Through the medium of Masonic trials many Masons have become very knowledgeable about their rights under a legal system, and have been quite adept at defending themselves when occasion warranted. When an expelled Indiana Mason pleaded before an Appeals Committee on the issue of reinstatement, he included in his defense many sophisticated legal arguments, among them the failure of the local lodge to present a list of charges, to allow defense counsel, the bias of the jury, and its failure to carry out the exact provisions of Masonic law.[7]

While the main roles in Masonic trials are played by local lodge members, or, on review, by the Grand Lodge committees, often a second level of "appeal" has existed by way of out-of-state Masonic opinion. Each Grand Lodge prints and distributes to its sister jurisdictions the record of its yearly general assembly. The responsibility for circulating the proceedings lies with the Chairman of the Committee on Foreign Correspondence (C.C.F.C.) of each state. Many of the C.C.F.C.s have taken upon themselves the role of Masonic constitutional authorities and have proceeded to judge the fairness and legality of actions taken by sister Grand Lodges. Exchanges between C.C.F.C.s on the importance of impartial trials have often been quite bitter. For example, the records of the Grand Lodge of California in 1912 include the words of the C.C.F.C. of Missouri attacking the Grand Master of Alabama, who while "always brave in his denunciation of those brutal followers of lynch law who are almost daily laying waste the homes and hearts of his Brethren, yet ... did nothing short of lynching" a brother when he illegally expelled him without benefit of a Masonic trial.[8] The C.C.F.C. of California, himself a major crusader for the sanctity of the Masonic trial, agreed wholeheartedly with his colleague's denunciation and had a goodly number of his own to contribute.

Self-government in Masonry, of course, means more than just conducting trials. It also means carrying on the normal

[7] *Proceedings* (New York, 1918).

affairs of the fraternity. On both the local and Grand Lodge level much of the work is done in committees. The number of committees in an average state Grand Lodge is nothing short of phenomenal. In New York in 1916 the following constituted the standing committees: Committee on Fraternal Correspondence (four members); on Jurisprudence (three members) on Finance and Banking (three members); on Subordinate Lodge Reports (five members); on Credentials and Proxies (three members); on Warrants and Dispensations (five members); on By-Laws of Lodges (five members); on Works and Lecturers (three members); on Foreign Relations (forty members); on Grievances (three members); on Appeals (Chief Commissioner and six others); on Revision of the Constitution (six members); on Sinking Funds (nine members); Jubilee Committee (thirty-three members). Other committees are created for temporary purposes.

The importance of these committees goes far beyond the practical work they accomplish. As can easily be imagined, with such a host of committees many of them accomplished very little. What they do is furnish large numbers of Masons with positions that not only boost their self-esteem but provide experience in how to function in the role of member, chairman, or secretary of an administrative committee. To the extent that the committees accomplish their official tasks they help to foster a sense of responsibility and leadership in the men who participate. On a local level the same sort of functions are served. In 1957 the Grand Master of New York told the leaders of his subordinate lodges that the best way to hold the interest of their members was to give as many of them responsibility as possible, to get them involved in the activities of running the lodge. Some of the devices he suggested included the formation of ways and means, investigatory, welfare and community liason committees.[9]

The Masonic fraternity offers its members more than just an opportunity to serve on a Grand or local lodge committee; it also provides a myriad of individual posts, many of which carry great weight in the government of the Order. The array

[8] *Proceedings* (California, 1912), C.C.F.C. reporting on Missouri.

[9] The proliferation of committees on all levels of Masonry has many dysfunctional aspects, and they will be dealt with in a later chapter. For the moment I am concerned only with their positive effects in creating social roles.

of offices that exist on the Grand Lodge level can most easily
be appreciated simply by listing the positions that existed in
a typical Grand Body: The Grand Master; Grand Senior and
Junior Wardens; Grand Trustees (two); District Deputy Grand
Master (eight); Grand Lecturer; District Deputy Grand Lecturer (eight); Grand Chaplain (two); Grand Marshall; Grand
Orator; Grand Registrar; Grand Historian; Grand Standard
Bearer; Grand Sword Bearer; Grand Senior and Junior Deacon;
Grand Senior and Junior Stewards (two of each); Grand Musi-
cal Director; Grand Pursuivant; and Grand Tiler.[10] All of these
positions serve an important ego-boosting function for the
Masons fortunate enough to obtain them. While many of them
are purely ceremonial offices and carry only limited power or
responsibility, some of them are very important and require
the occupants to possess or acquire a variety of administrative
and executive skills.

One of the skills Masonry tries to instill in its devotees is
an appreciation of and ability in business management. This
ideal receives practical expression in the determination of the
leaders of the fraternity to teach governing officials, if they
do not already possess it, the rudiments of "sound" business
procedure. The Grand Master of New York in 1935 made this
point when he said of the local lodge situation, "We must see
to it that we produce better business executives, to take care
of the many problems that confront us. This is very essential
and necessary as lodges cannot go doing slipshod business."
A Grand Master of Georgia happily observed that in his state
the local lodges were following the business practices that he
recommended, such as placing their funds in banks, having their
checks signed and counter-signed by officers other than the
treasurer, keeping records of votes on money matters and
records of checks signed. Not only would such procedures keep
the Craft sailing smoothly internally, but "When you do business that way it gives your lodge and its officers a standing
for square dealing in the [white] business circles in your town
and community."[11] A District Grand Lecturer of Alabama
probably best expressed the view of many Masonic leaders on
the importance of business in Masonry: "I might well compare
[seeing the local lodges working] to visits I have made into

[10] *Proceedings* (New York, 1918).
[11] *Proceedings* (Georgia, 1926).

some of our great industrial plants where wheels, belts, cogs and spindles, all in harmony, respond to the touch of the Master mechanic. . . ."[12] When a local or Grand Lodge fails to function efficiently because of an official's lack of knowledge of correct business form, there is always someone watching to point out the error of his ways. The C.C.F.C.s who are ever watchful for violations of Masonic due process are no less vigilant in defending good business practices.

The Prince Hall fraternity offers many opportunities for members to learn and exercise the business skills the Order values so highly. Besides the internal operation of the local and Grand Lodges, the fraternity engages in a host of business undertakings, all of which involve the membership, and especially its leaders, in business decisions and management. As I shall show later, most Grand Lodges have established some kind of relief, charity, or burial program, each working on a different system of collection or distribution for the benefit of the members, their widows, or orphans. These programs constitute major financial undertakings requiring great skill in their successful operation. Such programs provide a vast number of opportunities for ambitious and talented blacks. A list of the offices within an endowment department of a standard Grand Lodge would probably be as long as the list of positions in the Grand Lodge itself. Many of these posts are as demanding of time, thought, and skill as their equivalents in a "secular" insurance company. The larger state Grand Lodges have endowment funds which take in and give out hundreds of thousands of dollars a year. While most of the work of these departments require the exercise of business ability,[13] their smooth running requires men versed in other roles as well. For example, the Grand Lodge of Texas felt that to insure the just resolution of complaints against the endowment fund by disgruntled beneficiaries, they should set up an elaborate board of arbitration. The board included a Past Master[14] to represent the claimant, another appointed by the

[12] *Proceedings* (Alabama, 1925). See also *Proceedings* (New York, 1916), where the C.C.F.C. comments on New Jersey.

[13] The leaders of Masonry are very pleased about this. The Grand Lodge of Alabama has always been ready to laud its own business acumen. The Grand Master of that state in 1939 proudly boasted that through the endowment fund "the Masonic Grand Lodge has become a business as well as a Fraternal organization."

[14] The executive of the local lodge is called the Worshipful Master, and when he retires from office he is given the title of "Past Master."

Grand Lodge and a third agreed upon by the other two. The three together called witnesses, gathered evidence, and decided cases. Only after their decision was a still-dissatisfied beneficiary permitted to appeal to the civil court—where another Grand Lodge official, possessed of a law degree, protected the fraternity's interests.[15]

Besides endowment departments, many Grand Lodges have also run old age or orphan homes, banks or credit unions, farms, commercial buildings and printing presses. All of these projects have required able business administrators. For the Masons who occupy these positions, the fraternity performs two major functions: first, providing an outlet for the entrepreneurial desires which the larger white society creates and then frustrates, and second, providing training in business techniques which ultimately may be useable in the black community outside of Masonry.

While most of the more impressive opportunities for learning and exercising business expertise exist in the Grand Lodge, they are by no means absent on the local level. Many local lodges engage in building or buying their own lodge hall, or in conjunction with nearby lodges cooperate in buying a district temple. The preferred form for such ventures is a public corporation with ownership of the stock in the hands of individual members and the lodges as units.[16] The whole process provides countless opportunities for acquiring business acumen. In addition, it is not uncommon for the proponents of the combined temples to buy or build structures that house commercial or rental property on their ground floors which create a profit to ease the burden of paying for the building. The necessity of choosing and renting to tenants, and supervising their operation provides other jobs and experience for entrepreneurially-oriented Masons.

The building of Masonic temples is not only a local lodge activity. On the Grand Lodge level the building of a permanent home is often the most important, expensive, and time-consuming venture undertaken during the fraternity's lifetime.[17] The

[15] *Proceedings* (Texas, 1934).

[16] A perusal of the *Proceedings* of New York will reveal a large number of these local corporations.

[17] Booker T. Washington in *The Story of the Negro* (New York, 1909), pp. 156-157, discusses fraternal hall building with much enthusiasm. He points out that the Masons are especially noted as worthy for this activity, and most of his examples of fine and impressive black structures are owned by the Masons.

Grand Lodge temple is the crowning achievement of a state Masonic jurisdiction and frequently involves the expenditure of hundred of thousands of dollars. The preparations for, details of, and financing programs of such ventures entails the labor of Masons at all levels.

This chapter has dealt with a number of major roles that Masonry allows its adherents to play. Often the Order directly instructs members in social roles with which they have had no previous contact, other times it simply (but significantly) allows Masons to increase their proficiency at roles they have known but which the limited range of opportunities for blacks has denied them occasion to exercise. The Masons have long felt that the results of this training, in ideas and action, has been of great importance not only for the individual but for the race. When a committee of Texas Masons in 1927 said, "For more than fifty years we have striven both day and night to build a leadership who will make our Masonic organizations the most potent factor in the uplift of the Negroes of Texas . . . ," they expressed a sentiment felt by most Masons through-out the history of Prince Hall Masonry.

To what extent this belief has been true is difficult to accurately gauge. While the wealth of black leadership in the Order is impressive, the extent to which Masonry has been responsible for making its followers leaders, as opposed to simply attracting leadership-types, is hard to judge. What can be said is that the opportunities for expressing leadership qualities that exist in the fraternity are so great that its claim to having "produced" in some way or another leaders for the entire black race are not unfounded. Indeed, a case can be made that the simple act of becoming a proficient Master Mason, even when not ultimately striving for office or position, is effective in creating leaders for the community. The require-ments for becoming a Mason force the initiate to handle him-self calmly before a group of people, to speak well, to commit to memory and retain a substantial body of information, and to generally acquire "social grace." These same qualities are required for a man to become prominent in any social under-taking, and this gives the Mason an advantage in his relations outside the lodge.[18]

By providing Masons with an arena for the acquisition and

[18] Interview with Royal Towns, December 1968.

exercise of executive skills the Order has done for its membership what a wider variety of high-status occupations normally
would have provided them:

> Occupational differences ... have an effect on class-related be-
> havior through the kinds of skills that are exercised and main-
> tained in ... the occupation. Thus, [as an illustration,] ... higher
> socio-economic status jurors make more contributions to jury
> deliberation ... [because] higher socio-economic status occupa-
> tions require the exercise and maintenance of communication
> and negotiation skills. ... The occupational activities of upper
> socio-economic status individuals tend to reinforce and even
> extend the skills acquired during formal schooling ... ;

whereas lower status individuals disregard many of the habits
they have learned.[19] For blacks, Masonry and institutions like
it serve as a compensatory agency permitting the retention
of leadership skills.

In summary, Freemasonry serves two fundamental needs for
its followers. It caters to the subjective psychological need for
opportunities to act out social roles that enhance the individual's self-respect, and it objectively trains its members in skills
that will make them more effective leaders in the larger black
community.

Freemasonry allows its adherents to act as if they were
first-class American citizens. Within the safety of the fraternity
it allows them to bring aspiration and practice into harmony.
If one wishes to be an active participant in the democratic
political process and to carry out civic responsibilities, one can.
In the next chapter I will show that Freemasonry also allows
the Masons to carry out in practice the moral code they preach.

[19] Peter Rossi and Zahava Blum, "Class, Status and Poverty," in *On Understanding
Poverty*, edited by D. Moynihan (New York, 1969), p. 47.

Chapter VI

Social Ideals in Practice

The importance that Masonry places upon the values of work, thrift, charity, property ownership, and business efficiency has already been established. This chapter will deal with some of the practical steps taken by the fraternity to turn these ideals into reality for the benefit not only of its membership but of the entire black race, through insurance systems, charity funds, old age and orphan homes, farms, printing presses, credit unions, banks and scholarship funds.

Masons, like most of the black middle class, have believed that a fundamental difference between blacks and other American ethnic groups has been the black man's lack of a tradition of cooperative self-help. They have felt foreign groups such as the Jews and Italians have gained internal cohesion, external "white" respect, and group upward mobility because of the mutual support they have provided their own people. For many Masons their fraternity has presented the possibility that this supposed black failing could be rectified, first among the Masonic membership, then, by its example, throughout the entire community. This hope has been one of the major attractions of the Order for its adherents.

I pointed out in an earlier chapter that the Masons' perception of black deficiency in charity and communal cooperativeness has been strongly influenced by the existence in the general white community of organized, institutionalized philanthropy—a form of charity which has been relatively weak among blacks—and the simultaneous lack of recognition that the types of charity that do flourish among blacks (e.g., the adoption of stray children) has received from the dominant race. The Masons' view has also been negatively affected by a severely exaggerated concept of how generous and cooperative

133

white men, especially members of the foreign ethnic groups, have actually been. As a result of their faulty perceptions, Masons have dedicated themselves to creating from scratch a tradition of charity among black people. (Though despite Masonry's desire to convert the race to its concept of charity, most of the fraternity's practical work has involved the building of charity-providing structures only for its own members and their families. And these structures have been more impersonal and bureaucratic and therefore less "charitable" than the Masonic ideal calls for).

Charity begins for Freemasons with their duty to aid other Masons at times of acute stress. These are usually during periods of sickness and death, or when a Masonic widow or orphan is in need. Financial aid can come from either the local lodge, which is the usual source, or the Grand Lodge. On the local level when sickness and death strikes, the members donate money either to aid the ailing brother or to bury him.[1] Unfortunately, the Grand Lodge proceedings only give a glimpse of local lodge charity activities, and since in many states, for many decades, most charity was dispensed at that level, we are left with little information on how effective this work was. Infrequently one does find reports such as that given by the 1930 Texas Committee on Charity which stated that 231 people received $4,680 in local charity during the year,[2] or the statement by the Grand Master of Georgia in 1920 that the local lodges paid out $16,000 in funeral expenses, $10,000 for doctor bills, and $4,000 for medicine.[3]

Because local lodges were the primary source of charity, a major financial burden fell on the local membership. Charity

[1] An example of the requirements for Masons regarding charity to their members is given in the Constitution of Texas' Grand Lodge adopted in 1911 and amended in 1918. It included the following model for local lodges writing their bylaws: the Worshipful Master and the lodge Wardens shall be a Charity Committee and shall have power to draw upon the treasury for any sum, not exceeding X dollars for relief of a distressed brother, his wife, widow or orphans. Also, every member who dies in good standing is entitled to a burial, and the lodge must bury him. The lodge must go to the relief of his family. As part of every regular meeting there will be a report on sickness and distress among members and their families. In the 1919 Constitution the rules were slightly changed. Local charity had to be given only after a procedure that involved the Grand Lodge sending an Investigatory Deputy into the matter. The raising of charity in this document mentions the issuance of 'appeals' to local lodge members for charity, and they appear to have been mandatory.

[2] *Proceedings* (Texas, 1930).

[3] *Proceedings* (California, 1921), C.C.F.C. reporting on Georgia.

needs came at erratic and unpredictable times, placing great
strain on local resources. As a result, Grand Lodge plans were
developed to systematize the giving of charity and, if possible,
finance it at the Grand Lodge level. The plans usually called
for the Grand Lodge to establish a "Relief," "Endowment,"
"Benefit," or "Insurance" department (normally compulsory),
which would receive money from the entire membership of the
fraternity during the year and take the burden for burial and/or
aid to widows and orphans from the local lodges.

The strongest argument in favor of a Grand Lodge Relief
System emphasized the inability of the local lodge membership
on the spur of the moment to raise adequate amounts of charity.
Because of the relative poverty of the race, some means was
necessary to allow money to accumulate to meet the emergen-
cies of the moment. The only way to accomplish this, the
proponents claimed, was to establish some systematic and
compulsory plan; the compulsory nature of the plan was vital
because:

> ours, in many respects, is an adolescent Race, greatly in need
> of leadership. Even in those things that make for our own
> happiness, as a rule, without a guide, we neglect until too late,
> and the things of tomorrow seldom concern us until tomorrow
> comes....[4]

A Grand Lodge plan would also mean more adequate charity
than was the rule under the local system. J. H. Wilson of
California, the author of this statement, was furious at those
Masons who attacked the principles of the benefit system as
un-Masonic but who, when it came to giving charity, "dole
out two-bit pieces," fifty cents or a dollar, and then congratulate
themselves on their fraternal virtue. As a secondary benefit
of the system, one most Masonic leaders other than Wilson
never publicly acknowledged, it promised to enable Masonry
to compete favorably with other organizations—whether fraternities, sickness and burial societies, or "secular" insurance
companies—for members.[5]

The opponents of the Relief System idea were opposed to
the very qualities that men like Wilson thought admirable.

---

[4] *Proceedings* (California, 1919), C.C.F.C., J. H. Wilson commenting on Ohio's
Voluntary Benefit Associations.

[5] *Proceedings* (California, 1913).

Their major objection was that a compulsory system of charity was by definition not a voluntary act of giving, and therefore not charity at all. Since Masonry preached the idea of free-will giving with no thought of return other than moral satisfaction, any system that collected dues and gave beneficiaries the right to demand the payment of some stipulated sum was a business and had nothing to do with Masonry.[6] Also, since relief systems were compulsory it meant that an up-standing Mason who did everything morally required of him to stay in the fraternity could be expelled if he were unable to pay his endowment fund dues.[7] Lastly, the fact that the new relief fund idea was similar to the practices of non-Masonic organizations, and promised to make Masonry more competitive with those organizations, was repulsive to many opponents of the plan; innovations in Masonry which resulted from imitation of other groups they considered degrading to the fraternity.[8] The result of the disagreements within the Craft over the acceptability of a compulsory Relief System often created long delays in the enactment of such programs. The plans as they were established, however, often embodied features aimed at disarming the opposition. The history of the Relief System of California is representative of that of many other states.

In 1893 California established a Masonic Aid Association with compulsory fees. The organization lasted for five years and became inactive in 1898. A second attempt in 1907 also required compulsory dues and proved abortive. According to the Grand Master of California in 1915, the reason for these two failures was that the membership found the threat of expulsion from Masonry for failure to pay dues objectionable. He proposed that any future plan be optional or else it would likewise fail.[9]

[6] See *Proceedings* (California, 1911).

[7] *Proceedings* (California, 1908).

[8] *Proceedings* (California, 1919), C.C.F.C. commenting on Pennsylvania. As mentioned in Chapter II, Edward Palmer pointed out Masonry's reluctance to imitate insurance plans of other fraternities simply to become more competitive. While ultimately dues-paying insurance did become a widespread feature of Masonic life, the reluctance of the Masons to make charity impersonal and automatic shows that the Order was not simply an immature form of insurance company. Too many scholars have ignored fraternities such as Masonry except insofar as they were the precursors of "secular" insurance companies. Insurance, and business generally, are key elements of Prince Hall Freemasonry, but the fraternity cannot be reduced to it.

[9] Lack of funds and unwillingness to spend those that existed also had their effect on the failure of these plans. The comment made in 1898 when the first plan died was that "The Brethren felt that they could not afford the small amount of ten cents

Despite the Grand Master's recommendation, the committee set up to devise some sort of relief plan still insisted upon a compulsory one and reported to the Grand Lodge that the membership was still not "educated" to accept such a scheme.[10] Finally, however, sufficient support was obtained and the plan was established in the early 1920s, almost 30 years after the initial venture. The Relief Fund, as it was called, required each member to pay $3 per year and promised each beneficiary $125 to cover funeral expenses. At the end of the year any money left in the fund was to be divided equally among that year's widows and orphans. The authors of this plan were careful to disarm critics who saw any systematic collection of money as uncharitable, by leaving the total amount widows and orphans received indeterminant, dependant upon the size of the membership and the number of deaths per year, rather than a stipulated benefit. During the Great Depression, the fact that California Masonry was not tied to a rigid insurance-table of benefits saved it the fate of many Negro organizations that went into bankruptcy because of their inability to meet their obligations.[11]

California's plan was only one of many types that Masonic Grand Lodges adopted. One of the most ambitious projects undertaken, and one of the most successful, was that adopted by the Masons of Texas. Texas was one of the largest state jurisdictions, with a membership numbering in the tens of thousands, and it was able to take advantage of its size and a greater willingness of its adherents to pay dues, to give its membership a death-benefit far greater than any other state. For example, in 1918 when each man paid $8 in relief dues the death-benefit was over $300; by 1947 it was $500, and by 1953 it was $1,000.[12] Their plan was even more flexible than California's as far as the amount each beneficiary received, and like California saved Texas Masons from bankruptcy in the

---

per month . . . ." The Grand Master in 1915 pointed out that many members had "all the insurance" they could afford in other organizations and did not have the money to pay for Masonic insurance as well. C.C.F.C. J. H. Wilson in 1912 commented upon this last point by accusing Masons with outside insurance of being selfish and un-Masonic.

[10] *Proceedings* (California, 1916), report of Committee on Masonic Relief.

[11] *Proceedings* (California, 1921, 1922), report of Special Committee on Masonic Relief.

[12] *Proceedings* (Texas, 1918, 1947, 1953), report on relief system.

Depression. The amount of money that passed through the Relief Fund of Texas was quite impressive, often several hundred thousand dollars a year; as I shall show later, this money had other uses than simply paying relief.

The Masonic jurisdictions of Alabama and Georgia worked out endowment plans different from those of Texas and California. They attempted to run their systems as if they were insurance companies, with members choosing whatever level of benefit they wished and paying higher or lower dues depending upon the amount they chose. Alabama Masonry, which was extremely concerned about training businessmen and acting in a businesslike fashion, succeeded in setting up a viable plan in a way that Georgia Masonry did not. The Alabama Endowment Department took in hundreds of thousands of dollars a year and, since it did not annually distribute its money as Texas Masonry did, it accumulated reserves in the millions of dollars.[13] Ultimately, as in Texas, the endowment money was put to uses other than simply paying beneficiaries the $100-$500 that the system allowed.[14] It is interesting that despite Alabama Masonry's almost narcissistic pleasure in her "business-like" practices, and the claim by some of her devotees that her relief department was indeed a full-fledged insurance company, the Grand Lodge did not escape the necessity of having to justify her actions to those members who demanded that charity be voluntary. The Grand Master rebutted critics by insisting that since the endowment department was part of the Masonic Order it was far more than just an insurance corporation; thus "in the settlement of all our death claims decisions are based essentially on equity and justice rather than a too strict adherence to the letter of the law. Such a policy is not only right and brotherly, but in the long run the best policy."[15]

The Grand Lodge of Georgia wanted to run its relief fund in a manner similar to Alabama's; unfortunately, while it took

[13] See *Proceedings* (Alabama, 1938-42), for example.

[14] The extent to which the Alabama plan relieved the local lodges of the necessity of paying for funeral expenses, as it was supposed to in California, is not clear. In the records the system appears to have served the same purpose as that of other states, except that in the late 1930s the Grand Lodge set up a separate, voluntary burial plan which was designed to give beneficiaries an extra $30-$60 to cover funeral expenses and thus relieve the local lodges; this implies that the larger endowment plans did not do this. See *Proceedings* (Alabama, 1938).

[15] *Proceedings* (Alabama, 1938).

over many of the outward appearances of an insurance company, it neglected to acquire an understanding of actuary
statistics, an oversight it paid for by almost going bankrupt.
When the idea of a Grand Lodge Relief System was proposed
in 1906,[16] the committee established to consider the project
rejected the ideas as "un-Masonic" because it was ". . . competing with other beneficiary organizations, [and] thus seeming
to bid for a larger membership . . . ." Their negative report was
approved, but a year later the ideas were revived and passed.
From the beginning the system was defective because the rate
chosen to finance it was too small. According to Grand Master
Dobbs, who oversaw the reorganization of the system in the
early 1930s, the reason was that the brothers in 1908 had not
been "mentally prepared" to undertake a real "business venture." Thus they had a choice of a defective plan or none at
all. Even Dobbs believed some action was mandatory because
during those early years the Negro in Georgia was totally
unable to secure insurance from stable and recognized insurance companies. According to Dobbs, as long as the plan did
function it served its purpose of helping relieve want and
destitution among widows and orphans; but the system ultimately collapsed. When the day of reckoning came, and the
future of the Masonic fraternity was in doubt because of the
inability of the fund to meet its commitments, Grand Master
Dobbs reorganized it and set up a new plan based on the Texas
system: everyone paid a fixed amount, and the money collected
in a given year was divided among the families of the dead.
Each beneficiary was given two checks, the first for $100, which
was guaranteed, and a second one, of indeterminate amount—
normally larger than the first—which depended upon the ability
of the fund to pay. The first check would be an emergency
check for the funeral, but the second check would be a "real"
act of Masonic charity since the beneficiary could not require
the lodge to pay it.[17]

The Grand Lodges of New York and Illinois did not set up
a statewide form of Masonic insurance. The records of Illinois
show that over the years many men tried to establish such

---

[16] Actually a voluntary endowment plan was inaugurated in 1896, but it was not
successful.

[17] *Proceedings* (Georgia, 1933), Grand Master's speech.

a plan, but each time they failed.[18] New York in the nineteenth century also experimented with a variety of methods of meeting the problems of aiding widows and orphans.[19] The final result of their efforts was the establishment of the Hiram Masonic Relief Association in 1888. The system was voluntary and raised money by assessment on each of its members at the time of a brother's death. The plan provided both death and sickness benefits. It collapsed from lack of membership in the early 1900s.[20] With the failure of the Hiram Masonic Relief Association, the local lodges were left to carry the burden of burial aid once again.[21]

The Grand Lodge relief systems have played many functions for the fraternity. For most of the Masonic jurisdictions they have enabled the fraternity to live up to their obligations to their membership in a way that unsystematic giving on the local level was unable to accomplish. They have provided a form of cheap, easy-to-pay insurance which alone or incorporated with other policies have given some measure of security for Masonic families. The institution of these plans has also provided many Masons with important business training, enabling them to play roles they have been unable to play outside the fraternity. As pointed out in an earlier chapter, the endowment funds have created positions that have required men to play the parts of planners, secretaries, actuaries, treasurers, bookkeepers, investors, managers, etc. To obtain men to fill these offices, Masonry has both trained its members in the required skills and utilized members who already possessed them.

The relief systems have had negative as well as positive effects, many of which will be discussed in a later chapter. Here, however, it is important to point out that organized, compulsory relief plans may very well have damaged Masonry's

[18] See *Proceedings* (Illinois, 1925) for a discussion and review of the problem over time. Also see *Proceedings* (Illinois, 1959).

[19] Both Illinois and New York, like California, placed the emphasis on specifically relieving the local lodges of burial expenses.

[20] *Constitution and By-Laws of the Hiram Masonic Relief Association of the State of New York*, 1891, 1898, and other reports; and *Proceedings* (New York, 1882, 1883).

[21] Later, New York did attempt to establish "district-wide" programs where all the lodges in certain areas could aid each other. See *Proceedings* (New York, 1917, 1919). A successful system of "District Voluntary Immediate Relief Funds" was set up under Grand Master Louis Fair in the 1940s (see *Sentinel* (New York), 1, no.2 (Jan. 1944): 1-4, and 1943-53, passim.

ability to create a viable tradition of philanthropy among its membership. No matter what Masonic leaders have liked to believe, their systems have been a form of impersonal insurance, not unlike that purchased from private insurance companies. Men pay and ultimately expect, as their right, a return on their money. It is a rational form of investment in the future, not a free-will, selfless act of charity.

Perhaps the most important benefit that the statewide relief systems have provided the Masons, outside of its immediate one, has been the concentration of large amounts of money in the fraternity's hands—sums often reaching hundreds of thousands of dollars a year. The economic power these funds have offered Masonry has inspired many a Masonic leader to visions of glory. As a Grand Master of Alabama pointed out in 1909:

> The eternal shame of Negro secret societies is, that the most they are accomplishing is to take care of the sick and bury the dead. I am of the opinion that properly managed, through our Masonic lodges, reinforced by other societies, many of which most of us are members of, farms could be owned, teachers' trained to instruct us, soldiers trained to defend us . . . .[22]

Most of the more grandiose hopes of Masonic leaders have not materialized, but in some important instances Masonic relief money has been used for broader purposes than the ones for which the plans were ostensibly created.

Probably the most ambitious, and for years the most prestigious, project undertaken by any Masonic jurisdiction occurred in 1911 when the Grand Lodge of Texas decided to establish its own bank, the Fraternal Bank and Trust Company. The leaders of Texas Masonry, and especially Grand Secretary William McDonald, felt that Masonry was the perfect means for the blacks of Texas to raise the race by cooperative effort. In 1911 the Banking Committee of the Grand Lodge proposed that a bank be established with a capital of $100,000. Individual Masons and local lodges "acting as individuals" would be allowed to subscribe. Each lodge would use the bank as its depository for no less than 10 percent of its funds. Management would be controlled by the shareholders, but not by the Grand Lodge as a body. The proposal was enthusiastically passed.

[22] *Proceedings* (Alabama, 1909).

The Grand Master was proud to announce he was immediately "Acting in accord with the resolution adopted by the last Grand Lodge ... to organize a Banking House for the benefit of all loyal craftsmen and the Negro race in general."[23]

While the original proposal called for the Masonic Grand Lodge to own control of the bank, the Masons felt they lacked the money and asked both the Grand Lodge of Odd Fellows and the Grand Lodge of Knights of Pythias to buy 2,500 shares of stock. The Masonic Grand Lodge itself bought only the same amount; however, individual subscriptions by Masons brought the total up to 5,000 shares. Once the bank was operating the Grand Lodge made it the depository for all its funds, the bulk of which came from the endowment department.

In 1930, after eighteen years of successful operation, the Grand Lodge decided that it was strong enough to take over the majority of stock in the bank, and thus achieve its original goal of 1911. Total control of the bank promised that the Grand Lodge would receive all accumulated interest of the reserve relief fund, and thus would be able to advance loans to Masonic beneficiaries on the basis of the inheritance they would ultimately receive. (Until this date, beneficiaries received only $200 immediately on the death of a Mason and had to wait for over a year for the majority of their relief money. Many people needed the money desperately, and the Grand Lodge wanted to be able to provide this loan service, which only full control over the bank would provide.) When the Masons acquired total control, the bank had deposits of $600,000. The Masons hoped that all black people, and especially black Grand Lodges and Mutual Benefit and Insurance Societies, would use the bank as a depository for their checking accounts and reserve funds.[24]

The bank from the start was unincorporated, but in 1947 a proposal was made to change the organization from a private to a state bank. The proposal proclaimed that the institution had served the fraternity well for over 30 years and deserved to be elevated to a higher level.[25] While the resolution was not acted upon, it caught the imagination of many Texas Masons who had a vision of the Fraternal Bank and Trust

[23] *Proceedings* (Texas, 1930). Minutes containing reports and speeches relative to the discussion to establish a bank, reprinted from *Proceedings* (Texas, 1911, 1912).

[24] *Proceedings* (Texas, 1930). Speech of Past Grand Master Kirk reported in Minutes.

[25] *Proceedings* (Texas, 1947), recommendation found in Minutes.

Company becoming the first Negro State Bank of Texas. To achieve this, however, more support from the local lodges was necessary. As the Texas Grand Lodge Committee on Banking reminded the lodges in 1953, "We are but a minority group in America, but we are capable of operating banks and other business as successfully as other races" and thus maximum cooperation was needed from the membership.[26]

While the Grand Lodge of California did not actually establish its own bank, it was deeply impressed by Texas financial activities. As early as 1939, a California Grand Master dreamed of his jurisdiction following in the footsteps of the Lone Star State. California did partially embark on such a path when in 1952 the Craft set up a credit union in Southern California.[27] The plan was to have an organization which would enable Negro Masons to pay for their cars, lodge halls, place of entertainment, and so forth with their own money.[28] By 1953 the movement was well established and Prince Hall Credit Union (No. 1), serving San Diego, Imperial, San Bernardino, and Riverside counties had $35,000; a second union was also established. At this point, the first union asked the Grand Lodge to deposit some of its funds, which the Trustees refused to do since no money could be given to an institution not federally insured, even if it were so closely allied to the Order. (Nevertheless, and without further explanation, the records show that the Grand Lodge did deposit $3,500 in Prince Hall Credit Union No. 1.) By 1959 the two credit unions had $78,000 ($68,000 in the first and $10,000 in the second), and many Masonic leaders had expectations of even greater accomplishments. For instance, the public relations director of the Grand Lodge pointed out to the Craft that in the fifteen years since 1944, four separate white savings and loan associations with gigantic financial assets had been created in California. Every one of them had the use of Prince Hall Money, but "We do not own them" and thus "we must form our own savings and loan association." He informed the Grand Lodge that such a dream was not purely visionary, since he had pledges from members

---

[26] At some point around 1957, the bank after 46 years of service collapsed. The outstanding obligations of the institution—in the hundreds of thousands of dollars—were met in large part by the Masonic fraternity.

[27] The organization was legally separate from the fraternity.

[28] *Proceedings* (California, 1952).

totalling $80,000 already and would receive $170,000 more within 90 days if the Grand Lodge approved the plan. If this proposal seemed too radical, he said, it must be remembered that one other state already had such an institution and it was successful.[29] The available records do not record what action, if any, was taken on this proposal, but it provides a clue to the business ambitions of Masonic leaders.

While Texas had started to use its relief funds quite early in the twentieth century, the Alabama Grand Lodge waited until 1950. Before that date its main concern had been the security of its endowment funds, and while many wished to use the reserve fund constructively for any number of economic purposes, the Grand Lodge refused. In 1950, a proposal, not too different from others made over the years, asked that the endowment fund laws be revised and liberalized to allow surplus money to be loaned to members of the Order in the form of mortgages. The proposal called for loans to be made to individuals and lodges based upon 50 percent of the "reasonable value" of the real estate offered as security. This idea was hotly opposed by people who feared it would destroy the fraternity. One year later, a new resolution was presented which acknowledged the sincerity of those opposed to the old plan but felt it had a solution which would satisfy all parties. The resolution pointed out that by using the Federal Housing Administration, the Grand Lodge endowment funds could be loaned with 100 percent security behind them. The same thing could be done under the Farmers' Home Administration. The government agencies would make loans to the brothers and lodges who qualified on conditions even more generous than the 1950 proposal; and, as an additional bonus, the endowment fund would pay higher interest than United States Savings Bonds. This method, the resolution concluded, would enable the fraternity to truly aid its members.

The 1951 resolution worked; it disarmed the opposition. The Grand Lodge approved the liberalization of the endowment laws and gave the Grand Master power to carry out the new plan. In 1954, the Grand Master was pleased to note that despite the slow start of the program, owing to the difficulty of securing

[29] *Proceedings* (California, 1952). It is not clear what state is being referred to. Texas had had a bank, but by 1959 it had failed. The speaker may not have known that, or there may have been a third state involved.

satisfactory service agencies under the Federal Housing Administration and the apparent apathy of the government representative toward loans to black farmers, the Grand Lodge was doing fine; indeed, it was hard pressed to meet all the requests made upon it. In 1954, alone, the Grand Master continued, $144,790 had been loaned to black farmers and $161,000 had been given in urban loans, making a total of $306,000. He concluded by stating that the Grand Lodge's use of its money to provide loans was one of the Order's greatest services to the black race.

The example of Alabama seems to have been followed in other states and by other Masonic bodies. In the July 15, 1967 New York *Amsterdam News* an article noted that the Federal Department of Housing and Urban Development had lauded the Prince Hall Scottish Rite Masons as "a pace setter among a growing list of fraternal and social organizations committed to making decent housing available to low and moderate income families and individuals."[30] This statement was in reference to the decision of that Prince Hall body to extend its social concern to sponsor housing. HUD officials observed that the housing program had been started under John G. Lewis, head of the Scottish Rite, South (and also Grand Master of Louisiana) when that organization had set aside $300,000 as a revolving fund to assist local groups.

The Grand Lodge of Georgia also was interested in making its relief funds work for the betterment of the race. Though its plan was less ambitious than Texas' or Alabama's, it was unfortunately not less risky, and it worked out far less advantageously. In 1920 an amendment to Georgia Masonry's Relief Fund Report was presented which asked that all Colored banks of sound standing be made depositories for relief funds. The proposal reflected the spirit of those Masonic leaders who wished to aid, in all ways possible, the growth of black business. By making black banks guardians of their money, the Masons felt the fraternity would be doing a maximum of good with a minimum of effort. By 1926 the Grand Lodge had funds in eight banks, five black and three white; unfortunately, two of the black banks went bankrupt soon after. When Grand Master Dobbs in 1933 reviewed the reasons for the collapse of the relief fund he was forced to emphasize the placing of

[30] *Sentinel* (New York), 20, no.3 (July-Sept. 1967): 1, reprinted this article.

$250,000 in "weak banks, Negro banks though they were . . . ."[31]
Despite the ill-fated nature of Georgia's deposits, they nevertheless illustrate another way in which Masons attempted to
aid the black business community.

The practice of using Masonic funds, endowment or others,
to aid black business was not uncommon. In 1938 California
put $500 in the Liberty Building and Loan Association because
it was a good and credible "race organization." In 1957 the
Grand Lodge of that same state put approximately $200,000
in four black savings institutions. When asked why they did
so, the answer was: "We studied the situation on behalf of
the Grand Lodge and how we could help our people become
property owners and First Class Citizens. White financial
institutions are refusing to lend money to our Prince Hall
Family and minority race."[32]

Masonry's enthusiasm for business and its efforts to create
a business sector is part of the black middle class's general
optimism about "black capitalism." The constant references
to the power of business to raise the entire black group and
to solve the race problem which are made by Masons and
middle-class blacks generally, has occasioned much scholarly
comment. E. F. Frazier calls the whole phenomenon "Negro
Business: A Social Myth"[33] and emphasizes its fantasy aspects.
This position is concurred in by Earl Ofari,[34] Ivan Light,[35]

[31] By 1933 many more than two black banks must have gone bankrupt to make
the figure $250,000.

[32] *Proceedings* (California, 1957), Grand Master's speech. The key limitation on the
"progressive" use of Masonic money for general black community (especially business)
purposes has been the general financial conservativism of the Masonic leadership. The
Masons have wanted stability and security for their Order. Thus, government bonds
have formed a very large proportion of their investments. (This is in opposition to
the policy of black banks which, according to Abram Harris in *The Negro Capitalist*,
(Glouchester, Mass., 1968), p. 164, have suffered from too little money invested in
government securities.) And most of the money the Masons have placed in banks has
been in white not black ones. Masonic financial timidity has: restricted the amount
of money they have been willing to invest in non-Masonic black business; limited
the transferability of fraternally-learned business skills, since their experience has been
geared to maximize security not profit; and given added security to the widows and
orphans of the Order and protected the solvency of the Order as a whole. In the long
run, the conservative policy probably has proved more rewarding for the Masons than
a greater willingness to aid black business would have been.

[33] E. Franklin Frazier, *Black Bourgeoisie* (New York, 1957), pp. 129-145.

[34] Earl Ofari, *The Myth of Black Capitalism* (New York, 1970); the entire book argues
the weakness of black business.

[35] Ivan Light, *Ethnic Enterprise in America* (Berkeley, 1972), pp. 101-126.

Abram Harris[36] and others. Indeed, Light goes into great detail in analyzing the cultural reasons why black business has been doomed to failure (something other scholars have asserted but not really discussed). According to his interpretation the blacks have suffered from the destruction of a basic folk institution, the Rotating Credit Association, which is capable of generating the capital necessary for business success. Without this device, American blacks—unlike the Japanese, Chinese and West Indians—have been forced to rely upon white bankers for credit. The white banks have been reluctant to aid small businesses, especially those run by nonwhites. With neither a cooperative folk institution nor outside financial help, the black middle class has had to prematurely create its own banks in the forms of advanced credit institutions that it has lacked the skill to operate efficiently or the secure investment opportunities to support successfully. As a result, the black business community has suffered from the availability both of too little and too much capital, simultaneously. Thus, black capitalism has been a hope without substance.[37]

The efforts of the Masons in creating and supporting a business ethic, teaching business skills, setting up their own businesses, and aiding the entrepreneurial ventures of others may seem less than significant, given Light's analysis that the whole exercise has been doomed from the start. If Texas Masonry establishes a bank, it is not an achievement to inspire admiration but simply another ill-fated, economically unproductive venture that dissipates black resources.[38]

However, an emphasis on the unreality of black business aspirations, whether by Light, Harris, Frazier or others, can easily exaggerate both the uniqueness of the black middle class's position and the extent of its naivité or weakness. American capitalist ideology has always emphasized the power of the average man to achieve wealth through private enterprise. The mythical aspects of this image have been accepted as reality not simply by a naive black bourgeoisie but by most of the

---

[36] Harris, pp. x, 177.

[37] Light, pp. 45-61.

[38] Harris sees the middle-class black not simply as doomed to failure, but also as an exploiter of the black masses. In fact, he says the masses "have *no greater exploiter* than the black capitalist who lives upon low-waged if not sweated labor, although he and his family may, and often do, live in *conspicuous luxury*" (Harris, p. 184, italics added). The accuracy of this view is questionable.

American population; that the black middle class has been living in more of a fantasy world than the bulk of whites is problematic. It is true that there have been greater opportunities for some whites to succeed in business, even to join the economic elite; but real success has eluded all but a few aspirants, with the fortunate ones simply pacifying and misleading the majority. The free enterprise system has maintained itself by co-opting through tokenism the white majority as much as the black minority. The death rate of American businesses is in the tens of thousands a year—a fact that has not deterred a continual stream of new entrants into entrepreneurship, a stream that has not been primarily black. It is hard to find fault with a minority group that accepts the ideology that dominates the general society; that the black middle class has ignored the signs of its economic weakness (as Frazier, Light, Ofari, and Harris emphasize) does not readily differentiate them from the American public generally.[39] Thus, preordained to failure or not, the black middle class's (and Masonry's) efforts are more worthy of respect than of scorn or dismissal.[40]

[39] As for Frazier's negative evaluation of black business, Oliver Cox, who is not convinced even that black business has been a universal preoccupation of the black bourgeoisie, believes "even the limited achievements [of black capitalism] . . . should not be regarded as 'make-believe' " and simply dismissed (Cox's introduction to Nathan Hare's *Black Anglo-Saxons*, [New York, 1970], p. 21).

[40] Light, of course, does not scorn or condemn the black middle class since he avoids the pitfall of too close an emotional involvement with the problem. Light's dispassionate analysis of the weaknesses of black business is the most ambitious and stimulating treatment of the subject to date. In large part it is both brilliant and persuasive. However, there are problems in his discussion. The insights that come from the comparison of Oriental and black business are deceptive since they appear to answer questions they cannot. The key discovery Light made was the existence among non-European peoples of a capital-forming folk institution (the Rotating Credit Association) which foreign ethnic businessmen could use but which native blacks lacked. The discovery seems to give flesh to the vague explanation of black failure that Frazier and others have given when they have emphasized the "lack of a business tradition" without specifying components of that tradition. The problem with Light's analysis is that his insight tells us only half the story. True, the blacks have lacked the tight-knit folk community of Oriental-Americans, and this deprived them of useful socioeconomic resources. But what made this so disastrous? Light, p. 5, originally posed the question of why immigrants (especially *white* ethnics) had succeeded in business while the blacks failed. Yet, the white ethnics are much closer to the blacks in the looseness of their folk ties than they are to the Orientals. Even the Jews, a very successful and tight-knit European group, compared to the Chinese are an atomized, disunified mass of individuals. Jewish traditional society had already collapsed in the Old Country before they left for America, and even at its height was never organized as closely as the Orientals that Light describes. To know why the blacks failed in business we must compare

Masonry has engaged in other activities besides the creation of relief systems to meet its obligations to Masonic widows and orphans. Throughout the nation, black Masonic leaders have considered the establishment of Masonic old age and orphans homes as among the most important goals for the fraternity. Booker T. Washington in 1909 said that while fraternities generally were doing much charitable work to help orphans and the aged,

them not simply (*or even primarily*) to the Orientals but rather to the European-Americans. We must ask what the white ethnics did to generate business capital in the absence of Oriental solidarity and why American blacks were unable to duplicate that achievement. The lack of clan, province organizations, and Rotating Credit Associations closed one possibility for blacks, but not all.

Even if the Oriental-black comparison were the most useful one, there is still a basic flaw in the discussion. Light uses the Chinese as one of the models for what blacks wanted to achieve: business success and group upward mobility. However, he exaggerates the extent of Oriental business achievement and its effects. He makes it appear that prosperity from entrepreneurship benefited the whole group rather than a small part of it. This is questionable. Rather, the group's rise out of poverty appears to have depended upon their attitude toward education *and* the lessening of anti-Chinese occupational discrimination during and after World War II. That Chinese-owned businesses did not produce prosperity for the vast majority of Chinese is obvious from Light's own account. On page 7 he points out that the hours were long and the remuneration very low for the Chinese working in Chinatown. (In 1920 fully 50 percent of them were employed or self-employed in laundries and restaurants). When anti-Chinese discrimination lessened and "the labor shortages of World War II opened new employment opportunities for them" they grabbed them (Light, pp. 7-8). Without the lowering of the barriers to Chinese entrance into white-collar and professional occupations, and their success in school which enabled them to take advantage of the new opportunities, the Chinese would have remained poverty-striken. It is more likely that business helped a small elite, at the cost of widespread Chinese exploitation, much more than it helped the whole group. Family and clan solidarity subordinated the average Chinese to the economic well-being of his highest status kin. Light only hints at the plutocratic and oligarchic nature of Chinese-American society; but even he provides a glimpse of the price the Chinese workers paid for their ethnic business establishment: "[Oriental] business class leaders were usually in a position to squash serious dissenters by depriving those who made trouble of employment opportunities. Purges of radicals and trade unionists were fairly common among both Chinese and Japanese during the 1930s. By virtue of discrimination in the American labor market, Chinese and Japanese wage earners depended on ethnic businesses for employment" (Light, p. 175). He goes on to say: "Chinese and Japanese workers . . . could not readily control unresponsive territorial elites by playing them off against one another . . . Old World loyalties . . . tended to prevent disgruntled people . . . from making common cause against conservative elites . . . In this sense, the mutually exclusive immigrant brotherhoods of the sojourning generation endowed business class leaders with an enormous capacity to mold developing Chinatowns or Little Tokyos in the image of their conservative social and economic philosophy" (Light, p. 176).

The Chinese elite may have guaranteed a minimal level of subsistance, but at a terrible price. Stanford Lyman in "Strangers in the Cities: The Chinese on the Urban Frontier" (in *Ethnic Conflict in California History*, edited by Charles Wollenberg [Los

The Masons are perhaps leading in this respect ... [since] they
[have] established homes for the aged members ... in Georgia,
North Carolina, Illinois and Tennessee.[41]

One of the most successful was in the jurisdiction of Georgia.
The Georgia Masonic Home was proposed in 1897, and a
committee to determine the site was established. The cornerstone was laid in 1898.[42] The home that was erected was the
pride and joy of the jurisdiction; and a source of endless race
pride for her leaders. Grand Master Dobbs in 1933 put succinctly what the home meant to him when he said, "The significance
of this achievement is best understood when you realize that

Angeles, 1970]) says that "Chinatown also housed the Chinese elite—the merchants
of the ghetto—who acted as spokesmen for and protectors of the laborers and who
held the latter *in a state of political dependence and debt peonage*" (Lyman, p. 78,
italics added). While the first generation dreamed of obtaining riches and respect, "In
fact, this rarely occurred . . . . The promise of America's gold turned to dross, but
he labored still" (Lyman p. 84). Even today, Lyman goes on, old elites "continue to
hold sway at the expense of their subjects, over whom they exercise a benevolent
but despotic authority" (Lyman, p. 99). Chinese business did not bring success to these
people. According to Lyman, it was only the children born to the Chinese *after* 1930
that really succeeded in America. [The severe lack of Chinese women in America meant
that there weren't enough women available to create a "second generation" until this
extremely late date (Lyman, p. 98).] Even as recently as 1960, the effect of the very
slow upward mobility of the Chinese resulted in the following statistics: In California
in 1960, 40.8 percent of the male Chinese, 14 years old or over, had not gone beyond
the eighth grade in school. In 1959, 61.6 percent of the Chinese 25 years old or over
in California made under $5,000, with 33.6 percent making under $3,000. [See R. Daniels
and H. Kitano, *American Racism* (Englewood Cliffs, 1970), where the publication
Californians of Japanese, Chinese and Filipino Ancestry (San Francisco, 1965) is
quoted.] One cannot help but wonder if Chinese capital formation wasn't more the
result of the exploitation of the Chinese workers than of the Revolving Credit
Associations. If this is true, then the black middle class compared to their Chinese
equivalent suffered less from the disappearance of that folk institution than from their
inability to sufficiently exploit their brethren. In addition, Light appears to equate
group achievement not so much with obtaining widespread prosperity but with its
ability to keep people off public welfare rolls. If a group provides "internal" welfare,
its business and community structure is deemed a success. Yet the adequacy of Chinese
group relief was in large part a function of the lower class's abysmal standard of living.
The willingness of the Chinese worker to subsist on community-provided *rice* was an
advantage the more Western black population lacked (Light, p. 88). If Chinese
expectations had been more American the Chinese community would not have been
able to support its own. If the blacks would have accepted a level of relief as low
as the Chinese, they too might have "successfully" avoided public welfare. When it
is realized that the Chinese elite fought to prevent the lower class from obtaining
public aid, which would have raised their standard of living, their achievement vis-a-vis
the black middle class becomes even more problematic (See Light, p. 114).

   [41] Booker T. Washington, *The Story of the Negro* (New York, 1969), vol. II, p. 158.
   [42] "History of the Grand Lodge" (Georgia), Sol C. Johnson, 1920 (pamphlet).

we have begged money with which to build our churches and our schools, but this entire plant was built and paid for by the Masons of Georgia. Not one dime has been begged from any outside source."

The Masonic Home which Georgia built was actually an orphans home, an elementary school, and a farm. By 1933 the institution had three modern brick buildings as well as a barn and livestock. There was also a brick cottage for the girls built by the Order of Eastern Star, the woman's auxiliary to Masonry. While the school offered work in the elementary grades, Grand Master Dobbs hoped to start an agricultural and industrial school when possible.[43] The Masons of Georgia were very proud of their home and especially generous to it. In 1926 the Masonic home department had an income of $26,000 ($10,000 as dues from the local lodges, $10,000 from the Order of Eastern Star, and $6,000 from sources such as tuition at the school and farm profits). Besides this money, a special building fund to erect a boys' dormitory had an independent income of $5,000. For the Masons this was quite a prodigious sum of money.

The orphans home accomplished a whole range of Masonic goals. We have already mentioned that it served to dispense charity and to encourage race pride. It also provided the fraternity with an arena for the realization of its ideals of self-help, thrift, hard work, and cleanliness. The children in the home were raised to be model citizens, embodying as much as possible all the middle-class virtues in which Masons placed so much faith.[44] Of special concern to the Grand Lodge was that the home and farm "produce," that every "consumer be a producer" and create more than he himself used. As a result the products of the farm—250 bushels of corn, 300 bushels of potatoes, or whatever the harvest happened to be that year— was viewed with great interest by the fraternity members.[45] The establishment of a Masonic home, school and farm and

[43] *Proceedings* (Georgia, 1933). For various figures on the home see 1920, 1908, and 1926, among others.

[44] This probably was the case in most other Masonic homes, as witnessed by the situation in the Masonic Home of Tennessee: "A good religious atmosphere pervades its surroundings and the habits of cleanliness and industry are enforced." The home fought the high cost of living with its Masonic farm which produced much of the food for the home and probably a surplus for sale (*Proceedings* [California, 1917], C.C.F.C. reporting on Tennessee).

[45] *Proceedings* (Georgia, 1920), report of the Matron of the Home and School.

their efficient functioning were also important in once again proving to the Masonic leaders, and they hoped to the white community, that blacks could be successful businessmen.

The existence of an elementary school as part of the Georgia Masonic Home is also indicative of another Masonic ideal the fraternity wished to put into practice. Since education was viewed as the key to upward mobility and ultimately to racial equality, Masonic responsibility for the orphans of deceased Masons could not be complete without some provisions for their training. The records of Georgia's Grand Lodge show that the state's leadership took great interest in aiding talented orphans to enter schools of higher education after they completed the elementary school. They often intervened with officials of Negro colleges to assure admission of their wards. In 1933, for example, the trustees of the home sent two orphans to college because of their outstanding ability, and Grand Master Dobbs said he hoped some day the Grand Lodge would establish a regular scholarship fund for such bright students. Dobbs saw his desire fulfilled in 1946 when the Grand Lodge approved the establishment of a scholarship committee and an education fund in response to the outcry by many members that hundreds of qualified Georgia Negro youths were unable to get proper technical or higher educational training. The Grand Lodge was especially proud that its education committee was headed by a professor from Fort Valley State College and four other "outstanding" Georgia black educators.[46] In 1950 the Grand Lodge appropriated $5,000 to what was then called the John Wesley Dobbs Scholarship, making a total of $15,000 between 1946 and 1950; and another $1,000 was given the Negro College Fund. By 1958 the Grand Lodge was providing $15,000 a year in scholarships. Dobbs considered the scholarship fund the most important enterprise of Georgia Masonry in the post-World War II period, much in the way he had considered the Masonic Home in earlier years.[47]

Alabama Masonry saw the importance of educational scholarships quite early. By 1906 it was appropriating nine awards

[46] *Proceedings* (Georgia, 1959).

[47] From the material available it appears that Georgia's educational aid was not restricted to Masonic orphans, or Masonic children at all, [see *Proceedings* (Georgia, 1949)], but this was not the case in most states. Elsewhere the scholarship funds tended to be restricted to the fraternity itself.

of $50 each to children of deceased Masons.[48] What occurred between 1907 and 1937 the available records do not reveal, but in 1938 a department of education existed which was dedicated to aiding Masonic orphans. A tax of five cents per member per year was levied in order to fund the department.[49] A report delivered in 1948 reviewing the previous nine years reported that a total of seventy-seven grants of approximately $100 each, for tuition, had been dispensed. The interest that Georgia and Alabama have shown in providing educational opportunities for Masonic orphans has been representative of the fraternity generally, and by 1962 it was hard to find a Prince Hall Grand Lodge that did not distribute student scholarships.[50]

Some Masonic lodges, Grand and local, have found that employment bureaus are yet another way to give substance to their ideal of Masonic charity. When Georgia in 1937 began publishing its Grand Lodge magazine it proclaimed as one of its goals the establishment of an employment bureau for needy and worthy Masons.[51] As early as 1928 the Grand Master of New York recommended that an employment bureau be set up in his jurisdiction.[52] While this proposal was not acted upon for many years, it was viewed favorably by a number of New York Masonic leaders. In 1948 Grand Master Louis Fair announced that he hoped shortly to establish such an employment aid for Prince Hall Masons. The available records do not tell us the specific action taken by Grand Master Fair, but sometime thereafter the Grand Lodge set up a department of charity, education, and *employment.* In 1966, this department was modernized and changed into the department of social concern, with a committee of employment opportunity under it.[53] The committee adopted as its objectives far-reaching goals:

1. To inform the Craft of all known employment opportunities, private and government.

[48] *Proceedings* (California, 1908), C.C.F.C. reporting on Alabama and Georgia.

[49] *Proceedings* (Alabama, 1939).

[50] *Digest* (California), 10, no.3 (Sept.-Dec. 1962): 17.

[51] See *Review* (Georgia), 1, no.1 (October 1937): 3. This venture depended on the financial success of the magazine. Unfortunately, the journal did not make a profit and had to be largely subsidized by the Grand Lodge.

[52] *Fraternal Review* (non-Masonic journal published in New York), 7. no.6 (June 1928): n.p.

[53] *Sentinel* (New York), 19, no.3 (July-Sept. 1966): 3.

   2. To provide assistance for brothers in completing applications
      for jobs.
   3. To maintain a bulletin board announcing new openings and
      opportunities for training.[54]
   4. To establish liason with government agencies for exchange
      of labor and market information.

They also planned to consider the establishment of a placement
office where perspective employers might register and job applicants might seek employment, as well as a job clinic for
vocational guidance.[55] A few years earlier, in 1960, the Grand
Master of California told the fraternity that he believed employment agencies supported by the Grand Lodge should be
set up in strategic places in the state and an employment
opportunity foundation established to support and implement
fair employment practices. The head of Illinois Masonry, Ashby
Carter, in the late 1940s and early 1950s, while not directly
involved in creating employment agencies, did lead the fraternity in the fight for a permanent fair employment practice
committee in Illinois.[56] The records also show that employment
was a concern of many local as well as Grand lodges, with
many of the more progressive ones setting up employment
committees to aid members in locating jobs.[57]

    While the Order has provided formal channels for aiding
members to obtain employment, more significant has been its
function as a meeting place where individual members can
cooperate on an informal basis. In a manner similar to the
white Masons, members of the fraternity have used the organization to improve their economic status. Exactly how often
they have made use of the Order for this purpose is impossible
to determine, not simply because the activity is unofficial but
because Masons are reluctant to discuss it because of its
apparent manipulative, and therefore "un-Masonic," character.
A fascinating illustration of this reluctance to speak, and the
reality hidden behind it, was provided by C. L. Dellums,
President of the Sleeping Car Porter's Union. In an interview

   [54] The author saw the Grand Lodge of New York's bulletin board and found notices
of civil service openings predominant.
   [55] *Sentinel* (New York), 19, no.4 (Oct.-Dec. 1966): 7.
   [56] See the later chapters on civil rights for more details.
   [57] *Review* (Georgia), 12, no.4 (1948): n.p., reviewing a local lodge in Indianapolis,
Indiana.

with the author he stated that to use the institution for material gain was reprehensible conduct for a Mason. And it is almost never done, except by a "dishonorable few." Nevertheless, much to his own shame, he himself had inadvertently obtained his first employment on the railroad directly because of his Masonic membership. According to his story he was in a dire financial position when he went to the railroad office seeking employment. He was rejected. Since he was desperate he returned for a second attempt, even though he believed it would do no good. On his second appearance the *white man* in charge saw that he had a Masonic pin, and as a result of Masonic loyalty (across racial and institutional lines) pushed Dellums ahead of his competitors into the job.

Despite Dellums' feelings of guilt over the incident, the favoritism shown him in this situation was totally in keeping with Masonic values—as long as job seeking was not the major reason for joining or staying in the Order. For one brother to aid another is an important form of social unity—exactly what Masonry stands for. That in Dellums' case the unity should have existed across caste lines is simply a special and fascinating case. It is also by no means the only instance of interracial Masonic solidarity I have found. Royal Towns told me of obtaining employment in an industrial shop that required all of its employees, white and black, to be Masons; other Masons have talked of favorable discrimination by whites toward black Masons even in the South.

One local California official was considerably more willing than most members to admit the importance of job opportunities in inducing men to join the Order. He maintained that he saw nothing incompatible with being a good Mason and aiding one's life chances as long as one broadened his commitment to the Order after obtaining employment. When he joined the fraternity there were no trade unions and few civil service positions open to blacks. If a man needed a reference, someone to vouch for his good character, belonging to a respectable fraternity such as Masonry was mandatory. Not only that, if a brother knew of an opening where he worked he would let his fellows know, and "put in a good word for them."[58] This

---

[58] Bridges Interview, April 1971. The usefulness of Masonry for providing jobs or job information is long standing. The Grand Master of Texas in 1960 told his brethren that the first Texas Grand Master, N. W. Cuney, almost a hundred years before had

practice of aiding brothers in employment has been a very important function of the Order on an unofficial level. If blacks as a group were more economically secure and had businesses that employed more workers, it would have been even more important—as it is among whites. Unfortunately, Masons have been severely handicapped in the number of economic favors they have been able to dispense.

Returning to Masonry's role in providing more traditional forms of charity, it has engaged in many of the standard public service types of work. For example, many states have established Prince Hall blood banks which, while helping the general community, have been primarily intended for Masons.[59] This type of program has also served to enable the fraternity to cooperate with non-Masonic bodies such as the American Red Cross, and thereby obtain favorable publicity. During World War II at least one Grand Lodge, that of New York, set up a military and naval service committee designed to ease life for Masons or their sons in uniform. The committee attempted to locate out-of-state Masons stationed in New York and provide them with recreation; and they contacted other states to do likewise. The committee was also the agency through which the local lodges contributed aid to the families of dead or injured servicemen. Besides the committee, the Grand Lodge set up a Prince Hall Masonic War Fund. In 1944 the Grand Master thanked the individuals and lodges that had contributed to the fund and told them that since many brothers would return crippled from the war the fund should continue to operate.[60] Soon after, the Grand Lodge raised $1,000 for just such a crippled brother.[61]

While the Order has worked hard to make charity a reality, it has spared absolutely no effort or expense in its attempt to give its ideal of property ownership substance. When the Grand Lodge Masonic Temples are built, especially in the larger and richer jurisdictions, each state hopes that its edifice will

shown his love of Masonry through his private efforts to help the brethren: "That he believed implicitly in the Mystic Tie is evidenced by the fact that many of the men working for the Mallory Line Steamship Company under his contract were Masons and members of our organization" (*Masonic Quarterly* [Texas], 40, no.141 (March 1960): 1).

[59] *Sentinel* (New York), 5, no.9-10 (Nov.-Dec. 1952): 9, 12.

[60] *Sentinel* (New York), 1, no.2 (Jan. 1944): 2.

[61] *Sentinel* (New York), 2, no.5 (May 1945): 5.

be the largest and most expensive in black America. For the outsider who observes Masonic activities, the Temple Building fever appears decidedly dysfunctional. Men who sincerely wish to provide as much charity, give as many scholarships, build as many orphans homes, and open as many black businesses as possible, and who find their efforts restricted or thwarted because of financial difficulties, turn around and spend more money than most of these projects combined for a Temple of dubious utility. But such expenditures should not be dismissed simply as an example of fraternal waste and extravagance. The psychological importance of the Temple must be understood. For the Masons the Grand Lodge Temple is more than a material object. It is an indispensable symbol of black manhood; it demonstrates as nothing else "the mental ability and financial sacrifice . . . [and] evidence[s] the business genius and race consciousness of our group . . . ."[62] It "represents the thrift, industry and business tact" of both colored Masons and non-Masons,[63] and serves as "a source of pride and inspiration to the entire Colored Race."[64]

Masonic literature is full of the most extravagant claims about what a Grand Lodge Temple signifies. For example, in New York, leading Masons such as the noted bibliophile Arthur Schomburg invoked every ancient black hero, every emotion of race pride and dignity, and every noble feeling to motivate the membership to spare no expense in building a colossus which would stand forever.[65] Temple Building fever has stemmed from the belief (not totally incorrect) that in capitalistic America neither a man nor a race is anything unless he owns property; and the bigger, the more prominent, expensive and gaudy the better:

> The worth whileness [sic] of any group . . . [is measured by] the ability of that group to enter the business world and hold its own in the strong competition in that field,[66]

[62] *Review* (Georgia), 10, no.1 (Jan.-March 1946): 11, quoting a New York Mason about his home jurisdiction's Temple.

[63] *Proceedings* (California, 1952), C.C.F.C. commenting on Arkansas' Temple.

[64] *Review* (Georgia), 1, no.5 (Feb. 1938): 19.

[65] *Proceedings* (New York, 1920).

[66] *Proceedings* (Texas, 1939), report of Temperance Committee. In the Grand Lodge of Georgia's magazine (*Review*, February and March 1938), Grand Secretary McDonald of Texas and Grand Master Dobbs of Georgia argue heatedly over whether Texas, Alabama, or Florida has the largest Negro-owned building. The two rather crassly

notes a committee of the Texas Grand Lodge, and for many Masonic leaders a Temple has represented the black race's coming of age in *business* as no other single enterprise could.[67] With such psychological rewards, what could a few thousand additional scholarships or more adequate charity payments offer?

The Grand Lodge Temple has not been the only outlet for Masonry's desire to acquire real property. The ownership of local lodge halls has been only slightly less important. The local lodges have often felt it necessary to sacrifice much of their other work in order to raise money to build or buy their fraternal home. The records of the different states are full of local cooperative corporations established for the purpose of building single or multiple lodge halls.

Underlying most of the projects undertaken by Masons, whether establishing more efficient ways of providing charity, creating a home for orphans, or buying a Temple, one finds the constant desire to promote black business. Good business methods and a knowledge of entrepreneurial skills are always seen as indispensible for the accomplishment of worthwhile causes. For example, in their attempt to raise the intellectual level of the Craft and to bind the Craft together, many states have embarked upon journalistic ventures. These constitute yet another form of enterprise. Working on the magazines, members have been able to learn to exercise their knowledge of editing, writing, reporting, organizing, and distributing. Often the editors of the Masonic journals have been noted and experienced black newspapermen who have worked on major black "secular" papers. For example, Charles T. Magill, editor of the *Prince Hall Sentinel* of New York, though he worked in the Post Office for forty years, had gone to journalism school at New York University, worked for the Chicago *Defender*, the New York *Amsterdam News*, and the New York *Age*.[68] For men like Magill the Masonic organ was an opportunity, among the few that existed, for exercising his journalistic

throw building-cost figures at each other. The more expensive a building was, the more it proved the black group's worth.

[67] The reason why Temples rather than a more traditional form of commercial enterprise has been chosen to represent both black property and business *par excellence* will be discussed in a later chapter.

[68] *Sentinel* (New York), 5, no.1-2 (Jan.-Feb. 1952): 1, 3.

ability. For others, the Masonic magazines probably were the first and only chance to learn the skills of journalism.

Some Grand Lodges have gone beyond the act of founding newspapers and magazines, and have created Masonic printing establishments—among others, in Texas, Louisiana, and Mississippi.[69] Ownership of publishing plants has provided Masons with great satisfaction. Merely the existence of skilled black printers has occasioned much pride. For instance, in New York in 1916 the Grand Master proudly informed the Craft that the printing of the Grand Lodge proceedings had been given to a member of a local Manhattan lodge and "Most of this work was done by colored people." He felt compelled to point this out "because we have heard it stated that it was an impossibility to have the work done around New York by colored people properly." The existence of a Masonic printing press could remedy this suspicion and prove, yet again, to blacks and whites alike, that Negroes are as capable of doing skilled labor and running a business enterprise as anyone else.

The Masonic fraternity has engaged in many activities in its attempt to translate its values into practice. Many of these ventures have produced important material benefits for the membership. They have also produced nonmaterial benefits as well: pride, psychological satisfaction, and the opportunity to learn and exercise useful skills and roles. These nonmaterial benefits have outweighed the material ones in importance, and thus even if some of the enterprises have to a degree failed, they have nevertheless done much good.

While Prince Hall Freemasonry has worked to allow its members to bring their individual ideals to fruition, it has also enabled them to achieve a larger ideal: the creation of an integrated black middle-class community within black society. It is only through the existence of such a community that the black Masons have been able to obtain the total support necessary to live the middle-class lifestyle. In the next two chapters I will deal with the ways in which Freemasonry has interfaced with other black institutions to create an environment conducive to bourgeois life. Chapter 7 will focus on Masonry's links with the local community, and chapter 8 on its links to the national and international community.

[69] *Proceedings* (California, 1940), C.C.F.C. reporting on Louisiana.

Chapter VII

Black Masonry's Links
with the Local Community

Prince Hall Freemasonry is integrated with the major centers of black middle-class life, through its own activities and through those of its members. Traditionally it has maintained strong ties to the church, to business, and to other major fraternities. In recent years it has forged additional links with civil rights and general uplift groups. Through these ties it has acted as one of the major institutional foundations of the black middle class.

My contention that a fraternal organization can play such an exalted social role receives general support from the noted American historian Rowland Berthoff in his seminal essay "The American Social Order: A Conservative Hypothesis."[1] Berthoff contends that America society in the nineteenth century was in a state of social chaos and disintegration. But while the old forces of social integration grew feeble, there were signs of revitalization:

> Symptomatic of the need for a new sense of community was the fraternal order. It is customary for historians to dismiss the lodges of Masons or Odd Fellows which sprang up everywhere as an unimportant eccentricity of a 'nation of joiners,' and yet they were highly significant of the lack of other forms of community in American society in their day.... The invention and maintenance of any kind of social community was in itself a sufficient cultural achievement for their time.[2]

[1] *American Historical Review*, 65, no.3 (April, 1960): pp 495-514.

[2] Ibid., p. 507. Berthoff, much like E. Franklin Frazier (*Negro in the United States*, [New York, 1957]), Allan Spear (*Black Chicago* [Chicago, 1967]), and others, assumes that the fraternities declined precipitously after other institutions creating social integration were formed. He may be right for the whites; or he may be wrong. There

While Berthoff is talking of American white fraternities and the community-building functions they served, the general social disintegration and confusion for whites was little compared to the chaos among blacks. Black men had suffered the eradication of most of their African heritage, compounded by the social confusion which marked the end of slavery. The fraternities and lodges were certainly a means of forming a common society in the years after 1865. This was true of fraternities generally, though various groups operated among different segments of the black population. We are concerned, however, only with the middle-class fraternities, of which Masonry was the foremost representative. Since these Orders were concerned primarily with creating and nurturing a black bourgeoisie they did little to foster a feeling of responsibility toward the masses of lower-class blacks, their official credos notwithstanding. Therefore, while acting as a constructive community-building force, their successes were limited to the creation of a parochial subcommunity, which had its eyes turned more to the white bourgeoisie (whose life style it shared) than to the black masses. That Masonry was a key institution in the initial creation of the black middle class after the Civil War there can be no doubt. In addition, it continued to play an important though diminished role in the period 1900-1970.[3]

In trying to understand how Masonry has interacted with other pillars of the black community, how it has worked to create an environment in which black middle-class men can spend as much of their social life as possible among their own kind, one faces a major obstacle.[4] Masonry has throughout its history refused to participate as an institutional entity in the

has been almost no study of the importance or lack of importance of American white Masonry in recent times—or in the nineteenth century.

[3] It is probably true that it played a similar role in many Northern black communities in the period 1800-1865, too.

[4] The black middle-class community is of course anything but complete. Since its economic base has traditionally been so slim, its members have been forced to spend most of their working life in contact with the white world. It is only after working hours that most of the men have been able to retreat to black social institutions. Not only that but, within the Ghettoes, because of discrimination, general black poverty, and lack of middle-class wealth, they have been forced to be in constant contact with lower-class blacks. As St. Clair Drake and Horace Cayton point out in *Black Metropolis* (New York, 1962), p. 660, middle-class blacks were forced to create "middle class apartment houses" since they could not control whole neighborhoods. It was this very lack of physical insulation from the lower class that made fraternities such as Masonry important as class protective devices.

affairs of the community. The reasons are many. First, the Order is a secret society and has felt it necessary to remain aloof from other institutions. The secretiveness of Masonry has been functional for the organization since it served to attract nonmembers by the promise of "hidden" knowledge, ritual, and activities, a promise that has always proven attractive to Americans, black or white.[5] A second and more important cause of its aloofness has been the fraternity's fear of disruption if political or religious issues were allowed to enter the organization. As a result of the desire for total harmony, Masonry, both white and black, has forbidden the lodges to directly involve themselves with most of the issues or organizations deeply affecting the life of the community.[6]

Thus in a discussion of Masonry's role it is necessary to look elsewhere than into the direct activities of the fraternity itself. Instead, the connecting links which join Masonry to other pillars of society and form a network that can legitimately be called a black middle-class community must be found in the individuals who fill the ranks of the organization.

We have already seen the intimate relationship between the church and Masonry in the eighteenth and nineteenth centuries. Prince Hall, the founder of black Masonry, was himself a clergyman. When the fraternity spread out of his home state of Massachusetts, other clerics were in the vanguard of its growth. The Grand Lodge of Pennsylvania, the second black Grand Lodge in America, was established in 1815 by "two blazing meteors of the religious constellation," the Rev. Absalom Jones, founder of the Negro Episocpal Church, and the Rev. Richard Allen, founder of the African Methodist Episcopal Church, with Rev. Jones as its first Grand Master.[7] The movement of the Order into the South during the Civil War and Reconstruction was often accomplished by ministers simultaneously spreading Masonry and the African Methodist Episcopal Church.

Once established, North or South, the two institutions con-

<hr>

[5] See New York *Age*, October 31, 1931, for some of the dysfunctional aspects of secretiveness. The article points out that the public does not really clearly know who the Masons are. As late as 1968 the Grand Master of New York lamented that many men who wished to join the Masonic Order did not have enough information to differentiate between Prince Hall and its "illegitimate" rivals.

[6] This will be discussed in more detail in later chapters.

[7] *Proceedings* (California, 1917), C.C.F.C. reporting on Pennsylvania.

tinued to maintain their connecting links. The pages of Masonic literature are full of clergymen who occupied high rank in the Masonic Order, often the Grand Master's chair. Thus an event such as the dedication of the Grand Lodge Temple of Georgia in 1940 by Past Deputy Grand Master J. S. Flipper, a Senior Bishop of the A.M.E. church and Presiding Bishop of the Diocese of South Carolina, is not unusual.

Very often high-ranking clergymen have used their religious conventions as a means for fulfilling not only their church, but Masonic obligations as well. For example, in 1927, when Rev. J. H. Wilson, Grand Master of California, traveled to Florida for a Baptist conclave, he used the opportunity to create closer ties with the Florida Grand Lodge. He found himself treated "royally" by the Grand Master of his host state and felt "pleasantly at ease" within the network of social relations maintained by the Florida brethren.[8] The Grand Master of North Carolina likewise used the General Missionary Board of the Methodist Episcopal Church meeting in Los Angeles as a means of forging closer links with the California branch of the fraternity.[9] In 1937 the Grand Master of California told his Grand Lodge, "we are looking forward with pleasure to a visit from some of our outstanding Grand Masters, who are expecting to attend the National Baptist Convention—meeting in Los Angeles."[10] When Grand Master Moss attended that meeting he was pleased to discover the large number of Masonic brethren present. He listed twenty-five names, most of them clergymen's, many of whom were Past Masters of their local or state Grand Lodges, or were serving in the post of one or another high-ranking Masonic position.

The informal personal links between Masonry and the churches have been maintained not only by the clergymen who are adherents of the Order but by the even larger number of Masons who obtain important lay positions in the churches. It is primarily through noncleric Masons that the most formidable bonds between Masonry and organized religion have been forged. When the *Prince Hall Sentinel*, the official magazine of the Grand Lodge of New York, joyously celebrated the installation of Past Grand Master Henry Rhodes as Ruling

[8] *Proceedings* (California, 1927).
[9] *Proceedings* (California, 1916), Grand Master's speech.
[10] Not all the delegates were clergymen.

Elder of Silaom Presbyterian Church, while Rev. "Brother" Milton Galamison the Pastor officiated, it was indicative of the relationship.[11] The majority of biographical articles in the Masonic Journals dealing with prominent local and Grand Lodge members demonstrate the membership's interest and achievement in the church. For example, the *Prince Hall Masonic Review* (Georgia) in 1946 reported the passing of Past Grand Master D. D. Powell of Florida. He was, the article said, a major influence in fraternal and religious organizations. He served not only as the Chairman of the Board of Deacons of his church, but was "chiefly responsible" for the elevation of two or three "of his friends" to Bishoprics in the African Methodist Episocpal Church in Florida.[12] The *Sentinel* of New York in 1967 informed the Craft that Trinity A.M.E. Zion church had saluted Past Grand Master Leo Payne for his long years of service as the Chairman of the Trustee Board of the church, and also paid homage to his son Past Master Clark Payne for his work as church treasurer.[13] Another Masonic publication, in 1946, on the death of Grand Master John L. Webb, patriarch of Mississippi, pointed out that besides serving as Deacon of his church, he was Chairman of the Board of Trustees for 25 years, President of the National Baptist Laymen's Movement U.S.A., member of the Executive Committee of the Federal Council of Churches of Christ in America and superintendent of Sunday Schools for 27 years.[14] Examples like these are legion.

In an attempt to obtain some figures, even of a limited nature, on the connection between the Mason and the church, I consulted *Who's Who in Colored America 1930-1932*.[15] While over 50 percent of the men listed in its pages were members of the Masons, the ninety-four men who by reason of their high rank in the Order demonstrated more than nominal

[11] *Sentinel* (New York), 19, no.1 (Jan.-March 1966): 6-7.

[12] *Review* (Georgia), 10, no.1 (Jan.-March 1945): 1.

[13] *Sentinel* (New York), 20, no.4 (Oct.-Dec. 1967): 9.

[14] *Review* (Georgia), 10, no.4 (Oct.-Dec. 1946): 23-24.

[15] It is understood that a book such as this has severe limitations. The listings includes only the names of men who achieved, according to the authors, an unusual degree of prominence in the black community. It cannot provide salient facts about average Masons, or the average prominent Mason either. Nevertheless, since it does give a large listing of important blacks, chosen for reasons other than their Masonic standing, it can provide us with strong hints of the characteristics of prominent men who have also been influential Masons.

membership were chosen for intensive analysis.[16] Of the ninety-four men, thirteen were clergymen. Of the remaining eighty-one, twenty-four occupied lay posts in black churches. The majority were trustees; many were officials in religious conferences and conventions.[17] The two groups, clerics and active laymen, equal thirty-seven, or slightly less than 40 percent of the sample group. Research on the general Masonic membership also indicates that the rank and file have been fairly faithful church-goers; whether obtaining position in the fraternity or church, they undoubtedly have helped bind the two institutions together.

Masonry has maintained links not only with the churches but also with a number of other important national fraternal orders. While the situation in South Carolina around 1929 was certainly an exaggeration of the ties between Masonry and her sister secret societies, it is at least indicative of the actual state of affairs. In that year, there is a report that the Deputy Grand Master of Masons was also Grand Master of the Exchequer of the Grand Lodge Knights of Pythias; the Grand Secretary of Masons was Chairman of the Auditing Committee, Grand Lodge Knights of Pythias, and Grand Director of the Grand Lodge of Odd Fellows; the Grand Master of Masons was Grand Attorney for the Grand Lodge of Odd Fellows; while the Grand Chaplain of Masons was Grand Secretary of the Grand United Order of Odd Fellows and Chairman of the Committee on Law and Supervisions of the Grand Lodge of Knights of Pythias![18]

Evidence from many other Masonic records tends to reinforce the South Carolina case. For example, the *Proceedings* of California in 1949 reveal that a member of the Grand Lodge, S. C. Moore, was the Grand Master of the California Odd Fellows: when he was introduced to the general assembly in his capacity as leader of that sister fraternity, he was greeted by Deputy Grand Master Hopkins since he was a member of both organizations. Around the same time, the *Sentinel* of New York, which was honoring J. Preston Cumberbatch, a Past

[16] The number of "more-than-nominally-committed" could have been extended considerably if those possessing the special "33°" in Masonry were included, but I felt it would be best to limit the sample to office holders.

[17] The biographical material in the Masonic journals shows a very high percentage of the men discussed to have been deacons of their churches as well as trustees. The *Who's Who in Colored America* material has relatively few men mentioned as deacons.

[18] *Proceedings* (California, 1929), C.C.F.C. reporting on South Carolina.

Master of Masons, as their Man of the Month, pointed out
that he was not only an active and dedicated Mason but Grand
Secretary-Treasurer of the Reserve Fund Department of
Knights of Pythias, Brig-General, Uniform Ranks, of Knights
of Pythias, and head of his local Elks lodge. A few years later,
on the death of the editor of the *Sentinel*, Charles Magill, the
journal revealed that he had also been a member of the Joseph
R. Magill Lodge of Odd Fellows (named after his father) and
occupant of numerous national offices in the Elks fraternity
as well.[19] Similarly, on the death of New York's Grand Secretary, the *Sentinel* made known that he had been Past Grand
Exalted Ruler of the Elks Grand Lodge, in addition to holding
many other fraternal offices.[20] Thus, while the remarks of a
Grand Master of Texas that "We belong to all the other
[fraternal] organization" cannot be taken at face value, it is
obvious that interlocking among the fraternities has been of
formidable proportions.[21]

In order to determine which fraternities Masons have tended
to belong to, I again turned to *Who's Who in Colored America*
and included in my sample every tenth Masonic name listed.[22]
Thus of 620 Masons, the sample was 62. Of the 62 names, 23
were members of Knights of Pythias, 23 of Odd Fellows, and
23 of the Elks. These memberships were scattered among 46
different men (approximately three-quarters of the sample).
Slightly more than half of the men who belonged to one of
the three major fraternities (other than Masonry) also belong
to a second. In other words, it was more common to find a
man belonging to Masonry, Odd Fellows, and Knights of
Pythias (or Elks) than just to Masonry and one of the others.
The 62-men sample also listed other fraternities than these,
but the numbers for each were small. While these figures, based
upon *Who's Who in Colored America*, are not conclusive, they
are consistent with the evidence found in the Masonic records.[23]

[19] *Sentinel* (New York), 5, no.1-2 (Jan.-Feb. 1952): 1, 3.
[20] *Sentinel* (New York), 5, no.1-2 (Jan.-Feb. 1952): 2.
[21] *Proceedings* (Texas, 1927).
[22] This time the 1928-29 volume was used.
[23] The formal interactions between the major secret societies, as with all other
organizations, has been minimal. However, it is interesting to note the scattered
references to cooperative action among them. For example, when the Grand Lodge
of Texas in 1912 decided to organize the Fraternal Bank and Trust Company, the
Grand Lodge of Knights of Pythias and the Odd Fellows both bought 2,500 shares
each; in Louisiana in the late 1890s a joint stock company of Masons and Odd Fellows

While the churches, other fraternities, and the middle-class family have constituted the three main pillars of the black bourgeois community, Masonry has also maintained links with other important sectors of the middle-class community. One of these sectors is black business. Negro business taken as a whole has been an important segment of the middle-class world, even though its size and economic powers have been severely restricted. Ever since the failure of Reconstruction, a great deal of thought and energy has been devoted to the problem of how to create a viable black business sector, one which would solve the fundamental incompleteness of the black middle class by enabling its members to stay within their own community, not only during their leisure time but during working hours as well. It is in the area of business, unlike in its dealings with the church and other fraternities, that Masonry as an institution has allowed itself to be directly active. Masonic leaders have had very strong views of the importance and legitimacy of a link between business and Masonry. In 1916 the then C.C.F.C. of California (later Grand Master) J. H. Wilson said that what Negroes desperately required was that "Some organization ... teach the Negro by example as well as by precept the worth and power of the almighty dollar, the philosophy and utility of the combination and association of dollars." And that organization was ideally the Masons since "There are ... few Grand Lodges of Masons in this country but what [sic] has or handles money enough each year and has the power as no other organization in the world ..." to force the whites to grant blacks equality through their successful establishment of businesses.

Over twenty years later the Grand Master of Alabama saw the Masonic fraternity performing a similar function for the black race. He argued that economic independence from the whites is the key to real power and can only be achieved in one way:

---

was organized to rent and ultimately buy a building; the Grand Exalted Ruler of the Elks was invited to Georgia in 1938 to tour the state with the Grand Master of Masons, making speeches on fraternal and political affairs; the Grand Master of Georgia in 1912 attempted to organize a coordinated organization composed of Masons, Odd Fellows, Knights of Pythias, Knights of Tabor, Good Samaritans, and others called the United Friendly Society of Georgia.

By organization and real sincere cooperation. We must organize
and start more colored businesses along lines in which at present
we have no colored businesses. We must, since we cannot do
it individually, get together, choose honest and competent leaders
and start cooperative businesses and enterprises such as Department Stores; Manufacturing Plants; Banks, etc. ... Next, we
must more generously support the colored enterprises we already
have.[24]

The actual results of such exhortations will be dealt with later;
for the moment it is enough to say that Masonic support for
the business community, by helping to create it, and by supporting those which already existed, was and is the goal of
many of Masonry's leaders.

Masonic records provide information on two different groups
in the fraternity and their relations to the business community.
Substantial numbers of members, most of them presumably
never reaching the higher levels of fraternal power, entered
Masonry because of their outside business activities. Despite
the Order's concern for black business and the development
of black businessmen, this group has always been considered
by Masonic leaders a degrading influence because it was concerned only with manipulating the Order for personal gain.
The records are replete with complaints against these "Masonic" businessmen over a period of at least one hundred years.
In New York, as early as 1882 the Grand Master requested
that his brothers take legislative action to prohibit men from
having the emblems of Masonry printed on business cards or
painted on sign boards. Whether action was taken or not, and
it probably was, the practice did not abate. In 1932 a similar
resolution was adopted.[25] The Masons to whom these actions
were directed obviously continued to believe that the fraternity
was important for their businesses because in 1963 the Grand
Lecturer of New York was forced to note that it was "not
uncommon" to see a brother's business card blazoned with
emblems of two, three, or more Masonic bodies.[26]

The Grand Lodge of Illinois, not a body which normally
passed up any opportunity to aid Masons in their entrepre-

---

[24] *Proceedings* (Alabama, 1939).

[25] *Prince Hall Masonry in New York State*, Harry Williamson, vol. 3, see heading
"1932."

[26] *Sentinel* (New York), 16, no.3 (July-Sept. 1963): 8.

neurial ventures, was also upset by "card-carrying" Masonic businessmen. As one official said in 1946, while "There is every reason, all things being equal, for members of the Masonic Order doing business with each other whenever possible," there is no reason to expect that a brother will do such business at a sacrifice to himself, or by dishonorably breaking a contract with other men. "This thought is occasioned by the frequency with which some members of the Order . . . have been heard to comment more or less broadly upon business in connection with Freemasonry."[27] The official concluded by cautioning those who came into the fraternity for business gain that they would be soon shown the error of their ways. However, Illinois had no more control over this practice than New York, for the Grand Master of Illinois found himself reiterating the same warning in 1956.[28] Despite the hostility of Masonic leaders from Georgia to California, men who have seen Masonry primarily as a place to make contacts or obtain customers have continued to enter the fraternity. To the extent that they have succeeded in their purpose or, for that matter, failed, they have established a very real connection between the Order and black business.

While Masonic leadership has abhorred opportunists concerned with "what they can get out of Masonry" rather than "what they can give to Masonry," it has strongly favored the development of business enterprise among members of the fraternity—though they demanded that the beneficiaries of such activities be of pure (i.e., nonmercenary) heart. Thus the Grand Lecturer of Illinois in 1948 could say:

> Has it ever occurred to you as a member of the Fraternity to transact, so far as it is possible, business with your fellow member . . . ? You may think that this will lead to clannishness, and no doubt it will. Why should not Masons be clannish?[29]

In the same year the Grand Lodge of Illinois' journal included a Directory of Masonic Businessmen which contained 50 names, all apparently in Chicago, and recommended, by way of a slogan, "If I Can Do Business With A Brother Satisfactory To Myself, As I Can With A Stranger . . . Then I Would Patronize My Brother."[30] Around the same time New York's

[27] *Topics* (Illinois), 10, no.10 (Oct. 1947): 18.
[28] *Proceedings* (Illinois, 1956).
[29] *Topics* (Illinois), 11, no.12 (Dec. 1948): 4.
[30] *Topics* (Illinois), 11, no.5 (May 1948): 24.

Masonic journal exhorted the membership to support the magazine's advertisers, all of whom were Prince Hall Masons and "the cream" of their businesses.[31] Masonry's general pro-business orientation and its desire to help found businesses has made its policy of encouraging the membership to patronize their brothers in business quite logical. However, it has done little to discourage opportunism since it has made the line between legitimate and illegitimate desire for business gain through Masonry a fine one.[32]

In addition to the small entrepreneurs who have joined the Masons, many of the men who have reached positions of prominence in the Order have been intimately connected with more successful businesses in the black community—men like W. W. Allen, perennial Grand Master of Maryland and Head of the Scottish Rite Masons, South, who was President of Southern Life Insurance Company, Baltimore;[33] Grand Master John Webb of Mississippi, who made his wealth in contracting and building and then became director of Universal Life Insurance Company, Memphis, President and Treasurer of the Century Life Insurance Company, Arkansas, President of the Negro Insurance Men's Association, and First Vice-President of the National Business League;[34] Sol C. Johnson, Grand Secretary of Georgia for more than fifty years, who was Editor and Publisher of the Savannah *Tribune*;[35] William McDonald, "kingpin" of Texas Masonry, master businessman, and President of the Fraternal Bank and Trust Company;[36] or Grand Master Theodore Moss of California, who owned the Independent Plumbing Works and organized the Modern Order of Bucks, a progressive business club.[37] Thus the Leaders of Masonry have also served as informal links between the fraternity and business.

For this type of man, Masonry has not been a source of

[31] *Sentinel* (New York), 1, no. 7 (July 1948): 10.

[32] In the same way, the emphasis on business has promised to create group solidarity, while at the same time the business ethic with its individualistic underpinnings has exaggerated the lack of cooperation.

[33] *Who's Who in Colored America*, 1933-37.

[34] *Review* (Georgia), 10, no.4 (Oct. 1946): 23-24; *Who's Who in Colored America*, 1930-32.

[35] *Review* (Georgia), 11, no.1 (Jan.-March 1947): 10.

[36] See *Proceedings*, Texas, generally.

[37] *Review* (Georgia), 1, no.8 (April 1938): 4. Moss, unlike the others, was a small businessman, but very active in promoting business among blacks.

business gain, but rather the ultimate expression of his own entrepreneurial abilities. In many states the Masonic Order has been the creation of single men, men with incredible talent, executive ability, and driving ambition for themselves and their race. For them Masonry has offered a stage for putting into practice their ideas for racial advancement. Often these men have brought into the fraternity their concern with, and ideas about, business and have helped shape the pro-business tone that has permeated the Order.[38] The black capitalism orientation of Masonry has thus not only reflected the existing aspirations of the general membership but has also helped shape its attitude.

In summary, the fraternity's connection with black enterprise has run the gamut of possibilities. It has included in its membership a sizeable proportion of the black business population. Many small businessmen have entered it because it has offered the promisè of increased patronage and aid; many more successful entrepreneurs have entered because it has provided an arena for the exercise of their skills and a vehicle for their more ambitious plans for racial uplift; and for large numbers of talented and frustrated nonbusinessmen it has provided a school for learning skills and an opportunity for employing them in running both the fraternity itself and its many separate businesses.[39]

[38] Masonry in many states has been characterized by the presence of one charismatic leader who has dominated the fraternity for decades. These men are the driving force of the fraternity and the inspiration behind its many activities in their states. What is needed is research into the personal histories of a number of these leaders and the role they have played not only in Masonry but in the black community generally. Some of the men who deserve this in-depth study are William McDonald of Texas; John W. Dobbs and H. R. Butler of Georgia; John Lewis and family of Louisiana; John Webb of Mississippi; W. W. Allen of Maryland; Amos Hall of Oklahoma; and Walter Woods and Charles Hendley of Alabama.

[39] In attempting to get some statistical material on prominent businessmen in Masonry I have encountered major problems. Biographical information is limited on Masonic leaders in the available records. Thus, when the Board of Trustees of the Grand Lodge of California says: "we are following probably some of the greatest businessmen this state has produced among our people. Men like Past Grand Master George R. Vaughns, Past Board Chairman M. Earl Grant, Past Grand Master Roscoe Broyles, Past Grand Master Theodore Moss, Past Grand Master Sterling Hopkins," we cannot be sure if they are referring only to their "business leadership" within the Order or also to their activities in the larger society [see *Proceedings* (California, 1960)]. The biographical information in *Who's Who in Colored America* is far less useful on this point than on others because it is severely biased in favor of professionals and against businessmen. It is useful to the extent that over 25 percent of the 94

One of the more fascinating ways in which Masonry interacts with other black middle-class organizations, thus demonstrating how a secret society helps bind together various black institutions of which it officially takes no cognizance, can be found in its relationship to the federal postal service. The postal service has for many decades been one of the major economic supports for the black middle class. Thousands of Negroes have found postal work steady, decent-paying, prestigious, and far more accessible than most occupations in the American economy. Of these men, some of them in high postal positions, thousands have found their way into Prince Hall Masonry.[40] A perusal of Masonic journals supports the contention that the post office has provided a major economic base for large numbers of Masons. Biography after biography of leading Masons reports the same information: Grand Secretary (later Grand Master) Rhodes of New York, employed in the post office as a clerk for over thirty years;[41] Grand Master Vanderburg of Illinois, employed for forty-six years;[42] Charles T. Magill, editor of the *Prince Hall Sentinel*, employed for forty years;[43] Past Grand Lecturer Coles of New York, employed for twenty-five years;[44] and the list goes on.

Because of the large number of blacks in the postal service and the existence, despite its comparative fairness, of racial discrimination, the black National Alliance of Postal Employees was organized in 1913 in Chattanooga, Tennessee. This militant organization, drawing its membership from black postal workers, has shared many of its leaders with the Masonic Order. The importance of this sharing of members and leaders, and how it serves to bind together black men and organizations throughout the nation, are best illustrated in the activities of Ashby Carter, who simultaneously occupied the Grand Mastership of Illinois and the Presidency of the National Alliance of Postal Employees.

In Carter's rise to the top of the Alliance he was first elected

---

leading Masons mentioned in it were engaged in business activities (even though most were primarily professional men); and this figure is probably lower than a fairer sample would be.

[40] *Topics* (Illinois), 12, no.19 (July 1949): 14-16.
[41] *Review* (Georgia), 11, no. 1 (April-June 1947): 10.
[42] *Topics* (Illinois), First Quarter, 1964.
[43] *Sentinel* (New York), 5, no.1-2 (Jan.-Feb. 1952): 1.
[44] *Sentinel* (New York), 5, no.1-2 (Jan.-Feb. 1952): 5.

President of the Chicago Branch in 1941. In that post he helped raise the membership of the local organization from 250 to 1,000. He was largely responsible for placing the Alliance in the forefront of Chicago's militant race organizations during World War II, when Negroes were battling for integration in war industries and in the social life of Chicago. In 1945 he was elevated to the National Presidency of the Alliance, which then had 16,000 members. At the same time he was elected Grand Master of Illinois as the culmination of years of prodigious activity at such posts as founder and editor of the fraternity's journal *Past Masters Topics*.[45] In his position as leader of the postal organization, which maintained a home office in Washington, D.C. and had eighty-eight branches in thirty-two states, Carter was able to travel each year throughout the United States and meet prominent black men.[46] In 1949, for instance, he visited Pennsylvania, New Jersey, Washington, D.C., New Mexico, California, Oregon, Washington State, Tennessee, Georgia, Florida, Wisconsin, Texas, Ohio, Indiana, Missouri, and Kansas.[47] During such extensive trips he traveled not only as head of the Alliance but as Grand Master of Illinois as well. In each state he was received by the ranking officials of the Masonic Order and was accorded the honors of a visiting dignitary. He thus was able to help bind the fraternity together at the same time that he unified the Alliance, and not infrequently the same men were involved in both organizations.

The significance of the bond between Masonry, the Alliance, and the post office workers can be readily comprehended by looking at a resolution passed by the International Conference of Grand Masters of Prince Hall Masonry in 1950. At that meeting a resolution was submitted by Grand Master Carter, along with the leaders of Wisconsin, Virginia, Mississippi, and Alabama Masonry, calling for the elimination of Jim Crow in America. Very prominent in that resolution was an attack on dangers which the Masons considered severe threats to the black population:

> Among the trends we deplore and view as dangerous ... are (1) Continuing attempts to herd Negro citizens into ghettos ...; (2) the cry 'subversive' against almost every individual who ...

[45] *Topics* (Illinois), 11, no.2 (Feb. 1948): 4-5.
[46] *Review* (Georgia), 12, no.1 (Jan.-March 1948): 18.
[47] *Proceedings* (Illinois, 1949).

advocate[s] ... equality ...; (3) the diabolical attempt of some
of our government agencies, particularly the Post Office Department, to stifle ... the ... fight against racial discrimination ...
by charging employees, predominately Negroes and Jews, with
being guilty of disloyalty. ... The ... Post Office Department
... [is] of special concern to us because it is an agency that
employs the most people, some 40,000 of whom are loyal Negro-
Americans whose economic contributions to our various communities are of great importance![48]

The resolution was passed and disseminated in the press, and
copies were sent to the President of the United States and
to as many local, state, and city officials as the various state
Grand Lodges requested. It is in actions like this that the
importance of the informal, human links between the two
organizations is proved.

Until recent years the fraternity's main official tie to the
rest of the community was its presence in officiating at the
cornerstone-laying ceremonies of new churches, colleges, and
schools. Masons have always claimed and been granted the
exclusive privilege of leading the march to the site of new
institutions and laying the cornerstone of the new edifice. This
type of activity has often placed Masons in a conspicuous place
during the most important events in the life of the black
community. As a Grand Master of Texas put it, "The best
men of every community, town or city, are members of Masonic
Lodges, and the fact that they are found among the Lodge
members on parades" marching to cornerstone layings has an
important effect on convincing young men to join the Order.[49]
Outside of its prominence in this activity, Grand and local
Lodges have aided the community over the years by contributions to charities, such as local old age homes,[50] community
chests and local hospitals,[51] or campaigns to aid disaster victims,
though most of this public work has been small-scale.[52]

Another traditional direct contact between the fraternity and
the community occurs during Grand Lodge or Auxiliary Order
meetings.[53] For example, when the Scottish Rite Masons of

[48] *Proceedings* (Georgia, 1950).
[49] *Proceedings* (Texas, 1919).
[50] See *Proceedings* of California and New York.
[51] See *Proceedings* (Georgia 1926) for example.
[52] *Proceedings* (Illinois, 1925). See Chapter VIII for discussion of charity.
[53] Certain organizations which accept members only from among Masons or their

the Southern Jurisdiction met in Atlanta in 1944 with Grand Masters of nine states, along with 3,500 other Masons, they were greeted by the President of Atlanta University, in the name of the schools and churches, and the President of the National Negro Insurance Association and Assistant Agency Director of Atlanta Life Insurance Company, for the business community. The meeting was held in the church of "Brother" Martin Luther King, Sr. Since at the time of the meeting "Brother" Bishop Flipper, Senior Bishop of the A.M.E. church, had just died, the Council went as a body to his funeral. They then proceeded to Spelman College, where they were welcomed by the President, and where the head of the Scottish Rite, South, addressed the students and teachers of the college.[54] Such meetings, public occasions, and addresses were and are methods by which a "secret" organization such as Masonry keeps its community ties.

One of the Masonic leaders in the pre-World War II period most active in bringing Masonry into the community was John Wesley Dobbs, Grand Master of Georgia. In 1938, for example, he invited the Grand Exalted Ruler of Elks to visit Georgia and tour the state with him as he gave addresses. Together they visited 18 towns and cities and spoke at a total of 40 public meetings. The two fraternal leaders were received at local churches and then proceeded to speak at every high school and college in the area. The topic they chose was "The Fraternal and Political Outlook of the Negro Tomorrow" in which they stressed the power of the ballot and the necessity of its use by the black man.[55]

The Grand Master of Georgia was also responsible for other programs that brought Masonry into contact with the general community. In 1939 he invited W. W. Allen, Grand Master of Maryland and head of the Scottish Rite, South, to go to Georgia and deliver the Lincoln-Douglass Day Address at Bethel Church. When Allen had finished he was the guest of Grand Master Dobbs in the latter's capacity as President of the Civic and Political League of Atlanta. In his address to

female relatives but are not subject to the authority of the Masonic Grand Lodge—except in giving them the right to be set up—are "auxiliary" or "concordant" bodies. They include Shriners, Royal Arch Masons, Knights Templar, Order of Eastern Star, Heroines of Jericho and Scottish Rite Masonry, North and South.

[54] *Review* (Georgia), no vol., no number (Oct.-Dec. 1944): 8.

[55] *Review* (Georgia), 1, no.8 (April 1938): 3.

the League, Allen spoke of the mass-action techniques employed by Baltimore's black community in its fight for civil rights and argued that such effective action could be taken in Atlanta as well as in Maryland.[56] Georgia Masonry in the 1930s under Dobbs may have been exceptional in its leader's involvement in community affairs such as these. But in all probability other state leaders engaged in similar activities.

Nevertheless, it was not until after World War II that Masonry made an effort to revise its formal policy of aloofness and become directly involved in the affairs of the general community. Since most of the impetus for increased involvement revolved around the desire to be more effective in the realm of civil rights, and to be represented as an institution on the boards of leading militant organizations, much of the discussion of this change will be left to a late chapter devoted to civil rights. However, besides civil rights, there was a *general* desire for increased community activity in the years after 1945. The Masons increasingly felt they had to "justify" their existence to the community in a way they had not done before. The reasons are not hard to discover. While some states began to recover from the Depression membership decline even before the decade had ended, real recovery came only during and after the war. In the atmosphere of the postwar period, of increased sophistication and rising expectation about the black man's place in America, the Masons felt that they had to enhance their public image to win members.[57]

In their fight for membership Masons soon discovered the importance of public relations departments and the glories of publicity. As a leading official of the Grand Lodge of Texas put it, "Public Relations, for the most part, is a white man's vehicle whereby he gets where he is going. It has been his way of putting to the public the things he wants to do."[58] Texas Masonry decided to do likewise. The achievements of the Grand Lodge in 1964 illustrates the successful use of public relations techniques. First, the Grand Master was given a citation for his work in behalf of the Polio Fund at the Grand Masters' Conference—which was reported in both the white and black presses. Then the Grand Lodge was honored when a historical

---

[56] *Review* (Georgia), 2, no.2 (Jan.-March 1939): 4.

[57] This will be discussed in more detail in a later chapter.

[58] *Proceedings* (Texas, 1964), Report of Public Relations Director.

monument at Galveston was erected honoring the fraternity's
first Grand Master, N. W. Cuney. The monument highlighted
the fact that Grand Master Cuney became a school director
of Galveston County in 1871, was an alderman, inspector of
the customs and later collector of the Port of Galveston, all
of which the Texas Masons considered important in boosting
the prestige of the Order for potential initiates.[59]

Exactly when Texas discovered the beauties of "the white
man's vehicle" is not easily discernible, but other Masonic
bodies showed active concern with public relations in the late
1940s and throughout the 1950s. For example, a local lodge
in Indianapolis in 1948 already possessed its own Public Relations Committee whose goal was to cooperate with non-Masonic groups in the community which were working for a "Christian
Democracy" and justice for all citizens.[60] A Masonic official
of California in 1952 was determined that a "Community of
Public Relations" office be maintained so that Prince Hall
Masonry would be constantly in the public eye. This would
be facilitated, he said, by having representative speakers from
all phases of planned community activity—youth, education,
housing, and politics—speak to Masonic groups.[61] The importance of these activities for all Prince Hall jurisdictions was
a topic of discussion at the Grand Masters Conference in 1952.
At that meeting Grand Master Fair of New York argued it
was the "duty" of all Grand Lodges to further favorable
impressions of Masonry in the community, establish good press
relations, locally and nationally, and obtain a competent public
relations director. Fair noted that his jurisdiction maintained
public relations through contributions to worthy public causes.

The type of increased participation in the community—and
resulting favorable publicity—which Masons were after can
most easily be seen in the Scottish Rite Masons' 1953 cospon-
sorship with the National Urban League of three vocational
guidance institutes. Local Masons joined in planning and conducting the programs. The Scottish Rite helped plan the
demonstration as a pilot project to stimulate greater interest
in the guidance of young people. Each institute lasted three
days, and prominent people from all segments of the communi-

[59] *Masonic Quarterly* (Texas), 40, no. 141 (March 1960): 1.

[60] *Review* (Georgia), 12, no.4 (Oct.-Dec. 1948): n.p.

[61] *Proceedings* (California, 1952), Report of the Inspector for the 8th Masonic District.

ty—labor, the schools, N.A.A.C.P., Urban League, etc.—took part. According to Masonic observers the project was a great success, partially because "An important segment of the Negro community—Masonic leaders and members—became more acutely aware of needs in relation to the education, training and employment of Negro youth."[62] In the years that followed other Masonic bodies set up their own plans to coordinate their work with organizations such as the Urban League. The Grand Master of Illinois, for example, told the Grand Lodge in 1959 that by working with other community organizations interested in racial uplift activities the fraternity would gain both good publicity and prestige, allowing the public to know who the "real Masons" are.[63] In keeping with this aid the Grand Lodge approved a plan to coordinate its youth work with the Urban League. The Chicago Urban League cooperated with the Masons in their leadership-training program by providing trained personnel, sending information to the lodges, and generally aiding their youth program. At the time the Illinois Masons started this project, they also set up a Masonic Big Brother Committee as an affiliate organization of the Illinois Youth Commission which promised to provide the Grand Lodge with all the aid it required. The Big Brother program was an important step into the community because the Masons had previously been concerned only about their own children. The leaders of the Grand Lodge felt the need to make quite explicit for some of its worried members that the new social conscience program would not endanger the older middle-class oriented emphasis by saying "Our Junior Craft Organization works with boys who are potential Masons, from good wholesome families and who offer no anti-social behavior." Indeed, the Big Brother work would hopefully serve as an inspiration for the antisocial boy whom "we plan to rehabilitate . . . until we feel he is ready to be turned over to our Junior Craft Order for further development and then into the Masonic Body as a good Mason."[64]

The Grand Lodge of New York which, under Grand Master Fair in the 1940s, started to involve itself in the affairs of the

[62] *Digest* (California), 3, no.3 (July-Sept. 1953): 17.

[63] Prince Hall Masonry throughout most of its existence has been plagued by rival black Masonic lodges which do not claim descent from either Prince Hall or the Grand Lodge of England. Exactly how many adherents they possess it is impossible to say, but estimates range as high as 100,000.

[64] *Proceedings* (Illinois, 1959), Report of the Big Brother Committee.

black community continually increased its tempo until 1966, when the Chairman of the Grand Lodge Department of Charity, Education and Employment recommended that the department's name be changed to the Department of Social Concern and have its areas of interest expanded to cover children and youth, human rights, and civic affairs.[65] When the committees that comprised the new department met, the Grand Master told them that he wished each committee to formulate a program designed to involve the Masons as an institution in all aspects of community life. They agreed, they composed a statement in support of a civilian police review board for New York City, and they announced that they would work for increased black voter registration. Their statement in favor of the controversial board was presented by the Grand Master to Mayor John Lindsay of New York and then circulated to newspapers and radio stations in the city.[66] In a less controversial area the new Department established a new corporate structure to act as sponsor for such important community programs as child day care centers and educational and medical research projects. The new organization was named the Prince Hall Service Fund, Inc.[67] Soon after this innovation the Grand Master proudly announced that the Grand Lodge had become the sponsor of the Prince Hall Colonial Park Day Care Center in Harlem, an action he believed was the beginning of a new era in Masonry.[68]

While New York was establishing its Department of Social Concern, the Masons of California were creating a civic affairs committee as their vehicle for direct community involvement. The new committee's aims were exceptionally ambitious, and through it the Grand Lodge took a position on numerous controversial issues then agitating the black population. In a report by the Civic Action Committee called "Rights and Responsibilities" the group endeavored to explain its purpose, and in so doing spoke for all post-World War II Masonry:

[65] *Sentinel* (New York), 19, no.3 (July-Sept. 1966): 3.

[66] *Sentinel* (New York), 19, no.4 (Oct.-Dec. 1966): 14.

[67] *Sentinel* (New York), 19, no.4 (Oct.-Dec. 1966): 4.

[68] *Sentinel* (New York), 21, no.3 (July-Sept. 1968): 5. The Grand Lodge's action apparently served as a model for many local lodges, which proceeded to sponsor local day care centers, senior citizen programs, etc. of their own. See *Sentinel* (New York) 21, no.3 (July-Sept. 1968): 8.

As Master Masons we are looked up to by the community . . . .
Many of us in one way or the other take an active part in our
community but as a group we have sadly abdicated our responsibility. As a consequence many of our young men have become
disappointed with us and have sought other avenues in which
to work. . . . The Civic Action Committee of . . . California was
formed for the purpose [of helping] . . . Master Masons . . . realize
their desire to contribute . . . to our long sought goal of first
class citizenship for all Americans.[69]

The initiation of direct Masonic involvement in the community
throughout the Grand Lodges of Prince Hall Masonry demonstrates to what extent the fraternity in the post-World War
II period has not declined as a major institution in black society
but instead has expanded its influence.

Conclusion

Throughout its history Prince Hall Freemasonry has formed
links with the other pillars of the black middle class and thereby
has helped create a general social environment within which
its members could feel at ease, a social network where the
middle-class moral code and behavioral pattern could be maintained with a minimum of contact with alternative life styles.
Through most of its history these links were primarily supported by the individual members rather than by the Fraternity
as an institution. In recent years its role has been expanded
as the organization *qua* organization has augmented its own
role. In the next chapter I will investigate how Prince Hall
has been integrated into, and helped form, a larger national
and international middle-class "community."

[69] *Digest* (California), 11, no.1 (Sept.-Dec. 1963): 11.

Chapter VIII

Black Masonry's Links with the National and International Communities

The Masonic fraternity, along with its many auxiliary Orders, the middle-class churches, and other national fraternities, has created a social environment that has been conducive to the support of a black middle-class community. By moving from one institution to another, members of the black bourgeoisie have been able to spend much of their social life fairly insulated from the alternative life styles which have existed in the ghetto around them.[1] This has been on the local level. At the same time Masonry has also been instrumental in forming ties between local communities through its attempts to unify its own constituent parts, and thus has aided in the formation of a national as well as a local black middle-class community.

Prince Hall Masonry, since it lacks organization at the national level, has had a harder time forging bonds between blacks living in different states than have many other national fraternities, or its own centralized auxiliary Orders, for that matter. Nevertheless, it has devised means for overcoming the isolation that its decentralized structure creates. The different Masonic Grand Lodges have throughout almost all of their history been concerned with maintaining relations with their sister jurisdictions. To facilitate the exchange of information most of the Grand Lodges have cooperated in setting up an interjurisdictional representational system. Under this plan each Grand Lodge appoints individual members of the grand assembly to represent a particular sister state. That repre-

[1] This is not to say that the black middle-class world is not composed of many other crucial parts, such as social clubs, cliques, and general friendship groups.

181

sentative is required to communicate with his counterpart in the other state and forward information back and forth between the two jurisdictions. Exactly when the system was started is not clear, but the New York *Proceedings* of 1879-1880 reported that when the Grand Master visited a local lodge he met a visiting Louisiana Mason, who represented New York Masonry in his home Grand Lodge. A few years later, in 1883, New York announced it had established representation with twenty-four states and was in the process of negotiating with seven more.

The system has been an important link between the different parts of Prince Hall Masonry, though it has not always functioned perfectly. Often representatives have been slack in carrying out their duties, and many Grand Lodges have gone for years without realizing that the men representing them in other states have retired or died.[2] However, there is much evidence of attempts, often successful, to solve these problems and establish an efficient flow of communication.[3]

Because of the importance of the bonds between different states, the office of Chairman of the Committee on Foreign Correspondence became especially important in the fraternity. It came to be esteemed as the highest appointive office and the main route for information flowing between different Grand bodies.[4] While the C.C.F.C. has handled most of the correspondence of the Grand Lodges, their main influence has been felt by means of the printed proceedings of their jurisdiction.[5] It became a custom in many states for a large part of the yearly Grand Lodge proceedings to be devoted to a review and summary by the C.C.F.C. of proceedings from other jurisdictions. As we have seen elsewhere these pages became a forum for criticism and praise of the internal practices of other jurisdictions.[6] The keen interest taken in the workings of other

[2] See "Report of Chairman of the Committee on Foreign Correspondence," by Harry Williamson, New York, 1931 (manuscript).

[3] *Proceedings* (California, 1915), contains a letter from the Grand Masters of Michigan relative to making the system work more efficiently.

[4] *Proceedings* (California, 1952).

[5] Before 1900 many states had been sending their *Proceedings* to other Grand Lodges for years, but by that year the practice became pretty universal in Prince Hall Masonry (see *Proceedings*, [California, 1904-05], C.C.F.C. commenting on Massachusetts, 1902-04).

[6] We have seen how the C.C.F.C.s carried on major debates about the importance of due process and fair trial in the fraternity. However, by 1955, at least one observer

states by the C.C.F.C.s has helped to create a feeling of unity in the Order. Knowledge of what other states have accomplished has often led to both a sense of pride and a desire for emulation. For example, the Grand Master of California in 1909 found the proceedings of sister jurisdictions electrifying since they proved to him what black men could do even under the most adverse circumstances: the southern Masons were providing college scholarships and, in many districts where free school accommodations were inadequate, assisting in paying competent teachers. Through relief funds the fraternity was aiding widows and orphans and by general programs fighting intemperance and vice. The Grand Master felt California should be inspired to emulate these achievements as best it could.

Interjurisdictional correspondence has been only a part of the means for creating "unity" among the Prince Hall lodges. Also important have been the intra- and inter-state travels of black fraternal leaders and members. The pages of Masonic journals continually recount the travels of men such as the Grand Master of Georgia, who reported that in a cross-country expedition he was greeted everywhere by the "warm embrace" of Masonic hospitality. Such trips have often not been official Masonic visits. It has been common to hear of blacks attending church conclaves or union conventions who have spent much of their time visiting with local fraternity members. Until recently, few public accommodations were available for middle-class black people, and the network of local lodges and hospitable local brothers probably added a note of security for Masons away from home.

In addition to such informal relationships between traveling Masons and the Masonic lodges, the fraternity has maintained more formal ones. The Grand Lodge of every state holds the responsibility for offering aid to any Mason or his family who becomes ill or dies while in its jurisdiction. Illustrative of this obligation was a letter sent by Dr. E. T. Belshaw of Alabama to his New York brethren testifying that "There has not been to my knowledge, any Mason from your state during the last twelve months to fall sick, die or be imprisoned or otherwise suffer from lack of Masonic attention in this state."[7] In another

---

lamented that the new generation of C.C.F.C.s was too uncritical of abuses in other states (*Prince Hall Masonry in New York State*, vol. III, see heading "1955").

[7] *Proceedings* (New York, 1916).

instance a Grand Master of New Jersey was informed by the head of California Masonry that a visiting Mason was sick in New Jersey. He investigated, found both the Mason and his wife ill, and gave immediate aid. Sometimes the coverage was quite broad.[8] In 1914, for example, the Grand Lodge of California offered financial aid to the daughter of a deceased Ohio Mason who was living destitute in Oakland.

Masonry not only gives aid to travelers, it also serves to cushion the effects of permanent migration. The records of California, for example, are replete with the names of Masons from other states who emigrated and later affiliated with the Craft in California. The aid Masonry provides is best exemplified during the Great Migration (during and after World War I), when northern fraternal leaders were deeply concerned that their local lodges help southern migrants. They noted with chagrin that often southern Masons failed to reaffiliate, later took ill or died, and were thus unable to receive Masonic relief. The Grand Master of New York, for one, suggested that northern and southern jurisdictions appoint representatives to locate these men in order to rectify the situation.[9] Further records suggest that the attempt was successful. A phenomenal rise in Masonic memberships in areas where migrants settle (for example, Chicago) in the 1920s suggests that the fraternity also probably provided an important cushioning effect for middle-class blacks who had not been Masons before leaving the South.[10]

During the early years of the twentieth century, Masonic aid, psychological or physical, was restricted to Masonic members or potential members. Over the years since the Great Migration, however, the fraternity has come to see itself as playing a broader role in the service of all types of black migrants. In 1960 the *Prince Hall Digest* of California reprinted an article from a Michigan Masonic journal in which the author pointed out that Prince Hall Masons had a duty to aid Negro migrants fleeing the South to escape rural oppression. Since these men, mostly lower-class and new to urban areas, were easily disorganized, they had no ability to cope with the new environment. Therefore, "colored leadership has a special obli-

[8] *Proceedings* (California, 1913), C.C.F.C. reporting on New Jersey.

[9] *Proceedings* (New York, 1919).

[10] Though such men usually joined the Order only after they adjusted to a large extent on their own.

gation to contribute toward all means of alleviation [of this problem]. PRINCE HALL MASONS HAVE THE PARTICULAR RE-SPONSIBILITY which goes with the training, economic status and other qualifications for leadership" which the brethren possess.[11] In short, for at least some blacks the existence of Masonic lodges in their new communities has helped alleviate some of the personal and social disorganization that migration entails.

In addition to providing links for black Masonic lodges throughout the country, and helping to unify the black middle-class communities in which they are situated, Prince Hall Masonry has forged ties with black lodges (and their communi-ties) throughout the world. The most important non-American jurisdiction in Prince Hall Masonry is the Grand Lodge of Liberia. The position of Masonry in the Republic of Liberia is everything the black Masons could desire for their fraternity. The Grand Lodge and the Government of the Republic exist in an intimate embrace in which access to political power is tied to fraternal standing. While the exact details of the government-fraternal bond have not been studied, the records of the Grand Lodge of New York leave no question as to the existence of close ties. In the years from 1920 to 1960, New York Masonry greeted at least four Liberian Grand Masters on their visits to the United States. The first, in 1920, was the President-elect of Liberia; the second, in 1948, was the Vice President; the third, in 1954 was President Tubman; and the fourth, in 1960, was the Speaker of the House of Repre-sentatives.[12]

While there is no scholarly study of Freemasonry in Liberia, there is research on the neighboring African Masonic jurisdic-tion in Sierra Leone. Although this branch of the Order is not affiliated with the Prince Hall family, it does shed light on

[11] *Digest* (California), 9, no.1 (May-July 1960): 3.

[12] *Proceedings* (New York, 1920); *Sentinel* (New York), 1, no.9 (Oct. 1948): 5; 10, no.9-10 (Nov.-Dec. 1954): 7 (President Tubman did not actually stop in New York City on this trip); and 26, no.3 (July-Sept. 1960): 4. The Liberian leaders while in America used the occasion to further their Masonic careers. For example, Vice-President (and Grand Master) Simpson went to St. Louis in 1948 to be given the 33rd Degree. In 1954 President Tubman also came to the United States to be initiated into the highest degree in Masonry. The only explicit statement about the relationship between Prince Hall Masonry and the Liberian government was Vice-President of Liberia Simpson's remark that "all government" high officials are Masons (*Sentinel* [New York], 1, no.9 (Oct. 1948): 5).

the probable characteristics of the Liberian fraternity because Masonry in Sierra Leone forms an intimate part of the black elite's social structure, as it does in Liberia.[13]

According to Abner Cohen, Masonry is a crucial institution of the Creole minority of Sierra Leone.[14] These people, living in the capital city of Freetown, are a black professional and business elite made up of the descendants of British slaves brought into the country from Nigeria. They are ethnically and culturally different from the indigenous tribes of the area, and they look down upon the natives as inferiors. While the Creoles have Freemasonry as their fraternal organization, the natives have their own "bush" societies, one of which (the Poro) is a powerful political and social organization. Masonry is extremely prestigious, and all those who can afford to enter it and are accepted—about one out of three Creoles—do so. The cost of joining the Order is so high, and the "necessary banqueting" so expensive, that many non-Masonic Creoles protest at the fraternity's "snobbishness."[15] Within the Order, despite the official claims of equality, the socially and economically most powerful men within the Creole group dominate. The Order's membership thus constitutes an elite within an elite, and the highest leadership is even more exclusive.

According to Cohen's analysis Freemasonry has become exceptionally important in the last twenty years as the country has moved toward independence. As the protection of the Bitish has been withdrawn, the Creoles have realized their vulnerable position in Sierra Leone society. A small, ethnically distinctive elite is subject to severe discrimination unless it can organize to protect itself. In Sierra Leone political parties among the Creoles are weak and other institutions divided. Since the Creoles lack a tribal structure and there are many different leadership hierarchies (the church, the professional, etc.), all faction-ridden, unity is hard to achieve. In addition, the Creoles are a very competitive and individualistic bourgeois people and it is difficult for them to accept other men as leaders over them. Freemasonry provides a neutral place for all the groups and the leaders of the Creoles to meet in relative harmony. While

[13] Some of the Masonic lodges are affiliated with the Grand Lodge of England, others with the Grand Lodge of Scotland.

[14] Abner Cohen, "The Politics of Ritual Secrecy," *Man*, 6, no.3 (1971): 427-447. The Creoles equal 2 percent of the country's population.

[15] Ibid., p. 435.

Masonry is not consciously used as a political force, according to Cohen, it nevertheless serves as one because of the communications network it provides.[16] In its role as community unifier, Sierra Leone Freemasonry achieves the goal American black Masons have always dreamed of but never succeeded in obtaining. The Creole elite, however, has the advantage of solid economic and political power, a firm basis of social differentiation between themselves and outsiders, a small population living in one geographic area of the country, and increasing native pressure against them to force cooperation.

Besides Masonry's political and social role in helping to unify the Creole group, it serves many other functions. One of them is created by the Order's close association with Western civilization. The Creole are very proud of their adoption of Western culture, of which Masonry is a major symbol:

> From the very beginning of their settlement in Sierra Leone, the Creoles made a bid to have a new slant in their cultural life. They adopted English names, English styles of dress, education, religion, etiquette, art, music, and a general English style of life. [They are] ... more English than the English.[17]

Masonry offers Creoles not only the pleasure of identification with a Western cultural institution but acceptance as social equals by white men as well, a not insignificant psychological gain.

The Order also serves as "a mechanism for the development and maintenance of a 'mystique' which marks and enhances their distinctiveness and superiority vis-a-vis the Natives."[18] Cohen says that he constantly hears from Creoles the myth that "no matter how highly educated a Native may be," he will never have the level of civilization the Creole has. Freemasonry, as a European organization, is seen as the "hall-mark of superiority, in contrast to the 'bush' secret societies" of the natives. Cohen believes that the Order is as important for ego-boosting among the Creoles as it is for impressing the non-Creoles—a situation he believes is true for American and European white Masons as well.[19]

[16] The Order, of course, draws only upon the Creole population, and natives are not members except in a few token cases.

[17] Cohen, p. 429.

[18] Ibid., p. 435.

[19] Ibid., p. 436.

The benefits of Freemasonry do not end there. The Order also serves to aid its members in their individual economic and social affairs. For ambitious men, having "brotherly" ties to one's boss or superior is a major benefit of the fraternity.[20] Many non-Masonic Creoles claim that appointments and promotions are "cooked up" in the lodges. This is an accusation commonly heard in America and Britain, too.[21] American black Masons have hoped to reproduce these advantages in their own lodges but have lacked the economic and social rewards necessary to make the system work well.

Much of Cohen's analysis of Freemasonry in Sierra Leone probably holds true for Liberia. The major exceptions are that the Americo-Liberian aristocracy has not been on the verge of losing power to an ascending native population, and the Order probably has for a longer period of time been more intimately tied to politics than in Sierra Leone.

While the Masons of Sierra Leone have few contacts with Afro-American Masons, the visits of Liberian Masonic leaders have served to unite the branches of Prince Hall in both countries. And the ties with Liberia, and Africa generally, have not been one-sided. The Grand Lodge of Liberia, itself, was originally established under the authority of the Grand Lodge of Pennsylvania in the nineteenth century, and Liberians and other Africans have often received their initiation into the fraternity, or into the "higher" degrees of the auxiliary Orders, in the United States.[22] The Masonic records also show the existence of many individual connections between African and American lodges. For instance, the *Proceedings* of New York show that James Spurgeon, while a member of the American Legation in Liberia during the late nineteenth century, rose to the position of Senior Grand Warden in the Grand Lodge of Liberia. After his return to the United States, he affiliated with the New York body and became Junior Grand Warden of it.[23] More recently, in 1960, two of the most important Prince

[20] Ibid., pp. 434-435.

[21] Ibid., p. 435.

[22] *Proceedings* (Georgia, 1957). Earlier I mentioned that the Order in Liberia may have been started by Prince Hall Grand Lodge of Massachusetts.

[23] *Prince Hall Masonry in New York State*, vol. II, see heading "1905." Another American black who went to Liberia in the nineteenth century was Alexander Clark. He went there as the United States Minister. Because he was an active Mason (and Past Grand Master of his state) "he took with him his [Masonic] diploma as a passport;

Hall leaders, Grand Master W. W. Allen of Maryland and Grand Master John G. Lewis of Louisiana, in their capacities as heads of the Scottish Rite Masons, South, visited President Tubman in Monrovia and were awarded the Humane Order of Africa's Redemption.[24] The award was bestowed for their work in behalf of Prince Hall Masonry in the United States and on the African continent. (Plans had been made to organize units of Prince Hall in Ghana and Nigeria, both of which Allen and Lewis had visited.)[25] In 1957 another Grand Master, John W. Dobbs of Georgia, visited Africa as representative of his jurisdiction at the establishment of the Republic of Ghana.[26] Later he noted with pleasure the many prominent Masons he met while there, including Premier Nkrumah, who had joined the Order while at Lincoln University in Pennsylvania. From Ghana, Grand Master Dobbs journeyed to Liberia and was personally received by President Tubman.[27]

Prince Hall Masonry's concern with Africa is only one example of what might be called "black American Masonic expansionism." The black Masons, in keeping with solidly American principles, have always shown an inclination to carry the light of virtue to other lands. The oldest Grand Lodges started by establishing local lodges under their authority in the southern and western states in an attempt to spread the fraternity throughout the United States. Once they had accomplished this, they looked to neighboring nations for virgin territory. In 1898 the Grand Lodge of Illinois passed a resolution authorizing that body to establish lodges in the new, ex-Spanish possessions.[28] Two South Africans around 1917 were given

that would give him all the protection needed in a strange land." [Pamphlet: "Oration on the Life of Hon. Alexander Clark" by Reverend J. W. Laws of Grand Lodge of Iowa (no place, no date), early twentieth century]. For another interesting example of ties between Liberia and Masonry see *Review* (Georgia), 15, no.2 (April-June 1951): 4, where the efforts of American blacks to build a YMCA in Liberia bring them to Prince Hall for financial aid. Aid in the opposite direction came when the Liberian Grand Lodge sent money to aid black victims of the San Francisco earthquake (see Minutes of the 1908 *Proceedings* of California).

[24] Both were militant black leaders whose activities will be dealt with in detail in the chapters on civil rights.

[25] *Sentinel* (New York), 24, no.1 (Jan.-March 1960): 13.

[26] In 1922 Dobbs' immediate predecessor, Grand Master Dr. H. R. Butler, attended the Pan-African Congress and was greatly pleased with it.

[27] *Proceedings* (Georgia, 1957).

[28] *Proceedings* (Illinois, 1925), in a report that summarized the events of 1898. The spread of Prince Hall Masonry to non-American people sometimes resulted in friction.

permission to set up lodges in their homeland under the jurisdiction of the Grand Lodge of Connecticut.[29] New York Prince
Hall, not a Grand Lodge to be outdone by others, reported
in 1916 that her "First Masonic District" included Manhattan,
the Bronx and the Bahama Islands! New York ultimately
carried Masonry, and her authority, into Connecticut, North
Carolina, Halifax, Nova Scotia, the Bahamas, and Barbados,
and in 1968 finished off by establishing a lodge in Guyana, South
America. Today black Masonic lodges can be found not only
in the lands listed above but in Hawaii, Alaska, Central America, and Haiti.[30]

In attempting to tie the various parts of the fraternity closer
together, many other mechanisms have been employed. One
of the most important in the twentieth century has been the
International Conference of Grand Masters. This is a yearly
meeting of Grand Masters and other high-ranking Masonic
officials to discuss common problems. While helpful in coordi-
nating the jurisdictions in carrying out a number of activities—from creating uniformity in ritual to aiding the
N.A.A.C.P.—it is solely an advisory body for its Grand Lodge
constituencies. For many years it has been common for the
Grand Masters' Conference to meet in the same city as the
most important Masonic auxiliary Orders (i.e., Shriners, Scottish Rites, Royal Arch Masons, Order of Eastern Star, Heroines
of Jericho) and thus facilitate an even greater knitting together
of the different Masonic groups.[31]

Another means of creating bonds between the different
jurisdictions has been the various Grand Lodge journals, many
of which have appealed to more than local audiences. One of

According to the Masonic historian Harry Williamson there were a number of Spanish-
speaking lodges under the New York Grand Lodge's control. They withdrew because
of the "dictatorial" behavior of the special deputy placed over them by the Grand
Lodge (*Prince Hall Masonry in New York State*, vol. III, see heading "1937").

[29] *Proceedings* (California, 1919), C.C.F.C. reporting on New Jersey, which originally
had reported this.

[30] *Digest* (California), 10, no.3 (Sept.-Dec. 1962): 23.

[31] For many years after its creation in the early twentieth century, the Conference
was the subject of much opposition. Many important Masonic leaders felt it would
ultimately evolve into a central authority and attempt to impose its will on the state
Grand Lodges. To the extent that many states at first refused to cooperate in its
meetings, the organization was weakened. See Harry Williamson's report as C.C.F.C.
of New York, 1931, among other critiques of the Conference. The Conference, though
helpful in enabling Masonic leaders to meet together and form personal ties, did not
become really effective until after World War II.

the earliest of these journals was the *Pacific Appeal*, a newspaper published in San Francisco in the 1860s and 1870s. Though primarily a "secular" enterprise designed for the black community of the Bay Area, after the formation of the California Grand Lodge it was that body's official organ. Peter Anderson, editor, publisher, and Grand Master, dedicated a considerable portion of his paper to Masonic happenings in the eastern states; and its pages became a major forum for angry letter-debates among prominent East Coast black Masons over the fraternity's problems. In the twentieth century, among the many attempts at national magazines, two of the most notable were the *National Fraternal Review* (Illinois), started in the 1920s, and the *Prince Hall Masonic Review* (Georgia), started in the 1930s. Both journals devoted considerable space to the affairs of other states. The Grand Master of Georgia continually appealed to other jurisdictions for articles in order to broaden the magazine's appeal.[32] While neither journal achieved the large out-of-state subscribership it wished, both attracted as readers many of the most prominent leaders of Masonry.[33] It is through activities such as those reviewed in this chapter that the Masonic fraternity has maintained unity within its own ranks and, by so doing, has helped create bonds among the local black middle-class communities in which they have been situated.

The national and international "community" Masonry has helped form has been of crucial importance for the black middle class. This "community" unlike the local one, has not been a direct social support but it has been a vital psychological and intellectual reality. By its existence, middle class blacks have been able to identify with a larger social unit than their parochial geographical communities. They have been able to lessen the isolation of being a minority in the local black population by expanding the area of identification. For those blacks who travel from locality to locality or state to state,

[32] *Review* (Georgia), 1, no.5 (Feb. 1938): 3.

[33] Harry Williamson, the noted New York Masonic authority, writing as C.C.F.C. in 1930, was furious at the lack of support the *National Fraternal Review* received. He considered it an excellent journal and a credit to the fraternity, but the Masons outside Illinois refused to give it the financial support it deserved. He pointed out that for its first five years the *Review* (Illinois) occupied a prominent place in American Masonic literature, was recognized by white editors, and had an international reputation. Prominent Masons were quite willing to read it, but insisted on staying on its "free" list.

the national middle class "community" takes on a physical as well as intellectual form.

Freemasonry has expanded the horizons of its members not only by the links it forges between different communities. It also forces its members to look outward to the state and national levels by its concern with black civil rights. In the next two chapters we will deal with the role of Masonry in the struggle of Afro-Americans for their rights as first-class citizens.

Chapter **IX**

Integration as a Goal

Prince Hall has had a long history of involvement with the fight for black civil rights. Its very existence forces awareness of the race problem since it claims to be part of a worldwide, predominately white organization. In this chapter I will attempt to show how vehement the Masons have been in the struggle for racial equality and social acceptance from the larger white society. The Masons have never allowed hypocrisy or caste or black subordination to be accepted as natural. The fight for human dignity has been a hard one and not always successful; but the Masons have persevered, although white hostility, and even white "friendship," has left its marks on them.

Black fraternal organizations have long had a reputation for being escapist in nature, a way of temporarily forgetting the realities of a racist, segregated society. Whatever the validity of this view for other fraternities, it cannot be applied to Prince Hall Masonry.[1] The existence of black Masonic lodges is in itself a form of rebellion against caste, a refusal to accept the racial status quo. The Grand Master of Mississippi in 1936—a bad year for "uppity" black men—tells us succinctly why Freemasonry and Jim Crow have never mixed well:

> It is an institution that knows no Caucasian whiteness or Ethiopian darkness; an institution that knows only man and by the exercises of brotherly love, the rich and the poor, the high and the low, the black and the white ... meet upon one common level and are brothers; an institution where no man is above his brother except by intellect, charity, good deeds and education.[2]

[1] Though it can, of course, be applied to some individuals in Masonry.

[2] *Review* (Georgia), 1, no.4 (Jan. 1938): 15, quoting the Grand Master of Mississippi.

The head of Texas Masonry spells out the implications of this
universalist creed even more clearly when he says that Masonry
"recognized no superior race . . . . It is not an isolated exclusive
band of rigid class or caste for social stratification . . ." but
is open to all races and creeds. Freemasonry claims for itself
an applicability to all mankind and for its members a perfect
equality, regardless of "race, color, creed, religion, or politics."[3]
What could be more anathematic to white racists than the
white Masonic doctrines, taken literally and adopted by the
subject black race?

The prospect of complete social equality that Masonry has
held out for the black man has been a primary attraction of
the Order. Through Masonry blacks have been able to stand
on a common plane with millions of white men, bolstering their
self-esteem, and transcending their status as a persecuted and
oppressed minority race. The Grand Master of Alabama, whose
white compatriots may have been less than pleased had they
known his views, summed up the feeling perfectly when he
said:

> Ours is the fraternity that binds together two worlds while it
> anoints every ramification of universal citizenship. The Masonic
> Fraternity, and he alone marches down the feudal hall of Great
> Britain, grasps the stalwart Englishman by the hand and feels
> the warm response of fraternal greeting. He hails the German
> among his vine-clad hills, or in royal garb at the imperial court
> . . . . Ah, my brethren, the influence of the Gold links [of Masonry]
> has done much to soften the condition of our people.[4]

These words in 1925 came as an echo of those spoken by the
Grand Master of the same state fifty years earlier, at the birth
of Masonry among blacks in the newly emancipated South:
"the Masons of England, Scotland, and the Grand Orient of
France reaches [sic] forth their hand of Fidelity, and clasps
the ebon hand of the BLACK MASONS of Alabama, and
through me . . ." welcomes you into the brotherhood of Masonry.[5] It is not difficult to understand the pride, the hope, the

---

[3] *Proceedings* (California, 1920), Grand Master's speech.

[4] *Proceedings* (Alabama, 1925).

[5] *Proceedings* (Alabama, 1875), speech of Grand Master. Of course, everything I am
going to relate in this chapter contains certain "escapist" elements. But it is a type
of escapism that leads to a keen awareness and concern with racial discrimination
in America, and thus is basically not a retreat from reality.

self-respect that these men, only a few years out of slavery, felt as they found themselves greeted by white men as equals and as brothers through the medium of Freemasonry.

The original hope that Masonry offered black men was the integration of the races in a common brotherhood. The spread of Prince Hall Masonry from the northern states where it existed before the Civil War to the newly freed slaves of the South was greatly aided by that vision. Since white Masons, both North and South, refused admission to blacks during Reconstruction, the ex-slaves were forced to establish their own black Grand Lodges just as their northern brethren had done earlier, though they regarded this as only a temporary expedient. Peter Anderson, Grand Master of the California Masons and editor of the San Francisco *Pacific Appeal* spoke for black Masons everywhere when he said:

> We have established Grand Lodge organizations for several of the states not from choice, but on the principles of self-respect and self-preservation of the Masonic Order among colored Masons. ... We have been compelled to set up separate Grand Lodges ... the same way as we have been compelled to establish separate churches. The fault is not with us, and the remedy is with those who have for at least two generations failed to apply it.[6]

Earlier, Anderson had boldly proclaimed that "It is the policy of the Independent Colored Grand Lodge of New Jersey to dissolve, if all of its subordinate Lodges are taken under the jurisdiction of the white Grand Lodge, and it is the same policy of the other Independent Grand Lodges in the respective states, including ... California."[7] This desire for complete integration was echoed by the Masons of Florida and Washington, D.C. in the pages of the same journal.[8] Even ten years later, after the failure of Reconstruction and the collapse of many of the hopes for an early end to American racism, the black Grand Master of New York opened correspondence with his white counterpart by stating: "we stand ready now, as we have stood many years passed [sic], to obliterate any and all separate and distinctive features which we may possess and to join with you in cementing bonds of a perfect and complete fraternization

[6] San Francisco *Pacific Appeal*, January 4, 1873.
[7] Ibid., January 13, 1872.
[8] Ibid., September 7 and March 2, 1872.

under one grand lodge."[9] This letter was published in a number of New York newspapers and received favorable comment from white reviewers.

Unfortunately, integration with the American white Masons was not forthcoming. The dream that "black" Masonry and "white" Masonry would become simply "Freemasonry" had to be either abandoned, or more commonly, indefinitely deferred. Instead, the blacks concentrated upon obtaining "recognition" from whites rather than integration. Recognition required that the white Masons state that black Masonry, descending from Prince Hall of Massachusetts, was "legitimate," that it had received its charter from the English Grand Lodge and thus was entitled to all Masonic rights such as intervisitation between black and white lodges. Ultimately, many black Grand Masters implied, recognition would lead to integration; though, as the years passed, black Masons played down or totally ignored this final goal.

The significance of the "recognition controversy" cannot be overstated. The demand for recognition comes down to us through the decades as an unending, monotonous demand. One observer has gone so far as to say that "Negro Masonic literature deals almost entirely with arguments against the white Mason's charge that Prince Hall Masonry is clandestine [i.e., bogus]."[10] The reasons for the vehemence and persistence with which black Masons have demanded that the whites admit their legitimacy, even if they do nothing else, center on the psychological benefits the Negro membership has received from the fraternity. Freemasonry has presented the black man with a worldview that has aided in his creation of self-respect by supplying him with a history that is radically different from the traditional one associated with his people. The black Mason of America has traced his ancestry back to Prince Hall, a Massachusetts *free* man, and it is through him and the Masonic charter he received directly from the Grand Lodge of England that he claims Masonic descent. The importance of this historical lineage connecting the American black Mason with the past cannot be overemphasized. It has erased from the mind of the black Mason his actual descent from slaves; in fact, the whole

[9] *Proceedings* (New York, 1882), Grand Master's letter to white Masons.
[10] Edward N. Palmer, "Negro Secret Societies," *Social Forces*, 23 (December 1944): 212.

history of Negro servitude in America is ignored. Instead, the
black man is provided with an ancestry of freedom, from the
days of the Pyramids—which according to Masonic legend is
the earliest beginnings of the Order—through Prince Hall, a
free black man, to the present. In the proceedings of the Grand
Lodges, the history of Masonry, its antiquity and its power,
has been a constantly elaborated theme. While such discussions
have helped support the institution's claim to unsurpassed
greatness, it has also allowed the individual black Mason to
claim that same greatness as his own.

The need for the black Masons to see Masonic history as
their rightful heritage is illuminated by the changes they have
made in reporting general (i.e., white) Masonic history. Normally, black Masonry scrupulously has adhered to white Masonic ritual, ideas, and practice because of the necessity to fight
white charges that they are bogus and illegitimate. But in one
crucial place in the recitation of the early, legendary history
of the Order, the black Masons have markedly differed from
the whites. When discussing the most distant origins of the
fraternity, the Masons, white and black, have claimed descent
from the ancient Egyptians; but the blacks have seen this origin
differently from their white brethren, for "We learn from
science that the first man was the black man found in Africa,
then we concede the beginning of man was the black man."[11]
And it is also known that "the ancient Egyptians were the
original man—the black man. So out of Egypt and through
the black man, the world gains its first knowledge of the worship
of the deity and the cultivation of science . . . ." Thus the white
man received Masonry, both operative and speculative,
"through Egypt as the first man—the black man."[12] Not only
were "the Negroes . . . the founders of [the] arts, sciences and
[other] forms of culture instead of being only hewers of wood
and drawers of water . . . It must not be forgotten that Solomon,
the builder of the great Temple . . . is the great foundation
upon which Masonry the world over stands. Solomon was a
black man."[13] In a Grand Lodge of California report, the
authors, after announcing that the Egyptians were the first

[11] *Proceedings* (California, 1919), Report of the Committee on Research.
[12] Ibid. See also *Address* by John Edward Bruce (Grit) before the Craftsmen's Club,
New York, March 6, 1910 (pamphlet) for a similar view.
[13] *Co-Operation* (published by Illinois Masons), no vol., no issue (July, 1942): 17.

builder race, proclaimed that "This is true of the Black Race
unto this day ... [because Masonry] the principles of which
... our ancestors in Africa [originated] along the banks of the
Nile" is still carried on by the Negro of America.[14]

By this interpretation the black Masons have been able to
claim general Masonic history as their own, not just by a
tenuous thread, but boldly and completely. And that heritage
has not been a slave heritage, but a glorious history, a past
full of great ideals and great deeds. Masonry has been synonymous with culture; it has been the father of freedom, liberty,
democratic government, and the main support of mankind
when the forces of despotism have descended upon the world.
As the inheritor of the Masonic past the black man has ceased
to be a poor, insignificant member of an oppressed group and
has become a member of the most important and idealistic
institution the world has ever seen! Indeed, the black Mason
is not even a member of the "profane" world, since "In the
strict and ancient and technical sense of the word Masons are
a 'peculiar' people—a people dedicated and set apart." And this
chosen people has been given special knowledge and a special
mission to lead the world. As one Grand Master said, the Bible
tells of things to come though the Revelations are hidden from
normal man, "But ... these Revelations are not meant for the
world in general now, but merely the elect [i.e., Masons]. To
you is given to know the mystery. To the profane these things
are spoken in parables and dark sayings."[15]

[14] *Proceedings* (California, 1933), Report of the Committee on Foreign Correspondence. Martin Delany in his treatise on Freemasonry, (*The Origins and Objects
of Ancient Freemasonry, Its Introduction into the United States and Legitimacy Among
Colored Men* [Pittsburgh, 1853]), takes a slightly different tack. He sees the Ethiopians
as the leading race of mankind, with the Egyptians as a branch of that race. This
position makes it easier to maintain the black origin of Freemasonry: "In the earliest
period of the Egyptian and Ethiopian dynasties, the institution of Masonry was first
established. ... The Ethiopian early adduced the doctrine and believed in a trinity
of the Godhead. ... Had Moses not lived in Africa, the mysteries of the wise men
of the East would never have been handed down to us." He goes on to say, "From
whence could Moses—he leaving Egypt when young—have learned his wisdom, if not
from the Ethiopians? ... For the Egyptians were a colony from ... the former. ..."
Thus, "to deny to black men the privileges of Masonry is to deny to a child the lineage
of its own parentage. From whence sprang Masonry but from Ethiopia, Egypt and
Assyria—all settled by and peopled by the children of Ham?" (Delany, pp. 15, 16,
37, 39, 40).

[15] *Proceedings* (California, 1936), Report of Research Committee, and *Proceedings*
(California, 1914), Grand Master's speech. Most of these ideas are not peculiar to the
black Mason; they are shared by the white Masons as well. The important thing,

Because of these psychological effects, the institution of Masonry has done for the black middle class in a moderate way what the heterodox religious cults have done for the black lower class—cults like the Black Muslims, the Black Jews or Father Divine's movement. Both perform the important role of stripping their adherents of their slave past and giving them a new identity and sense of self-respect (sometimes to the extent of giving them a new name); and providing a philosophy-history that explains their past (which is glorious), their present (which is meaningful and pregnant with prospects), and their future (which is apocalyptic and millennial), and which foresees the black man inheriting the earth.[16]

The psychological benefits that Masonry has offered the black Mason have been severely threatened by the refusal of white Masons to recognize their black counterparts as legitimate. As a result, one repeatedly finds remarks like, "The doors of Freemasonry were open to the Sons of Africa and they were practicing the same in America when some of the ancestors of our Southern friends were feudal slaves and vassals to the lords of Europe," in Masonic literature.[17] In this remark we see an interesting turning of the tables; the Negro is not a descendant of slaves, the white man is.

One way in which the need for black Masons to prove their Masonic regularity is demonstrated by the practice of many Grand Lodges of starting each year's proceedings with a restatement of the original Charter that Prince Hall received. This is usually accompanied by a chronological history of black Masonry from 1775 to the present. In Grand Lodge reports and in Masonic magazines the authors never tire of repeating the history of the Order in great detail, often presenting involved historical-legal arguments to prove the legitimacy of Prince Hall Masonry—discussions that would make a Constitutional lawyer proud.

---

however, is that they play a special role for the Negro which is either not necessary or, more likely, less necessary for his white brethren.

[16] See Essien Udom's *Black Nationalism* (Chicago, 1962).

[17] *Proceedings* (California, 1909), Grand Master's speech. The Grand Lecturer, Western Division, of Alabama in 1925 put it this way: "Now, history tells us of the many dark-skinned kings and rulers as being among the first and foremost ancient Masons like the couchant [sic] sphinx whose lips are sealed. They left us in doubt as to the unsolved mystery of the whiteman's claims as to his lawful right to our inheritance [Masonry]."

For over 200 years the black Mason has sought recognition
from the white, but until recently to no avail. Throughout most
of American history, white men have degraded or at best
ignored blacks. White Masons were certainly no exception. The
white Grand Secretary of Mississippi is undoubtedly representative of the period in which he wrote (1909), when he said,
"Scopio Africanus is simply a brute, with no revenge or resentments, and no regard for the truth or the purity of women.
Whiskey and cocaine and miscegenation are his bane and until
some remedy is found for these great evils, the poor fellow
will continue to go down lower and lower in the social scale
. . . ."[18] Nor was bigotry limited to the South. When the C.C.F.C.
of Virginia boldly stated that the Negro was no better than
"a mule," the C.C.F.C. of Iowa commented favorably on the
analogy.

The unrelenting, ubiquitous white racism that permeates
American Masonry has led to continuous black protest and
to bitter verbal attacks upon white Masons.[19] As a result,
Masonry has never offered a fantasy land of pomp and pageantry, to which blacks could escape from the racial problems that
have afflicted their people in America. A black Masonic leader
by definition has always had to ram his head against the wall
of racial discrimination. One *cause célèbre* early in the twentieth century which provoked the united wrath of the black
Masons involved the white Grand Master of Mississippi's belat-
ed discovery that the white Grand Lodge of New Jersey allowed
a black local lodge under its jurisdiction:

> It is an open secret that virtue and morality, which are indis-
> pensable qualifications to [sic] membership [in Masonry], are
> foreign to the race. I felt it my duty . . . to cut loose [i.e., withdraw
> fraternal relations from New Jersey] from any who dare to open

[18] This quote and the following one come from *Prince Hall Primer*, Harry Williamson
(New York, 1946), items 216-218. In the Illinois *Proceedings* (white) of 1899 it was
said, "We know that Masonry is not only close in fellowship, but it is perfect in morals
. . . . And we know that the Negroes of the South are wholly incompetent to enhance
it. They are ignorant, uneducated, immoral, untruthful, and, intellectually, they are
more impotent than minority or dotage." Obviously, some white Masons disagreed
with such views, as is witnessed by the Fraternal Correspondent of Virginia (white),
1913, who said, "Now, to a brother in Western Australia, and equally to one in Maine,
no doubt it is natural that a Negro seems to be simply a black white man . . . , but
how utterly wrong they are in their disregard of scientific ethnology. No Negro ever
born is the social, or moral peer of a white man." (see items 217-218).

[19] For a disucssion of relations between white and black Masons which counteracts
and modifies the basic racism of American Freemasonry, see Chapter XI.

the door of Masonry to a people whose standing for virtue is a mockery to civilization.[20]

The black Grand Master of California in outrage lashed back, saying:

> It is not only an open secret, but an open fact, that in ... Mississippi there are living examples of the price these Southern moralists put upon the virtue of unprotected Negro maidens, who are forced to succumb to their vicious and animal nature, and if ... he has found Negroes who are unfit to assume the responsibilities ... of Masonry, they are those who are assimilated with the blood of his race and have inherited their vicious habits.[21]

The difference between the hope of universal brotherhood which Masonry has held out to the American Negro and its reality has always created bitterness. When a black Mason in 1876 proclaimed that "the mission of American Masonry is to oppress the oppressed, to keep a struggling people down, to yet continue to trample underfoot a people who have already been most fearfully wronged, outraged beyond conceptions,"[22] his view, while more alienated than most, was still indicative of a constant undercurrent of thought among black Masons. White Masonic hostility and discrimination have seemed small reward for the black men who have been promised the Kingdom of God on earth.

The actual state of American Freemasonry, which has not been universalist, has not believed in or practiced the equality of men and races, but rather has been a major support of racism and segregation in America, should reasonably have turned most blacks against it. But it did not. The promise of brotherhood was there, and despite the disillusionment, anger, and frustration, faith would not die. Hope sprang from two important sources.[23] The first was the belief that justice and righteousness would of divine necessity prevail. In 1875 Prince Hall Grand Lodge of Massachusetts informed all the black Masonic Grand Lodges in America of God's plan in establishing black Masonry:

> That this Act of communicating Light was a part of His great plan in the liberation and elevation of our people, is evident from

[20] *Proceedings* (California, 1909), quoted in Grand Master's speech.
[21] *Proceedings* (California, 1909), speech of Grand Master.
[22] *Pacific Appeal*, November 25, 1876.
[23] For a third source of hope, see Chapter XI.

the fact that those who sought the continuance of our enslave-
ment have refused, and do yet refuse, to recognize ... us as
Masons. Hence the struggle between light and darkness which
has been continued for the last hundred years; a struggle between
the class of Masons who fail to discern that a denial of the
brotherhood of man strikes a fatal blow at the whole Masonic
system and those who accept true Masonic landmarks ....[24]

In this monumental struggle, the Grand Lodge of Massachusetts was confident that the cause of "equity and justice shall
become ... supreme" and the "hateful spirit of caste" will be
destroyed.[25] In a less religious vein the Grand Master of Ohio
in the same year placed his trust, as Masons did then and
still often do, in the secular promises of enlightened white
Masons that their lodges are or will soon be willing to recognize
the black Masons because of the obvious "justice of our
cause."[26]

Throughout their history Prince Hall Masons have worked
to establish connections with the European Grand Lodges. In
so doing, the importance of striking down the caste line has
always been prominent—both as a vindication of the promise
of Masonry and in order to achieve the self-respect that comes
from being treated as an equal human being.[27] When a black
chairman of a committee on fraternal relations could say of
a white Masonic body: "The Grand Lodge of Scotland seems
to have a very warm Masonic heart, whose flames extend to
all mankind .... They bar no man's color from the folds of

[24] *Pacific Appeal*, January 9, 1875.

[25] Ibid. Seventy-five years later the Grand Master of Georgia echoed this view when
he said, "The good will ultimately triumph over evil because God Almighty is on the
side of right. His side will never lose," and thus racism in America will be ended
[*Proceedings* (Georgia, 1949)]. It is interesting to note that Dobbs was a militant Grand
Master who often forcefully cried out against American hypocrisy and injustice. In
this speech he turns around and says, "Here in America a man has the chance to
be free. He has a chance to work, to save, to own something and to develop his
personality." This pronouncement goes against both the facts and the interpretation
he placed on them on many other occasions. This paradox will be discussed in detail
in a later chapter.

[26] *Pacific Appeal*, January 2, 1875.

[27] As was the case with the Jews of Germany, there was also a hope that foreign
recognition would force local acceptance. Indeed, a sympathetic white Past Grand
Master of Ohio, Lucius Bierce, in 1870 advised the blacks to petition Europe because
"If the lodges of Europe recognize you, the lodges of America will be compelled to
..." (Davis, p. 112). This hope was not groundless since a white Grand Master of
Ohio in 1875 did in fact urge recognition and emphasized that he did so at least partly
because of the position of European Masons (Davis, p. 112).

Masonry," he could do so with a feeling of pride.[28] When a white Grand Master of the Bahama Islands could come to the black Grand Lodge of Illinois in 1881 and congratulate the brothers on their progress as citizens and Masons, and say "I know no difference on account of color, if such is the American idea of Masonry I do not desire to learn it. In England and the Bahama Islands color would be no barrier against a man as a Mason," then Masonry really had delivered what it promised the American Negro.

Both the pledge and the actuality of racial equality in the Masonic Lodges of Europe have been a constant source of inspiration for the black man.[29] For example, Grand Master H. R. Butler of Georgia in 1926 felt greatly honored to be one of the four black members of the Masonic Research Lodges in England. And his hope was that the great black Masonic historian Harry Williamson would publish articles in "French, Spanish and other European tongues" to help establish Prince Hall's reputation abroad. Williamson did just that and wrote countless essays for non-American Masonic journals designed to familiarize the Europeans with black Masonry and to tell the world of the hypocrisy, racism, and viciousness of American whites to their darker brothers.[30]

The importance of official recognition by Europeans, not easy to come by and sometimes not obtained, is illustrated by the extremes to which some black Masons went in achieving it, or at least in convincing themselves that they had achieved it. Around the turn of this century the Grand Lodge of Louisiana decided to establish a subordinate lodge in British Honduras. It did so, Louisiana claimed, because for many years a number of "colored Honduras gentlemen" had desired to become Masons but could not do so. But of greater importance was the belief "that it would go a long way in cementing the fraternal ties between us and the Grand Lodge of England."[31] In a similar though more far-fetched move, the Grand Lodge

[28] *Proceedings* (California, 1915).

[29] Prince Hall Masons visiting Europe are allowed to sit in on the lodge meetings. The Creoles of Sierra Leone, like their American brethren, find this sign of fraternal acceptance very attractive (Abner Cohen, "The Politics of Ritual Secrecy," *Man* 6, no.3 (1971): 436).

[30] See Harry Williamson's collected articles in the Schomburg Collection, e.g., "Prince Hall Masonry" from "The Freemason" of London, November 9, 1912.

[31] *Proceedings* (California, 1900), C.C.F.C. reporting on Louisiana.

of New York tried to convince itself that relations between it and the Grand Lodge of England—which did not officially recognize Prince Hall Masonry—were very close by using a letter addressed to one of its members from an English Mason thanking him for the "personal favors" he received while staying at a Schenectady Hotel![32] Instances such as these demonstrate the psychological importance of the European connection.

However, while black Masons have not been above inventing ties with European whites to boost their self-esteem, they have not normally had to do so. Reality has been on their side. Grand Master Peter Anderson of California was realistically able to announce in 1870 that "Any American Mason, be he black or white, can gain admittance to any of the European lodges, providing he can prove himself to be a Mason. . . ."[33] The Grand Master of Alabama was also able to point with pride to the Grand Orient of France's statement that racial discrimination was un-Masonic; and even when he went on to say that the Europeans would "Teach the American Mason that though they may not recognize us, the time is coming when the Masonic world will, and then it will be too late, when the Vox POPULI will recognize us," there were legitimate grounds for his optimism.[34]

Nevertheless, in applying for recognition by European Grand Lodges the blacks have faced great difficulties. Despite the strength of their case for legitimacy as a Masonic body, foreign Masons have risked the disfavor of the mass of white American Masons when they have dared recognize the blacks. On more than one occasion, such as the famous New York (white) Grand Lodge versus the Grand Lodge of Hamburg, Germany, controversies have raged for years between American and European whites over the color question. In the Hamburg case, the Germans did recognize the black Grand Lodges of Ohio and Massachusetts, with the result that the white Grand Lodge of New York severed relations with them for fifteen years.[35] But for the blacks, the nondiscrimination that European recognition has implied to colored Americans has justified any expenditure of energy to achieve it.

[32] *Sentinel* (New York), 1, no.4 (April 1948): 3.

[33] *Pacific Appeal*, October 1870.

[34] *Proceedings* (Alabama, 1874).

[35] See *Prince Hall Primer* and *Pacific Appeal*, July 26, 1873, January 17, 1874, July 3, 1875, July 10, 1875.

While almost all dealings with the European branch of Masonry have tended to be positive assets, there have been a few negative encounters. In 1916 the C.C.F.C. of New York broadened the black Mason's usual sympathy for colored minorities to a general sympathy for the unjustly maltreated of any race when he commented adversely on Masonic activities in the British Isles:

We read with interest how the Grand Lodge of England passed a resolution ... prohibiting persons of German, Austrian, Hungarian or Turkish birth attending any meeting of [their] Grand Lodge ... and they are hereby required to abstain from such attendance during the progress of the Great War .... How like our beloved land of 'equal opportunities' that sounds, with this only difference, that the prohibition by the Grand Lodges of the States is only directed against the people of one race. Masons in whatever clime, has [sic] a right to look for plain dealing from all members of the Craft ... be they of the black or Caucasian race. ...[36]

In a second and much more important case, the black Grand Lodge of New York came into direct conflict with the English. During the Second World War the English Grand Lodge asked foreign Masonic bodies to send financial aid because of the terrible suffering from German bombing. Though the English Masons specifically asked several American white Grand Lodges, the Prince Hall Masons of New York felt duty-bound to send their own donation of $50 since they traced their ancestry back to England. The Grand Lodge of England refused the money and, with a brief, curt note, returned it. The black Masons were outraged and humiliated by what they considered a gratuitous insult, an insult certainly caused by the English Grand Lodge's fear of alienating the mass of white American Masons at a time of great need. While the incident did not lead to closer European-black Masonic relations, nevertheless the original donation was in keeping with traditional black attempts to create some feeling of fraternity and equality between themselves and the Masons of Europe—whether official or unofficial in nature.[37]

Despite the crucial role European whites have played for American black Masons, the most important relations for

[36] *Proceedings* (New York, 1916).
[37] *Prince Hall Masonry in New York State*, vol. III, see heading "1941."

blacks have been with white Americans. While European recognition has been both ego-gratifying and useful, American acceptance has always been the ultimate hope. In demanding recognition from their compatriots, the blacks have utilized a number of different approaches. "Recognition" is a vague term, and over the years Masonic leaders have interpreted it flexibly. Depending upon the racial climate of the country they have given it different public meanings, emphases that would allow at least some hope of achievement; underneath the official explanations, however, the desire for an end to segregation in the Order has been constant and strong. In the years after the Civil War, recognition was simply a gentle way of asking for complete integration; as the American race system hardened it increasingly came to mean inter-visitation between lodges in the manner of the colored and white churches, where ministers were able to speak at each other's meetings. With the full flowering of segregation, the official definition of recognition was narrowed to a simple declaration of "legitimacy" that the blacks could use in fighting the "bogus" black Masonic organizations that sprang up all over the country and competed with the Prince Hall Fraternity for members. During the history of black Masonry it is usual to find all three of the public interpretations of "recognition" being discussed simultaneously, though with one or another predominating.

One factor that has affected the official emphasis has been the element of race pride among blacks. Even at the height of integrationist aspirations in the 1870s some Masonic leaders protested against those blacks who "humiliated" the race by demanding recognition too vehemently. Past Grand Master of Massachusetts, De Leon, writing in the San Francisco *Pacific Appeal*, said:

> As a race we are too exquisitely sensitive and as individuals exquisitely punctilious to 'crowd' ourselves where we are not wanted; all we ask and shall continue to DEMAND as our inherent right, is a recognition upon the broad, cosmopolitan ... basis of Masonry which knows neither clime nor color. ... When this recognition is accorded upon perfect equality ... your 'social gatherings' will not be intrusively visited, as we do not propose to become ... worshippers of white men.[38]

[38] *Pacific Appeal*, March 11, 1874.

The importance of not humiliating the race while asking for fraternal acceptance is illustrated by the actions of the Grand Master of New York who wrote to the white Masons of his state in 1882 saying that he looked forward to the union of the two Grand Lodges, to, in other words, complete integration. However, a year later, after the Chairman of the Committee on Foreign Correspondence of Washington, D.C. had commented upon that letter, the Grand Master claimed that he had asked only for "recognition" (i.e., legitimization) and not amalgamation, since that was up to the whites and he would not "degrade himself" by requesting it. What we see here is how truly delicate the problem actually was; the Grand Master wanted integration, but as a right, not as a condescending, paternalistic favor. He had to be careful not to cross the line between pride and humiliation, and it seems that he came quite close to crossing that narrow divider.

The difficulty of pursuing integration while not degrading oneself has continued ever since. Almost fifty years later the fiery and militant Grand Master of California, Rev. J. H. Wilson, attacked the black Masons of his time who went through the country demanding recognition by white Masons: "Be it well understood, I, for one want NO recognition from ANYBODY, from ANYTHING, or from ANYWHERE that will destroy or in the least effect my identity as descendant of Prince Hall Masonry...."[39] Perhaps the classic statement of this sentiment was written by George Crawford in 1914 in a book entitled *Prince Hall and His Followers*. He rejected the idea of any social interaction with whites on any terms when he said:

It is not surprising that a white Mason is not able to conceive of the vindication of Negro Masonry without coupling it with 'recognition' by white members of the Fraternity. Reward as the justly earned approbation of the superior white race is the unconscious mental attitude from which scarcely any white man can escape. That is the offense which our sincerest white friends ... commit against us and to whom our intolerance of the same is understandable only as race consciousness. The Negro Mason is not interested in the vindication of his legitimacy merely as a means ... to recognition by white[s]. ... A man would be interested in removing the stigma of bastardy, not so much

[39] *Proceedings* (California, 1924).

because it might bar his reception into polite society, but to
vindicate himself in the eyes of his own self-respect.[40]

Statements such as these, which can be found in all eras,
are important as demonstrations of black race pride and self-respect. However, insofar as they appear anti-integrationist, at
no time have such views been the predominant expression of
black Masonic desires; and even for the speakers themselves
their words must be taken at less than face value.[41] The internal
logic of Masonic philosophy has demanded total integration
of the races; and throughout its history the actual interest
of their race has led black Masonic leaders in the same direction.
The Grand Master of Wisconsin expressed the real thrust of
Masonry when he asked, "How long can we go on mouthing
vain babblings about the universality of Masonry while tolerat-
ing what we know to be the denial of the basic concept and
cornerstone of Masonry, [the division into] one section white,
one section black."[42] A similar position was taken by the leader
of Texas Masonry in 1947 when he protested, "it is not only
treason against the true spirit of American democracy, but the
height of absurdity seriously to suggest the possibility of our
segregating ourselves from one another."[43] The races, he went
on, must live together, and Masonry, based as it is on the
Fatherhood of God and the Brotherhood of Man, can help.

It is easy, especially in today's electrically-charged atmosphere, to confuse black dignity with black nationalism. The
records of the Grand Lodge of Texas provide an illustration
of why some Masonic statements must not be accepted in the
exact form they are given. In 1960 the Grand Master of Texas
corresponded with the white publisher of a Masonic journal.
After praising him for his work in fighting racial prejudice, he
went on, "If you could only implant in the minds of white
Grand Lodges that Prince Hall seeks no inter-visitation, no
participation in social events of white Masons . . . , [only] public
recognition of . . . regularity and legitimacy," he would be
satisfied.[44] The white editor in a reply praised the Prince Hall
Order and said he hoped for the day when there would be no

[40] Quoted in *Review* (Georgia), 14, no.1 (Jan.-March 1950): 9.
[41] Grand Master of California J. H. Wilson's ambivalent and contradictory feelings
about whites will be dealt with in detail in a later chapter.
[42] *Digest* (California), 1, no.4 (Oct.-Dec. 1951): 18.
[43] *Proceedings* (Texas, 1947), speech of Grand Master.
[44] *Proceedings* (Texas, 1960), speech of Grand Master.

black, white, or yellow Masons, only one unified fraternity. The Grand Master of Texas was overjoyed at this comradely Masonic aspiration, and he informed his Craft that he "approved it totally."[45] He did so despite his loud protestation that black Masons wanted no integration, no social inter-visitation, nothing but a formal, purely technical announcement of recognition.

Over the years the reasons for anti-integration statements by black Masonic leaders have not solely been due to adverse white words or actions. Black leaders have often feared that many of their followers lacked pride in their race—the more they have believed this, the more strongly they have played down their own desires for Masonic unity. Typical is an article written by the Grand Master of Michigan in 1960 who took a strongly antiwhite position and recommended that black Masons completely ignore the white fraternity rather than waste time worrying about integrating with it. Part of the reason for his belligerent stand was the obvious fact that "in the fore-seeable [sic] future, men like Talmadge, Eastland, [and] Faubus ..., Masons all," will never accept blacks as fraternal equals. But much of his belligerency stemmed not from white hostility but from the refusal of a large proportion of the black Masonic membership "to adopt the ... attitude of dignity demonstrated by our young adults, that expresses itself ... [as] 'we do not give a damn what others might think ...,' " and thus terminate their humiliating concern with white "approval." The lack of race pride among some Masons, now and in the past, in and of itself has forced men like Grand Master Greene to make explicit anti-integrationist statements for the sake of self-respect.[46] Despite such statements, the goal of union between the white and black branches of the fraternity has remained fundamental to Prince Hall Masonry.

The tendency toward integration receives support not only from the doctrines and purpose of the Order itself, but also from the pull that American nationalism exerts on the membership. Black Masons are extremely patriotic and as a result their expressions of race pride have come only within the narrow limits set by such loyalty—to wit, within an integrationist framework. The Masons glorify black heroes as super Ameri-

[45] *Proceedings* (Texas, 1960), speech of Grand Master.
[46] *Digest* (California), 9, no.1 (May-July 1960): 3.

cans, as proof that blacks have the right to claim American history as their own. This kind of ego-boosting can be quite effective and can create a whole gallery of black models, but it gives little support for anti-integrationist sentiment. The glorification of black Americans has been more compatible with the movement for assimilation than useful in providing a basis for ethnic separatism.[47] The Masonic *Proceedings* are replete with references to black Masonic heroes of the past. Leading the list, of course, is the founder of black Masonry, Prince Hall, followed by Richard Allen, Absalom Jones, and many others. While the objective activities of these men are praised (and since the 1950s primarily for their civil rights activities), to a large extent they are more important as links to the general American past, sometimes specifically to *white* heroes, than they are in themselves. For example, Prince Hall is often mentioned in conjunction with important white leaders; and while his own legitimate and inspiring accomplishments are highlighted, there is usually an attempt to merge his accomplishments with those of the whites around him. In one Prince Hall Day Address the speaker pointed out,

> our Reverend Brother Prince Hall ... along with *his contemporaries*, served as a founding father of our American Idealism. ... [He fought for many causes.] Such [also] were the spiritual drives of those, *his contemporaries*, good men and true who were masons, who served in moulding ... our Declaration of Independence, and the Constitution ....[48]

The speaker goes on to say why he keeps linking Prince Hall with the phrase "his contemporaries":

> As I have indicated ... the founding fathers of our documents of freedom were contemporaries of Prince Hall. Some were associates, others were Brothers in the Bond of Masonry. Because of the factor of reciprocity in nature, wherein the age has a positive influence upon the life of many, by the same token, the man, be he beggar, prince or potentate; master or slave, has just as positive an influence upon the age. Let us then examine ...

---

[47] Most of the white ethnic minorities have done the same thing in "discovering" great Jewish, Polish, and Italian patriots who have single-handedly made America great. For white ethnics these heroes have created increased group self-respect, but only as part of the process of identifying more closely with standard American history and of furthering the process of cultural assimilation.

[48] *Digest* (California), 7, no.2 (no month 1958): 3, 4-5.

the life and activities of Prince Hall in the light of reciprocity
so as to determine the influence that our Grand Master Prince
Hall may have had [on] ... our lives as free men.[49]

The result of this is the merging of Prince Hall with the select
group of American Founding Fathers. In this speech, as in many
others, the black hero is linked to more "standard" white heroes.
After the speaker mentions Hall's dedication to Negro education in Boston, he goes on to praise the deeds of white Masonic
leaders who fought for education, such men as George Washington and De Witt Clinton. As a result, the black Mason is
able to identify with white leaders who otherwise might seem
to have no relationship to him. He can feel that he, like other
Americans, is the direct spiritual descendant of Washington
and Jefferson, of the founding fathers and the American past.

The integrationist use of black history is nowhere more
evident than in the fact that when the Grand Masters' Conference created "Prince Hall Day Observances" they specified that
during services honoring the founder, "the theme of 'Americanism' was to be expanded and enlarged upon."[50] As a result,
when the state jurisdictions set up the celebration many of
them called it "Prince Hall Americanism Day." While a black
hero is often used as the means of entry into the American
past, he is not mandatory; often the identification is made
simply by stressing that important white leaders have been
members of the Masonic fraternity. Given the known hostility
of white Masons to the Prince Hall group, and the constant
attacks made upon the whites for their hypocrisy, it is interesting that much glory and pride is claimed by the Prince Hall
group through identification with white Masons of the past.[51]

The power of American nationalism to restrict black race
pride and prevent the growth of strong separatist sentiment
within Masonry is quite striking. Why this nationalism is as
strong as it is considering the objective reality of black oppression is a complex problem one cannot solve here. At least part
of the answer—besides the obvious and powerful one proposed
by one Masonic Grand Master that "we know no other land

[49] *Digest* (California), 7, no.1 (no month 1958): 3, 4-5.

[50] *Digest* (California), 7, no.1 (no month 1958): 3.

[51] Long discussions of white Masonic notables are ubiquitous in the black Masonic
proceedings. See William H. Grimshaw's *Official History of Freemasonry among the
Colored People in North America* (New York, 1903), pp. 362-368, for a listing of
illustrious white Masons.

than this"—is the relation between the black and white bourgeoisie. The attractiveness of the white middle class, its values, life style, and promise of ultimate acceptance to those who conform to the "good life," has always had an irresistible quality for the black Masons. As long as they have accepted the basic promise of American life as true, their race pride has been allowable only insofar as it has demonstrated that blacks have lived up to white standards of heroism and accomplishment, thereby furthering black claims to acceptance as 100 percent Americans.

That black pride is shaped and limited by the white standards of what one should be proud of is strikingly illustrated where black Masons have traditionally attempted to be most aggressive in their self-image: their claims that the blacks are the descendants of the ancient Egyptians.[52] On the face of it the proposition seems a manifestation of quasi-nationalistic pride: this is our true heritage, we are a great, independent and ancient people, not simply Americans. But there is a strange quality to this supposed heritage. It is not that the Egyptians are not black—despite white claims, the Egyptians are an extremely mixed race, many of whose members would be considered Negro if they lived in the United States; rather, the identification of American blacks with the Egyptians verges on sacrilege. The folk heritage of American blacks has been the identification with the heroes of the Old Testament, the ancient Jews. The Bible has also provided them with the option of choosing to claim descent from the ancient Ethiopians. Both identifications are indigenous expressions of black pride and black self-consciousness. How then did the black middle class, and especially the black Masons, come to associate themselves with the archetypal enemy of the Jews, the nation of slaveholders *par excellence*?

The answer is clear. To the whites the Egyptians were the great builder race, the fathers of Mediterranean and, therefore of Western civilization. To claim descent from them was, first, to accept white values of what greatness was and, second, to present oneself to whites as deserving of their solicitude. (The fact that the Egyptians held the Jews in bondage and were

---

[52] As I have pointed out earlier, the black claim to an Egyptain past is not simply a black Masonic invention; the idea has been maintained by black intellectuals for generations, and the Masonic position only reinforces the general belief of a significant minority of the black middle class.

slaveholders, not slaves, may not, on some deeper level, be displeasing to many middle-class blacks who want to forget their history of bondage in America.) The identification with Egyptians by blacks cannot be an indigenous surfacing of race pride (since the black "folk" would never have the opportunity to see Egyptians in any light other than the Old Testament portrays them), but rather must be seen as a defensive reaction of educated blacks to white hostility. The linking of Afro-Americans with Egyptians makes sense only in terms of the silent dialogue between whites and blacks in America. It means that middle-class blacks accept white evaluations of what civilization and culture are (i.e., Pyramids "yes," Bantu villages "no"), and gains its nationalistic and prideful quality of turning the tables on the dominant race only after the white man's ground rules have been accepted.

The influence of the white middle class in defining for blacks what constitutes good and bad, moral and immoral, civilization and savagery, means that the black bourgeoisie is constantly on the defensive. They must be continually self-conscious of "big brother's" standards. Behind the appearance of self-contentment and self-glorification lurks a desire for acceptance and approval.

One recent change in the black Masonic fraternity which might appear to represent a greater independence from the whites and a movement away from integrationist goals is the widespread adoption by state jurisdictions of a new name: Prince Hall Grand Lodge. For most of their existence the individual state grand lodges made no mention in their titles of any distinctive ethnic quality that might differentiate them from other Masonic groups. Indeed, in the nineteenth century when whites requested that blacks call themselves "African Grand Lodge" or some equivalent, the black Masons fiercely protested. They maintained that any such "preface" would *ipso facto* admit to the world that they were less than 100 percent legitimate.[53] The adoption of the name Prince Hall in the last

[53] The Grand Master of Texas proudly told his Grand Lodge in 1934 of the refusal of the Texas black Masons in 1870 to compromise their Masonic claim to universality: "our Masonic predecessors refused to change the original characterization of our Order from its actual appellation by calling the Order 'Colored'. . . . Therefore, they safely and intelligently incorporated our Grand Lodge under the name, 'Free and Accepted Masons,' that possessed no tinge of racial [,] national or other differentiated characterization."

few decades can be seen as a change in this view. Indeed, some
leaders have emphasized an explicit "nationalistic" element in
the change:

> Several [Grand Lodges] have changed their names in the last
> few years to such and such PRINCE HALL GRAND LODGE. This
> move is promoted by a desire to become unified but mostly by
> just PLAIN RACE PRIDE. Our ideal is changing his COMPLEXION
> slowly but surely. Where we once saw it personified in WHITE
> RECOGNITION, we are no[w] viewing with pride the life and works
> of the Great Soldier, statemen, diplomat and the outstanding
> Master, of his time, our first Grand Master, Prince Hall of
> Massachusetts.[54]

However, this view in 1936 and even today is a minority one.
The records show that the name change is overwhelmingly
justified in terms of the necessity of combating "clandestine"
black Masonry, which thrives on the inability of people to
recognize the legitimate group by name. The leaders of the
different state lodges have hoped that by maintaining a uniform
nomenclature their rivals would suffer.

Nevertheless, the name change does reflect at least a minimum of increased self-confidence. Masons are willing to make
their distinctiveness more official than in the past. Indeed, some
black leaders have taken great pride that a number of West
African Masonic groups who could have affiliated directly with
European Grand Lodges have associated themselves with the
Prince Hall Fraternity instead. This willingness to talk about
the black fraternity as a unit—which, of course, reflects social
reality—has not been done, however, at the expense of black
claims to Masonic equality or their long-range goal of Masonic
inter-racial unity.[55]

Black Freemasonry, unlike the black church, has not lent
itself to the growth of a unique Afro-American culture or to
nationalistic tendencies because while the autonomy of the
black Order on a social level has been quite real, it has been
severely restricted in its innovative powers by the need to
conform to the "universal" (i.e., white) laws, ritual, and organization of the institution. Masonry, like more truly independent

---

[54] *Proceedings* (California, 1936), Grand Master's speech.

[55] Actually, the fact of black-white conflict and legitimate-illegitimate black Masonic
conflict led to the use of the generic name "Prince Hall Fraternity" for generations
without any separatist overtness.

black institutions, could aid black pride, but only within the
guidelines that the Euro-American middle class set down, not
in terms of any specific values produced by indigenous Afro-
American experience. The limits on the ability of the black
Masons to become a separatist order is nowhere better illustrated than in the continued present-day use by most Prince
Hall Grand Lodges of Masonic legal texts which are fundamentally racist in their attitude toward blacks. Some of the most
widely used and highly respected Masonic guides are those
written by Albert Mackey. Mackey, one of the greatest white
Masonic law interpreters, was an antebellum Charleston gen-
tleman who believed in the innate inferiority of Negroes and
the absolute ineligibility of blacks to join the Order. His books
explicitly state his view of the race question. Despite a long-
standing undercurrent of hostility to the use of texts by such
a man, the importance of Mackey for understanding general
Masonic law has forced blacks to use him. The growth of a
true separatist position among black Masons would necessitate
not simply the rejection of Mackey but of the entire Masonic
institution, which is irrevocably intertwined with Euro-American white history.

The fact that black Masonic leaders have predominantly
desired integration rather than ethnic segregation is in no way
a slur on the black man's racial pride, though today many
might take that position and feel compelled to force black
Masonic material into a mold emphasizing a nationalistic and
separatist tradition. During most of the history of Prince Hall
Masonry the demand for integration, not separation, has been
the militant, racially proud position. The real alternative for
the black Mason has not been go-it-alone Afro-American Nationalism, but quiet acceptance of his "place" in the American
caste system. The type of race pride that has enabled some
black leaders today to turn their back on white America has
not been a viable option for the majority of men who have
become Masons. For those with a powerful sense of antiwhite
race pride, the Euro-American institution of Masonry has been
the wrong type of fraternity to which to belong. A purely local,
Afro-American fraternity would have been more congenial.
From the beginning blacks have insisted upon copying the most
important Euro-American fraternal organizations for a reason:
they have wished to be identified with, and accepted as equals

by, whites. Given the race prejudice of the Caucasian majority
this has not been a humiliating or submissive desire. Rather,
it has demonstrated a healthy amount of self-pride and has
been a direct attack on the doctrine of white supremacy. While
it is true that the prointegrationist argument has sometimes
been used by blacks who have lacked any sense of race pride,
who have wanted nothing more than to lose their racial identity, and have been quite willing to humiliate themselves in
the process of achieving their goal, this has not been the normal
situation. Rather, the average Mason's desire for integration
has resulted from his refusal to be either humiliated or kept
in an inferior status.

The emphasis in this chapter on the integrationist thrust
in Prince Hall Freemasonry contradicts the position espoused
by E. Franklin Frazier and others that the black middle class
is basically separatist and not integrationist.[56] Frazier argues
that significant segments of the black population (especially
businessmen, professionals, and to a lesser extent white-collar
workers) have a vested interest in segregation. They reap
monetary, social, and psychological rewards from having a
captive black market. Not only do they benefit positively from
the ghetto walls, but they fear that white competition resulting
from integration will show up their relative incompetence.
Segregation has allowed low levels of skill to exist in the black
community without external pressure to improve. The logic
of Frazier's position implies that Freemasonry as a source of
prestige, power, status, and income would likewise foster prose-
parationist feeling. This view certainly receives support from
one white Masonic observer friendly to the black fraternity.
In 1959 he said, "Prince Hall leaders are wise enough to know
that they would be reduced to 'zero' if white Masonry took
over .... They want nothing like it ...; they are a great
fraternal power among their own color" and want to keep it
that way.[57]

Doubtless, Prince Hall Masonic leaders, like the leaders of
most black organizations, have some vested interest in segregation. That is hard to deny, though there is no discussion of
such motives in the Masonic records themselves. But the degree

[56] See "Human, All Too Human" in *The Rise of the Ghetto*, edited by B. Rudwick
(Belmont, Calif., 1971), for an example of Frazier's view.
[57] Van Cott writing in the *Digest* (California), 7, no.4 (Oct.-Dec. 1958): 7.

of vested interest and the practical effects it generates are easily exaggerated, in Masonry as in any other institution. Frazier, it must be remembered, did not make his observation from a detached perspective but as part of a general indictment of the black middle class. It was the "incompetence and mediocrity" of black professionals and businessmen, and the resulting white "patronization" of blacks (which worked to humiliate men of talent such as Frazier himself) that infuriated him. His hostility to the black bourgeoisie on this point was only a specific instance of his general negative evaluation of the group.

Frazier was right in pointing out a tendency in the black community that liberals might too easily have overlooked. But he failed to emphasize the countervailing pressures working against the black middle class's actively taking steps to protect their interest. G. Franklin Edwards seems closer to the truth when he discusses the attitude of black teachers in South Carolina in the middle 1950s. He points out that these blacks had a vested interest in segregation and a strong fear of job displacement if integration occurred. However, the fears were countered by an ideological commitment to desegregation and a realization of the importance for blacks and the country that integration promised. According to Edwards, the result of the contradictory pressures was a marked level of ambivalence and mixed emotions. Yet, he concludes, "It is not likely that these attitudes [i.e., fear of integration] strongly counteract tendencies to change."[58] To the extent they maintained social distance from whites, teachers did not act out of petty self-interest but from the fear that whites would unjustly use their power and refuse to implement integration in good faith.

The same can be said of Prince Hall Freemasonry. On the one hand the Order has an ideological commitment to integration. On the other hand, many Masons receive benefits from segregation that would be threatened by the merging of the black and white branches of the fraternity. The two must create ambivalence, but the ideological aspect is more basic. The gains in ego from the promise of universal brotherhood and equality are too great for short term advantage to outweigh them. Man's

[58] G. Franklin Edwards, "Community and Class Realities: The Ordeal of Change," in *The Negro American*, edited by Talcott Parsons and Kenneth Clark (Cambridge, Mass., 1966), p. 299.

ego does not live by narrow self-interest alone. In addition, the reality of white prejudice has meant that the possibility of immediate Masonic integration has been small and thus the danger to self-interest has been limited, while the attack on self-esteem because of white Masonic rejection has been extensive and constant.[59] Such a situation has strengthened the integrationist thrust while keeping active separatist tendencies à la Frazier at a minimum.[60]

Prince Hall Freemasonry has been forced to take a stand on civil rights questions simply because of its claim to Masonic status, regardless of its desires to get involved. But the Order has also willingly involved itself in the racial fight. The next chapter will deal in detail with the specific battles for human dignity fought by the fraternity over the years.

[59] The Chairman of the Committee on Research of California's Grand Lodge, 1920, clearly illustrates the fundamental importance of Masonry's worldwide unity for the black man: "[all that we have shown] prove[s] beyond the shadow of a doubt that Masonry from its earliest conceptions was intended to be universal in its applications. That the known world has always been its field and the members of every nationality its subjects. . . . Investigations up to this point prove conclusively that in the principles and practices of Ancient Free Masonry, race, color, creed, religion, or politics were unknown. That in the various countries of today no line is drawn, except here in our Free America [where] . . . the greatest universal organization, except the church, known to all the world . . . [is divided] . . . . In this land of the free and the home of the brave, where our sons have shed the most blood at the altar of democracy . . . our path to improvement is mostly obstructed. Only our own Masonic white brethren say to us, 'You shall not be men,' 'You shall not advance.' " Given an interpretation such as this, for the black Masons not to fight for integration would be evidence of a lack of race pride and self-respect. The strength of the black Masons' hostility to Freemasonic segregation is also well illustrated by the words of the Grand Master of Arizona: "Negro Masonry has been challenged. We live in a country where we as a group, have been set apart in every endeavor of life. The meanest racial programs of Europe do not equal this systematic persecution and exclusion that has been practiced from top to bottom in the civic and political set-up in this great country. Thus, it was deemed necessary, even to separate on a racial basis, the *one organization that offered true fellowship to all men of the world*" [from *Proceedings* (Arizona), no date (probably 1939), reported in *Proceedings* (California), C.C.F.C., 1940; italics added].

[60] Nothing that has been said here is to deny the actual "separate" character of Prince Hall Freemasonry; American Masonry is a segregated institution and always has been. I am concerned with the social ideal of the black Order, not with the present and past reality.

Chapter X

Black Masonry's Civil Rights Activities

If Prince Hall Masonry's claim to fraternal equality had not already precluded its being escapist, its leadership would have. The leaders of the Order have always been deeply concerned with the problem of civil rights, not only as it affects Masons but for the entire black community. In 1907, Grand Master Tinsley of California spoke to this point when he addressed his constituents on "The Race Question." He bitterly argued that while the gravest problem before the public involved race, the American people refused to solve it because that would require them to treat "the Negro as a man." While the black man had fought in every war for American freedom, the only justice the government had provided him was "to allow him to be lynched, burned at the stake or sacrificed in some way to appease the savage appetite of the dominant race."

Tinsley's lament was not meant for an audience that saw Masonry as a refuge from the realities of American life, and his brethren reasoned as he expected they would. His views struck a cord in Masons from coast to coast. The C.C.F.C. of Georgia reprinted verbatim a large portion of the address for the benefit of his jurisdiction (another illustration of the close links between Grand Lodges). The C.C.F.C. of Texas did likewise and added to it a resounding "we agree," while the C.C.F.C. of New Jersey felt compelled not only to approve Tinsley's sentiments but to expand upon them by providing a "solution." He told the Grand Lodge that "The allusions of the Grand Master [of California] on the race question were not only right, but deserve high commendation, for the time is come when a great and highly important organization like this of ours should step to the very forefront of the battle to both defend and direct a defenseless people."[1] The C.C.F.C.'s belief that Masonry had a major role to play in defense of black liberties was not unique but, as we shall see, represented a widespread sentiment in the Order.

While the deteriorating racial situation in America during the early twentieth century continually forced individual Masonic leaders to speak out against injustice, the event that brought out a universal reaction among the brethren was America's entrance into World War I. For black Masons the immediate effect of the Great War was rising hopes and expectations that reached a peak in 1918, reflected in the words of the Grand Master of Texas: "We believe that our second emancipation will be the outcome of this war. If the world is to be made 'safe for democracy,' that will mean us also." If white Texans had any doubt about what constituted a "Second Emancipation" for a black Mason, the Grand Master resolved them by saying "we are expecting to be free—free from segregation; free from ostracism, free from . . . mob violence. . . ." Neither the Texas Grand Master nor the black Masons generally accepted "their place" in the American caste system. The fact that they were adherents of Freemasonry was not irrelevant to their stand because, as the Grand Master was quick to point out, "Masonry has contended, from the beginning [for] equal rights to all; special privileges to none."[2]

By 1919, when the Chairman of the Committee on Foreign Correspondence of the Grand Lodge of California commented upon the Grand Master of Texas' speech, the situation had changed radically. The expectations that the war created were not only left unfulfilled, but race conditions had deteriorated. As a result, when C.C.F.C. J. H. Wilson did review the speech, he felt impelled to supplement it. When the Grand Master of Texas said the black man had much to fight for in this war he was right,

> But . . . not in Germany, nor yet in Europe, but right here in Texas and the rest of these United States, is the bloody or bloodless battlefield where the Negro has the most for which to fight. If the Negro could afford to . . . die . . . to liberate the

[1] *Proceedings* (California, 1908), C.C.F.C. quoting New Jersey; *Proceedings* (Georgia, 1908).
[2] *Proceedings* (Texas, 1918).

serfs of Europe, and to make permanent the rule of the Anglo
Saxons, can he afford to do less to protect his own home and
loved ones from the insults and ravages of the brute force of
the degenerates of America. . . . We have been fighting the wrong
fellow. The low American and not the German, is the brute who
has ravished our women, lynched, flayed, burned and massacred
our men and women.[3]

The militancy of J. H. Wilson did not abate with this outburst
of frustrated alienation from white America. In 1920 he broadened his attack on racists and drew some conclusions on how
to implement the fight against them:

> If the darker races of the earth are to ever check the encroachment
> of this proud, arrogant, intolerant, white race, and force them
> to see and acknowledge the Brotherhood of Man, it will come
> only when . . . the darker races . . . become united . . . . It is because
> the white race sees into the future, that he has as part of his
> program in his world conquest for mastery, the keeping apart
> of the darker races of the world.

The first step to uniting the colored races, argued Wilson, was
for the American Negro to develop some intraracial solidarity,
and he, like many other Masons, felt the fraternity could be
the major instrument for creating it.[4]

While J. H.Wilson was vehemently protesting race conditions
on the West Coast, his New York brethren were equally engaged
in raising their voices in protest. Though no more effective
in solving the problems confronting the race than was C.C.F.C.
Wilson, they did make their voices heard at the very highest
councils in the land. In 1919, the Grand Lodge of New York
sent a resolution to President Wilson and the Congress demanding that the federal government intervene to stop the
lynching, burning, and oppression of black people in the South.
In 1920, Arthur Schomburg, Grand Secretary of the New York
Masons (and founder of the Schomburg Collection of Negro
Literature of the New York Public Library), opened a correspondence with the United States Justice Department dealing
with the problem of mob violence. He informed the authorities
that the Masons of his state were deeply concerned with
lawlessness in the South, that many of their sister jurisdictions

[3] *Proceedings* (California, 1919).
[4] *Proceedings* (California, 1920).

had seen their Masonic Temples burned down without any possibility of redress. He specifically emphasized the need for a federal anti-lynching law, not only to further justice but to forestall the possibility of black despair leading to black revolt. He argued that if neither of these considerations moved Washington, the government must at least realize that mob violence "pictures to the other nations the low estimate which Americans have for the majesty of the law . . . ."[5] The Schomburg appeals provoked two letters from the Justice Department, the second of which curtly ordered him to inform members of his race "once and for all" that lynching was a local matter and of no concern to the federal government; blacks should stop annoying the Department with their incessant complaints.

Despite white officialdom's hostility to black protest, it continued. The Grand Lodge of Pennsylvania went on record in 1920 in support of a federal anti-lynch bill, a position that was copied by other Masonic Grand Lodges. Ten years later the Masons of New York were so horrified by "the wholesale execution of colored youth in Alabama" that the Grand Master felt compelled to appoint a committee to send a telegram of protest to the Governor of that "bloody state." In the mid-1930s the California Masons sent telegrams to all the state's representatives and senators in Congress asking support of the anti-lynch legislation before that body. It was the hope of the Grand Lodge that the bill to end the "un-American and barbarous practice" of lynching would be passed with the active support of all law-abiding citizens who wished to maintain America's reputation as a Christian country.[6] Such attempts to sway the leaders of white America were not uncommon, despite their lack of success.

Disillusionment and protest in the immediate aftermath of the First World War were by no means confined to the Masons of the North. One of the angriest leaders of the fraternity was the Grand Master of Georgia, Dr. H. R. Butler. His speech to the Grand Lodge in 1920 may very well have been the most ominous and threatening of any presented in the period. Butler began by saying that though the Great War in Europe was

[5] *Proceedings* (New York, 1920), reprinting the Schomburg letters.

[6] *Proceedings* (California, 1934-35), reprinting the telegrams. An identical resolution was sent in 1921 in support of the Grand Lodge of Pennsylvania's protest [see Report of the Committee on Resolutions, *Proceedings* (California), 1921].

officially over, the fight had not ended. There still existed on the continent the Bolshevik Army, which was pledged to conquer the world in the name of the "toiler." Many Americans claimed that this was not true, but it was. And just as true was the existence in America of more poor and hungry people than rich, despite the land's abundance. Soon, he said, the class war would reach the United States—the proof of which was the "unjust" jailing of the "candidate for radical social change," Eugene Debs. His jailing had kindled a fire that could not be put out until all the laboring people of America had achieved their rightful reward. Butler ended by saying the blacks must be prepared for the great class war when it came.

Conditions in Georgia in the early 1920s in no way alleviated the initial sense of alienation that the end of the war created for Grand Master Butler. As a result, he more than once felt it imperative to loudly protest the continued state of affairs. One of his more biting attacks on racial conditions in Georgia came in 1925 when he told the Grand Lodge that those who blamed the great northern migration primarily on such neutral factors as the boll weevil and the low price of cotton were distorting reality.[7] Rather, he protested, the mass exodus from Georgia was caused by injustice in the courts, poor schools, poor wages, taxation without representation, segregation, lynching, and general debasement of the blacks by the whites. If the white image of the "good" black man in Georgia was a man who saw no evil, heard no evil, and spoke no evil, Grand Master Butler in the 1920s had certainly forgotten his "place."

Another outspoken opponent of the continuing oppression of blacks in the years between the two world wars was also a southern Masonic leader, Grand Master Charles Hendley of Alabama. Despite his place of residence, Hendley, like Butler, refused the white man's version of the black man's place in Alabama society; and he was not afraid to let his fellow Masons know it. As he saw it, the continued degradation of the Negro by American "democracy," if not reversed, would cause the entire system to "fall of its own rottenness" because "it is freedom and equality and liberty for all or freedom, equality and liberty for none." The best way to correct the evils of racial oppression was for the Negro to "regain his right of a

[7] The emphasis on causes other than racial discrimination for the great migration that Butler protests against are again in favor among scholars today.

free effective and untrammeled use of the ballot in Mississippi
as well as Massachusetts; in Alabama as well as Arizona; in
South Carolina as well as New York."[8] This was a view common
to Masonic leaders everywhere. The unique quality in Hendley's belief in the importance of the vote was the powerful
imagery he employed when he proclaimed to his Grand Lodge
that, "Little as we may think of it, next to the Church, there
is nothing which so intimately concerns and affects the life
of people as politics. Politics is as essential to temporal salvation, as religion is to eternal salvation."[9] His reasoning
in this was not dissimilar to that of some important white
Americans of an earlier era, "To live under laws in the making
of which we have no part; to be subject to officers in whose
selection we have no voice is slavery, call it by whatever other
name you wish."[10]

The importance of the ballot has been continually emphasized by Grand Masters throughout Prince Hall Masonry.
However, because of the Masonic doctrine that the Order must
abstain from partisan politics, the problem of voting has usually
been discussed without reference to any specific election or
personality. When direct political conflict has entered the lodge
halls, the response has usually been similar to that of the Grand
Master of Illinois in 1916:

> Brethren using Masonic Lodge literature for political purposes
> and for publishing and circulating lodge emblems of masonic
> cuts, and titles, and numbers of other things which are unmason-
> ic, are liable to discipline. You must refrain from using the lodge
> rooms for political meetings.

The prohibition on partisan politics in Masonry, while inhi-
bitory, has never been universally enforced. Among the most
frequent "offenders" in this matter have been the Masons of
Illinois, which may explain the pronouncement just quoted.
The official journal of the Illinois Masons in the 1920s, the
National Fraternal Review, took an active interest in "un-Ma-
sonic" political activity. In a 1927 editorial the journal spoke
out against one of the front runners in the race for the
Democratic presidential nomination, Senator James Reed of
Missouri. The article suggested that Prince Hall Masons and

[8] *Proceedings* (Alabama, 1938).
[9] *Proceedings* (Alabama, 1939).
[10] Ibid.

blacks generally should realize that the man was an expert manipulator of Negrophopia and a danger to the American black man.[11] The next year the *Review* engaged in a campaign to convince its readers that the blacks of Chicago should elect their own black congressman. The very fact that whites had discriminated against blacks and pushed them into a ghetto now provided them with the means for self-protection, if only they would vote as a united group.[12] A few months later, the journal went even further, beginning to sprinkle throughout its pages articles and "fillers" supporting specific politicians, and pointedly noting their Prince Hall Masonic affiliation. There were recommendations for the Craft to vote for "Brother" William Dawson, "If you would have your own representation" in Congress; "Brother" Kersey from "Universal Lodge No. 65" for State Representative, and for Sanitary Trustee, Morris Eller, who, the article proclaimed, was already "Popularly endorsed by Prince Hall Brethren."

The Grand Lodge of California, which was more wary than Illinois of partisan politics in the Order, was not above making exceptions when the opportunity presented itself. In 1919 the Grand Master announced with great pleasure that Delta Lodge member Frederick M. Roberts had been elected to the state legislature, the first black man ever elected to that body. While the Grand Master's statement gave no clue as to what part the fraternity played, or should play, in such elections, a few years later his successor left the brethren with no doubt. Since the only black man in the legislature was a Mason, as were "the best men of the state," it was the duty of every member of the Craft to keep him in office and to elect additional men "who by united effort may look well to the interest of the group."[13]

In the same year, 1928, the *Fraternal Review* (a New York-based journal) informed the Craft of the political activities of William McDonald, absolute ruler of Texas black Masonry and an important figure in the Republican party of Texas. The editor felt that a letter McDonald had written to the head of the Republican National Committee, Colored Division, would be of interest to the Masons of New York. McDonald

[11] *National Fraternal Review* (Illinois), 4, no.12 (June 1927): 2.
[12] *National Fraternal Review* (Illinois), 5, no.9 (March 1928): 2.
[13] *Proceedings* (California, 1928).

was obviously not adverse to such publication since he began his letter "Through you, I wish to speak to all the Negroes of the United States." McDonald went on to charge that Ku Klux Klanmen in the South had joined the pro-Hoover committees, that the Republican party was in the hands of the lily-white faction, and that blacks were denied the right to participate in nominating conventions and primaries. While conditions deteriorated on the local level, the situation was equally oppressive on the federal level, with "the Departments at Washington . . . honey-combed and dominated by the humiliating policy of separating government employees because of color . . . ." McDonald also protested that while the federal government had the power to stop segregation on inter-state carriers, end the slavery of peonage, and stop lynching, it had done none of these. McDonald ended by warning the Republicans that "No party has a mortgage on us. No party, no political organization has any deed or trust," and if the presidential candidate does not stand firmly for black rights he will lose the black vote.[14]

Examples such as these, appearing with even greater frequency after World War II, show that Masons have often been directly involved in partisan politics. Nevertheless, it is far more common to find exhortations to register and vote as a general duty than to find political electioneering. The Grand Master of Virginia in 1932 was quite representative when he told his Grand Lodge that Masons, as the leaders and advisers of their communities, had a duty to teach the race "that the time has come when we must look upon the ballot as a personal responsibility"; all blacks must register and vote, but it is especially incumbent upon Masons.[15]

The ballot has promised the Masons an infinite variety of rewards when used properly by the black population. Not the least in importance has been its power to improve the quality of black education, which Masons like most Americans have considered the single most important factor in achieving success. Throughout their history the Masons have tried to put pressure on local educational officials. Most Grand Lodges have maintained committees on education which each year make recommendations to the membership. It has been quite com-

[14] *Fraternal Review* (New York), 8, no.10 (Oct. 1928): n.p.
[15] *Proceedings* (California, 1933), C.C.F.C. commenting on Virginia.

mon for such committees to recommend that all subordinate lodges encourage the local authorities to provide longer school terms, better school buildings, and increased salaries for black teachers.[16] Often they have recommended that special local lodge committees be organized in order to champion such reform.[17] When this pressure proves unsuccessful, they suggest that the brethren resort to the polls and pick men who are responsive to their wishes.[18]

While the Masons have traditionally been willing to attempt to persuade the whites to provide better educational facilities, their position has not been meek, as is witnessed by the firm stand taken by a committee of the Grand Lodge of Texas in 1939. The committee enthusiastically reported on the Southern black teacher's fight for equal salaries for equal work. They noted that what Negro teachers in Louisville, Kentucky had accomplished by a strike could be achieved everywhere. Alabama, Tennessee, and Louisiana teachers had already followed Kentucky's example, and the committee hoped to see the movement spread throughout the South. It concluded by reminding the Masonic membership "that the only way to get justice in any field of labor is to fight for it, plan for it and pay for it."[19]

In their efforts to improve Negro education, the Prince Hall Masons have found that pressure on local officials, and voting for progressive school administrators and politicians, were complemented by direct lobbying in the state legislatures. For example, in 1932 the Committee of Education for the Grand Lodge of Missouri, after collecting data to demonstrate the inferior conditions in black schools, repeatedly sent representatives to the state legislature until they persuaded it to raise the appropriation for black education. The significance of such activities was not lost on other Grand Lodges, as is

[16] *Proceedings* (Alabama, 1925).

[17] *Proceedings* (Texas, 1934).

[18] *Proceedings* (Texas, 1947), Report of Committee on Education.

[19] *Proceedings* (Texas, 1939), Committee on Education. In 1949 the Grand Master reminded his brethren of the traditional Masonic interest in good education. He pointed out that "one of Prince Hall's significant contributions to the progress . . . of his day was his valiant fight for the right of the Negro children of Colonial Boston to full participation in the educational [process] . . .; you know of the part played by Masons, most especially that of Past Master and State Representative Corneal A. Davis, in the matter of equalization of teacher's salaries in the schools of southern Illinois. Our interest in education must ever be kept alert and active."

witnessed by the favorable comment in the *Proceedings* of California. The C.C.F.C. of that state recommended that all education committees in the Prince Hall Masonic family emulate Missouri tactics in their fight for black youth.[20]

While civil rights, voting, education, and racial uplift were all of concern to Prince Hall Masons in the decades before World War II, there has been a proliferation of such activities and discussions in the postwar period. It was similar to the heightening of civic and racial concern which took place after World War I, except that it was part of a civil rights revolution that gained strength and flourished, rather than one which bloomed and died without results.

In the years immediately after World War II many Masonic leaders saw what they felt to be a rising tide of reactionary sentiment in America, a new form of fascism.[21] They hoped Prince Hall Masonry would be in the forefront of the fight against this new threat from the Right. Unfortunately, the new reaction that appeared upon the American scene took the form of an anti-Communist crusade, a movement the Masons found difficult to combat because of their own class fears of Communism and the danger that they would be Red-baited. As a result, in the 1950s Masonic bodies and their main national forum, the International Grand Masters' Conference, continually passed resolutions attacking the Red menace in order to prove their loyalty. They even had their views read into the Congressional records. Nevertheless, they always mixed their standard anti-Communist rhetoric with strong statements in support of civil rights, and vehemently attacked those who manipulated anti-Communism in order to prevent racial equality. Quite representative of their approach in these years was

---

[20] *Proceedings* (California, 1933). The concern for quality education was not the only problem which forced Masons to trek to their state legislatures. For example, in 1915, when the state of Michigan proposed to pass an antimiscegenation law the Grand Master of Michigan appointed a delegation to go to the legislature and protest the gross insult to the race [see *Proceedings* (California, 1916), C.C.F.C. commenting on Michigan]. The Masons sometimes found that they could work best by dealing directly with the local power centers rather than the state legislative. For example, in the early 1950s a Past Grand Master of Ohio spoke at a Grand Masters' Conference of the need to attack segregation on the local level. He accused the Los Angeles, California, Fire Department of discrimination and then "stated that similar conditions had existed in Columbus, Ohio, but it was broken up and that the Prince Hall Masons played an important part in doing so" [*Digest* (California), 3, no.4 (Oct.-Dec. 1953): p. 18].

[21] *Review* (Georgia), 1, no.1 (Jan.-March 1947): 14.

the view expressed in the *Prince Hall Masonic Review* of Georgia. In an article in 1950 it argued that while blacks must fight Communism abroad, they must also fight it at home. This could only be done by strengthening democracy. Since czarist excesses led to Stalin, the same could happen here if racial discrimination was not ended:

> Let those who fear that the forgotten man in our own country may listen sympathetically to the enticing claims of the Communists, also remember that to a black sharecropper in Mississippi it can little matter whether the heel on his neck belongs to a white man speaking ... Slavic ... or to a white man speaking ... with a Southern drawl. Communism is not merely a word, it is a political idea. You cannot destroy an idea even with an atom bomb.[22]

It can only be beaten by a more valid idea. A year earlier the C.C.F.C. of Georgia had gone even further, saying that it was anti-Russian sentiment in America which made world affairs unsafe, not the Communist menace, and he coupled this with the observation that reaction was "riding high in Georgia" with bigotry and lawlessness experiencing a full resurgency.[23] Basically, the Masons were willing to support anti-Communism as long as it did not endanger their own efforts for civil equality; and when necessary they used it to achieve their goals. As a Grand Master of Alabama said, he had the right to expect and demand that the leaders of the West live up to their precepts at least to the extent that the leaders of totalitarianism lived up to theirs. If the Communists oppressed on principle, the democracies must liberate on principle as well.[24]

The most important event in the post-World War II era for Prince Hall Masonry in its fight for civil rights was the relationship that the Order established with the National Association for the Advancement of Colored People. Before the war, many Masonic Grand Lodges had looked favorably upon the organization and had contributed money to its local branches. As early as 1922 the Grand Master of California had told his brethren that the spirit of the abolitionists was not dead because the N.A.A.C.P. carried it on, and thus it deserved the financial support of the fraternity. Nevertheless, its relations

[22] *Review* (Georgia), 14, no.3 (July-Sept. 1950): 22.

[23] *Proceedings* (Georgia, 1949).

[24] *Proceedings* (Alabama, 1952).

with Masonry as an institution, rather than with Masons as individuals, were meagre. In 1951 this situation changed drastically when the International Conference of Grand Masters in cooperation with Thurgood Marshall (a Mason) created the Prince Hall Masons Legal Research Fund under the control of the N.A.A.C.P.

The establishment of the fund made a deep impression on many Masonic leaders. The president of the conference summed it up well when he proudly announced that by their action, "we have assumed a place of leadership unequalled by any other organization. We have moved out of the seclusion of our halls ... into the community to serve the country, the race, the community and God."[25] This high opinion of their achievement soon received confirmation from outside sources. A few years after the inception of the fund the *Chicago Defender* presented the Grand Masters' Conference with an award for service to humanity for setting up the Legal Research Bureau.[26] At the same time Thurgood Marshall announced that the Masons had every right to be proud of their contribution to the N.A.A.C.P. since the only organization to surpass them in the amount donated was the Congress of Industrial Organizations (CIO). In 1958 Marshall paid the Masons the highest possible tribute by publicly saying that without their financial support many of the cases won before the Supreme Court could not have been fought. "Whenever and wherever I needed money and did not know of any other place to get it, Prince Hall Masons never let me down." In that year the Fund had received $142,000![27]

One of the most noteworthy aspects of Masonic support of the N.A.A.C.P. was the role played by the southern branch of Prince Hall Masonry. Two of the most prominent leaders working for the link between Masonry and the N.A.A.C.P. were Grand Masters John Wesley Dobbs of Georgia and John Lewis, Jr. of Louisiana. We have already seen some of Dobbs' activities in the 1930s, such as his 1938 speaking tour of Georgia with the leader of the black Elks championing the power of the ballot, and his invitation to the Grand Master of Maryland, W. W. Allen, to address the Civic and Political League of

[25] *Proceedings* (California, 1952).
[26] *Digest* (California), 3, no.4 (Oct.-Dec. 1953): 16.
[27] *Proceedings* (California, 1958), report of C.C.F.C.

Atlanta in 1939 on the power of black mass action protest movements to achieve civil rights. In the 1940s he headed the Georgia Voters' League, an organization dedicated to regaining the ballot for the black man. According to Grand Master Ashby Carter of Illinois, in 1948, "When 25,000 Negroes, despite intimidation and threats, marched to registration places in Georgia and qualified to vote," it was the result of "the sterling work of Grand Master J. Wesley Dobbs, who organized and led the campaign . . . ."[28] John Lewis, Jr., who received awards in Africa for his Masonic work, became a member of the National Board of Directors of the N.A.A.C.P. in 1953 and served on it for many years.[29] While the grand Masters' Conference in 1951 pledged to raise $20,000 in the first year, both Georgia and Louisiana contributed far more than their quotas. By 1958 Georgia alone had given $32,000 and Louisiana $24,000.[30] In 1962 the annual N.A.A.C.P. report presented at the Conference took special note of "The Grand Masters and the Prince Hall Masons throughout the Southern jurisdiction [who] have provided moral and financial support for their Research Department . . . [and] have stood up to be counted in the economic, education and social crises of the times . . . ."[31]

While the fraternity as a unit was endeavoring to aid in the struggle for civil rights through the Grand Masters' Conference, Masonic leaders on the state and local level were far from idle. While the post-World War II period saw such older Masonic statesmen like the Grand Masters of Georgia, Alabama, and Maryland continuing their prewar activities, it also witnessed the rise of many new faces. One of the most prominent of these was Louis Fair, who became Grand Master of New York in 1943. Fair was deeply embroiled in the fight to end segregation in the New York State Militia. He announced his intention to make this discrimination in New York a paramount issue in the fraternity—long before the problem of segregation in the National Guard became a major political issue—because he felt that Prince Hall Masonry had a duty to be in the vanguard in the fight for equality.[32] Fair wrote articles and made speeches attacking military segregation. In 1948 the Grand Lodge's

[28] *Proceedings* (Illinois, 1948).

[29] *Topics* (Illinois), 16, no.2 (April-June 1953): 4.

[30] *Proceedings* (California, 1958).

[31] *Digest* (California), 10, no.3 (Sept.-Dec. 1962): 17.

[32] *Sentinel* (New York), 1, no.3 (March 1948): 2.

official organ, the *Sentinel*, entered the fight alongside the Grand Master with a biting editorial demanding that the Governor of New York take immediate action to desegregate that part of the National Guard which lay under his, rather than federal, control.[33] Response to the editorial was heavy. One writer, Major William G. Holly, former head of the Third Separate Infantry Batallion, New York Guard (Colored), informed the editor that when "the stigma of segregation will be removed . . . much of the credit will rebound to you" because of your "pitiless publicity."[34] A black lawyer in Massachusetts commended the editor for his bold and effective attack on the outrageous situation in New York.

While Grand Master Fair and his brethren concerned themselves with segregation in the East, Grand Master Ashby Carter of Illinois was active in the Middle West. Carter, who was also president of the militant National Alliance of Postal Employees, was probably the most outspoken advocate of civil rights among the Masonic leaders in the twentieth century. The type of leadership he brought the fraternity is best illustrated by the four events that he himself considered the high points of his life: marching in an N.A.A.C.P. picket line in 1940 in the fight for integrated war work for Negroes; his membership in the Chicago Council for Negro Organizations and their 1941 pilgrimage to Washington to fight for integration; his 1945 election as Grand Master of Prince Hall in Illinois; and his appearance before the judiciary committee of both houses of the Illinois legislature in 1947 to fight for a fair employment practices committee.[35]

Carter's total commitment to active civil rights agitation made him, unlike some Masonic leaders, contemptuous of those who denied Masonry's right to intervene in political and civic activities. The most important fight that the Grand Master led the fraternity in was the battle for the Fair Employment Practices Committee (F.E.P.C.) of Illinois. He demanded that the Masons work as members of the Order, not simply as concerned citizens, for the necessary legislation. By June of 1949 he felt that the campaign for the F.E.P.C. was assured

[33] The State War Military Disaster Corps attached to the National Guard was state-controlled.

[34] *Sentinel* (New York), 1, no.11 (Oct. 1948): 11.

[35] *Topics* (Illinois), 11, no.2 (Feb. 1948): 2, 4-5.

of success, and it was time to congratulate the membership on its role in the victory. He specifically praised Past Master James A. Green, a delegate to the legislature who helped keep the fraternity and those working to pass the bill in constant contact.[36] When the bill unexpectedly went down to defeat, Carter counseled the brethren to work even harder to force the legislature to reconsider it. In keeping with his wishes Masons from twelve southern Illinois communities attended an important F.E.P.C. meeting held in 1950. Carter unexpectedly died in office in the early 1950s, with the fair employment practices legislation still unenacted, though his work was continued by his successor.[37]

Another one of Carter's major activist programs was his 1947 proposal to establish a Grand Lodge civil rights fund.[38] He saw his project as the means for allowing each local lodge to pay its share in the fight for freedom. The money raised was allocated for all types of civil rights activities, and some of it was used in the Grand Lodge's fight for the F.E.P.C. Under the Grand Master's leadership the Masons became deeply involved with many non-Masonic organizations. They worked with the N.A.A.C.P., Urban League, *ad hoc* protest committees, and newspaper campaigns, among others. Often cooperation between the fraternity and outside groups was facilitated by the presence of prominent Masons heading the non-Masonic organizations. For example, when Carter informed the Craft in 1947 that the Masons of Chicago were actively aiding the N.A.A.C.P. in the fight for adequate housing, he pointed out that "Brother" Henry McGee, President of the Chicago N.A.A.C.P., was actively engaged in working with them; a similar situation prevailed in Masonic cooperation with the Citizens Committee on Housing headed by "Brother" John H. Sengstacke, editor and publisher of the *Chicago Defender.*[39]

Of the Masonic jurisdictions, Illinois, for many decades, has notably been the most politically involved and civil rights-oriented. At the very least, its militant *National Fraternal Review* in the 1920s and early 1930s, its *Co-Operation* magazine in the early 1940s, and its bold leaders like Ashby Carter and

---

[36] *Topics* (Illinois), 12, no.19 (July 1949): 3.
[37] *Proceedings* (Illinois, 1959).
[38] *Topics* (Illinois), 10, no.1 (Jan. 1947): 5.
[39] *Topics* (Illinois), 10, no.4 (April 1947): 4.

his successor are all outstanding in Masonry. This activity is not totally unexpected considering the high level of political activity and general race consciousness traditionally associated with the black community of Chicago which has made up the heart of Illinois Masonry.

New York State, which should also have been a militant leader of Masonry, whether in its traditional role or its more progressive pursuits, did not live up to that expectation. For many years New York Masonry was numerically small, and its activities were limited, not only in the matter of civil rights but in other areas as well. It was not until the late 1950s and early 1960s that New York took its place in the forefront of Masonic Grand Lodges, especially in working for racial equality. One of its most notable activities took place in 1963. The Grand Master of New York, in an attempt to make the voice of Prince Hall Masonry on civil rights heard in the community, appointed the then Junior Grand Warden Edward Lawrence to head a new committee, the Freedom Fund Committee. The first effort of this committee was to plan a historic, public, *Freedom Now Fund Rally*. They hoped that Martin Luther King, Jr. would speak, and they planned space in the armory where it was to be held for local branches of the N.A.A.C.P., CORE, and other civil rights groups. The rally was held and the $10,000 profit was divided in part among the major civil rights organizations, while the rest was given to the local lodges for distribution locally.[40] At the rally the first New York Grand Lodge Medgar Evers Memorial Award was presented to the Reverend "Brother" Milton A. Galamison, Pastor of Siloam Presbyterian Church and a major black leader in the fight for school desegregation in New York. (Galamison was later prominent in the fight for community-control of the schools.) The award was created to honor those fighting for black rights. At the time of Evers' assassination New York Masonry sent its condolences to the Grand Master of Mississippi as well as to the family. After the 1964 rally the New York Grand Lodge voted to send $500 to his widow.[41] The *Freedom Now Rally*, which was well publicized in New York by the mass media, was originally proposed after the Grand Lodge, parading as a unit, had returned from the March to Washington in 1963. The march

[40] *Proceedings* (New York, 1964).
[41] *Sentinel* (New York), 16, no.3 (July-Sept. 1963): 2.

itself had been a historic step for the New York fraternity in its effort to take a more active role, as an institution, in civil rights protest. In the 1960s the local lodges of New York increasingly attempted to expand their activities in the community, especially their ties with the N.A.A.C.P. and CORE.

The leaders of the New York Order, who have always been vocal in their support of Masonic involvement with current social problems, have recently become even more outspoken. The most prominent new Masonic leader to appear in the fraternity in the 1960s was Edward Lawrence, editor of the *Sentinel* and later Grand Master. Grand Master Lawrence, one-time executive director of the New York Council for a Sane Nuclear Policy, helped give New York its increasingly militant tone during the 1960s. Many of his pronouncements on civil rights demonstrate a dedication that few of his brothers could match. An editorial he wrote in 1967, when editor of the *Sentinel*, is an indication of the type of militancy he brought to the fraternity. The country, he said, is headed toward destruction, and

> On the way, the White Power Establishment seems more concerned with the search for scapegoats than with remediation of the causes .... The brotherhood of all men, in which we believe as Masons, cannot be gained by violence, but the FIREBRANDS of S.N.C.C. did not create the ghetto slums. They did not invent poverty or unemployment .... There is more blood on the hands of those who had the power, but did little to relieve the agony of life in the Black ghettoes, than on the hands of any Black Firebrands. ... There is more provocation in the words and deeds of those who are willing to spend Billions EACH MONTH killing non-WHITES in Vietnam, BUT NOT ONE CENT TO KILL THE RATS THAT THREATEN BLACK BABIES IN SLUM HOUSING, than the words and deeds of any Black Nationalist, however misguided.[42]

In the same year Lawrence wrote an editorial on Adam Clayton Powell, Jr., entitled, "IS HE JUSTLY REPREHENDED? LET THE WORLD SEE HOW MASONS LOVE ONE ANOTHER." Powell, said Lawrence, was stripped of his chairmanship because of blatant racism, because "An example had to be made of this Black Man who thought and acted as though he was 'as good as any White Man ....' 'Good' Blacks KNOW they cannot use Power. 'Good' Blacks know they must even permit

[42] *Sentinel* (New York), 20, no.3 (July-Sept. 1967): 3.

themselves to be used to put an 'uppity' Black in his place."[43]
When the community power movement started to shake the
New York Public School system, Lawrence, then Deputy Grand
Master, put himself on the side of those fighting for innovation
in education. He told his Masonic audience that black children,
"victims of . . . educational genocide," must be helped, that
"Black parents must insist that they be given a voice in the
policymaking which will determine whether our children continue to be crippled for life in ineffective schools or begin to
achieve their fullest potential," and that "The fantastic myths
which are taught . . . as American History must be exposed
. . . . Our children . . . must no longer be brainwashed . . . that
our forefathers were happy and contented in slavery. . . ."[44]
Later as Grand Master, Lawrence felt privileged to give the
Grand Lodge's Medgar Evers Award, whose only previous
recipient had been Rev. Milton Galamison, to Rhody McCoy
of the Oceanhill-Brownsville Experimental School District.[45]

As we have seen in these last two chapters, Prince Hall
Masonry over the years has not been a fantasy world in which
blacks have escaped from the problems besetting their race.
There have been fun and games, parades and costumes, incredible titles, and much else. Some of the effects of these things
have been dysfunctional, and they will be discussed later. But
despite them, the Masons have been concerned and involved
in their communities, especially in relation to the white society.
The role Prince Hall has played is one the Masons can be proud
of; its achievements no one can take away from them. However,
the picture has not been only one of achievement, or even of
valiant (if doomed) effort. There has been a basic problem
within Masonic and middle-class thinking which has severely
restricted their accomplishments. The next chapter will deal
with the obstacles to effective civil rights activity.

[43] *Sentinel* (New York), 20, no.1 (Jan.-March 1967): 3. This editorial was considered
of such note that the North Carolinian Masonic journal reprinted it in full.
[44] *Sentinel* (New York), 20, no.4 (Oct.-Dec. 1967): 3.
[45] *Sentinel* (New York), 21, no.4 (Oct.-Dec. 1968): 2.

Chapter XI

Civil Rights—Contradictions

Prince Hall Masons have constantly found their highest aspirations for the fraternity and its role as a civil rights leader frustrated. Time after time dynamic potential and effective action have been agonizingly dissipated. As will be seen, part of the problem is the result of conservative, backward-looking elements in the Order. But a more fundamental problem is created by the attitudes of more militant Masons toward whites, poor blacks, and themselves. To a large extent the Masonic leaders were neutralized before they began by the conflicting pressures of being black and bourgeois in American society.

In 1933 the Chairman of the Committee of Foreign Correspondence of California reprinted a letter written by "Brother" Oscar DePriest, a black congressman from Chicago. Congressman DePriest expressed the hope of many Masons that the Order, along with others, would play an active role in civil rights and activities for racial uplift:

> Since I have been in Congress I have been greatly impressed by the potential power in the Negro race that rests in its fraternal organizations. Organizations that meet regularly from two to four times a month; organizations that meet in grand session periodically every year or every two years; organizations that are in touch with the 12 million loyal Negroes scattered throughout the United States and the Isles of the Seas. I have [en]visioned what could come of that power if it intelligently addressed itself to the uplift and progress of the race.[1]

W. W. Allen, patriarch of Maryland Masonry and head of the Scottish Rite, South, expressed a similar sentiment in a speech

[1] In 1967 Oscar DePriest was Grand Master of Illinois Masonry.

before the Grand Lodge of Virginia in 1939 when he said that all modern uplift organizations should avail themselves of the services of Masonry and similar fraternal bodies since "with their disciplined membership" they have great potentiality "to further progressive causes."[2] Yet despite the high aspirations and demands for action, the dream of the fraternity leading the community in the struggle for freedom never materialized. Masonry never fulfilled its potential as a radical agency of racial uplift. Why did it fail?[3]

Part of the problem was and is ideological. A significant part of Masonic leadership has always adhered to those traditions of the Order which forbid involvement in non-Masonic affairs. The basis for their position has been the Masonic Landmarks, which forbid the entrance of partisan politics and sectarian religion into the lodges, a taboo rooted in the fear that such public disputes would divide the fraternity and void its claim to universality. The traditionalists have interpreted this prohibition literally and have refused to make modifications—not only with regard to politics and civil rights but to economic projects and general racial uplift enterprises as well. Grand Master Broyles of California was typical of a large part of this faction when he attacked the "progressive" or "materialistic" Masons of 1940 California: "We must be a very poorly developed race indeed if we are not big enough to support one organization devoted to our spiritual needs [i.e., Masonry] without inviting and dragging in our greeds, low desires and deceits ...."[4] Traditionalists have also believed that concern for government and the community is important for the individual—but not in his capacity as a Mason.[5]

Over the years progressive factions in Masonry have used countless arguments to persuade the traditionalists to support their activist programs. These arguments have all produced the same stubborn responses. Though the post-World War II era has seen a clear strengthening of the progressive position

[2] *Review* (Georgia), 2, no.2 (Jan.-March 1939): 4.

[3] By asking this question we are taking the aspirations of Masonic leaders seriously. Observers like St. Clair Drake and Horace Cayton who note that most black social clubs, as a matter of form, try to appear interested in racial uplift, probably would not. Perhaps for social clubs, bridge clubs, and the like, their "interest" in civil rights, etc. is purely ritualistic; but this is not the case for Masonry. St. Clair Drake and Horace Cayton, *Black Metropolis* (New York, 1962), p. 688.

[4] *Proceedings* (California, 1940).

[5] *Sentinel* (New York), 2, no.2 (Feb. 1945): 1.

and a heightened attack on the traditionalists, the issue is still far from dead. As late as 1964 the Grand Master of Texas could feel secure in correcting "the idea in the minds of some Masters and members that they must justify the existence of their Lodges in the community by engaging in an organized way to solve local, social, political and religious problems . . . which must not, and should not, concern Masonry."[6]

In their effort to win over the traditionalist element in the fraternity, progressive Masonic leaders have attempted to prove that the prohibition against politics and religion in Masonry applies only to "partisan" and "sectarian" disputes, not to the general problems of the community. Civil rights, they have argued, is not a divisive issue in a black lodge but a unifying one. When this argument has failed, progressives have tried to prove that while the Masonic lodge may not be allowed to engage in civic activities, a "service" organization established by the lodge and attached to it, but not Masonically convened, may. Many Grand and subordinate lodges have made use of just such a distinction to win support of increased civil rights activity.

A common technique employed by the progressive faction against their opponents has been to quote tradition against them. The records of the Grand Lodges are full of references to the deep involvement of nineteenth-century Masonic leaders, such as Prince Hall, Absalom Jones, Richard Allen, and others in the protest activities of their era. If the "founding fathers" could become involved so can their descendants. As a last resort, the activists have always been able to threaten the traditionalists with the collapse of Masonry if the Order did not adjust to new conditions and attract new members. Throughout the twentieth century changes in the general black community have created continual challenges to the fraternity; and in each of the ensuing battles, whether it was to set up an insurance plan, create an old age home, invest in commercial enterprises, or become active in the fight for civil rights, the traditionalists have been threatened with institutional disaster if they refused to accomodate.

Nevertheless, the old guard position has remained potent; and this requires an explanation. While a logical case based on Masonic Law can be made for the conservatives, an equally

[6] *Proceedings* (Texas, 1964).

legal, and far more moral, argument can be made for their opponents. The Masonic records are unclear as to why many Masons have continued to adhere to the antiactivist position. Most of the evidence available reflects progressive views and draws a rather inaccurate picture of the opposition. Progressives have tended to categorize all of their enemies, those who have consciously and unconsciously obstructed social action, as traditionalists. Thus: "politicos," who are ever jockeying for Masonic office; "utilitarians," who see Masonry primarily as an insurance company, burial society, or business office; and "ritualists," who are attracted only by the secret handshake, colorful garb, and exotic ritual, are all identified as being part of a single group. While these types have been of great importance in diluting Masonry's potency, and probably have desired the victory of the old guard in order to avoid being forced to engage in civic activities, they are not traditionalists. Rather, they are outside the ideological debate, and their main contribution to the fight has come in the form of apathy and inactivity, which frustrates the goals of both ideological camps.

The real traditionalist leadership has been that element in Masonry which, while totally dedicated to the Order as a *serious* undertaking, has used it to avoid the unpleasant realities of the racial system in America. They have found Freemasonry a philosophical and metaphysical system of values, morals, ideals, and secret wisdom which in and of itself has been the total justification for the existence of the Order.[7] For them Masonry has provided a place where the black man could withdraw from the world and live in a purified and dignified cultured atmosphere. These men have never been the major element in the fraternity, nor dominant in its leadership, but they have been powerful obstructors. While they have not

[7] The metaphysics of Masonry has always attracted devoted adherents. Abner Cohen, "The Politics of Ritual Secrecy," *Man*, 6, no.3 (1971): 432, says, "Like many other ritual systems, Freemasonry offers a body of beliefs and practices which have intrinsic value. ... In Freetown I met young Masons who spent a good deal of their spare time reading Masonic literature for sheer intellectual satisfaction." Many of the progressive leaders are themselves deeply attracted to Masonic philosophy, but the traditionalists do not wish to go outside that area of concern. Jacob Katz also comments on the great attraction of Masonic philosophy and mysteries for gentile Europeans in the eighteenth and nineteenth centuries as an end in itself; interestingly enough, he felt that the Jewish Masons were less concerned with such matters than they were with social acceptance. Jacob Katz, *Jews and Freemasons in Europe, 1723-1939* [Cambridge, Mass., 1970] pp. 26-53).

escaped into a land of fun and games, they have hurt the Order just as much as those brothers who have seen Masonry as simply an amusement and an escape from reality. And it has been the traditionalist leaders who have provided the ideological cloak which has given legitimacy to those Masons who have simply not wanted to expend the effort necessary to make Masonry an effective protest and "uplift" force in the black community.

But there is more to Masonry's failure. Traditionalist obstruction can explain why Prince Hall never developed its potential to be a fraternal version of the N.A.A.C.P. Yet the most militant leaders of the Order have desired a much more revolutionary and dynamic role for the fraternity.

They have believed Masonry could provide the institutional framework, leadership, and moral ideas to awaken, inspire, unify and mobilize the energies of the entire black population—considerably more than Masonry as civil rights organization could accomplish. This ambitious goal has always been impossible to attain because of the emotional and psychological problems of the militant Masonic leaders themselves. No leaders, committed as they have been to the "bourgeoisification" of black people, to racial uplift through moral suasion and exhortation, have been capable of providing radical or unified leadership to the entire black community. Such men have been prisoners of their own value system. As long as they have continued to believe in the basic promise of a bourgeois life style, and have seen the world through the restricted perspective of those values, they have been incapable of facing the true nature of either the American race system or the black masses; for them to have done so would have threatened the basis of their own psychological and social integration.

The black middle class's adherence to the Protestant ethic has been influenced by three interrelated and mutually supportive beliefs: first, that bourgeois standards are morally good and therefore should be obeyed; second, that the difficult sacrifice of present pleasure which the life style demands are acceptable because they will ultimately bring concrete material rewards (money and property) and social rewards (equality and acceptance); third, that the rewards which faithfulness to middle-class behavior promise are guaranteed by the white community. (The last point is based upon the belief that whites discriminate against blacks not because of their *race* but because of their *class* and *cultural* differences; to the extent that blacks adopt middle-class behavior, white "prejudice" will dissipate and blacks will be granted true equality in America. This is the essence of the American "promise"). All three parts of the formula are crucial. Part one, without part two, asks more sacrifice from people than they will give. Part two (the promise of reward) without part three (white cooperation) is almost impossible since active white discrimination will severely retard or destroy the achievement of material and social rewards which adherence to bourgeois behavior normally would bring.

For a militant Masonic leader to fully admit that the material and social rewards promised are not forthcoming because Caucasian prejudice is in actuality determined by *race* and not by *class* would be to undercut the justification for his life style. Since no Masonic leaders, no matter how outspoken and alienated they may sound, have ever been willing to pay the full psychological price of total rejection of the white community's supposed flexibility on the race issue, they have always been forced to ignore the implications of their own assessments of the American scene.

The retreat of militant Masonic leaders from the realities of the race system is nowhere better illustrated than in the speeches of the radical Grand Master of California, J. H. Wilson. If there has been any Mason who at times has appeared to have held no illusions about the nature of American prejudice it has been him. In 1918 he wrote that the values and standards of white men are totally false and hypocritical since "her theory makes the lot I own adjoining a white man's, the farm I own lying alongside the one he owns, of less intrinsic value because the title is vested in a Negro, [and because] he contends that the religious training, the moral attainments, the oaths and obligations are of less, or no value, when the Negro is concerned."[8] Two years later he broadened his attack on the whites by saying that reason and morality have no effect on them. And thus,

> If the dark races of the earth are to ever check the encroachment
> of this proud, arrogant, intolerant white race, and force them

---

[8] *Proceedings* (California, 1918).

to see and acknowledge the Brotherhood of Man, it will come only when ... the dark races ... become united .... It is because the white race sees far into the future, that he has as part of his program in his world conquest for mastery, the keeping apart of the dark races of the world.[9]

Wilson sounds modern and perceptive and appears to break through the deceptiveness of false optimism as he searches for a consistent militant position.

But Wilson could not maintain that position. At the same time that he saw the truth of racism he still believed—had to believe—that it was not true. The very intensity of his outrage sprang from his continued faith in the American "promise." The result was that after denouncing white perfidiousness and hypocrisy, he could turn around and say, as he did in 1922, that "To a large extent we are largely responsible for our condition today. To agitate and complain ... will never solve our problem. ... When we learn to fight conditions and obstacles with dollars and not with tongues, the seeming impregnable barriers that confront us will melt as the morning mists before the rising sun." Despite Wilson's increased disillusionment, this sentiment was a perfect echo of his belief in 1914 that the acquisition of property by blacks would bring equality since by such activity "the leopard will have done much to change his spots and the Ethiopian his skin."[10] In spite of all evidence to the contrary, this faith was something Wilson and Masonic

---

[9] *Proceedings* (California, 1920).

[10] Wilson, in 1916, while Chairman of the Committee of Foreign Correspondence of California, expressed at length the middle class's faith in money and business to end race prejudice. The occasion for his comments was a 1915 speech of the Grand Master of Missouri in which he said that recent Supreme Court decisions on suffrage heralded an improvement in black prospects: "We share with him [the Grand Master] ... this optimistic view, and believe with him that the [white] public conscience must be reached, aroused and educated; but we have more faith in the power and influence of the American eagle [on money] to accomplish this feat than all the courts in the land .... we need ... that business acumen, that business sense, that business stamina that can blaze the way and enlist the cents and dollars of the race ... where they will make not only business, place and wealth for stockholders and patrons; but at the same time will do more than all else in moulding and educating public sentiment favorable to the race." Wilson at this point in time deceived himself into believing that other nonwhite people proved the power of money to destroy race prejudice. He asserted that in California both the Japanese and Chinese had won influence and respect because of their wealth: "It is what they are to their surroundings in material wealth, in cents and dollars, organized for the interest of the races, that says to this American hell-born prejudice 'This far shalt thou go, and no further.' " Masonry has the power and money "as no other organization in the world ... to set in motion

leaders generally were not able to reject, for to have done so would have struck at the foundation of their entire bourgeois life style. Demoralization and anomie, not revolution, was the probable consequence of an unqualified rejection of the white man's ultimate good faith.

Continued adherence to middle-class respectability and the belief that discrimination is primarily a class not a race problem have severely restricted the militant Masons from being able to view the black masses objectively. Despite the desire of men like Wilson for intraracial solidarity and their dream of Masonic race leadership, they have not been able either to prevent the repulsion that lower-class behavior provokes in them, nor to suppress the feeling that white hostility to the black middle class has been basically the fault of the black masses. The extent of the divisiveness within the black community brought on by adherence to an "ethnocentric" bourgeois worldview based upon value and behavioral codes most blacks have been unable to practice, is epitomized in a speech of the Grand Master of California in 1960:

> One of the growing problems in our cities is the irresponsible element ... the lazy, irresponsible element who does not want progress. ... It is most regrettable that the law-abiding, decent members of the group are judged by the worst element by and large. ... Our fight [for Civil Rights] is not for the undesirable, irresponsible element who does not ... contribute to the social and economic welfare of the community.[11]

---

the machinery that will do more in eliminating prejudice and bring the Negro race into its own than all the courts of the land" [*Proceedings* (California, 1916), Chairman of Committee of Foreign Correspondence].

[11] This speech shows remarkable continuity with one given fifty-seven years before by the Grand Master of Illinois. As the result of an outbreak of lynching in the United States the earlier Grand Master felt compelled to arouse the Craft to its duty to protect the race. However, he felt it necessary to point out how some elements among the blacks themselves were the cause of all the trouble: "There are two classes among our people. There are those who are willing to work and make an honorable living and are proving themselves to be respectable citizens. From this class we must draw our members and this class only. There is another class that spends too much time in saloons and gambling. To this class is due much of our trouble. They are dragging us to degradation. We must shun them as we would a viper" (Speech of Grand Master of Illinois, 1903, reprinted in *Past Masters' Topics*, (Illinois), 19, no.3 (July-Sept. 1955): 8-12. A similar view, though from a more recent period, can be found in the words of the Grand Master of Texas in 1949. The Grand Master expressed his belief that the achievement of racial equality required not only prudence, frugality, and temperance, but also "social graces." The Masons must be very careful about their membership

The middle-class black has been forced by his own successful adherence to his code to assume that if he can struggle to maintain it, so can everyone else. To the extent that others have not, they must be judged morally culpable. Such a harsh attitude flows logically and inevitably from the beliefs that Masons, militant or not, have stood for over the years—a judgment strengthened by the belief that white Americans value economic achievement and social manners more than anything else.

How could men such as Wilson both condemn whites as liars and hypocrites and still maintain faith in the promise of equality and acceptance? The paradox inherent in maintaining these contradictory estimates of American society is partially resolved by reference to two other aspects of the black world which until now I have slighted. The first is economic. Despite discrimination, prejudice, and the illusiveness of the American Dream, the black Masons have to a limited but significant extent made it in America: their bourgeois values and behavior have paid off in tangible ways. They have not succeeded to the degree that they were promised, or in line with their abilities or talents, but they have received at least a *minimum* level of rewards. The benefits they have received have not been great enough to deaden criticism or even totally control outrage at white betrayal, but they have created counterpressures that hold hostility within bounds. The Masons have not been unlike the Irish of Stephan Thernstrom's *Poverty and Progress*. Trying to explain why the poor Irish in the nineteenth century accepted their degradation without some violent reaction, Thernstrom maintains that despite their plight they received enough material rewards and upward mobility to make the system tolerable:

> the laborers of Newburyport had abundant evidence that self-improvement was possible. To practice the virtues exalted by the mobility creed rarely brought middle class status to the laborer, or to even his children. But hard work and incessant economy did bring tangible rewards—money in the bank, a house to call his own, a new sense of security and dignity.[12]

if they want to receive their reward for being virtuous. It is very unfair to "condemn a whole society for the irregularities of a few individuals" and the Texas Masons must be careful that no such excuses for rejection exist.

[12] New York, 1970, p. 164.

By practicing their moral code the Masons were able to obtain and keep jobs that provided at least a minimum of security, pay, and status. The jobs were not the best, but they were not the worst, either. Many Masons could take legitimate pride in their occupations despite their longing for something better. Most Masons could boast of material possessions as the result of their life styles, often the ownership of their own homes.[13] While the difference between what they had and what whites had, or between what they achieved and what they wanted, was great, they were aware of how little the majority of blacks had compared to themselves, of how much progress as individuals they had made. To this extent the promise of material reward for bourgeois behavior was not a total lie; there was enough truth in it to insure a significant degree of co-optation.

The promise of social acceptance and equality rather than economic success has proved considerably more elusive; but even here the black middle class's faith in white good will has reflected reality to a limited degree—enough to keep black hopes (continually) alive, but little else. While most white Masons have rejected black men regardless of life style, some whites have tried to fulfill their part of the American (or Masonic) promise. The Masonic records are replete with references to American whites whose friendship to middle-class blacks has rekindled faith in white intentions. As early as 1875 Grand Master Batten of Ohio (white) announced to his Grand Lodge:

> Shall it be because his skin is not colored like our own we shall spurn the colored Masons with contempt? ... But whether he comes from the jungles of Africa, the swamps of Carolina, the plains of Hindoostan ... or from whatever nation or clime he may have traveled, if he is a Mason ... he should be welcomed as a man and a brother into our Lodges .... Is it not right and proper that we, as Masons, shall at least attempt to bring about ... a union of these two Grand Lodges [black and white] in ... [Ohio].[14]

The Grand Master's position was seconded by F. J. Werner of Cincinati, a white who reflected German-American Masonic

[13] Unlike the nineteenth-century Irish-Americans, the blacks did not achieve home ownership at the expense of their children's education or social mobility.

[14] Quoted in Charles Wesley, *The History of the Prince Hall Grand Lodge of Free and Accepted Masons of the State of Ohio 1849-1960*, (Wilberforce, Ohio, 1961), p. 66.

attitudes. He demanded that a committee to investigate Prince Hall Masonry's claim to fraternal status be formed and if the claim was found to be true that they be treated as brothers.[15] A decade later Grand Master Clark of Ohio (white) published the "Negro Mason in Equity," in which he, too, pleaded for fraternal recognition of the blacks.[16]

The most important white champion of black equality appeared at the turn of the nineteenth century in the person of William H. Upton, a prominent white Mason of the state of Washington who headed a committee investigating the status of black Masons. After thorough research, the committee decided that subordinate lodges had the right to accept into membership blacks claiming Masonic descent from Prince Hall of Massachusetts. From that time forward Upton became the major fighter for Masonic justice for black men. The intensity of his feeling was shown by a provision in his will asking that no monument be placed over his grave until both white and black Masons could place it there as brothers.[17]

These white Masons, like liberal whites generally, have been unable to fulfill the Masonic (and American) promise of brotherhood or equality since they have not represented a wide sector of their communities. All they have been able to do is to keep the hope of racial unity alive—an achievement that has often had more negative than positive consequences for the black population. This liberal friendship has worked to confuse, divide, and mislead black leaders, keeping them from a consistent evaluation of American society. For many middle-class blacks the *system* of racial oppression has been reduced to a

[15] Harry E. Davis, *A History of Freemasonry Among Negroes in America*, (n.p., 1946), p. 142, and Wesley, p. 68. Harry Davis said of these men that "These leaders [of white Masonry] were of an unusually high type ... and they were willing to waive possible embarrassing consequences in the ultimate interest of the institution. The basic tenets of Masonry meant more to them than policy or expediency" (Davis, p. 147).

[16] Wesley, p. 98.

[17] Davis, p. 158. The Grand Master of California, 1909, said of Upton and his contribution to Prince Hall Masonry: "We shall always cherish the name of Wendell Phillips as an abolitionist, and Abraham Lincoln as the emancipator of our race, but both of these great men by political restriction or public sentiment, failed to live to carry out their ideals, but Hon. William H. Upton, being inspired by the unpretended sense of truth has sounded the depth of Masonic history, and in the face of adverse sentiment and prejudice, has proven ... that Negro Masonry" is legitimate. The Grand Master also said that Prince Hall Grand Lodge of Massachusetts in appreciation of Upton's work was raising money for a monument to him—a monument "to the best friend the colored Masons ever had."

problem of hostile versus sympathetic individuals.[18] White America has loomed Janus-like over the black man, and he has had trouble dealing with its contradictory faces: friendly, humane, tolerant and/or hateful, spiteful and bigoted.

The Masonic records reveal that despite widespread white racism it is almost impossible for blacks to miss some signs of white good will. Earlier we saw how C. L. Dellums, president of the Sleeping Porters Union, received preference on his first railroad job because of his Masonic pin. Hylan Lewis in *Blackways of Kent* says that among fraternity members "Nominal identification and expectation extend across race lines, [and] particularly in the case of the Negro Masons . . . some differential treatment . . . by white Masons is expected [and received] on the basis of parallel status."[19] Lewis relates a black Mason's explanation of why a black man who was beaten by a white mob was not killed:

'He [the black man] was a Mason; one of the men in that [white] crowd was a Mason and he wouldn't let them hurt him any more. If it hadn't been for that, they would have killed him.'[20]

Booker T. Washington in *The Story of the Negro* relates a similar incident a hundred years before Lewis'. In 1850 the first Kentucky black Masonic lodge, Mount Moriah No. 1, was organized in Louisville. Because of the "black laws" it had to meet across the river in New Albany, Indiana. After three years under this policy, the lodge started to assemble in Louisville itself, where it was raided and twenty-one members were arrested. At the prison, however, the jailer refused to receive them and the judge allowed them bail on their own recognizance. When they returned for trial the courthouse was locked and barred by the police. They were told to go home quietly and they would not be disturbed. The explanation appears to

[18] See Erdmann Beynon's "The Voodoo Cult Among Negro Migrants in Detroit," *American Journal of Sociology* 43, no.6 (May 1938): 894-907, for a discussion of how some Southern blacks only realized the existence of a system of racial oppression after they went North and later returned home for a visit. Also see Ezra Mendelsohn's *Class Struggle in the Pole* (Cambridge, Engl., 1970), Chs. 5 and 7, for a picture of the difficulties the socialists faced in convincing the Jewish proletariat that there existed a czarist system of oppression rather than only individual friends and enemies of the Jews. I am not claiming that the prospect of total black-white polarization is attractive; but without it the degree of black unity necessary to demand and win real equality from whites is severely limited.

[19] Hylan Lewis, *Blackways of Kent* (Chapel Hill, N.C., 1955), p. 271.

[20] Hylan Lewis, p. 271.

have been that the jailer and judge were Master Masons.[21] Martin Delany in his antebellum treatise on Freemasonry, written at a time when his feelings for white men were anything but cordial, also reports with pleasure the cordiality of some Caucasians:

> Southern Masons recognize and [have] fellowship [with] colored men, as such, whenever they meet them as Masons. The writer has more than once sat in lodge in the city of C—, with some of the first gentlemen of Kentucky, where there have been present ... a distinguished lawyer ..., one of the first alderman of the place, and [the] ... President of the Judges' Bench. This is a matter of no unfrequent [sic] occurrence, and many of our members have done the same.[22]

It is significant that this type of interracial experience has created warm feelings between blacks and whites, but the bonds have been forged more often with the white elite than with the middle or working classes. The effects on black leadership are apparent in the many comments found in Masonic and general black records explicitly praising the white upper-class attitude toward blacks while contrasting it with middle- and lower-class bigotry.[23] This supports Eugene Genovese's contro-

[21] Booker T. Washington, *Story of the Negro* (New York, 1909), vol. II, pp. 151-152.

[22] Martin E. Delany, *The Origins and Objects of Ancient Freemasonry, Its Introduction into the United States and Legitimacy among Colored Men* (Pittsburgh, 1853), pp. 28-29. That Delany's experience was not unique is testified to by Harry Davis: "[I]t is fair to say that well informed white Masons privately concede that colored Masonry ... is legitimate. ... This attitude is reflected in the really cordial feeling existing between both officers and members of white and colored lodges. Colored grand officers frequently, though unofficially, report conferences with white grand officials ... and fraternal advice freely given" (Davis, p. 148). California Masonic records show that in the 1930s the white Masons were very friendly and cordial toward their black "brethren" whom they tried to help but could not formally recognize. Indeed, Davis testifies that many white Grand Lodges have had an informal entente with Prince Hall which clearly differentiates them from truly "bogus" lodges of blacks (Davis, p. 149). Even Southern white lodges have often informally shown a fraternal regard for Prince Hall. A Grand Secretary of Virginia (white) aided "leading colored members of this [Prince Hall] organization in establishing it in Virginia believing it would be helpful to Negro citizenship. His text book was used as their guide for years" (Davis, pp. 150-151). And it has not been unknown, according to Davis, for Southern white Grand Masters to attend, as honored guests, Prince Hall Grand Lodge meetings as a sign of fraternal feeling (Davis, p. 148).

[23] Prince Hall himself also showed the same attitude three-quarters of a century before. In a sermon he delivered attacking the slave trade and the unfair treatment of blacks, he pointed out that insults and daily harassment came from ex-servants and immigrant "low-life people" but not "gentlemanly Bostonians." (The Sermon was reprinted in *Digest* (California), 7, no.2 (no month, 1958): 19.

versial contention that black leaders have been prey to elite paternalism, that they have been open to manipulation by those upper-crust whites who have appeared to be "above" petty racial prejudice.[24] Even when black leaders have not actually been co-opted by the white elite, incidents such as these have contradicted the implications of most encounters with Caucasians and thus have tended to reinforce the black middle class's basic love-hate ambivalence toward whites.

In summary, the ability of Prince Hall Freemasons to effectively fight for racial equality has been compromised, restricted by powerful forces from many directions. On the one hand, the Order's committment to a bourgeois view has made it difficult to deal with white racism as it actually exists. This in turn has affected, and been affected by, the middle class's alienation from the black masses. It has been difficult to know where the problem lies—is it the whites or the "no-good" lower-class blacks who are to blame? And finally, the obvious decency of a highly visible minority of whites has further clouded the picture. The result has been a severe restriction on the effectiveness of black Masonic civil rights leadership.

The problems which cripple the Masons' potential for civil rights leadership also affects their leadership in the black community generally. Some of the same forces of love-hate ambivalence (to whites and poor blacks) which we have just examined are at work there as well. And their negative effects are compounded by distrust, competitiveness, and envy within the Order. This will be seen in more detail in the next chapter.

---

[24] This tendency is not unique to the black minority. The Jews also have had a tendency to see aristocratic gentiles as friendly to them in contradistinction to the hostility of the masses of Christians. See, for example, Milton Himmelfarb, "Jewish Class Conflict?", *Commentary*, 53, no.1 (January 1970): 39.

Chapter **XII**

The Problem of Leadership

Masonry has always seen itself as a unifying and binding force in the black community. The fraternity has felt that by its ideals and practices it has been able to heal the divisiveness among black groups. Though Masonry's emphasis on respectable public behavior has forced the Order to restrict its work to the black middle class, it has believed itself successful in its efforts both to integrate the diffuse groups that make up the black bourgeoisie, and to provide individual leaders for that class and for the race generally. To an extent this success has been real, as we have seen in past chapters. Nevertheless, Masonry's constructive efforts have had to counteract powerful centrifugal forces, not only within the black population generally and the black bourgeoisie specifically, but within its own membership as well.

In this chapter I will discuss the strong antileadership currents within the Masonic membership. I will show the conflict generated by the attempts of some to overturn recognized leaders and others to maintain them. There is a struggle between anarchy, authoritarianism, and democracy in the Order, a struggle that reflects the status anxieties of the members and of the black middle class generally. The anxieties and hostilities underlying the conflict are generated by the contradictions inherent in being black in a racist society.

Backbiting, envy, and jealousy are not traits restricted to any race or people. They are found universally. It cannot be proved that Afro-Americans have suffered from them more than other ethnic groups; however, blacks have believed that they have, and in that belief has lain an element of self-fulfilling prophecy. The Masonic documents record a continuous outcry

251

against the disruptive forces that fragment the black group.
The Grand Master of Texas in 1911 bitterly pointed out that,

> The progress of the colored people is not only contested by other
> races, but there are impediments in our own ranks .... Most
> curious of all the races of men, you can depend upon some one
> or two [blacks] riding it roughshod over and neglecting and often
> abusing the very men trying hardest to help the race ... ; you
> must also prepare for this development. Not once (for you never
> get vaccinated from the tendency of the colored man to lambast
> those working hardest for him) but time and again.[1]

The need to combat the disunity caused by these alleged traits
among blacks has been one of the major rationales for the
existence of Masonry. The Prince Hall Masons have seen their
institution with its ideology of brotherhood, charity, and cooperation as the perfect means to bind the race together. While
they have admitted that the church has attempted to accomplish the same function, they have believed that Masonry, since
it recognizes no sectarian divisions, can heal many of the
wounds that organized religion itself engenders.[2] The healing
nature of Freemasonry has been seen as capable of curing not
only the personal problems of envy, pride, and malice, but all
social divisions among blacks as well:

> [I]f the acerbities and asperities alive ... in the breasts of men
> aroused by opposing views resulting from different political
> alliances, economic combinations, religious creeds, or dogmatic
> declarations dangerously fume, is there not the need for the
> ameliorating, passion assuaging, equilibrating influences of Free-
> masonry, that strives to bring together men of upright life. ...[3]

Masons believe that internal unity among blacks is vital not
only because internal conflict is itself a terrible evil, but because
it has left the race prey to white oppression and control. One
of the most articulate proponents of race unity through Masonry was the writer John E. Bruce, who in a 1919 address laid
the problem of black conflict squarely before his brethren. He
argued that the Spirit of Brotherhood,

> is the spirit which ought to prevail among ... Negroes generally
> ..., the spirit that actuates white men to-day ... to go to the

[1] *Proceedings* (Texas, 1930), quoting 1911.
[2] *Proceedings* (Texas, 1934), speech of Grand Master.
[3] Ibid.

relief of white men. The white race is organized on the family principle, no matter what their religious or political differences ... they are ONE people with ONE purpose, ONE destiny.

The only way, according to Bruce, to black brotherhood was fraternalism, with "Negro Masonry the medium through which to give the right direction to the thought and policy which is to govern and control the race."[4] While the desire to create black unity has been important for Prince Hall Masonry, the Order has generally failed in its purpose. The envy, pride, malice, and revenge that Masons have believed existed among blacks has continued to flourish, while brotherly love, compassion, and cooperation remain words often spoken but rarely practiced. Masonry not only has failed to spread its Gospel to the "profane" world but, more important, it has failed to create unity in its own ranks.

Over the years Prince Hall has been plagued by severe interpersonal hostility which the organization has neither eliminated nor channeled into constructive activities. The fundamental area of conflict has been the attitude toward the established leadership. A committee of the Grand Lodge of California highlighted this problem when it argued:

Perhaps the greatest single drawback, we have as a group, is our unwillingness to follow acknowledged leadership. We create leaders, by our free choice, then set about in every way possible, oftimes [sic] dishonest and unmanly efforts, to discredit the leaders we ourselves have set up.[5]

In Masonic eyes such antileader attitudes are among the prominent traits of the general black community which they have hoped to combat. A Grand Master of Georgia early in this century lamented that, "In many ways we, as a people, have not arrived at that high station of appreciation to our leaders for services faithfully rendered" which a race must achieve, though he hoped that with increased black "maturity" the problem would be overcome.[6] To Masonic observers the

---

[4] Address: "The Significance of Brotherhood," by John E. Bruce, 1919 (pamphlet).

[5] *Proceedings* (California, 1932), report of Committee on Grand Master's speech. Reverend (Brother) Boone of Texas, in 1934, "electrified" his audience when he pointed out that "Your Grand Master is a deacon at my church, a trustee and chairman of the financial board [yet] ... we are great on killing leadership. I find *more hypocrisy among Negroes than any other people*." (Italics added.)

[6] *Proceedings* (Georgia, 1920).

passing years evidenced no improvement in the general Negro community; and conditions in Masonry itself were so discouraging that a New York Masonic official thirty years later felt compelled to state as a matter of form that, "In accepting this office I fully realize the many obstacles to be surmounted; the many words of ridicule to be expected; the many hypocritical expressions of praise [by backbiters] to be listened to."[7] The antileadership attitudes and disruptive activities which plagued the fraternity in 1900, 1925, or 1940 are just as prevalent today. In 1968, the newly elected head of New York Masonry found it necessary to tell his audience that Masonry would move forward "despite those whose every effort has been to sow doubt, to promote discord, to create disunity, and to spread confusion among the Craft."[8] Many leaders of the fraternity have felt that conditions have been so hopeless among black adults that the only remedy has lain in disregarding them and concentrating on youth. By teaching the young respect for leadership, Masonry would help not only itself but the race as a whole.[9]

To the extent that antileadership attitudes among Masons mirror a similar situation within the general black population, the phenomenon must be partially seen as a problem in legitimacy. Masons, and the black population as a whole, have found it hard to grant other black men legitimacy as rulers over them. In much the manner of the disgruntled colonists of seventeenth-century Virginia studied by Bernard Bailyn, many blacks who have accepted the need for leaders and followers in theory have not been able to believe that the men around them, coming from the same race, class, and social circumstances, could possibly meet the requirements for power.[10] Just as Virginia colonists "knew" that a "real" aristocrat had to possess a social, economic, and political pedigree which their *nouveau riche*, erstwhile neighbors could never have, the blacks have known that those who could rightfully claim to exercise leadership over them could certainly not be other Negroes. It

[7] *Proceedings* (New York, 1941), speech of the District Deputy Grand Master of the First District.

[8] *Sentinel* (New York), 21, no.3 (July-Sept. 1968): 2.

[9] *Proceedings* (Texas, 1927), speech of Grand Master.

[10] Bernard Bailyn, "Political and Social Structures in Virginia," in J. M. Smith, ed., *Seventeenth Century America, Essays in Colonial History* (Chapel Hill, N.C., 1959), *passim*.

is difficult enough occupying the bottom rung in a racial caste system without willingly giving up the only advantage that such a system offers—the forced equality of the oppressed group.[11] The importance of the race system for creating distrust in the black community is well illustrated by the remarks of a California Grand Master in 1920. He maintained that, "As race people we will never accomplish the desired end until we learn to trust each other as we do the other race." The race system has fostered, consciously and unconsciously, a lack of faith in the ability, honesty, and legitimacy of black leaders by making the white race the model for all the qualities a leader must possess.

This thinking helps explain not only the antileadership attitudes prevalent in Masonry but also the omnipresent hostility that manifests itself in continuous backbiting, gossiping, talebearing, and general disharmony. The Masonic records are full of laments over the pervasive envy that is found (in and out of Masonry) toward black men who raise their heads above the mass. The Grand Master of Alabama in 1939 was representative when he demanded:

> Let us stop being so narrow and envious. Stop tearing down and holding back worthwhile efforts. Stop going into business with the idea of closing up some other colored fellow's business of a like nature. Do not be afraid to build up colored men and enterprises ....

The head of Texas Masonry a decade earlier felt compelled to lash out at the same problem when he protested that in Masonry "There must be ... no ill towards that brother because he is making a success in the world. Thou shalt not covet comes down through the ages today as clearly as when given on the mount."[12] Unfortunately, for both Grand Masters, the pervasive envy and resentment that inferior status in a competitive yet caste society creates among those at the bottom cannot

[11] Some observers claim that this type of disunity does not really exist in the larger black population. St. Clair Drake and Horace Cayton, for example, in *Black Metropolis* (New York, 1962), dismiss the ubiquitous complaints about Negro disharmony which they heard from Chicago residents at all levels of black society as nothing more than "ritual condemnation" which is not really meant; and to the extent that it is meant, is based upon an erroneous belief in white unity (pp. 723-730). The latter is certainly true, but I do not think all the evidence of intra-black conflict can be dismissed by calling it "ritual," if for no other reason than the belief in disunity creates disunity.

[12] *Proceedings* (Texas, 1927).

be combatted by moral platitudes. American capitalism with its individualist ethic gives rise to a disruptive competition which for blacks has been aggravated by racist restrictions on their opportunities.[13] Since there is only so much "success" that the race and economic systems allow a colored man (though there is no limit to his expectations), everyone else is a potential competitor. Under such circumstances resentment and envy are directed primarily at other members of the subordinate group, as everyone scrambles for his share of the pie. The same socioeconomic situation that makes lower-middle-class whites battle blacks as if blacks were the real cause of their social insecurity, has also been effective in shoring up the capitalist system by dividing the blacks among themselves. It not only undercuts claims to legitimate leadership by other black men, but it destroys faith in the honesty, ability, and integrity of blacks who do achieve leadership positions by making them the most dangerous competitors of all.

While Prince Hall Masonry suffers internally from a marked tendency toward anarchy, based upon continual challenges to established authority, it suffers from the opposite tendency as well. While a large minority of the fraternity is in constant rebellion against their leaders, many of the objects of their assaults, far from demonstrating the qualities one would expect of democratic leaders in an egalitarian brotherhood, behave like petty despots. The proclivity of black Masons to either anarchic rebellion or ruthless authoritarianism is a constant

[13] As I pointed out in Chapter II, Abner Cohen, "The Politics of Ritual Secrecy," *Man*, 6, no.3 (1971): 443, in discussing disunity within Creole society sees such hostilities as common among the bourgeoisie (white or black) generally. I however, believe that this conflict while not unique to Afro-Americans is exaggerated among them. Ivan Light, *Ethnic Enterprise in America*, (Berkeley, 1972), though talking about an organization different from Masonry, presents a view supporting mine. He contends that the capitalistic ethic which is basic to black middle-class business aspirations is inimical to group solidarity: "Ironically, the archtypically entrepreneurial characteristics persistently interfered with the . . . [National Business League's] capacity to stimulate Negro-owned business, its *raison d'etre*. As a result, an undercurrent [among probusiness black spokesmen] of racialism ('buy black') competed with the official bourgeois ('buy cheap') ideology" (Light, pp. 115-116). The Masons have faced the same problem: the exhortation to buy from brother Masons conflicting with the demand to buy from the cheapest and most efficient seller. Light went on to say that, "the black business population which arose was composed of unrelated competitors. These persons cooperated only on the basis of shared interests . . ." narrowly conceived (Light, p. 125). Masonry has tried to create a supportive "fraternal" bond to bridge the gap among black businessmen, but again its emphasis on individual self-reliance, hard work, and efficiency has tended to encourage competition, not comradely cooperation.

cause for recrimination by the members of the fraternity who stoutly believe that Masonry is the great bastion of democracy in America.[14]

For many years one of the most vocal opponents of fraternal dictatorship was Bertram Baker, one-time Masonic corre-spondent for the New York *Age*, and today a leading black politician in New York State. In a column written in 1933 he pointed out to his readers that,

> Contrary to the opinions of some, Freemasonry is not a despotic institution. It is unfortunate ... that some men, and I am speaking now of colored men, holding high positions in the fraternity would assume the attitude of despots, taking unto themselves the ... doctrine of the 'divine right of Kings.'[15]

Baker argued that these petty lords of creation were not only violating the basic principles of the fraternity, crippling its ability to forge unity in its own ranks, but were responsible for the bad reputation that the entire black race had among the white majority. He felt that white stereotypes of black fraternal leaders as "De Grand, ALL Powerful, Invincible, Most Supreme, Unconquerable Potentates" received too much veri-fication among Masonic jurisdictions.

Baker's remarks were in agreement with the observations of many of the most dedicated Masons throughout the country. However, Baker's column was not an impersonal and objective account of the seamier side of Masonry either, for during 1933 Baker was in the midst of a major power struggle that created a tragic rupture in the New York fraternity. The details of the Baker case are worth recording, not only because they illustrate an instance of executive autocracy, but also because they demonstrate in action how personal feuds and animosities grow and how they divide Masonic lodges.

The series of events that ultimately fractured New York Masonry began simply enough during the 1932 meeting of the Grand Lodge. At that meeting, District Deputy Grand Master Rawlins of Brooklyn humiliated the members of Carthaginian Lodge, one of the local lodges under his supervision and the home lodge of Bertram Baker, when he claimed the lodge had not paid all of its Grand Lodge taxes. It was a minor incident,

---

[14] See *Sentinel* (New York), 1, no.6 (May 1944): 4, for a good statement of this belief.
[15] New York *Age*, February 4, 1933.

a minor humiliation, but it created bad feelings between the lodge and Rawlins and threatened the chances of future cooperation between this prominent group—one of the most important and civic-minded in the New York fraternity—and the Grand Master's deputy. Some time later the issue appeared settled when Rawlins publicly admitted he had erred and the lodge was not guilty of negligence. A few months later, during a campaign to aid the poor of Brooklyn in which Rawlins was soliciting the active cooperation of all the local lodges, but especially Carthaginian, he informed the brothers that in his capacity as president of the local lodge Unified Temple Association, he was bringing civil action in court against Carthaginian Lodge. Baker, writing in the New York *Age*, was outraged by this second seemingly unprovoked slap in the face aimed at his lodge, and after condemning Rawlins called publicly for his removal from office. Rawlins, said Baker, was a good example of a constructive and hardworking man who had allowed power to go to his head.

Baker's column provoked swift counteraction by the Grand Master of New York. He wrote a letter to Baker informing him that he was in violation of fraternity law by publicly exposing problems of the Order, and that henceforth he must allow all of his articles for the *Age* to be censored by the Grand Master. Baker indignantly refused to concede to such a gross violation of freedom of the press, and was promptly suspended from Masonry.

The suspension of a Mason without a trial by a Grand Master is one of the most frequently cited proofs that a Masonic leader has laid claim to autocratic power. As J. H. Wilson of California said,

> it is subversive of all jurisprudence for one to play the part of comainant [*sic*], prosecutor, judge and jury all at one and the same time, and in Masonic jurisprudence the law is universal that no form of Masonic punishment be inflicted or imposed upon any brother without giving ample opportunity for defense.[16]

The trial of an accused Mason must be conducted in the local lodge, and neither the Grand Master nor the Grand Lodge, except on appeal, can interfere.

---

[16] *Proceedings* (California, 1933), C.C.F.C. commenting on the Grand Master of Michigan's suspension of a man without trial for "contumacy and insubordination."

In the events that followed the suspension of Baker, the hand of authority and the power of personal animosity were leveled against both the columnist and all of his brothers in Carthaginian Lodge. By the end of the fight many of Baker's closest associates had been suspended for periods ranging from one to fifteen years for their defiance of the Grand Master's authority. The original cause for these suspensions came from the local lodge's refusal to punish Baker on the Grand Master's demand. They insisted that the Grand Master had no right to usurp the rights of a local lodge to original jurisdiction. Not only did they refuse to punish Baker, but at the next lodge election they made him an officer of the lodge.[17]

The lodge's action in defying the Grand Master ultimately led to the splitting of the membership into two factions, one pro- and the other anti-Baker. As the result of personal animosities emanating from that election, a group of anti-Baker Carthaginians, aided by Grand Lodge officials, decided to get their revenge, and ultimately won control of the lodge.[18] Once in power they established a trial commission to investigate the activities of certain of Baker's supporters to see if their actions in his defense passed the acceptable and honorable bounds of freedom. In one of these trials, a prominent Mason, Louis Jeppe, was found to have indeed gone beyond what was acceptable and to have committed "an unwarranted public defiance of vested authority" for which his penalty was long-term suspension.[19]

The ruling faction of Carthaginian Lodge represented a type of Mason that J. H. Wilson had warned the fraternity against in 1912:

> There are still a few of those in the Masonic world, who are swayed more by passion than by reason ... those who seem to think that the Grand Master is the Grand Lodge ... to differ with whom is to die—and this without judge or jury. This class of Masons constitutes, what might properly be called the mobocrats of Masonry.[20]

The extent to which members of the New York fraternity were willing to go to support "vested authority" against all assaults,

[17] New York *Age*, April 2 and 9, 1933; May 13, 1933.
[18] *Prince Hall Masonry in New York State*, vol. III, heading "1933."
[19] New York *Age*, August 5 and 12, 1933.
[20] *Proceedings* (California, 1912).

justified or not, was most revealingly demonstrated when the
Grand Lodge in response to an outcry for an appeals commission
did look into the original suspension of Baker by the Grand
Master. That commission, despite its bias toward the Grand
Master who appointed it, found the original suspension illegal
and void. However, since Baker protested so vehemently, they
felt he was attacking the dignity of the Grand Master's office
and demanded that he apologize. He refused and was expelled
for being "overly indignant" over an illegal suspension![21]

The Baker case, a *cause célèbre* which ultimately led not
only to his exit from Masonry but also to the resignation of
the noted black bibliophile Arthur Schomburg, to the suspension of the internationally known black Masonic writer Harry
Williamson, and to the alienation of many others, is a flagrant
example of the tendency toward despotism in the fraternity.
The major difference between this incident and countless other
suspensions without trials in other states was that columnist
Baker and his allies were a highly articulate and forceful group
and for years refused to allow the issue to die.

The fact that the New York case was not an isolated
phenomenon but symptomatic of a widespread problem in black
Masonry was attested to by Harry Williamson long before the
Baker incident. Writing as Chairman of the Committee on
Foreign Correspondence for the Grand Lodge of New York in
1931 he had this biting comment to make on conditions within
Prince Hall Masonry:

> Reading the reports issued by our various grand jurisdictions,
> one is greatly appalled to read of the autocratic powers that
> so many of our Grand Masters presume to take unto themselves.
> These do not hesitate to make and unmake the laws of this
> jurisdiction nor to hesitate in going into constituent Lodges and
> 'running' things much to suit their own fancy .... Our Grand
> Lodges appear to be dominated by their Grand Masters and the
> body of the Craft makes no effort to compel a strict conformity
> with Masonic Law and the Laws of the jurisdiction affected.[22]

The type of authoritarian rule exercised by the highest
official in Masonry, the Grand Master, has been present on

[21] "Supreme Court of Kings Country, Bertram L. Baker for a Mandamus Order
against Francis F. Giles and Most Worshipful Grand Body, etc." (unattached document).

[22] "Report of the Fraternal Correspondent," Williamson, June 1931 (unattached
document).

lower levels as well. It is not unusual to hear outcries against
the despotism practiced by the leader of the local lodge, the
Worshipful Master.[23] For example, the Grand Master of New
York in 1935 felt forced to admonish the Worshipful Masters
of the fraternity to be less arbitrary in their rulings since the
brothers they were alienating were dropping out of Masonry.
An effective Master, he contended, should use reason and intel-
ligence, not the gavel, to get things done.[24] A few years earlier
the Grand Master of Georgia felt compelled to admonish some
of his local leaders to stop suspending members without a trial
and forcing their lodges to illegally pay the Worshipful Master's
Grand Lodge and insurance dues.[25] The monetary rewards that
despotism brought some local leaders in Georgia was also a
cause of concern for the Grand Master of New York quoted
above. He told his Grand Lodge, "I, also, stress . . . the principle
that the officers, Grand Lodge and Subordinate, should interpret the office as an opportunity to render service, rather than
for the enjoyment of personal aggrandizement."[26]

The tendencies in Prince Hall Masonry toward antileadership rebellions and leadership autocracy have reinforced one
another. The politics of control from the top have complemented the politics of anarchy from the bottom, reinforcing
antileadership attitudes among the membership. The Grand
Lodge of Texas tried to solve both problems, or at least publicly
state the ideal it sought, when it composed a sample booklet
of bylaws for local lodges, demanding cooperative behavior on
the part of both the rulers and the ruled:

> Each officer of the Lodge shall [make sure] . . . his office is filled
> with dignity, honor and correctness, and that its various duties
> be performed without haughtiness, or tyranny, but according
> to love . . . Due respect, [and] obedience shall be paid by the
> members of this lodge to the officers according to their rank
> and station.[27]

Such a scheme, while laudable, ignored actual social conditions.
The tendency toward autocratic rule in Masonry has had

[23] See, for example, the Grand Master's speech in *Proceedings* (Texas, 1939), and
Proceedings (Georgia, 1926). See also the Report of the District Deputy of New York's
First District, *Proceedings* (New York, 1935).
[24] *Proceedings* (New York, 1935).
[25] *Proceedings* (Georgia, 1926).
[26] *Proceedings* (New York, 1935).
[27] *Proceedings* (Texas, 1939).

obvious dysfunctional effects on the fraternity's fight to create a harmonious and cooperative spirit among its members, let alone the black population generally.[28] An angry Grand Master of Texas spoke about the noncooperative, hostile Masonic leader (or candidate for leadership) who has been all too common in the Order when he noted:

> I happen to be acquainted with some [Masons] who are letter perfect in ritualistic ceremonies of Free-Masonry, who are the personification of selfish, hellish, hypocritical, malicious living, Masons who are so obsessed with personal, ambitious desires for self-advantages and promotion ... they would sell the Order out for any material advantage, that would place them where their incomes and position would enable them to place their feet on the necks of any Mason who do[es] not humble themselves to their rule and control. They are rule and ruin, so-called Master Masons.[29]

Such men are the natural result of a society that emphasizes individual aggrandizement and then blocks most of the normal avenues of achieving it.

One problem that a review of Masonic despotism raises is why the democratic leaders of the Order—and they have always been the majority—have not been more successful in their fight against this un-Masonic situation. The literature is full of their laments against the subversion of Masonry through the violation of democratic procedures, but these seem to have been of no avail. The reason is as simple as it is unfortunate. When the democratic leaders of Masonry have been confronted with what they have seen as the black man's tendency toward either antileadership anarchism or iron-fisted despotism, they have usually chosen the latter. Since the most thoughtful Masonic leaders have been preoccupied with the necessity of creating a tradition of obedience to authority for the race, they have often found themselves sacrificing their commitment to democracy in order to achieve that more pressing goal. The result has been the creation or adoption of an autocratic philosophy within Masonry by many of the men most committed to the fraternity's ideals.[30]

[28] However, "autocracy" has had its uses too. Booker T. Washington pointed out that the fraternities "seem to be democratic in their organization, although, as a matter of fact, I think that has seldom been true where the organizations have been successful" (Booker T. Washington, *Story of the Negro* [New York, 1909], vol. II, p. 169).

[29] *Proceedings* (Texas, 1939).

[30] Much of the philosophical and practical justification for Masonic autocracy comes

One of the earliest speeches that provided a rationale for Masonic despotism was delivered by the Grand Master of New York in 1856. He informed the fraternity that the power of the Grand Lodge and its Grand Master is "supreme" and "despotic." If Masonic power were not totally centralized in the Grand Lodge, and from there further concentrated in the Grand Master, Masonry would never have survived the fall of countless empires. The power of the Grand Master, he went on, is completely unlimited: "Therefore, my brethren, when you select one ... to fill that station he must be obeyed, he must be sustained in his government." If the brethren make a mistake in electing him, they have no recourse but to wait until his term expires and he can be replaced.[31]

Another Grand Master, John Wesley Dobbs of Georgia, almost a century later gave a similar view, expressing his belief that respect for authority was of paramount importance for the black Masons:

In the discharge of his duty as Grand Master of Masons, he is clothed with almost absolute power in the enforcement of Masonic authority and decisions. ... Discipline is the very foundation stone of Peace and Harmony. Without discipline there would not long be obedience to law ... it is entirely incumbent upon him ... to see to it that the laws of FREEMASONRY are strictly ENFORCED and OBEYED.[32]

---

from white Masonic sources. White Masonry has material that can be used to justify anything from perfect representative democracy to dictatorship, depending upon who does the selection of laws. What we are concerned with is why many black Masonic leaders, who usually emphasize the democratic traditions in Masonry, have also turned around and highlighted the opposite. It would be very enlightening to know to what extent white Masonry has emphasized autocratic or democratic aspects in its government, the social reasons for doing so, and whether the situation is similar to or different from that of black Masonry. Unfortunately, I have undertaken this study of black Masonry before anyone else has written on its white counterpart. This leaves me open to explaining certain situations in a black framework that may be more accurately described in a general Masonic (white and black) or American framework. For the moment, however, I believe that even similarly appearing situations in the two parts of the fraternity—for example, the prevalence of politicking—are actually different phenomena. White Masonic politics are more realistically motivated—because of the very substantial economic and business rewards available for the victors—and less demoralizing for the group, than the similar situation in the black fraternity. This is not to say that there have not been real monetary benefits, etc. for Prince Hall leaders too. But the degree of hostility generated has been greater than the rewards have justified—this is especially clear in states such as California which afford their leaders few monetary rewards.

[31] Williamson, *Prince Hall Masonry in New York State*, vol. II, heading "1856."

[32] *Digest* (California), 4, no.1 (1954-55): 3, 17. This was said in a speech given by

According to Dobbs, recognition of the absolute power of the Grand Master was imperative not only in order to force blacks to respect established leadership but also to create order and stability within the fraternity.

The type of argument that could be made for the authority of the Grand Master over the entire Craft could also be made for the Worshipful Master in the local lodge. In a speech worthy of John Winthrop aboard the *Arabella*, the Grand Orator of California in 1933 set forth his views on the power of the local lodge leader: "Once he ascends the three steps of the dais, he speaks NOT for himself. All of his utterances are inspired by ancient law." Once so inspired, "He pledges himself to observe the usages and established customs, and to strictly ENFORCE these within his own lodge. This is not a reference ... to his autocratic powers, but his autocratic CHARACTER." In dealing with their leader the local lodge membership must always understand its position: "if there is one thing that members of a Masonic lodge MUST learn, it is the ironclad fact that a Worshipful Master does not TAKE orders from his Craft, he GIVES them and the powers that make him are NOT the powers that break him."[33]

This Winthropian view of government has appealed to many thoughtful leaders of black Masonry, not only because it helps create a tradition of respect for authority but also because it rests on a view of human nature which has been widespread among the leaders of the Order. That view has proclaimed the general inequality of Man:

> All men in Masonry meet, we are taught, upon a level, upon the footing of absolute equality, and the doctrine ... that all men are created equal, finds in Masonry ... an *intelligent interpretation* [italics added]. From among the members of the human family there is not now, there has never been ... equality of mind, or manners, or strength or stamina, of privileges or position ... of aims and ambition .... All men are eternally and everlastingly unequal ....[34]

Dobbs at the Grand Masters' Conference called "Powers of a Grand Master—To Discipline." See also *Proceedings* (New York, 1915), where the District Deputy Grand Master of the 1st District says: "He who best can obey [,] best can rule ... ; some must rule, others must, of necessity, obey. We fear there is growing disposition among those who call themselves 'progressive Masons' to show utter disregard for masonic authority. ... They assume to interpret the law without first knowing the law." This Mason, in fighting lack of discipline, laid a foundation for undemocratic leadership.

[33] *Proceedings* (California, 1933).

[34] *Proceedings* (California, 1932), speech of Grand Master.

The only true equality, the Grand Master went on to say, exists in equality of "industry"; any working man is as good as any other; the hard-working laborer is the equal of a prince or a captain of industry. As a result of the basic inequality of man, except insofar as the laws of the land justly require equal treatment under the law, it naturally follows that "All men were not born to govern, for it is a principle ... that 'some must of necessity rule and teach, and others learn to submit and obey.' "[35] Masonic leaders have considered it imperative to convince the undisciplined masses of black people, both in and out of Masonry, of this fact.

This secular belief in the innate differences between men has received added support from religious ideas, a support that has also served to justify autocracy, though tempering it with paternalism. In a speech given to the 1947 meeting of the Grand Lodge of Alabama, the Grand Master of that state presented the old Puritan concept of "stewardship" and applied it to the Masonic Order. He announced that the fraternity was required to utilize to the fullest "men of ability" because their talents were not theirs alone but gifts from God; and they would be judged by God on how well they employed their talents. One important aspect of their "stewardship" which the Grand Master felt compelled to emphasize was the necessity to allow such men to wield authority over others. As stewards of "talent" from God, they had to be stewards of men. In return they would exercise their powers honorably, as did the Grand Master himself, who had a "stewardship" both from God and the fraternal electorate.[36] While the Grand Master of Alabama was good enough to point out that his stewardship came not only from heaven but from his earthly Masonic constituency as well, we have seen that, once elected, a Grand Master, like the Puritan governors of Massachusetts, had to be obeyed without question. For life to be bearable for those under the Grand Master's rule, given this theory of power, a great deal of self-restraint by leaders is necessary. As a head of the Texas Craft has said, "Full well do I know that in order to attain a definite goal it is imperative that one person should do the thinking and commanding and carry most of the responsibility. But those who are led should not be driven . . . ."[37]

[35] Ibid.
[36] *Proceedings* (Alabama, 1947).
[37] *Proceedings* (Texas, 1939).

Despite all the philosophizing and theorizing about how to combat anarchism, success has been anything but universal. Paradoxically, the reason for this has been that the anarchists have been too well organized! This organized chaos goes under the rubric "un-Masonic politics." All of the destructive, competitive, antileadership feelings that abound among the membership, and which if left unorganized could probably be kept under control by the determined minority trying to establish order, are given expression through the medium of factional politics. Masonic history is full of the formation of factions attacking different men in power, or of attacking the economic, social, moral, or political undertakings of the Order as carried out by the Grand Master or the Worshipful Masters. Though the founders of Masonry, just like the founding fathers of America, did not recognize the legitimacy of political parties and factions, such are ubiquitous in the fraternity. In fact, the belief that politics should not exist in the Order has been one of the primary reasons that it has never been controlled or put to constructive use.[38] Instead of trying to harness this activity and to use it to help govern the Craft, the response to factional politics has always been to seek its total suppression.

The energy for factional politics comes from the great reservoir of frustration, envy, jealousy, and distrust of leaders which has always existed among the Masonic membership. Men suffering from these feelings are organized into powerful factions by individuals, usually possessing marked leadership abilities and experience, who are ambitious for office. The irony of the situation is that these "antileader" leaders often use their followers to gain power and then find themselves the object of hostilities much like those they so successfully manipulated.[39]

The importance of prominent Masons in leading rebellions

[38] Of course the extent to which political factionalism could really have been controlled, given the context of a racist capitalist system and its corollaries of hate and envy, was always quite limited.

[39] Ivan Light says that the competition among black leaders is so great, and diversity of opinion so wide, that no single leader can represent the population. He sees this as a reflection of "the democratic, popular, and fluid quality of black American urbanism" (Light, p. 173). The same situation can be found in many Masonic Grand Lodges. The problem is that it leads both to disruption and to attempts to force authority on followers, willing or not.

against the established leadership is continually noted in Masonic records. The comments of the C.C.F.C. of California in 1908 are typical of observations elsewhere: "insubordination, or rebellion against constituted authority ... are usually lead by some Past Grand Officer, or by some brother who has stood high in the council of his lodge." The rebel chieftain launches his attack by spreading rumors, making accusations, and generally creating an atmosphere of distrust and suspicion in the Grand Lodge. The Grand Masters, as a result, are continually on the defensive. It is quite common to find them defending themselves against charges of immorality or thievery. In almost all situations in which the leadership is actively engaged in buying or selling property, building a temple, or setting up a charity fund, accusations of dishonesty abound.[40]

Attacks on Masonic leaders can be found in every state and in all periods. As Harry Davis points out, in the nineteenth century black Masons already were quite given to disunity since "the colored brethren early developed a tendency toward quarrelling and schism over questions of authority and discipline ...."[41] The so-called "National Compact" of the mid-nineteenth century was supposed to be the solution to the problem, but it gave rise only to far worse conflicts in the Order.[42] During the 1920s and 1930s, California, for example, was racked by continual skirmishes over the Grand Master's attempt to implement a progressive program of activities: a charity fund for widows and orphans, and an old age home. At the end of a decade in office, Grand Master J. H. Wilson reviewed his attempt to establish a Grand Lodge charity fund and the "insidious" opposition he experienced. First, some members "covertly sought to retard or prevent" the new fund's functioning by calling it an illegal and un-Masonic innovation. Then "the cheap, low, unprincipled and un-Masonic politician[s] ... sought to destroy the faith of the Craft in the constituted officers ... by creating a suspicion of graft." When that tactic also failed, they started the rumor that the leadership was

---

[40] See *Proceedings* (California, 1914), C.C.F.C. commenting on South Carolina; *Proceedings* (Illinois, 1954); *Proceedings* (Texas, 1934); and *Proceedings* (California, 1923, 1927, 1930, and 1932).

[41] Harry E. Davis, *A History of Freemasonry among Negroes in America*, (n.p., 1946), p. 98.

[42] Davis, p. 99.

planning to "barter away rights of this Grand Lodge, and sell
... out to an Insurance Company."[43]

As soon as Wilson was voted out of office, his successor found
himself in a similar situation. He protested to the Craft the
outrageous rumors being spread that there was graft in connection with his purchase of a Grand Lodge old age homesite.
He denied that any Grand Master ever had a personal interest
in the property, "although this is contrary to a report circulated
through this jurisdiction by certain persons through ignorance,
jealousy and un-Masonic principles" who have claimed that
the Grand Master was "unloading" the property on the fraternity.[44] That rumors such as these could circulate in Grand
Lodges and gain support among the membership again demonstrates how ready many Masons have been to believe the worst
of their leaders. Such a disposition on the part of the mass
of Masons has created opportunities for ambitious Masonic
politicians to succeed in their attacks on the established leadership. The records of most of the states are full of denunciations
of the "whining, complaining, non-constructive" obstruction-
ists who have continually plagued Masonry. And when the
situation reaches such proportion as it did in California, where
the Grand Master was forced to protest that he was not getting
the respect due himself and his office, it was both pathetic
and destructive to the Order.[45]

Rumors and insinuations have been common not only on
the Grand Lodge but on the local lodge level as well: "In too
many instances, our Past Masters [ex-leaders of the local lodge],
when they pass out of office, also pass from their period of
usefulness to the Craft, or else feel that it is their inherent
right to run the lodge, or the entire Jurisdiction."[46] The ambition and hostility of Past Masters who disrupt local lodges or
form "political machines" in the Grand Lodge (of which they
are members) have been a constant source of anxiety in Masonry.[47] They create factions in an attempt to regain power, or
simply refuse to obey the new leaders as a means of boosting
their own egos. The men who should understand the need for

[43] *Proceedings* (California, 1930).
[44] *Proceedings* (California, 1932).
[45] Ibid.
[46] *Proceedings* (California, 1926). See also *Proceedings* (Alabama, 1925).
[47] *Proceedings* (California, 1926).

authority have often been the first to demonstrate a lack of support for leaders.

The fact that Past Masters are usually articulate, talented, and experienced makes their disruptive activities very effective. It is not uncommon for their successor on the local or Grand Lodge level to be unable to deal with them. When a Grand Master of Alabama demanded that his subordinate lodge leaders govern their lodge without fear of Past Masters and force them to exhibit both respect and obedience, he did so in the hope that his lieutenants would demonstrate the backbone which he, like many other Grand Masters, felt they lacked.[48]

Unfortunately, whether the Worshipful Master had backbone or not, the difficulties facing him in his attempt to create harmony and order in his lodge have been very great. The reservoir of hostility easily tapped by any disgruntled ex-leader is often great. A poem in the Prince Hall Masonic Digest of California in 1964 gives us a glimpse of one type of man who has always been ready to support challenges to the elected leadership. The poem asks,

> Are you an active member, the kind
> that would be missed,
> Or are you just contented that your
> name is on the list?
> Do you attend the meeting, and mingle
> with the flock,
> Or do you stay away—and criticize
> and knock?
> . . . .
> Do you ever go to visit or call a
> member that is sick,
> Or do you leave the work to just a
> few and then call them the
> 'clique.'[49]

These men, who do little themselves, and at the same time distrust the men who do gain power, are convinced that they can do a better job, at half the price, if only they are given the chance.[50] While lacking the ambition to personally chal-

[48] *Proceedings* (Alabama, 1925); see also *Proceedings* (Illinois, 1916).

[49] *Sentinel* (New York), 17, no.2 (April-June 1964): 3-4. The Masonic "disunity" poem is one of the ubiquitous features of Masonic literature. Also see *Proceedings* (Georgia, 1922) and *Review* (Georgia), 2, no.4 (Oct.-Dec. 1939) for examples.

[50] See *Review* (Georgia), Fourth Quarter, 1939, for an excellent short story dealing with this problem.

lenge the leadership, they are easily persuaded to support their more ambitious brothers.

The worst period is election time when, as one Missouri leader put it, friendships are severed, untruths told which can never be lived down, and some men imitate the tricks of the ward politician to gain office.[51] All too often, elections are a time for criticizing and belittling the incumbent rather than praising the virtues of his opponents.[52]

The weapons that opponents of the incumbent leadership have had at their disposal, besides the usual rumor, accusation, or political faction, have been many. One of the most interesting is an institutional technique that a Grand Master of California found widespread in the Order. He lamented that "There has been a spirit in our Masonic system for many years which prompts secretaries and treasurers to arrogate to themselves" powers unknown to the fraternity, and by so doing "subjugate the actions of the Master to their will and pleasure."[53] This custom was even more appalling because it had become common for retiring Masters to seek these offices, which they easily obtained, and place the new and inexperienced Master directly at their mercy. This "pernicious custom," the Grand Master went on, was seeking to invade the Grand Lodge, as witnessed by his own unfortunate experience with two Past Grand Secretaries and a Grand Treasurer.[54]

On the local level another important weapon that the faction leaders have wielded against the incumbent regime has been the "blackball." In the voting to admit new members, individual personal resentments and organized factional politics have neatly blended. The records of Masonry are full of outcries against the "un-Masonic" use of the veto against new members. While pure personal spite has played its part in the abuse of the blackball, of more significance has been its use as a means of embarrassing and attacking the Worshipful Master or one of his officers when they have tried to bring new members into the lodge.[55]

[51] *Proceedings* (California, 1914), C.C.F.C. commenting on Missouri. See also C.C.F.C. of California 1909 commenting on Missouri 1908.

[52] See *Review* (Georgia), no vol., no.3 (July-Sept. 1940): 3; *Proceedings* (Georgia, 1908); and *Proceedings* (California, 1909), among others.

[53] *Proceedings* (California, 1942).

[54] Ibid.

[55] See *Proceedings* (California, 1915), C.C.F.C. reporting on Texas, among countless examples.

While this chapter's emphasis has been on the disruptive elements in Masonry, the normal situation has not been one of chaos. Most states demonstrate a remarkable degree of stability in their leaderships, despite the threats to it. It is not uncommon to find states reelecting the same Grand Master for twenty to twenty-five years! Scores of men in dozens of states have served their Grand Lodges at least a decade. This stability has existed not only among Grand Masters but among Grand Secretaries, Treasurers, Chairmen of the Committee on Foreign Correspondence, and others. The same names appear year after year, decade after decade, and if not in the same post, then in equally prominent ones.

The striking amount of stability at the highest levels of Masonry can be accounted for by many reasons. The most important has been the simple effectiveness of appeals to the Masonic electorate by the leadership against its opponents. Though the leaders have often found themselves harassed, humiliated, and frustrated by continuous assaults, at the end of each year they have been victorious. Often their plans for constructive programs for the lodges have been defeated or crippled by outcries from the dissident elements, but even then they have usually experienced more mental torment than concrete obstacles.

Some leaders of Masonry, especially those whose rule is measured in decades, have maintained themselves in office not so much through democratic (i.e., established electoral) procedures, as through charismatic appeals, for example the by-passing of institutional safeguards by "unanimous" consent. While Masonry has found it difficult, but not impossible, to create a tradition of democratic respect for authority, it has found it easy to capitalize on a tendency toward hero worship among the membership. The records are replete with Masonic hero figures, men who have been looked upon as saviors of the race, whose every word and deed has been a cause for praise and adoration. Many of them might be classified as despots because of their trampling on Masonic Law, but their ability to stay in power has usually been straightforward and honest personal magnetism rather than political trickery. A white observer of Prince Hall Masonry commented on the importance and power of such leaders by saying that black Grand Lodges "seem to revolve around the personality, genius, and strength of one or two men in each jurisdiction."[56] While this cannot be said of every state, it has certainly been true of many. A list of charismatic leaders in Masonry would include scores of names, men who maintained stability and order for decades in their jurisdictions. Some of the more interesting who warrant individual study—such as William McDonald of Texas, John Wesley Dobbs of Georgia, John Lewis, Sr., and John Lewis, Jr., of Louisiana, Charles Hendley of Alabama—have been briefly mentioned already. Each of these men was the Mr. Masonry of his state, and was treated accordingly by his followers. It is not uncommon to find tributes to men like these preceded by such accolades as "Savior of our People," the "Moses of the Race," and to find them showered with gifts of money, cars, and vacations.[57]

This type of leader can be found not only in Prince Hall Masonry but in other black fraternal orders, in religion and politics. Unfortunately, the Masonic records provide us with little concrete information about such Masonic leaders and how and why they have received the adoration and power they wield. To what extent pure charismatic magnetism or political manipulation, or a combination of both, has been at work in unknown. Since they almost never lose power, we do not have easy access to the views of their opponents, who could provide inside information on their tactics. According to the records, all power simply flows to them naturally as a sign of their constituents' affection. When they are elected by acclamation, the normal

[56] *Proceedings* (California, 1936).

[57] See *Proceedings* (Alabama, 1925). Grand Master Woods, patriarch of Alabama Prince Hall Freemasonry is called another King Solomon because he built the great Masonic temple. He was elected unanimously after the rules were suspended, and was given a Buick as a sign of the Grand Lodge's love and affection. In the *Proceedings* (Georgia, 1956), the Committee on the Grand Master's address praised Wesley Dobbs in no uncertain terms: "We are happy to say that our Grand Master, though privileged, is one of the people .... He is a unique combination of aristocracy and democracy .... Even when he speaks and writes of great ideas and noble ideas, the illiterate and ignorant, no less than the cultured and erudite, feel the impact of his magnetic personality ...." After the report was made, it was recommended that in addition to the Grand Lodge's normal donation of $500 to Dobbs for his vacation, $2,000 be added. It was approved. A biography of Dobbs would be exceptionally rewarding since he has the distinction of being the grandfather of the first black mayor of Atlanta, Maynard Jackson. According to Peter Ross Range in "Making It In Atlanta: Capital of Black-Is-Bountiful" (*New York Times Magazine*, April 7, 1974), p. 74, Jackson's relationship to Dobbs was a feather in his cap since people recognized that "Maynard Jackson was pedigreed. He was a Dobbs (people are more prone to mention his maternal ancestry than his father's side of the family)."

rules of Masonic election having been suspended (something the C.C.F.C's of some states, especially California, have always been outraged by), one can only wonder if suspension of the rules was political manipulation or a simple formality. All that we can say is that these powerful men deserve special study in order to understand not only black Masonry but black society generally.

What can be determined is that these leaders have helped maintain a marked degree of stability in the fraternity. However, while these "democratic despots" have helped counter the tendencies toward anarchism in Masonry, they have been far less effective in creating a lasting respect for authority than have their more democratic, noncharismatic colleagues. The heroic leader has been looked on as such an unusual man that neither he nor his followers have thought to train any successor; more important, no tradition of support for nonheroic leadership has been built. Also, insofar as they maintain themselves in office for long periods of time, charismatic leaders discourage the most talented and ambitious young men from preparing themselves for active leadership in Masonry.[58] Traditional democratic and charismatic leadership in Masonry accounts for the relative stability of the Order over time despite the great pressures toward disruption that exist. For this reason Masonry does not fit the stereotype of black fraternities, constantly changing leaders, organizing, reorganizing, and finally dying.

The disharmony this chapter has emphasized must be viewed in perspective. While there is a striking amount of conflict within Masonry, and its effects are quite debilitating, exactly how severe the situation in the Order is, remains unclear. It is possible that much of Masonic disunity is a function of black perception rather than social reality, and the level of relative conflict should not be taken at face value. The Masons do not complain about disharmony simply because of its absolute intensity but rather as it compares to their vision of white cooperation. The Masonic proceedings show that blacks *expect* organizations to function with almost no internal friction and

[58] The more successful noncharismatic Masonic politicians who gain office and keep it through electioneering, patronage, favors, threats, or the creation of cliques of allies, also force many potential leaders among the young either to lose interest in the Order or turn to factional politics and antileadership rebellion.

to operate at the peak of efficiency in pursuit of the official institutional goals. This is how they perceive the situation among the Anglo-American and white ethnic groups. Because their reality deviates markedly from this ideal, they see disorder engulfing them, and their anxieties have become a prime topic of discussion in Masonic literature. Before we can truly assess the relative intensity of black internal conflict we must know more about the level of harmony in nonblack ethnic organizations in order to find a point of comparison. Until then all we can safely say is that the *belief* that blacks are more disunited than whites has a tendency to create additional emotional anxiety within the group. Since Masons are convinced that blacks are comparatively untrustworthy, they interact with each other on the basis of that presumption. Fears of conflict, even if based on a faulty perspective, probably lead to less actual cooperation than is found among other groups.

Some additional light is shed on this problem by research I am currently engaged in on the Knights of Columbus and their role in the adjustment of Catholics to Protestant America. While the records of the Knights show that politicking and backbiting are indeed present, the level of dissension and conflict is only a fraction of that which is found in black Freemasonry. Not only is the actual level lower but, equally important, the perception of conflict and the perception of the membership as contentious are a good deal more limited. Part of the difference may come from the organization's Catholicism. The Knights of Columbus, like the Masons, have a very idealistic vision of their role in society, but that idealism, and the expectations it generates, is tempered by a strong belief in original sin. The Knights expect that high ideals will be qualified in practice, that high sounding generalities have to coexist with human frailty. The confessional is always at the back of their minds.

The black Masons, on the other hand, drawing on Protestant idealism and Masonic idealism, are less prepared for the realities of group endeavor than are the Knights. When hostility rather than cooperation surfaces in Prince Hall the Masons are likely to blame themselves, as black men, rather than human nature. The lack of intercourse between blacks and whites (i.e., European ethnic groups) limits their ability to adequately judge what is natural or unnatural in organizational life. The false perception of how others behave then feeds upon itself and helps create the reality it initially only imagines.

This chapter's discussion should not be seen as a negation of the more positive aspects of Masonry that have been presented in earlier chapters. The problems dealt with here restrict and qualify Masonry's power to aid its members and the black group generally, but they do not destroy it. They simply make achievements much harder to obtain. The next chapter will conclude this discussion by showing some of the other areas in which Masonic hopes are compromised by internal disunity, status anxiety, and general black frustration.

Chapter **XIII**

Other Failures

In the last two chapters I have dealt with the failure of Masonry to live up to many of its most inspiring promises. It did not become the unifying, healing, uplifting force for the entire black community that its adherents hoped it would be. Its moral, political, and leadership goals were continually thwarted, frustrated, or limited. The same fate befell the dream that Masonry, through economic enterprise, would save the race. The pages of the Masonic records are full of men who saw Masonry leading the way to economic prosperity and racial dignity. When Grand Master Wilson of California argued in 1922 that "This is imminently an age of combination and cooperation, and the extent of our ability to combine our earnings and cooperate along business and commercial lines, will be the measure of our success, and decide the future status of the organization [i.e., Masonry] and of the race," he expressed the deepest hopes of his colleagues. The Grand Master of Alabama almost two decades later saw the same need and the same solution. He told his Grand Lodge that economic independence and respect for black people in the world only come "By organization and real sincere cooperation." Since blacks as individuals could not achieve the results needed, "We must . . . get together, choose honest and competent leaders and start cooperative businesses and enterprises such as department stores; manufacturing plants; banks; etc."[1]

But the economic enterprises they hoped to see, the pooling of finances they believed necessary, and the leading role Masonry was to take in the process did not materialize, save in a few cases and on a restricted scale. All of the reasons given

[1] *Proceedings* (Alabama, 1939). See also *Proceedings* (Texas, 1930), where Grand Master Kirk supports William McDonald's belief that Masons should help provide employment for brothers. The race, he said, needs a chain of stores and other businesses to give the young work, and Masonry must do something about it.

for Masonic failures in the last two chapters apply here as well: traditionalism, backbiting, the lack of respect for or trust in leadership, the spirit of selfishness and ego-centrism, and the lack of an organized charitable tradition. When the Grand Master of Alabama, as pointed out in the last chapter, had to say to his brethren:

Let us stop being so narrow and envious. Stop tearing down and holding back .... Stop going into business with the idea of closing up some other colored fellow .... Do not be afraid to build up colored men and enterprises . . .[2]

he spelled out why Masonry's most ambitious schemes for economic uplift had to fail.

In an earlier chapter it was argued that Masonic Grand Lodge Temples were *the* symbol for members of the fraternity that the black race had reached maturity and that the fraternity deserved white respect. The Temples possessed a significance which the establishment of Masonic business should more logically have had. The reason Temples, not business, received most of the Order's attention was that the latter has activated the envy and distrust the Grand Master of Alabama condemned. Building a Temple, despite its own set of problems and hostilities, was far more unifying an enterprise than any business venture could be.

The grandiose economic schemes that many Masonic leaders projected for the Order were not the only casualties of the internal problems plaguing the fraternity. Many plans of far more modest scope were also retarded or crippled before they could be carried out. Earlier I dealt with the successes of Masonry in fulfilling many of its immediate goals, such as providing aid for widows and orphans; now I must deal with the less attractive side of this same picture.

While the records of Prince Hall Masonry contain many examples of the Order's successful accomplishment of its intentions to aid the needy among its members and their dependents, they also report many instances of failure or unconscionable delay. For example, though the Grand Lodge of New York decided to establish an old age home for Master Masons and their widows around 1900, and received concrete proposals on where to build it—in 1902, 1911, 1912, 1921, and throughout

[2] *Proceedings* (Alabama, 1939).

the 1940s—the project never materialized. The closest the plan came to realization was after World War II when the idea of an old age home was combined with a scheme for establishing a recreational facility for all Masons in up-state New York. The Grand Master went so far as to buy a magnificent estate near Roscoe, New York, which was rapidly developed as a Masonic retreat. Although Masonic leaders continued to emphasize that "the real purpose of this property is to house our aged and indigent members," the development of an old age home alongside the recreational facilities has never occurred.[3]

The history of the Grand Lodge of California's old age home is not dissimilar. Although it took up the problem of aid to the aged in 1907, and discussed it heatedly for many years, it was not until twenty-five years later, in 1932, that the homesite property was actually purchased. While the property was immediately used for farming and commercial speculation, the old age home was never built. As late as 1960, fifty-three years after the original proposal, the Grand Lodge was still debating whether to sell the homesite, build houses, or a motel, on it, or, last but not least erect an old age home!

In both California and New York the plans dragged on for fifty years, full of high hopes and little results. Committees were appointed time and time again, and either did nothing at all or talked, resolved, reported, and went away.[4] This pattern has been repeated for countless other enterprises, some of which were never achieved, others which were delayed for decades. For example, in 1858 a New York Grand Lodge Committee was established to report on the expediency of establishing a Masonic Library. It recommended favorably, the Grand Lodge adopted the proposal—and did nothing about it.[5] The idea came up frequently in the years between 1858 and 1959 (!), when it was established. Even if one forgets that it took over one hundred years between the original proposal and the institution of the library, one cannot help noticing that the Grand Lodge

---

[3] See *Sentinel* (New York), 1, no.1 (Jan. 1948): 5; 1, no.11 (Dec. 1948): 3; 6, no.7-8 (Sept.-Oct. 1952): 8-9, and *passim* in the years since then.

[4] Of course, many states did establish, quite early in the twentieth century, rather fine old age homes and maintained them for many decades, down to the present. See *Proceedings* (Illinois), during the entire century for good illustrations; the discussion earlier of Georgia's Orphans' Home which, while failing as an old age *and* orphans' home, was also quite successful.

[5] *Prince Hall Masonry in New York State*, vol. II, heading "1858."

got serious about the project a full decade before it materialized; indeed, the Grand Master went so far as to appoint a
"Grand Librarian" in 1954, five years before there was a library
to supervise.[6]

The type of inefficiency, procrastination, and lack of concert-
ed effort that is demonstrated by New York's library and old
age home experiences also plagued many Masonic jurisdictions
in the far more important work of establishing youth orders,
which have been viewed as part of Masonry's effort to aid both
its members and the community. At least as early as 1923,
California's Grand Master pointed out the need for a children's
organization among blacks which would operate like white
Masonry's De Molay to teach the young to follow in their
fathers' footsteps. By 1932 some action had been taken on the
local level and a Junior Masonic Club had been established
in San Bernardino. Its object was to act as a feeder for the
lodge and to allow Master Masons to instill in the youths a
belief in right principles and clean living. As a result of this
success a committee on youth clubs was set up in the Grand
Lodge. Two years later the Grand Lodge even established the
Order of "B" Square Junior Craftsmen. The Order experienced
a nominal degree of success in the San Francisco Bay Area,
but interest around Los Angeles died when the Reverend N.
P. Greeg, the founder, died. The southern part of the state
was without a youth movement until 1948 when the Grand
Lodge appealed for the establishment of a Prince Hall Youth
Association as an adult financing organization. In 1951 the
Grand Lodge adopted the nationwide Knights of Pythagorus
as California's youth fraternity.[7]

During the same years, youth activity in northern California
was not much better, as is witnessed by comments in the
Proceedings of the 1930s. In 1937, for example, it was pointed
out that youth groups could work only if adult members gave
a great deal of attention to them, but that too often when
adults did and things got under way, petty jealousy among
the men interfered with organizational growth. Many years
later, in 1952, the Director of Youth for Northern California
was forced to inform the Grand Lodge that Masons in local
lodges were not cooperating with the youth movement by giving

[6] *Sentinel* (New York), 24, no.1 (Jan.-March 1960): 4.
[7] *Digest* (California), 1, no.4 (Oct.-Dec. 1951): 13.

the names and addresses of boys between the ages of 15 and 20 to the district inspector. He also pointed out that the work needed adult cooperation and could "not be done by a few" working alone.[8] Unfortunately, adult Masons from 1933 on had shown nothing more than a casual interest in the youth movement.[9] According to the reports available in the Grand Lodge *Proceedings*, youth-oriented activities in the 1950s were far more successful than they had been before.[10] However, even this modicum of success was slow in coming despite the obvious importance of the work.[11] The type of problems that have led to failure, or at least severely retarded success in these Masonic activities, have effected practically everything the fraternity has attempted, even when the results have proven more positive. The Order has suffered from inefficiency and wasted energy.

In an earlier chapter mention was made of the committee system in Masonic Grand Lodges and of the positive function it has served in providing large numbers of Masons with the opportunity to play a variety of important roles in the fraternity. But the same system has had dysfunctional effects as well; it has often made the efficient operation of the Grand Lodge impossible. It is not uncommon for resolutions, plans, and proposals for the fraternity, which have been sent to committees by the Grand Master, to never be seen or heard of again.[12] Not atypical is the case of the Committee on Revision of the Grand Lodge Constitution of California in 1904, whose members were "unable" even to get together, let alone produce constructive work. A similar committee in New York in 1919 after more than seven years of reporting from time to time, never passed the discussion stage. The Grand Lodge family grew so weary of the inefficient group that it appointed a new committee, which actually completed a revised Constitution;

---

[8] *Proceedings* (California, 1952).

[9] Ibid.

[10] See *Proceedings* (California, 1954, 1955, 1956, 1958, 1959), reports of Youth Inspector.

[11] See *Review* (Georgia), 15, no.2 (April-June 1951): 20-22. for an article on the youth movement by the Grand Master of Ohio which shows that the movement lagged in many states all over the country. For specific states, see *Prince Hall Masonry in New York State*, vol. II, heading "1940"; *Proceedings* (Illinois), 1925, 1954; (Georgia) 1959; and (Texas) 1934.

[12] *Prince Hall Masonry in New York State*, vol. II, see heading "1884" for general comment on this.

however, it was so poor it was impossible to adopt. While some committees never met, or met and accomplished nothing, other committees did their work in the most incredible fashion. When a New York committee charged with supervising the reports of the Grand Secretary and Grand Treasurer could highlight a nine cent discrepancy between the two reports, and when the Grand Lodge could busy itself deliberating on whether or not to give the janitor six dollars or buy a typewriter, things were not being done efficiently![13]

Even with many inefficient Grand Lodge committees and incompetent committee members, Masonry could still have achieved far more of its aims had it not suffered from one last ailment. Despite everything, Masonry's "efficiency" problems have stemmed less from its executive and legislative organization than from its rank and file membership. Masonry, like almost every voluntary organization in America, has suffered from the lack of commitment from a substantial proportion of its members. Unfortunately, Masonic leaders have never really adjusted to that simple fact of organizational life in the same way that they have refused to recognize that a fraternity based upon high ideals could suffer from politics, indeed needed to harness political energies to work most effectively. All of the visions and hopes for the role of Masonry in the black community which the leaders have entertained have drawn strength from the numerical size and financial resources that a very large and supposedly committed membership possessed. Grand Masters have been exhilarated by the knowledge that almost any project the fraternity set out to achieve, whether establishing a bank, gas station or orphans home, could be easily accomplished with only a small per capita tax on the membership. A jurisdiction with 30,000 Masons (which includes a number of states) could raise $36,000 for any project it desired with only a 10 cents per month tax for a year. By raising the levy to only one dollar per month they would have $360,000. It has been because of this easily tapped wealth, at least in part, that Masonic leaders have foreseen a great role for the fraternity. The only problem has been that the schemes have always depended upon a committed membership.

Exactly how many black Masons have wholeheartedly concerned themselves with the fortunes of the fraternity is impos-

[13] *Proceedings* (New York, 1914).

sible to determine. A figure often given by despondent leaders
is 10 percent,[14] a figure similar to that which a white Masonic
publication in Oregon gave for its membership.[15] When a Grand
Master of Georgia in 1926 said that of 25,000 Masons in his
state only 3,000 were "real" Masons, he gave added support
for this approximate estimate. However, what the Masonic
leaders have considered a "genuinely" involved member is
obscure, and probably suffers from gross over-exclusiveness.
The figure of 10 to 15 percent may be accurate for the most
dedicated, but another 30 to 45 percent has probably been quite
committed by ordinary standards. One can look at attendance
at the local lodge meetings, but the exact correlation between
attendance and willingness to support the Order financially
in important undertakings is not known. Drawing conclusions
from average attendance, other than to say it is only a fraction
of the membership, is difficult. For example, in 1916 the local
lodges of Illinois varied drastically in their attendance records;
with averages of 11 percent, 25 percent, 40 percent and 50
percent. The Grand Master of California in the same year
complained of attendance, especially in larger lodges, which
he claimed was much worse than in smaller ones. However,
his figures were 10 to 30 percent attending the big lodges and
50 to 75 percent the small ones. A Grand Master of New York
in 1957 was disappointed with "only a 30% attendance record."[16]
Impressionistically, figures for attendance are governed by the
general rule that large lodges have a smaller percentage attending regularly than do small; similarly, attendance in urban
lodges is proportionately lower than that of their rural counterparts; but it would take a great deal of work to prove this
and to discover any other controlling factors.[17] What can be
said with certainty is that a large proportion, and probably
the majority of Masons, do not attend their lodges regularly.
   Many factors account for the lack of full commitment on

[14] *Topics* (Illinois), 12, no.18 (June 1949): 10.

[15] *Topics* (Illinois), 14, no.4-6 (April-June 1951): 23.

[16] *Sentinel* (New York), 14, no.1 (Jan.-March 1957): 2.

[17] Many Masonic authorities believe that large lodges have less committed memberships than small. However, many states have trouble with lack of commitment in
small lodges, too. Interestingly enough, the 1916 figures for Illinois show that the lodge
with the largest average attendance, 40 to 50 percent, was the largest lodge of those
given, with 218 members. Two of the other lodges with almost identical memberships
(105 and 96, respectively) showed the first with 40 percent attendance and the second
with only 20 percent. Obviously, many factors other than size come into play.

the part of a large proportion of the membership to the Masonic fraternity. The Grand Master of Illinois in 1951 felt the most important were three:

> Some [of the uninterested] are Masons because their fathers were and it's a family tradition. Others are members because they feel their social standing is enhanced. Still others, a minimum, present petitions for mercenary reasons despite their denials [i.e., business and insurance reasons].[18]

One would imagine that the second reason, to enhance their social standing, has been the single most important reason for most half-hearted Masons, though in many states, especially those with large memberships and thriving insurance plans, the third has also been vital. In the 1930s Alabama, for example, was plagued by local lodges which did not meet regularly, nor initiate new members, but simply existed to act as insurance agents and collect dues for the endowment funds.[19] Other jurisdictions, even far smaller ones, have also suffered similarly, as is witnessed by the complaint of the Grand Master of Minnesota that men were entering the fraternity who saw it only as a benefit organization.[20]

It may seem odd, but Masonry has also suffered greatly from competition for the interest of its membership with other Masonic organizations. Attached to the basic Masonic fraternity are many "higher" degrees or organizations that draw their memberships exclusively from members of the local Masonic lodges. These Orders, which are not under the jurisdiction of the state Grand Lodge but are recognized as Masonic "auxiliaries" by them, include Shriners, Knights Templar, Scottish Rite Masonry, and Royal Arch Masonry, among others. They compete for the time and money of the Masonic membership, and often win. The reasons are varied. According to the Grand Master of California in 1922, many Masons have been under the misapprehension that the "higher degrees" give the initiate real secret knowledge that the local Masonic lodge does not possess, and thus the "blue lodge," as it is called, is only a stepping stone upward. For others, the pomp and pageantry of the auxiliary groups appeal to them more than the activities

[18] *Topics* (Illinois), 14, nos.4-6 (April-June 1951): 23-25.
[19] *Proceedings* (Alabama, 1938).
[20] *Proceedings* (California, 1932), quoted in the Report of the C.C.F.C.

of the local lodge.[21] The Masonic records are full of suggestions of how the blue lodge can make its program more interesting and thus hold its members more tightly. The boredom of a badly conducted local lodge is a constant problem, according to the records.

The Masonic lodge has also experienced competition from non-Masonic sources. The same social forces mentioned in an earlier chapter which have made it difficult for the Order to recruit new members, have also put a strain on her ability to keep the old ones committed. Masonry must compete with television, radio, movies, automobiles, church groups, business and professional associations, and social and welfare projects for the attention of the membership.[22] All of these factors have severely limited the commitment of many Masons to their fraternity, as has the almost universal social fact that the majority of people who join a voluntary organization, be it the Young People's Socialist League or the Rotary Club, lack the motivation to take an active part in its work. The result has been that Masonic plans which have called for the fullest cooperation in money, time, and effort of the entire Masonic membership have collapsed or been retarded.

It has been lack of commitment and cooperation, not lack of money or skill, which has defeated or restricted so many of Masonry's grander dreams for social and economic uplift. The black population, Masons included, has been relatively poor. But the Masonic leadership has been correct in its contention that the amount of money required of each member in order to carry out most of the Order's plan has been quite small. For example, the state of Alabama in the late 1930s provided a tax of 5 cents per member per year to maintain its scholarship fund, a fund it was extremely proud of. For years, the Committee on Education recommended that the tax be raised to the sum of 10 cents per member per annum, but they never got it.[23] Such penny-pinching has unfortunately not been atypical. Obtaining money has often been extremely difficult, despite the fact, as many Grand Masters have pointed out, that the brother who begrudged the scholarship fund an extra 5 cents would turn around and throw money away on

---

[21] See *Proceedings* (California, 1936), Report of Department of Research, for example.

[22] See *Sentinel* (New York), 10, nos.9-10 (Nov.-Dec. 1954): 3 for example.

[23] "Report of Fraternal Correspondent," Williamson, June 1931 (mimeographed).

one entertainment or another. Even when members have been willing to give money to the fraternity they have often shown a lack of commitment to its ideals through its allocation. As Harry Williamson bitterly pointed out in 1931, "There are Lodges that will spend a hundred or so dollars for a jewel for a retiring Master or a banquet on election night but when sometimes it comes to a matter of dispensing charity . . . the brethren will argue for no little length of time about a mere five or ten dollars."[24] The Chairman of the Committee on Foreign Correspondence of California echoed the same sentiment when he complained, "Is it not to be the eternal shame of our profession[s of charity] that . . . nearly all of our jurisdictions . . . , [after] we have given a small pittance to our sick, doled out amity to our widows, 'paid our debts,' we flatter ourselves that we have done well."[25] (The rest of this statement is of interest because its solution to the problem is to build local lodge halls and thus give Masonry something solid to show for all its years of existence!)

Despite the fact that in the realm of charity Masonry has accomplished a great deal, there is continuous evidence that the basic goal of the fraternity to teach its members the value of giving generously has never really been achieved. Ubiquitous in Grand Lodge proceedings are notices of charity donations for exceptionally needy widows and orphans which are ludicrously small. The Grand Lodge of New York in 1934 was quite typical when its Committee on Charity "opened its heart" and voted eleven men and women five dollars each. But what kind of charity for "exceptionally" deserving widows and destitute Master Masons is five dollars? Of course, Grand Lodge funds were limited, but not *that* limited. The Masonic records reveal not only that Grand Lodge charity has been pitifully low, but often that no one has noticed; indeed, a tone of self-congratulation is not uncommon. For example, in 1906 the California Grand Master devoted a large part of his annual message to discuss "The Old People's Home at Beulah, Alameda County." He told the Masons that this was the only old-age home for colored people north of the Techachapi Mountains, a home to be proud of: "We, as Masons, should do all that lies in our power to aid and assist it morally and financially." He went

[24] Ibid.

[25] *Proceedings* (California, 1920).

on to say that the greatest "adjunct" of the institution was Masonry's own beloved "Brother" J. C. Rivers; and for all these reasons he (the Grand Master) recommends that the Grand Lodge "continue to make a liberal and charitable donation, as it has hitherto done in the past." The only trouble with this sentiment is that the normal "liberal and charitable donation" from the Grand Lodge was ten dollars! When the majority of the uncommitted Masons have shown a lack of understanding concerning the meaning of Masonic charity, it is quite understandable. It is much harder to explain how many leading and committed Masons, including the Grand Master of California mentioned above, could wax so eloquent about such inadequate donations to worthy causes.

While the Grand Master of California in 1906 did not notice the problem inherent in Grand Lodge charity, the head of New York Masonry forty-five years later did. He told the Craft that New York had been sadly remiss in not establishing a fund for Widows and Distressed Master Masons, an Annuity Fund for Aged Brethren and an institution for worthy, aged Freemasons and their widows:

> It is my sincere belief that our inability to support general charities, as outlined, mitigates against our recognition by other Masonic Bodies. Of course, we as Prince Hall Masons, realize that the real bars to recognition are delivered from Race Prejudice. But, we must admit that in spite of our economic condition, we have fallen short.[26]

He went on to say that while the race and fraternity were not financially able to set up a trust fund or maintain an extensive institution for the indigent, there could be no doubt that much more could be done than was being done. And he was quite right. However, it was one thing for thoughtful Masons to realize the problem and another to get the majority of Masons to rectify the situation with increased financial aid. The result has been that Masonry has accomplished far less than it has hoped, and the ultimate losers have not only been the fraternity and its membership but the entire black race.

In the last few chapters we have discussed a number of problems Masonry has faced which have severely limited its ability to achieve its stated goals, especially the goals of elimi-

[26] *Sentinel* (New York), 5, no.9-10 (Nov.-Dec. 1952): 2, 6.

nating black disunity in economic undertakings and in facing
white racism. Ivan Light's study of black business pinpoints
yet another weakness of Masonry. It is Light's thesis that, as
a result of slavery, the blacks lack traditional ascriptive organizations, whether tribal, clan, or territorial, upon which a "moral
community" can rest. Since a sharing of moral values (the
creation of social trust) is necessary for most group processes,
the blacks have been forced to create by means of conscious
choice a noncompulsory moral community. The mechanism
they have had to utilize is the voluntary association. Their
success or failure in this has been dependent upon the strengths
and weaknesses inherent in that type of social organization.
Light maintains that the weaknesses of voluntary association
vis-a-vis ascriptive organizations are much greater than most
observers have realized. Since Masonry is an archetypical voluntary association which aims to create a moral community
among its members, his thesis has obvious relevance to this
study.

According to Light, the burden placed on nonascriptive
organizations by black needs is greater than their capacity to
bear. When strangers come together and attempt to create trust
and confidence, which have little or no previous foundation,
from scratch, they must fail unless they produce an all-inclusive
social environment where total commitment of the individual
can be obtained. Anything less than this total experience—as
achieved in religious and political sects—can achieve only a
limited form of solidarity, a form not great enough to overcome
the disunity that exists where primordial ties are lacking. Light
argues that for voluntary associations such as

> churches and fraternal orders to create and sustain intense
> internal solidarity depended on their ability to impose an ethical
> discipline upon the membership. The more rigorous the ethical
> discipline, the more intense would be the internal solidarity of
> the moral community. In general, the imposition of ethical
> discipline required the churches and fraternities to achieve a total
> rather than segmental control over members' motives, beliefs,
> associations and conduct. This total level of control voluntary
> associations are notoriously unable to achieve without Draconian
> measures.[27]

[27] Ivan Light, *Ethnic Enterprise in America* (Berkeley, 1972) pp. 131-132.

The exceptions to this situation are elitist organizations appealing to higher status groups on the basis of "snobbery" which can use exclusion as a threat.

According to this interpretation, scholars place too much faith in the rational ability of men to come together for utilitarian purposes and achieve them; with far too little argument, voluntary associations are assumed to be progressive urban replacements for traditional ties, and of necessity superior to what they replace. In fact, Light maintains, modern American society is not the voluntary association society *par excellence* it is thought to be. Rather, it rests upon many traditional solidarities, and it is those ties which supply the voluntary associations with the minimal trust and moral agreement necessary to insure their functioning. If no ethnic, religious, kin, or class groups permeated white society, many of the most successful utilitarian voluntary associations would fall apart since the organizations would fail to create the minimal trust necessary for cooperation.[28]

In Light's view the blacks come closer to lacking traditional ascriptive bonds than any other major group, and thus the weakness of voluntary associations to create a moral community without outside aid are more obvious. For black organizations to overcome their limitations they must create an emotional enthusiasm far stronger than is normally necessary. The emotional commitment, if strong enough, can forge a mystic tie similar in power and usefulness to the missing ascriptive ones.[29]

Using Light's analysis, we may view Prince Hall Freemasonry as an institution concerned with the creation of solidarity and moral community and possessed of a strong nonrational, mystic element that could conceivably overcome the weakness inherent in nonascriptive organizations. Unfortunately, it must deal with a problem endemic to black society, the unrestrained competition among organizations for members. According to

[28] See Light, p. 183, where he says that the American urban center is neither an "occidental" nor an "oriental" city (using Max Weber's ideal types) but leans more toward the latter than the former.

[29] Light believes that the blacks are closer to Weber's "condition of urban society in which a plurality of competing voluntary associations constituted the exclusive basis of social solidarity" than any other group. Since Weber never saw a purely "occidental" city, he did not realize that a society of voluntary associations without other ties tends to atomize and demoralize the poor and weaken social cohesion generally (Light, p. 184).

Light, the only way to get the necessary commitment to an association to build a moral community is to require a marked degree of isolation between the membership and the rest of the society, especially other organizations.[30] The more that members have a choice of associations, the more they will require the institution to dilute the requirements and responsibilities it places on its members. Black society generally is inundated with voluntary groups competing for members. This is because the black population is relatively "culturally undifferentiated"—that is, there are few ascriptive or achieved divisions which make a potential membership pool easily distinguishable from a nonpotential one. This encourages competition among voluntary associations rather than specialization and coexistence.[31] Except for a few heterodox, extremist groups, the result is that all such organizations find that their ability to bind their members together and to create trust and cooperation are undercut. Nonheterodox organizations, according to Light, can get the necessary power to control the behavior and morals of their members only if they are "exclusive" enough and prestigious enough to make rejection for nonconformity a real threat, only if the potential member wants admittance more than the organizations wants him. Only through social snobbery or its equivalent can it protect itself from the corrosion of competition.[32]

Prince Hall Freemasonry has always been a fairly exclusive and prestigious organization, and it has benefited from that fact. The number of associations directly competing for its membership is lower than it could have been had not Masonry aimed at attracting a comparatively select middle-class audience. However, it is not a small, elite Order, but a mass, middle-strata one. It thus partakes of some of the key weaknesses of organizations which lack the selectivity and prestige needed to maintain control over their membership.

Although Masonic literature speaks as if the fraternity is a tight-knit mystic brotherhood, like the Black Muslims or Jehovah's Witnesses, Masonry is too much in the mainstream of Western society to demand or receive the fierce devotion and loyalty such groups obtain. Given Light's analysis, Mason-

[30] Light, p. 29.
[31] Ibid., pp. 131-133.
[32] Ibid., pp. 185-186.

ry as a nonfanatical voluntary association with only a moderate level of charismatic and mystical appeal or social exclusiveness, has been incapable of achieving its more ambitious goals. To rise above the moderate level of success it has achieved there would have to be greater unity and trust already existing among its members from other sources; or it would have to move toward the heterodox extreme and make itself a real secret society; or it would have to become a more elitist social institution. It cannot be an orthodox foundation of the greater black middle class and simultaneously create a moral and social revolution among its adherents.[33]

None of this is to deny that Prince Hall Freemasonry does help forge solid lines of trust and cooperation among its members and between its members and other parts of the middle class. Rather, it means that the depth and strength of the community created is definitely limited—and at a level below both the organization's goals and the objective needs of the black group.

In order to put the last three chapters into proper perspective, it is important to realize that the negative aspects of Prince Hall Freemasonry do not contradict or negate its positive features. Many readers would prefer to see Masonry, and the black middle class, in a consistently positive or negative light. For some the book should have ended at chapter 11, for others it should have started there. But simple consistency is not the key to understanding the black Masons or the black bourgeoisie.

The positive accomplishments of the fraternity and its members have developed out of the agonized efforts of the black middle class to achieve dignity and self-respect, to live by the standards of manhood that American society projects. The Masons have had to sacrifice individually and as a group to succeed even marginally. The antagonism of the black bourgeoisie to the black poor develops naturally out of this very process of class differentiation, of adoption of the middle-class

[33] It should be pointed out that Light's discussion of black voluntary associations really focuses on the black lower class. The exceptions he makes for his generalizations are for small and elite groups (e.g., college fraternities) and extremist religious and political groups (which appeal to the poor). The black middle class is left out. The middle class's organizations seem to combine some of the strengths and some of the weaknesses of the other two groups. They create more moral solidarity among their membership than lower-class organizations and less than elite or extremist ones.

moral ethic, and of sensitization to the attitudes of the value-setting white group. The backbiting, envy, and hostility to leadership within Masonry are the direct result of the Masons' aspirations as they are distorted by the racial and class realities. Even the petty failures of Masonry, such as stinginess and penny pinching, flow from the Masons' constant striving for a secure middle-class status which their restricted and narrow economic base frustrates. The black bourgeoisie is trapped in the middle between prosperity and poverty, between the lower class and solid middle class, between white and black. Marginality hurts; it hurts the black bourgeoisie, it hurts the black population as a whole, and it gives a tragic quality to black middle-class life.

Conclusion

The black middle class deserves better treatment at the hands of academic observers than it has previously received. Too often it is portrayed as a pathological social strata, mindlessly and crudely mimicking the white middle class without benefit of the economic resources, social manners, or cultural "good taste" to do it well. All too often the black bourgeoisie is seen as selfish and irresponsible, living in a fantasy world that incapacitates its members and betrays the entire race. In the eyes of such commentators, it exists as a parasite on both the white and black communities.

More sympathetic observers have been no more objective in their effort to deal with the black middle class. To these supporters the black bourgeoisie has no real social existence, no three-dimensional quality. It is rather a column of statistics (all favorable) demonstrating that blacks are well on their way to total acceptance in the larger society, that they are economically, occupationally, and educationally upwardly mobile. They are a vanguard proving that the "black problem" is well on the road to solution.

I have questioned the accuracy of both of these extreme positions, and at the same time have sought to give the black middle class the serious investigation it deserves. Without denying the element of truth in both of the former viewpoints, I have challenged their general usefulness by illuminating other, more important, aspects of life among the black bourgeoisie. As I have demonstrated, this group's most salient characteristic is its alienation from both the black lower and white middle classes. As an emerging class, seeking to define and solidify itself, the black bourgeoisie has been acutely self-conscious, particularly in its awareness of the differences which divide it from the black masses. Not far removed from the lower class in time or space, the middle-class black has, of necessity, come to view his lower-class counterparts as a negative reference group—of vital importance to defining what the black bourgeoisie is by demonstrating what it is not.

The inevitable social alienation inherent in the process of class differentiation is compounded by the black middle class's commitment to mainstream (i.e., Euro-American) bourgeois values. Regardless of the attractiveness of much of Western middle-class morality or codes of conduct, aspects of those values exaggerate intrablack disunity. Even in its watered-down, consumer-oriented version, the Protestant ethic, for example, emphasizes individual competitive effort and achievement; it promises rewards for the hardworking, ambitious, and resourceful man. At the same time, it morally condemns those who fail to succeed and attributes to them personal responsibility for their fate. Members of the black lower class have been America's classic losers. For those who have succeeded (no matter that their success is marginal) the validity of the bourgeois ethic is convincing. Not only does their achievement prove that the competitive spirit is justified, it actively inhibits sympathy with those who have failed to make the grade. While this ethic allows the successful black man to take pride in his own accomplishments and to justify his efforts to put social distance between himself and most blacks, at the same time it compels a loss of empathy with those left behind, those who "wilfully" refuse to exert or discipline themselves in order to seize the opportunities that readily await them.

If the resulting natural estrangement of middle- and lower-class blacks were not enough, the process of estrangement is aggravated by the attitudes of middle-class whites. Not only are they the black bourgeoisie's class peers, they are the interpreters of a shared moral code. The antipoor sentiments inherent in the general middle-class work ethic are exaggerated by white prejudices to which the black cannot help but respond. (While the black middle class can react negatively or positively to white opinion, it cannot act as if it has never heard the accusations leveled against the black race.) The most common defense against racist slurs aimed at the morals and culture of black people has not been to deny them outright—because the black middle class in its self-conscious opposition to the black masses has felt that many of them are true—but to attribute nonbourgeois, allegedly "immoral" conduct to the lower class, and then to emphasize intraracial class differences.

The hostility between the black middle and lower classes, however, has been far from total. The forces for unity as well as for division have been considerable. The continued existence of white racial prejudice, which has failed to discriminate between classes, has required the black bourgeoisie to develop race consciousness and to engage in the general fight for civil rights and race uplift. Indeed, the middle class has publicly assumed the role of champion of the ideal of universal racial equality and has refused to restrict itself to pleading for narrow class benefits. The result has been a significant modification of the antagonisms resulting from class differences. Unfortunately, these two views of the black lower class—"our poor oppressed people" and "the rabble who give us a bad name"— have not blended to form a consistent position. Instead, they coexist, creating an unstable and contradictory love-hate relationship between the black classes.

Interaction between the black and white middle classes has been no less complex or ambiguous. On the one hand, the black middle class has been attracted to its white counterpart. The white bourgeoisie, as the dominant group, has been the model for upwardly mobile blacks, setting standards of morality, manners, art, and culture. Alternative models have not been viable. The black folk culture has not been a "workable" model since the emergent bourgeoisie has not wished to be identified with its rural and lower class past. Even if identification had been desired, the folk culture has a far too limited and parochial repetoire of roles and concepts to fulfill the needs of a rising urban-oriented middle class. African cultural models, regardless of their possible adaptability, have been unavailable to American blacks.

It must be pointed out that middle class blacks have not been unique in finding the "white" world attractive. The Jews of nineteenth-century Europe, emerging from their own traditional culture, also found their world view and value system too parochial and limiting to be a useful guide to the world they were attempting to enter. The Jews, like the blacks, aspired to acculturation into and acceptance by Western secular society. For them, the attractiveness of the white Christian bourgeoisie and its value system stemmed, in large part, from its explicitly universalist message. The rising middle class's value system claims that all those who live by it are equal and will be rewarded according to individual merit, not group ascription. This notion of equality of opportunity has been irresistible to Jews and blacks alike.

The refusal of white America to honor the ideal of equality and, in fact, its vehement support of anti-individualist corporate ascriptiveness and its refusal to reward blacks who live by the middle-class ethic, have created powerful antiwhite antagonisms among the black bourgeoisie. As we have seen in great depth, the black bourgeoisie has not been able to resolve the tensions inherent in its attraction to and repulsion from white middle-class society. The rival attitudes coexist uneasily, leading to basic contradictions in black bourgeois thought and action.

The alienation and ambivalence of the black middle class vis-à-vis the larger social groups, black and white, which surround it, has been its basic tragedy. Prince Hall Freemasonry, as a major foundation of the black bourgeoisie, has allowed us to view that predicament with unusual clarity. The study of Freemasonry has permitted us to see the isolation of the black middle class more clearly and in greater depth than would have been possible by focusing on institutions or people more traditionally the object of academic inquiry—such as the black press, civil rights groups, or major political and intellectual spokesmen. Masonry permits the examination of a crucial "secondary" level of black opinion-leaders, people more directly in touch (emotionally, socially, and intellectually) with the black middle class than are highly placed and more well known national leaders of the "first rank." Determining the relationship between W. E. B. DuBois, Booker T. Washington, Roy Wilkins, the Chicago *Defender*, or the National Association for the Advancement of Colored People to black middle-class society presents problems that are minimal in a study of a "grass roots" institution like Prince Hall and its leaders. The fact that Masonic leaders do not speak to a large public audience, that they are not as skilled or professional as are more prominent black leaders, that they are closer in their capacities to their "electorate," makes a study of them rewarding in ways that investigations of more "important" subjects are not. The ability to see black spokesmen operating within a functioning social institution, which is simultaneously the object of analysis, allows a comparison to be made between thought and deed.

Fraternal organizations can help one also to understand the experience and attitudes of significant numbers of people below the normal level of academic observation. For example, my

investigation of the Knights of Columbus and the Catholic
response to America has pointed to both marked similarities
and dissimilarities with the Prince Hall Freemasons. The lower
level of internal division within the Catholic Order has already
been discussed. In addition, the leaders of the Knights show
relatively little concern with the moral conduct of the members
(except insofar as adherents must be practicing Catholics, a
characteristic that is more a function of attendance at Mass
and Confession than a specific type of everyday lifestyle) or
with recognizing and fostering class consciousness. When the
Knights say they are interested in all Catholics as potential
members they are really not more accurate than the Masons.
However, the key divisions are not class but ethnic.

If the Knights differ significantly from the black Masons in
these respects, they are nonetheless identical in a more fundamental one. The Catholic Order has been deeply preoccupied
with the attitude of the white Anglo-Saxon middle class toward
Catholics in much the same way as the Masons have been
concerned about attitudes toward blacks. Protestant "Big
Brother" has been a constant specter haunting the Knights.
The Knights like the Masons have been continually "looking
over their shoulders" for outside approval. They have been
especially hard put to prove to native Americans (and themselves) that anti-Catholic slanders are false. The most provoca-
tive accusation against the Catholics for many years was that
they were an intellectually benighted group whose bigoted and
superstitious clergy kept them cowed. The Knights dedicated
themselves to proving that education and Catholic faith are
not only not mutually exclusive but, further, that one cannot
exist without the other. The need to prove themselves to
Protestants on this score was so great that they undertook
one of the largest and most expensive private adult educational
experiments in American history—the creation of an education
network for the American armed forces in France during World
War I. Like the black Masons, concern with Protestant opinion
permeates the Knights' records. I hope that my research, when
completed, will reveal a new dimension of the Catholic adjustment to America and shed light on similarities and differences
between the white ethnic groups and the Afro-Americans.

The study of Prince Hall Freemasonry has shown more than
middle-class alienation and marginality. Freemasonry as an

institution provides insight into the means by which the black middle class has attempted to create solidarity and self-consciousness among its membership, provide social and psychological support for the bourgeois life style, facilitate social and physical distance between itself and other classes, and transmit its values to others. The study has attempted to cast light on the ways in which middle-class institutions as a group work together to create a viable subcommunity within black society which can provide protection against the demoralization caused by a racist society or the seductions of rival ghetto life styles. It shows the many benefits that flow from black middle-class institutions. Prince Hall Freemasonry has helped provide security, friendship, and unity to its members. It has helped develop a tradition of organized charity, self-help, and self-reliance, and has trained individual members not only for Masonic leadership, but for leadership of the entire black population. It has allowed middle-class blacks to play social roles and acquire technical skills that American society has denied them. While its role in creating and maintaining a bourgeois community within Afro-American society has not been an unmixed blessing for the race, to a large extent its role has been vital to the survival and development of the black group in white America. Masonry and its sister institutions have given the economic, social, political, and organizational leadership necessary for existence. The history of Prince Hall Freemasonry is also the history of the fight for civil rights and for an end to racial discrimination in America. Its accomplishments as well as its failures offer insights into aspects of the black middle class which for too long have gone unexplored.

Bibliography

The following is a selected bibliography. Much of the material found in the Schomburg Library's Black Masonry Collection (New York Public Library) will not be listed separately. All materials, with the exception of the *Proceedings* of the Grand Lodge of California and the *Prince Hall Masonic Digest* (California), are located in the Harry Williamson Masonic Collection, Schomburg Library, New York Public Library.

Newspapers and Magazines

The Colored Tribune.
Co-Operation (magazine published by the Grand Lodge of Illinois).
Doric Magazine (published by the Masons of California).
Fraternal Review (New York City).
The Masonic Quarterly (published by the Grand Lodge of Texas).
National Fraternal Review (published by the Grand Lodge of Illinois).
New York Age.
Past Masters' Topics (journal published by the Grand Lodge of Illinois).
Phyorony (magazine of Prince Hall Lodge of Research).
Prince Hall Masonic Digest (published by the Grand Lodge of California).
Prince Hall Masonic Review (published by the Grand Lodge of Georgia).
Prince Hall Sentinel (published by the Grand Lodge of New York).
San Francisco *Pacific Appeal.*
The Savannah *Tribune.*

Directories

The Dictionary of American Biography, 1932.
Negro Who's Who in California, 1948.
Official Directory of Most Worshipped Sovereign Grand Lodge State of California Jurisdiction (n.d., but probably between 1920 and 1930).
Thompson's East Bay Colored Business Directory, 1930.
Who's Who in Colored America, 1928-29, 1930, 1931, 1932, 1950.

Manuscripts

Edward N. Palmer, memorandum for Gunnar Myrdal's investigation,
The Negro in America (original manuscript).
Harry Williamson, "Report of the Chairman of the Committee on
Foreign Correspondence," New York, 1931.

Constitutions

By-Laws of Progressive Lodge, No. 17, New Brunswick, New Jersey.
Constitution and By-Laws of Grand Lodge of Georgia, 1924.
*Constitution and By-Laws of the Hiram Masonic Relief Association
of the State of New York*, 1891 and 1898.
Constitution and By-Laws of Prince Hall Square Club, Inc., New
York City, 1930.
Constitution of Grand Lodge of California, 1918.
*History, Constitution and By-Laws of Excelsior Lodge No. 11, Free
and Accepted Masons*, Cleveland, Ohio, 1926.
Members' Dues Book and By-Laws of Carthaginian Lodge No. 47,
1914.

Proceedings and Reports

Annual Report of the Secretary-Treasurer of the Hiram Masonic
Relief Association, 1900-1901 and others.
Proceedings of the Grand Lodge of Alabama, 1873-1954.
Proceedings of the Grand Lodge of California, 1890-1970.

Proceedings of the Grand Lodge of Georgia, 1908-1959.
Proceedings of the Grand Lodge of Illinois, 1889-1959.
Proceedings of the Grand Lodge of New York, 1897-1971.
Proceedings of the Grand Lodge of Texas, 1880-1964.

Addresses

"Address delivered by John Edward Bruce (Grit) before the Craftsmen's Club," March 6, 1910.
"Prince Hall, The Pioneer of Negro Masonry Proofs of the Legitimacy
of Prince Hall Masonry," John Edward Bruce (Grit), 1921.
"The Significance of Brotherhood," John Edward Bruce (Grit), 1919.

Histories (by Masons)

Butler, Dr. H. R. *History of Masonry Among Colored Men in Georgia.*

Grand Master of Georgia, 1911.

Davis, Harry E. *A History of Freemasonry Among Negroes in America.* Published under the auspices of Scottish Rite, North, 1946.

Delany, Martin. *The Origins and Objects of Ancient Freemasonry, Its Introduction into the United States and Legitimacy Among Colored Men.* Pittsburgh, 1853.

Grimshaw, William. *Official History of Freemasonry Among the Colored People of North America.* New York, 1903.

Johnson, Sol C. *History of the Grand Lodge* [Georgia Grand Lodge]. n.p., 1920.

Wesley, Charles. *The History of the Prince Hall Grand Lodge of Free and Accepted Masons of the State of Ohio 1849-1960.* Wilberforce, Ohio, 1961.

Williamson, Harry. *Prince Hall Masonry in New York State,* 3 volumes. Manuscript at Schomburg Library.

Williamson, Harry. *Prince Hall Primer.* New York, 1946.

Williamson, Harry. *The Story of Carthaginian 1904-1947,* n.p., 1949.

Interviews (Conducted by Author)

Interview with Adrian Bridges, Secretary of an Oakland, California, Lodge, May 1970 and April 1971.

Interview with C. L. Dellums, May 1971.

Interview with Royal Towns, November and December 1968.

Interview with Richard Wilson, Secretary of Good Hope Lodge, Oakland, California, May 1971.

Secondary Sources

Aptheker, Herbert. *The Negro in the Abolitionist Movement.* New York, 1941.

Bacote, Clarence. "Some Aspects of Negro Life in Georgia, 1880-1908." *Journal of Negro History* 43, no.3 (1958).

Bailyn, Bernard. "The Political and Social Structure of Virginia." In *Seventeenth Century America, Essays in Colonial History,* edited by J. M. Smith. Chapel Hill, N.C., 1959.

Bernard, Jesse. *Marriage and Family Among Negroes.* Englewood Cliffs, N.J., 1965.

Berthoff, Rowland. "The American Social Order: A Conservative Hypothesis." *American Historical Review* 65, no.3 (April 1960): 495-514.

Beynon, Erdmann. "The Voodoo Cult Among Negro Migrants in Detroit." *American Journal of Sociology* 43, no.6 (May 1938): 894-907.

Brown, Jr., William. "Class Aspects of Residential Development and Choice in the Oakland Black Community." Ph.D. dissertation, University of California, Berkeley, 1961.

Cohen, Abner. "The Politics of Ritual Secrecy." *Man* 6, no.3 (1971): 427-447.

Crawford, George L. *Prince Hall and His Followers*. New York, 1914.

Daniels, R., and Kitano, H. *American Racism: Exploration of the Nature of Prejudice*. Englewood Cliffs, N.J., 1970.

Davis, Allison, and Gardner, Burleigh and Mary. *Deep South*. Chicago, 1941.

Davis, David B. "Themes of Counter-Subversion: An Analysis of Anti-Masonic, Anti-Catholic, and Anti-Mormon Literature." *Mississippi Valley Historical Review* 47, no.2 (September 1960): 205-224.

Dollard, John. *Caste and Class in a Southern Town*. New Haven, 1937.

Drake, St. Clair, and Cayton, Horace. *Black Metropolis*, 2 volumes. New York, 1962.

DuBois, W. E. B. *The Philadelphia Negro*. Philadelphia, 1899.

———. *Some Efforts of American Negroes for their Own Social Betterment*. Atlanta, 1907.

———. *Economic Co-operation Among Negro Americans*. Atlanta, 1907.

Edwards, G. Franklin. *The Negro Professional Class*. New York, 1959.

———. "Community and Class Realities: The Ordeal of Change." In *The Negro American*, edited by Talcott Parsons and Kenneth Clark. Cambridge, Mass., 1966.

Foner, Philip. *The Life and Writings of Frederick Douglass*, vol. 4, New York, 1955.

Frazier, E. Franklin. *Black Bourgeoisie*. New York, 1957.

———. *The Negro in the United States*. New York, 1957.

———. *The Negro Family*. Chicago, 1966.

———. "Human, All Too Human." In *The Rise of the Ghetto*, edited by B. Rudwick. Belmont, Calif., 1971.

Gans, Herbert. "Culture and Class in the Study of Poverty: An Approach to Anti-Poverty Research." In *On Understanding Poverty*, edited by D. Moynihan. New York, 1969.

Gans, Herbert. *Urban Villagers*. New York, 1962.

Genevese, Eugene. "The Legacy of Slavery on the Roots of Black Nationalism." *Studies on the Left* 6, no.6 (1966): 3-65.

———."On Antonio Gramsci." In *For a New America*, edited by James Weinstein and D. Eakins. New York, 1970.

Greene, Lorenzo. "Prince Hall: Massachusetts Leader in Crisis." *Freedomways* 1, no.3 (1962): 238-258.

Hannerz, Ulf. *Soulside.* New York, 1969.

Hare, Nathan. *Black Anglo-Saxon.* New York, 1970.

Harris, Abram. *The Negro as Capitalist.* Glouchester, Mass., 1968.

Himmelfarb, Milton. "Jewish Class Conflict?" *Commentary* 53, no.1 (January 1970): 37-42.

Hobsbawm, E. J. *Primitive Rebels.* New York, 1959.

———. *The Age of Revolution, 1789-1848.* New York, 1962.

Johnson, Charles. *The Negro College Graduate.* Chapel Hill, N.C., 1938.

———. *Growing Up in the Black Belt.* Washington, D.C., 1941.

Jones, Mervyn. "Freemasonry." In *Secret Societies,* edited by Norman MacKenzie. New York, 1971.

Katz, Jacob. *Jews and Freemasons in Europe, 1723-1939.* Cambridge, Mass., 1970.

———. *Tradition and Crisis: Jewish Society at the End of the Middle Ages.* New York, 1971.

Kinzer, Robert, and Sagarin, Edward. *The Negro in American Business: The Conflict Between Separatism and Integration.* New York, 1950.

Lewis, Hylan. "The Negro Business, Professional and White Collar Worker." *Journal of Negro Education* 8 (July 1939): 430-445.

———. *Blackways of Kent.* Chapel Hill, N.C., 1955.

Liebow, Elliot. *Talley's Corner.* Boston, 1967.

Light, Ivan. *Ethnic Enterprise in America.* Berkeley, Los Angeles, and London, 1972.

Lyman, Stanford. "Strangers in the Cities: The Chinese on the Urban Frontier." In *Ethnic Conflict in California History,* edited by Charles Wollenberg. Los Angeles, 1970.

———. *Chinese Americans.* New York, 1974.

McWilliams, Carey. *Brothers Under the Skin.* Boston, 1964.

Meier, August, and Lewis, David. "History of the Negro Upper Class in Atlanta, Georgia, 1890-1958." *Journal of Negro Education* 28 (Spring 1959): 128-139.

Mendelsohn, Ezra. *Class Struggle in the Pale.* Cambridge, Engl., 1970.

Moynihan, D. *On Understanding Poverty.* New York, 1969.

Muraskin, William. "An Alienated Elite: Short Stories in The Crisis, 1910-1950." *Journal of Black Studies* 1, no.3 (1971): 282-305.

———. "The Harlem Boycott of 1934: Black Nationalism and the Rise of Labor-Union Consciousness." *Labor History* 13, no.3 (1972): 361-373.

———. "The Moral Basis of a Backward Sociologist: Edward Banfield, the Italians and the Italian Americans." *American Journal of Sociology* vol. 79 (May 1974): 1484-1496.

Ofari, Earl. *The Myth of Black Capitalism*. New York, 1970.

Palmer, Edward N. "Negro Secret Societies." *Social Forces* 23 (December 1944): 207-212.

Range, Peter Ross. "Making It In Atlanta: Capital Of Black-Is-Bountiful." *New York Times Magazine*, April 7, 1974, pp. 28-78.

Raper, Arthur. *Preface to Peasantry*. Chapel Hill, N.C., 1936.

Rodman, Hyman. "The Lower-Class Value Stretch." *Social Forces* 43 (December 1963): 205-215.

Rollin, Frank. *The Life and Public Services of Martin R. Delany*. Boston, 1883.

Rossi, Peter, and Blum, Zahava. "Class, Status, and Poverty." In *On Understanding Poverty*, edited by D. Moynihan. New York, 1969.

Spear, Allan. *Black Chicago*. Chicago, 1967.

Thernstrom, S. *Poverty and Progress*. New York, 1970.

Ullman, Victor. *Martin R. Delany: The Beginnings of Black Nationalism*. Boston, 1971.

Udom, Essien. *Black Nationalism*. Chicago, 1962.

Valentine, Charles. *Culture and Poverty*. Chicago, 1968.

Washington, Booker T. *Story of the Negro*, 2 volumes. New York, 1909.

Wilson, James Q. *Varieties of Police Behavior*. Cambridge, Mass., 1968.

Woodson, Carter. *The Negro Professional Man and the Community, With Special Emphasis on the Physician and the Lawyer*. New York, 1934.

Index

Abolition: Masons worked for, 35, 53; opened up Masonry, 37-39, 161; social change after, 79-81

Acacia Lodge: oldest in Oakland, 87; occupations in, 91-92; property ownership in, 103

Acculturation: through Masonry, 24-25, 82-83, 85, 110-111

Achievement: as value, 22-23; dysfunctional aspects, 83-84

Admissions standards: use of blackball, 15n, 41, 270; exclusiveness of, 26, 40-41, 43; of first lodge, 31-32; lowered, 40-41; behavioral, 43-48, 51, 117; economic, 47-51; age, 51, 117; importance of maintaining, 70-71n, 244-245n

Adonis Lodge: 87; property ownership in, 103

Adultery: expulsion for, 73n

African Benevolent Society, 66n

African Lodge No. 1, 31-32

African Lodge No. 459, 32, 34

African Masons: Liberia, 185, 186, 188-189; Sierra Leone, 185-188; Ghana, 189; West Africa, 214

African Methodist Episcopal Church: ties with Masonry, 35, 38-39, 52, 162, 163, 164

African Methodist Episcopal Zion Church, 38, 39

Age: standards for admission, 51, 117

Age, New York: on Masonry as luxury, 50; on power struggles, 257, 258

Alabama: membership growth, 29; Masonry began, 37, 38n; admissions standards, 41n, 44; initiation fees, 48; business skills taught, 128-129, 138; endowment plan, 138; loan plan, 144-145; scholarship fund, 152-153, 284; ties with business in, 167-168; supported teachers' strike, 227; lodges as insurance agents, 283

Alabama, Grand Master's statements: on charity, 65, 66-67; criticized, 126; on need for economic cooperation, 141, 276, 277; on Masonic universalism, 194; on acceptance by European Masons, 204; on anti-Communism, 229; on leadership, 255, 268, 269

Alaska: Masonry in, 190

Alienation: from lower class, 5, 27, 43, 58-59n, 74-85 *passim*, 292-294; from white middle class, 221, 292, 294-295. *See also* Ambivalence

Allen, Richard: founded African Methodist Episcopal Church, 35, 162; as activist example, 210, 239

Allen, W. W.: as businessman, 170; as charismatic leader, 171n; community activities, 175-176; honored by Liberia, 189; on mass action, 230-231; on fraternal power, 238

Alliance, Ohio, 55

Ambivalence: of black middle-class position, 5, 27, 78, 207-213, 216-218, 241-250 *passim*, 290-295. *See also* Alienation

American Dream: paradox of, 245-246

American Missionary Association, 39

American Red Cross: Masonic blood banks cooperate with, 156

American Revolution: Prince Hall Order founded during, 29

Amsterdam News: on loan program, 145

Anarchy, 256, 261, 266-270. *See also* Anti-leadership

Anderson, Peter, 191, 195, 204

Anti-Communism: Masons' relation to, 228-229

Antileadership, 251, 253-255, 261, 266-270, 277, 291

Anti-Masonic movement, 36

Anti-culture-of-poverty theories, 9-11, 12n, 15-16, 58-59n

Appeals Committee, 126

Aptheker, Herbert, 52-53

Archibald, Julius A., 54

Arizona: Masonry began, 38n

Aristocracy, 23. *See also* Elite

Arkansas: Masonry began, 38n; competition for members in, 40-41n; ties with business in, 170

Ascriptive organizations: commitment compared, 287-290

Assimilation: with white Masonry, 194-196, 206-218 *passim*. *See also* Acculturation

Association: middle-class patterns, 8, 18

Atlanta, Georgia: lodge established, 109; ties with community in, 175-176

Attendance, 282-283